P9-CBG-725

MEDIA PSYCHOLOGY

MEDIA PSYCHOLOGY

David Giles
Coventry University

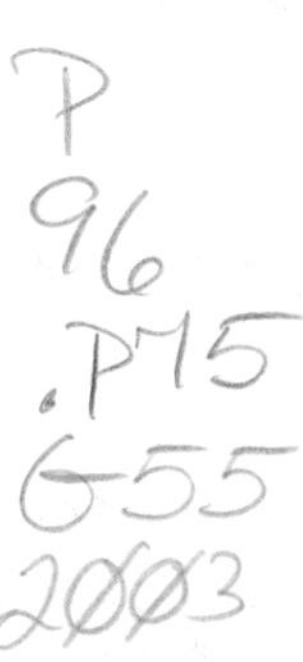

LEA LAWRENCE ERLBAUM ASSOCIATES, PUBLISHERS
2003 Mahwah, New Jersey London

Lawrence Erlbaum Associates, Inc., Publishers
10 Industrial Avenue
Mahwah, New Jersey 07430

Cover design by Kathryn Houghtaling Lacey

Library of Congress Cataloging-in-Publication Data

Media psychology by David Giles.
ISBN 0-8058-4048-6 (cloth : alk. paper); 0-8058-4049-4 (pbk. : alk. paper).
Copyright information for this volume can be obtained by contacting the Library of Congress.

Books published by Lawrence Erlbaum Associates are printed on acid-free paper, and their bindings are chosen for strength and durability.

Printed in the United States of America
10 9 8 7 6 5 4 3 2 1

Contents

Preface

As with so many academic texts, the idea for writing this book stemmed from a specialist final-year option that I developed at Coventry University. Simply put, there was no single text that covered all the material to which I wished to introduce students in the year. Most relevant texts were aimed at media and communication students, and assumed a lot of background knowledge about media history that psychology undergraduates rarely possess. Others failed to go beyond the basic "effects" paradigm, or were largely concerned with cognitive processing of media rather than placing them in a social and cultural context. Others, typically those in the European media studies tradition, erred in the opposite direction, blandly dismissing psychology as at best a relic of behaviourism, at worst as fascist propaganda! The idea for this book, then, was to navigate a gentler course in between the two traditions, arguing that serious study of the psychological influences of media should be rooted in the scientific tradition, but that good science requires the ability to look beyond the laboratory and use appropriate methods of investigation in the "real" world.

I hope that the resulting text is not too much of a fudge, playing the experimentalists off against the social constructionists, trying to balance discourse and cognition, but I really think it is important for psychologists to study the whole picture rather than sinking lazily into the comfy chair of an established paradigm. (I blame the Ph.D. process for this!) I apologise, too, for my Anglocentric perspective throughout the text, particularly in chapter 13 ("Sport"). I know that readers in North America and continental Europe (and many in the United Kingdom) may scoff at my use of examples from the sport of cricket, but I would never have had the time to learn the mysteries of baseball (or sumo, or whatever) in order to conjure up parallel examples that would have wider appeal. And the examples are important, so do bear with me on this one.

Several figures have played an important role in shaping the development of the book. Emily Wilkinson, my editor at Lawrence Erlbaum Associates, has been fantastic throughout, never interfering in the creative process but always helpful and encouraging. I owe a great deal to Jeffrey Goldstein and Barrie Gunter for their positive and constructive criticism at various stages in the writing process, and I would also like to thank Jennings Bryant for some very useful feedback on the initial proposal. I would also like to thank two cohorts of undergraduate students at Coventry for their willingness to engage with the lecture material that forms the content of this text.

Part I

MEDIA PSYCHOLOGY IN CONTEXT

Shortly before I began writing this book I attended a party at the home of some friends. It was a highly civilised affair, populated mostly by professional couples in their 20s and 30s and one or two single people, all graduates of some sort or other, although with little in common other than their friendship with the hosts. I was not wearing my psychologist's hat; far from "analysing everybody," as nonpsychologists would have it, I was simply chatting away in my usual friendly style when the topic of conversation turned to a television show that had been broadcast the previous evening. Suddenly, I stopped chatting and started listening. I felt my psychologist's hat materialising on my head, and it stayed there for the remainder of the evening, as the conversation ebbed and flowed. After about an hour or so, the content of the conversation had almost exclusively concerned media—specific shows had been discussed and critiqued; various personalities and celebrities had been gossiped about and evaluated as though they had been guests in the next room; when cultural matters had cropped up, even they had concerned subjects like football and pop music, which rely heavily (and in some cases exclusively) on media consumption. When the conversation ended and we played a game, this game was based entirely on a popular television quiz show.

A popular cliché states that television has destroyed the art of conversation. Yet here we were, not "consuming" media at all (although the stereo may have provided a quiet aural backdrop), conversing away artistically, indeed playing parlour games as our Victorian ancestors had. However, this roomful of near-strangers were able to discuss an enormous breadth of topics in intimate detail, requiring a degree of shared cultural knowledge that would have astonished past generations. Far from robbing us of social activity, some would argue that the mass media have enriched our cultural lives over the last century in ways that could have never been imagined. For others, they have simply filled our minds with trivia and junk, some of it poisonous. Either way, in 2002 it is seemingly impossible to ignore mass media's influence on any but the most remote communities on earth.

Statistically, the use of television has been widely reported—we often hear that much of our lives is spent watching the box, for so many hours a day. Harris (1999) claimed that 98% of U.S. homes have television (this figure has remained constant since 1980), and that 96% of U.S. homes have video recorders. It is even estimated that there are more television sets in the United States than there are toilets (Bushman, 1995). Television's role in communicating world events is so integral that it is easily forgotten, but nobody will forget the live transmission of the terrorist attack on the World Trade Center on September 11, 2001, broadcast in all its horror to living rooms across the world. In Manhattan itself, the television almost assumed the role of a mirror, reinforcing the reality of the disaster. Writer Jay McInerney described how he watched the events unfolding with his attention split between the window and the TV set, and could not even recall which source he was following when the second plane hit the building (*The Guardian*, 15/9/01).

Why have psychologists shown so little interest in the media up to now? In chapter 1, I outline a number of possible explanations. I then lay the foundations for a psychology that has media as its focus from the outset, identifying important questions that a media psychology might address, and attempting some broad definition of "media," which is essential for marking out the boundaries of the field. Developing a media psychology requires the synthesis of many diverse theoretical and research literatures, so in chapter 2 I give readers a broad overview of the many approaches to media research in both North American and European traditions (and, indeed, work from other parts of the globe). This wide range of perspectives derives in part from a huge and eclectic toolbox of research methods; hence, in chapter 3 I review a range of methods that have been used to study the media that would be appropriate for a media psychology.

Chapter 1

What Is Media Psychology, and Why Do We Need It?

Why has it taken so long for a psychology of the media to evolve? The answer lies in the history of the discipline, and of academic developments in general. In this chapter, I sketch a number of ways in which a distinct field of psychology might be defined. No field of psychology can emerge without a significant number of psychologists simultaneously addressing the same issues and identifying commonalities in each other's work. I think there are plenty of reasons why, at the start of this century, a diverse but identifiable field is beginning to take shape. The task now is to knit together these diverse literatures and practices.

DEFINING THE TERRITORY

Specialist fields of psychology have appeared at an ever-increasing rate throughout the history of the discipline. Many of those fields are defined by practice—three examples are clinical psychology, educational psychology, and industrial psychology. They emerge due to a social or commercial demand for the application of psychological theory and research in a non-academic environment. Within academia, broad fields have been defined in attempts to classify general approaches to psychology—cognitive psychology, social psychology, and developmental psychology, for instance. Other fields may be defined by a particular methodological approach or theoretical perspective, such as connectionist psychology, critical psychology, or behaviourism. These are often described as "schools of thought" rather than subdisciplines in their own right. Finally, there are fields that can be defined on the basis of topic, such as parapsychology, (cross-) cultural psychology, or the psychology of music. These fields may incorporate perspectives from broader fields (e.g., cognitive, social, and developmental psychology) but do not have to be dominated by any particular theoretical or methodological approach.

Media psychology is probably closest to this final, topic-defined type of field. Such fields are brought into being as a result of books (such as this one), journals (Lawrence Erlbaum Associates publishes a journal entitled *Media Psychology*[1]), conferences, and specialist teaching modules (such as the one I teach at undergraduate level at Coventry University). Media psychology potentially covers an enormous scope—wider, for example, than the psychology of music. This is partly because there are already a number of established fields that could be accommodated within media psychology, such as the psychology of advertising and the psychology of the internet (see chaps. 7 and 16).

What makes media psychology unusual among specialist psychology fields, however, is that much of the work has already been done in disciplines outside psychology. In North America, most universities have a department of media and communications that carries out research into broadly psychological aspects of media. These departments employ many staff members who have been trained as psychologists in the quantitative science tradition. Their work is referred to as "communication science" or "media research" and is published in journals such as the *Journal of Broadcasting and Electronic Media*[2] and the *Journal of Communication*.[3] Each year, the International Communication Association hosts a conference at which many papers are presented on media psychology topics. It is rare, however, to see media psychology on the curriculum in a North American *psychology* department.

In 1991, the psychology/communication distinction formed the basis of a special issue of the journal *Communication Research*.[4] Here, Reeves and Anderson (1991) discussed the ways in which psychological theory could inform media studies and vice versa, arguing that it was difficult for either field to ignore the other. For media researchers, the cognitive processes involved in watching film or video cannot be dismissed; for psychologists, cognitive and developmental psychology could be enriched by a consideration of media use, much in the way that studies of reading have influenced general theories of cognition. Reeves and Anderson quoted the famous cogni-

---

[1]http://www.erlbaum.com/Journals/journals/MEP/mep.htm

[2]http://www.beaweb.org/jobem.html

[3]http://joc.oupjournals.org/

[4]http://www.sagepub.co.uk/frame.html?http://www.sagepub.co.uk/journals/details/j0078.html

tive psychologist Ulrich Neisser (1976) as saying "a psychology that cannot interpret ordinary experience is ignoring almost the whole range of its natural subject matter" (Reeves & Anderson, 1991, p. 599). The implications of media studies for developing social psychology, although not considered by these authors, are potentially greater still.

In Europe, the academic relationship between psychology and media studies is rather different. There has been a limited growth in media psychology as such, largely concentrated in Germany (where a German-language journal, *Medienpsychologie,* has flourished), and two edited volumes have been published based on the proceedings of workshops that brought together European media psychologists during the 1990s (Winterhoff-Spurk, 1995; Winterhoff-Spurk & van der Voort, 1997). These workshops attracted psychologists largely from Northern Europe, most of whom work within the North American communication tradition of laboratory studies of the cognitive and behavioural effects of screen media.

However, this small field is not typical of the European tradition in media and communication research. In most academic institutions, "media studies" has evolved as a specialist branch of cultural studies, and is rooted in the qualitative social science research tradition. Psychologists are rarely found in European media studies departments; indeed, the word *psychology* tends to carry negative connotations in this field (Livingstone, 1998a). However, recent developments in media studies have paved the way for a psychological treatment of some aspects of audience research. David Gauntlett and colleagues recently published a collection of studies examining the internet, arguing that media studies' focus on traditional media (mostly television and print media) threatens the discipline with redundancy (Gauntlett, 2000).

In particular, pressure is being placed on media scholars to concentrate as much on audiences as on the media texts themselves, a prospect that, as far as Gauntlett was concerned, requires a level of empirical research that may be beyond the interests (and methodological capabilities) of cultural scholars. He maintained that media scholars should, instead, concentrate on cyberspace and other new media, which offer new and exciting avenues of cultural exploration. Gauntlett's views are in no way typical of those of media scholars in general, European or American. However, they do highlight a growing concern for media studies in their need to consider new technological forms. They also reflect the suggestion of Livingstone (1999) that audience research has reached a "crossroads" whereby it is no longer sufficient to merely study the content of media; one must now engage at a social level with the practices of media use in general. I would argue that this is a project that is ideally suited to social psychology.

How, then, to chart the territory of media psychology? To begin with, there is a danger of media psychology becoming so broad that it begins to swallow up other topics in which the media plays an important role, such as political psychology. Clearly, there are important issues around the dissemination of political propaganda or government policy, and media influences on voting behaviour and the popularity of politicians. But it must be remembered that politics is, to some extent, a *pre*media phenomenon. Admittedly, the presentation of electoral candidates has been shaped by the media in democratic societies, and of course political action has always depended on some form of medium in order to mobilise communities. However, the nature of politics itself—and the psychological processes that govern political thought and opinion that constitute the field of political psychology—require many philosophical, theoretical, and methodological considerations that may be beyond the scope of media psychology.

We can go no further, then, without first establishing a boundary. What do we mean by "media," and what elements of media are, or should be, of interest to psychologists? If political psychology is excluded from media psychology on the grounds of its status as a premedia phenomenon, this suggests that *history* is a prime consideration. However, behaviours such as aggression and sex, or fundamental social and psychological processes such as discourse and cognition, are universal human phenomena that would occur—or so we assume—under any historical conditions. Thus, the key issue is: How might the media have influenced these behaviours and processes?

DEFINING "MASS MEDIA"

Media studies textbooks usually distinguish media (*mass* media, to be precise) from other forms of communication, in relation to one of the many models of general communication that have been developed over the years (McQuail & Windahl, 1993). This allows us to distinguish communication technologies, such as the telephone, from mass media, in which communication is (ostensibly) unidirectional, such as the television. However, the emergence of the Internet and other interactive media networks have forced us to reconsider our concepts of media.

According to Marshall McLuhan, perhaps the most famous of all media scholars, this is only to be expected, because each new medium shapes society by its own terms, so we can never have a universal definition of "media"—the concept is forever in a state of flux. He cast the net as wide as possible by defining a medium as an "extension of ourselves" (McLuhan, 1964, p. 11), using electric light as an example. Media are effectively ciphers (i.e., empty of meaning) until we perceive some form of content, which is then treated as a message. The electric light is devoid of content until it is used to convey an explicit message, such as an advertising slogan or brand name, or until we credit it with a particular meaning (such as "light pollution").

From such reasoning came McLuhan's much-quoted expression, "The medium *is* the message."

But none of this really helps much. If we are to define a specialist field from psychology in relation to media, we need a definition that will be understood within that discipline. For this, we need to consider the relation of media to two broad aspects of civilisation—*technology* and *culture*. These two aspects are common to all human societies throughout time and space. Mass communication, however, is an intrinsically modern concept, emanating from the invention of printing and boosted by the discovery of electricity. The term *mass* is usually taken to refer to the size of the potential audience of a communication medium, typically 10% to 20% of the given population (Morris & Ogan, 1996). Mass media—the kind of media that are of interest in this book[5]—could be seen as the intersection of mass communication, culture, and technology. This would incorporate all media that rely on electricity, such as television, but exclude media that have a solely communicative function, such as the telephone. Newspapers and magazines are included, even though they require no technological input from their readers.

This leaves a number of grey areas, which is only to be expected with such a vast and difficult concept. First, where do we draw the line between mass media and popular cultural products? CD players and video game consoles satisfy all the criteria—they are electrical devices that communicate cultural material—but should they be treated any differently from more traditional cultural forms, such as books? This problem would not have bothered early media theorists, such as the Frankfurt School (see chap. 2), who made a sharp distinction between traditional culture and what they referred to as the "culture industry" (Adorno, 1991). Electronic cultural products were seen as part of a new dark age in which traditional culture was being, to use a thoroughly modern phrase, "dumbed down," and used as political propaganda. Today, however, the sheer diversity and ubiquity of electronic cultural material mitigates against such a view, blurring the boundary between culture and media. Nevertheless, the relation between the two—particularly in fields such as cinema and popular music—is so close that the study of media is practically synonymous with the study of contemporary popular culture.

The second grey area concerns new developments in technology that have already begun to transform the 21st century social landscape. The Internet has been described as a *multifaceted* medium because it comprises a

---

[5]This raises some questions about the status of some media, particularly in their early stages; for example, it is estimated at the time of writing that only 10% of the world's population has access to the Internet, although that figure rises close to 50% for the United Kingdom and United States. Thus, the Internet is undoubtedly a "mass" medium in Western Europe and North America, but not in other parts of the globe.

number of distinct functions, each with its own characteristics (Morris & Ogan, 1996). The World Wide Web is the function that most closely resembles traditional mass media—an *information* medium in which cultural material is communicated electronically to a defined audience; however, its other communicative functions are purely social (e-mail, and outlets such as chat rooms). Strictly speaking, e-mail is no more a "mass medium" than the telephone or the letter.

These grey areas mean that identifying a clear boundary for the field of media psychology is no easy task. To address the issue, during the 1990s the American Psychological Association changed the name of its Division of Media Psychology to the Division of Media Psychology and Communications Technology. Although I take issue with the APA's definition of media psychology later in this chapter, the new name at least acknowledges the distinction between media and technology. However, this is not always the case, and it is important to recognise this distinction in developing a psychology of media.

I illustrate this distinction with an example from academic research. This deals with an area of new technology that Biocca and Levy (1995) described as the "ultimate [communication] medium"—virtual reality (VR). Although an enormous amount of research is being conducted on the development and potential uses of interactive virtual environments, the VR experience is restricted to laboratory settings, in which users typically don a headset and gloves or hold "wands" for tactile simulation. The psychological responses to these environments have been a focus for VR research—in one study, for instance, participants were required to skirt round the edge of an apparently steep drop (although in actuality only a few inches) and displayed physiological responses that were consistent with the anxiety produced when faced with a real drop of several feet (Meehan, 2000). The term *new media* is frequently applied to new technologies for human–computer interaction. However, such laboratory-bound experiences can hardly be classified as "media use." While Web-based virtual environments may become commonplace in the future, we can presently only speculate about the course of their social and cultural applications, no matter how knowledgeable we are about the capabilities of the technology. Until such environments become part of everyday experience, we cannot regard them as "mass" media, certainly not if we apply Morris and Ogan's (1996) definition.

To some readers, this caveat may place unwelcome restrictions on the field of media psychology; however, as I argue shortly, part of psychology's reluctance to deal with media may result from caution about the historical permanence of media culture. Furthermore, the dazzling speed with which technological development occurs (witness the growth of the internet) is out of all proportion to the speed of academic research. Although the latter may adapt to meet the demands of the changing technological world, at present a rigorous, well-funded, and well-conducted piece of research can take at least 5 years from theoretical conception to successful funding to eventual analysis, so even a rapid turnaround in academic publishing practices would make little difference to the currency of the findings. This can be illustrated by the rapid redundancy of an excellent European study of children's media use (Livingstone & Bovill, 1999). This report, based on research carried out between 1997 and 1998, was already dated at the time of its publication, because it narrowly missed the explosion in mobile telephone use during the following year.

This is not to say that the *findings* of computer-mediated communication such as VR have no interest or implication for media psychology. Indeed, the concept of "presence" (see Lombard & Ditton, 1997), in which the user experiences the sense of actually being present in the simulated or virtual environment, has been applied to studies of "immersive" television (Freeman, Lessiter, & IJsselsteijn, 2001). Other important issues, such as the status of "cyber-identities," are very much part of any psychology of media. Chapter 16 explores these issues in detail.

PSYCHOLOGY AND MEDIA: AN UNEASY RELATIONSHIP?

Why do so many psychologists still regard television as nothing more than a tin box generating visual stimuli, while the rest of the world is constantly digesting and regurgitating its contents? One of the reasons for psychology's slowness in picking up on the influence of media is that, as a young science, it has been cautious in its selection of topics for inquiry. Partly this caution derives from its uncertain status as a science, so there has been a neglect of topics that do not easily lend themselves to measurement, preferably in the context of the laboratory. This caution is not peculiar to psychology. Within academia in general, the media are not considered a fit topic for academic research; many media researchers can recall snooty comments from colleagues about their interest in the "trivia" and "junk" of media culture. This attitude has trickled down to the student body. One of my third-year students reportedly said to another, "Surely you can't be studying reality TV for your final year project?" These are not stuffy, fogeyish young people, but they feel that academia is no place in which to pick apart their leisure pursuits.

Negative attitudes to the serious study of media pervade far beyond the academy: in the United Kingdom, even as recently as 1993, the Education Secretary of the Conservative government referred to media studies as "cultural Disneyland for the weaker minded" (O'Sullivan, Dutton, & Rayner, 1998, p. ix). Furthermore, the media themselves are not above pouring scorn in serious attempts to study popular culture. Every few months, on quieter news days, an end-piece story will appear about a Ph.D. student at some university who is conducting a thesis on Madonna or "Big Brother," and newsreaders will raise a quizzical eyebrow and wonder which government body is chucking away taxpayers' money on such frivolous pursuits.

Although cultural snobbery and concerns for psychology's scientific credibility may partly explain its lack of interest in media, there are other factors as well. The pace of technological change over the last century, and the rapidity of associated social upheavals, have made it difficult for serious research to get to grips with either. The current climate of speculation about the future social consequences of the internet and virtual reality echo the speculation that initially surrounded radio and television. Every decade in the last 50 years has seen major developments in mass communications and media. Keeping a finger on the pulse of change is difficult when you are trying to discover universal truths about human nature.

It would be unfair to claim that psychology has ignored *all* aspects of media. A quick trawl through North American social psychology journals in the 1970s and 1980s reveals a large number of research papers dealing with the "effects" of television and films. Most of these studies were instigated by a concern that, far from being a harmless box of tricks in the corner of the living room, the television is a source of imagery and information that is capable of turning acquiescent and innocent little children into gormless zombies, or, worse, mass murderers. This research is largely the legacy of behaviourism, and is discussed in full in part II of the book.

It is, however, symptomatic of much psychological research that it is essentially *problem* driven, rather than curiosity driven. In other words, the research has been conducted in response to calls for scientific evidence for the harmful influence of media, rather than an intellectual need to understand how media in general might influence behaviour. As a result, studies have been devised that have the best chance of securing a statistically significant outcome for a causal relationship between violent media and aggressive behaviour. The resultant literature enabled Leonard Eron, one of the leading researchers in the area, to claim that the causal link between media violence and aggression is as powerful as the link between cigarette smoking and lung cancer (Eron, 1993).

Despite widespread agreement as to the shortcomings of much experimental research on media violence, its legacy has been bequeathed to the media themselves, and to politicians, who continue to make unsubstantiated statements about the direct relationship between media violence and antisocial behaviour (Barker & Petley, 1997). Meanwhile, in the United States in particular, media violence research has moved on, exploring means of curbing the argued effects of violence, through advisory warnings, labelling, and blocking devices such as the "V-chip." The consensus here is that Eron is right: There is no need to prolong the experimental investigation because it has already proved the causal link beyond doubt. Nevertheless, there are pockets of research into media violence that draw on contemporary theories and methods in social psychology (e.g., Shaw, 2001), and to many minds the issue is far from settled.

What is interesting is that Eron himself never set out to investigate media influence per se. His initial field of research was aggressive behaviour (Fowles, 1999). Due to the lack of any established media psychology tradition, this pattern of career development is likely to apply to most psychologists who have conducted research on the influence or effects of media. The exodus of staff from psychology departments to media and communications departments in North America has given psychology the perfect excuse to ignore media: It is now another discipline's concern.

Despite the disappearance of media psychologists from psychology over the last century, the influence of the media on everyday behaviour is so insidious that it has been impossible to dispel it completely. Indeed, its effect on social change has been so rapid that references to media phenomena now abound in psychological research, and their status as media phenomena is often completely ignored. A good example of this comes from a paper on self-concept by Aron, Aron, Tudor, and Nelson (1991) who, in a study on close relationships, happened to mention that their participants found it easier to generate vivid visual images of the pop star Cher than of their own mothers! Historically speaking, this is a truly remarkable psychological finding, worthy of more than a casual comment in a Method section.

Perhaps the most surprising thing of all is that, despite the rapid expansion of psychology toward the end of the last century, no applied field of psychology has welcomed media under its wing. For instance, cultural psychology has emerged as a clear field within the discipline (e.g., Cole & White, 1996), and it might seem that this would be the natural home for the study of the influence of media culture on psychology. However, textbooks on cultural psychology barely give the media a mention except for the occasional remark about television's deleterious effect on "traditional" cultures.

Overwhelmingly, cultural psychology draws its data from premedia cultural contexts and from parts of the globe where media influence is less evident than in the West. There is a clear bias toward "cultural durability," implying that technologically oriented cultures are fleeting and insubstantial, and that "culture" is not worth studying unless ingrained over several centuries. Any contemporary theory of the role of culture in psychology ought to take media culture into consideration. In effect, this book is about *not* ignoring media, or taking them for granted, in the study of psychology.

PRACTISING MEDIA PSYCHOLOGY?

One final consideration in this introductory chapter is about the notion of media psychology as a practice rather than, or as well as, a field of academic research. The latter is broadly the approach of the American Psychological Association (APA), who have had a Division (number 46) of Media Psychology since 1986. The interests of the division are split between, on the one hand, providing training and advice for psychologists appearing in the media, and on the other, promoting findings of research on psychological aspects of media. The APA have published two edited books about psychology and the media (Kirschner & Kirschner, 1997; Schwartz, 1999). These follow the interests of the division in that they are split into sections dealing with research and practice. Most of the "practice" chapters consist of anecdotal material from psychologists working in the media and sound advice for psychologists appearing on radio or television.

The idea of media psychology as a practice may seem a little strange, because there is not much a psychologist can do within the media apart from the usual practices of occupational psychology, such as advising on organisational practice, or offering counselling or human resource management services. Appearing on a television show as a psychologist barely constitutes "applied psychology," because the professional psychologist immediately becomes another media figure—talk show guest, news programme interviewee, or generic "expert." Nevertheless, certain individuals regard themselves as "media psychologists," such as Toni Grant, a psychologist who has hosted a television chat show and written books urging "a return to traditional feminine values and morals" (Friedland & Koenig, 1997, p. 130). The qualifications for being a media psychologist of this type seem to consist of any media work—journalism, performing, writing, or consultancy—but these activities are not organised into a practice in the tradition of clinical psychology, educational psychology, or counselling psychology. Nobody works in an office with a sign on the door that reads "Media Psychologist."

Why should the APA concern itself with media employees and guests in this way? One important reason is to safeguard the interests of the discipline. Much of the training and advice offered in the APA's publications are geared to promoting the media image of psychology as a profession, and this carries with it a powerful degree of ideological responsibility. For example, Sheras and Sheras (1999) described their function as media psychologists as promoters of "the healthy couple" in an attempt to stem the rising divorce rate. It is hard to imagine the APA supporting a psychologist whose research concerned the positive aspects of divorce. The APA places no curbs on psychologists' freedom of speech, although both they and the British Psychological Society (BPS) issue guidelines to members that regulate their performance in the media. For example, the BPS discourages members from discussing psychological topics outside their field of expertise. The object of these guidelines is sensible enough—to prevent "quackery" and the promotion of individual interests above those of the discipline.

However, there are many occasions when psychologists appear in the media not as representatives of the discipline or profession, but as individual authors or academics. There is a difference between being interviewed as "David Giles, author of *Media Psychology*," "David Giles, senior lecturer in psychology at Coventry University," and "David Giles, psychologist." Only in the final role would I feel pressure to abide by BPS guidelines, unless I was interviewed in connection with a presentation at a BPS conference or a paper in a BPS journal. The situation is even less clearcut in countries like Norway and Sweden, where university researchers are required by contract to present their findings to the media, potentially leading to a three-way conflict of interests (Griffiths, 2001).

In the future, professional bodies may feel the need to exert greater control over the appearance and conduct of their members in the media. It may be that psychologists will eventually require chartering in order to call themselves psychologists in the media (although the media apply their own labels regardless). Only then would media psychology fully constitute a *practice* in its own right. Such a development would not, in my view, be a step forward for psychology. Providing advice is one thing, but controlling performance may deter all but the most narcissistic from entering the media circus. If we really want to honour the call from former APA president George Miller in his 1969 address to "give psychology away," a certain amount of flexibility—and respect for academic psychologists as independent thinkers, authors, and researchers—is called for.

Chapter **2**

Theoretical Issues in Media Research

The evolution of media research has produced two markedly different bodies of literature, dotted with small islands of convergence. The primary goal of this book is to sift through this work and extract the elements that prove most useful in building a theoretical basis for a fully comprehensive psychology of the media. However, the first task is to provide the reader with a brief overview of major developments over the years in general media theory.

EARLY APPROACHES TO MEDIA

The history of media research begins in the period leading up to World War II, when radio was beginning to make an impact on the cultural landscape on both sides of the Atlantic. Two important early works were Cantril and Allport's *The Psychology of Radio* (1935), a look at the possible psychological effects of mass communication, and Cantril, Gaudet, and Herzog's *The Invasion From Mars: A Study in the Psychology of Panic* (1940), which examined the implications of the outbreak of hysteria induced when a dramatised version of H.G. Wells' *War of the Worlds,* complete with realistic news bulletins, was broadcast on American radio one evening in 1938. These authors were disturbed by the prospect of radio as a potential vehicle for propaganda during a politically unstable period. A popular metaphor in this period for the psychological effects of media was the "hypodermic needle" (Lasswell, 1935), which likened the effects of propaganda to an "injection" of ideological bias that contaminated radio listeners, rather in the manner of "brainwashing," an expression still widely used today to refer to the apparently hypnotic effect of media.

Much of the academic literature about media in the early days of radio and television had a strongly negative flavour. The two biggest influences on media theory were North American sociology and the Frankfurt School, the latter being a group of social theorists who moved from Germany to the United States in the 1930s in order to escape Nazi persecution. The emerging discipline of communication science advocated the use of quantitative experimental methods to investigate topics such as political communication and marketing (e.g., Hovland, Lumsdaine, & Sheffield, 1949). Leading figures in this tradition included Robert Merton and Paul Lazarsfeld, who sounded alarms about the threat of mass media to the arts and "narcotising dysfunction" (Lazarsfeld & Merton, 1948), a media-induced state of apathy in which people were content to *know* rather than to do.

Although broadly negative about the media, Lazarsfeld and Merton were not quite as scathing in their criticisms as the Frankfurt School, whose Marxist-inspired approach regarded the media as "mass deception." Like the functionalists, the Frankfurt School feared for the future of "high culture," and believed it to be under threat from what they called the "culture industry." For these scholars, mass media and popular culture were indistinguishable, a recurrent theme in the history of media theory. Prominent among the Frankfurt writers was Theodore Adorno, whose work is worth reading if only for its spirit of invective (for an edited collection of his writings, see Adorno, 1991). Junk culture is far from harmless, he claimed; it promotes conformity and anti-intellectualism, risks reducing adults to the level of 11-year-olds, and impedes the development of "autonomous, independent individuals." Like Milgram's research on obedience in the same period, this work is permeated with the fear of a potential resurgence of fascism.

Meanwhile, British writers began to voice similar concerns about the influence of television as it was introduced into homes after World War II. The popular image of a media future in this period was Orwell's *1984*, which presented a vision of television as an instrument of social oppression. The literary critic, F.R. Leavis, had already railed against prewar cinema as "cheap" and emotional (Leavis & Thompson, 1933), and Raymond Williams continued to work in this tradition in the postwar period. Rather than the sledgehammer approach of Adorno and the Frankfurt School (although he shared their political views), Williams made a clear distinction between mass media and new cultural forms, arguing that the cinema was already starting to compete with theatre in the dramatic tradition, but that art was under threat from being absorbed by mere "entertainment" (Williams, 1962).

One of his major concerns was that entertainment was increasingly filling the gaps in everyday life, so that people were watching television rather than doing nothing; not only did this mean that they were perhaps subject to the "abuse" of advertising, but also that they were sucked in by the "flow" of television, unable to break the spell of viewing (Williams, 1974). Like Leavis, Williams was a firm advocate of media education, training the public in the art of media criticism as a way of suppressing media's unpalatable effects.

McLUHAN AND POSTMODERNISM

The negativity of the early media theorists was soon under attack from several fronts. First of all, Marshall McLuhan issued his famous statement "The medium *is* the message," and, as discussed in the previous chapter, challenged the notion of media as inherently dangerous. Each new medium, he argued, forced a radical reappraisal of what media *were*, and affected social change accordingly. For example, although the car did not change society simply through its function or meaning, it opened up social mobility and this, in turn, transformed the way we live (McLuhan, 1964).

Seen in this light, it is television itself—not the political machinations of governments—that has turned the world into a "global village." Critics of McLuhan labelled his vision "technological determinism"; others, such as Hans Enzensberger (1974), went further, calling him "reactionary," a "charlatan," and his views "idiocy." Enzensberger was a Marxist but rejected the pessimism of the Frankfurt School, instead exploring the possibilities of mass media for a radical "challenge to bourgeois power," a sentiment later echoed by many minority political groups with regard to the potential of the Internet.

In some respects, McLuhan's comments about the postwar mass media are more applicable to contemporary cable and digital communications than to "terrestrial" media. The state has always had to regulate traditional broadcasting, because in any country the portion of electromagnetic spectrum suitable for broadcasting is limited, and radio and television have to compete with other users such as the armed forces and emergency services (Scannell, 1989). Nevertheless, there are now hardly any communities on the planet that have not found a use for television or, more recently, Internet technology; as with the car, these media have created *possibilities* for social change. However, whether they have *determined* these changes is arguable. In historical terms, the problem is that the rise of the mass media have coincided with so many other profound social and political developments that causation is impossible to infer, although their association with these developments is undeniable.

McLuhan's theories, "apolitical" to many, have echoes in later postmodernist theories of media. *Postmodernism* is a problematic term because it is used to describe a historical period (the period after "modernism"), an artistic phase of development, and a theoretical position; one can be a "postmodernist" thinker or artist, but this does not necessarily mean that one is living through a "postmodern" age. Many writers prefer the term *late modernity* to describe the current point in history (Giddens, 1991). In artistic terms, *postmodernism* usually refers to a break with tradition characterised by the collapse of the former canon of values—for example, mixing and matching architectural styles from previous periods—and its use in theory or philosophy has similar connotations. In psychology, postmodernism has been invoked in order to challenge traditional scientific methodologies and theories, and to urge a more eclectic approach (Kvale, 1992).

Postmodernism has been applied to the media in a variety of contexts. To begin with, grand social theory has looked at the changes wrought by media on an international scale; for example, the work of Jean Baudrillard (1988). Baudrillard was one of the first writers to discuss media and communications as systems circulating, above all else, *information* (as opposed to "messages," images, or propaganda). Whereas McLuhan saw media themselves as apolitical, Baudrillard argued that they have depoliticised the masses, creating a "lack of will," so that people are content to sit back and luxuriate in the "ecstasy of communication" (Baudrillard, 1985). This is not the same thing as "opium for the people," however; like McLuhan, Baudrillard is no Marxist—the effect of this excess of information is to collapse the media and the masses into one, so that the traditional communication model of sender–message–receiver is no longer appropriate.

Again, perhaps, Baudrillard's vision has more pertinence with regard to Internet technology than to traditional media, which after all are still mostly under state control or the ownership of multinational corporations such as Time-Warner (although this company's integration with AOL may have important implications for the regulation of Internet technology, too). Nevertheless, postmodernist thought has been highly influential in European media research, where it has fed into a number of contemporary fields such as feminism, "queer theory" (Jagose, 1996), and more general theories of popular culture (McRobbie, 1994). Much of this work takes a more optimistic, positive perspective on postmodernism than did Baudrillard, who talked of the "obscenity" of a culture that is all "image, surface and transparency" (Baudrillard, 1985, p. 126). For many writers, postmodernism is seen as liberating, something to be celebrated. This has much to do with the way media have been credited for breaking down social boundaries to allow women and minority groups a more prominent voice in contemporary culture—or, in postmodernist terms, collapsing the processes of production and reception so that the old establishments no longer have any power or meaning.

Like McLuhan, postmodernist thinkers have been criticised for ignoring political and economic realities (Billig, 1999). The preferred term in cultural studies, at the level of theory at least, is often *poststructuralism,* which implies a postmodernist dissolution of high and low culture, and rejects essentialist (and scientific) notions of truth and knowledge, but is more guarded in its conception of "reality." This approach also falls under the more general banner of "critical realism" (for an application of these ideas to media psychology, see Blackman & Walkerdine, 2001).

DEVELOPMENTS IN MEDIA RESEARCH

These shifts in theoretical thinking about media have not necessarily been reflected in all developments in media research. Postmodernist thought has had little obvious impact in North America, although it has had more influence in Europe. There is some evidence that the two traditions have begun to converge; positivist science has found some of the postmodern and cultural studies research hard to ignore, whereas on the cultural studies side there are increasing attempts to reevaluate some of the empirical work (Ruddock, 2001).

Media research has been focused on a number of areas, some of which are more obviously relevant to psychology than others. Issues concerning the ownership of the media are of specific interest to news (chap. 4) and advertising (chap. 8). Technical matters such as production techniques, and the structure of media texts, have implications for the study of media content and will be alluded to in the chapters on representations (chap. 10). The remainder of this current chapter concentrates on research that has direct relevance to psychology—notably, studies of the "effects" of media, which stretch from the 1930s to the present day, and studies of audiences, which range from psychometric studies of media use and large-scale surveys of audience behaviour to postmodernist analyses of the reader–text relationship.

THE "EFFECTS" TRADITION

The "media effects" tradition has probably had the greatest impact of all media research on public life in the last 50 years. Concerns about the negative psychological effects of media are so commonplace that they are barely questioned outside academia, except by some producers of media, such as pop stars and film directors, and fans of the media material under attack. By far the most frequently voiced assumption is the causal link between violent media and violent behaviour, and there are numerous instances in recent years of media products being blamed for random outbreaks of violence. The media violence debate is covered in detail in chapter 4.

The earliest studies of the psychology of media were driven by the concerns of the time (e.g., the influence of radio advertising and propaganda), but it was in the 1960s and 1970s that media effects research really began to take off, with numerous laboratory-based studies measuring short-term responses to media stimuli. It is unfortunate in a way that this body of literature has become known as the "effects" tradition, because the word *effects* covers a wide range of behavioural processes. To some academics (typically from the cultural studies camp), *effects* is virtually synonymous with *psychology*, and both are to be avoided entirely. However, it is important that we evaluate the experimental research in its historical context and treat it as a valuable, if limited, body of work that needs to be balanced alongside findings of more contextual and cognitive approaches to audience behaviour.

Most of the experimental work in the 1960s focused on the *negative* effects of media. Typically, a group of undergraduate students was "exposed" in the media laboratory to media material (usually recorded on video) that contained a certain quantity of the undesirable content under investigation—mainly sex and violence. The students then performed some other activity—completing a questionnaire or scale, such as a mood inventory, or participating in an experimental manipulation, or working together on a task while under observation. These designs are often referred to as "dose-response" studies, because the hypothesis is usually that the degree of exposure (dose) is related to the amount of aggression displayed or negative mood reported (response).

Such designs can be traced back to the behaviourist tradition in psychology, because they are based on the principle that rigorous experimental control can eradicate confounding variables (e.g., social context) to such a degree that a direct causal relationship can be demonstrated between media content and human behaviour. The strength of this relationship is often a function of the rigour of the experimental design. A truly behaviourist explanation for significant results in dose-response experiments might be that human beings learn through imitation, and if certain social acts are rewarded in films and even cartoons, people will imitate those acts in real life.

Behaviourism is at its most persuasive when children are concerned, and so it is not surprising that the most popular behaviourist media research was that carried out by Albert Bandura during the 1960s. In a series of studies, children were exposed to some violent behaviour (either performed "live" in the laboratory or recorded on video) and then subsequently observed playing with a variety of toys, including a "Bobo doll" (an inflatable figure that, after being punched, returns to an upright position). Bandura found that children who had been exposed to violence—either live or recorded—performed significantly more aggressive acts toward the Bobo doll than did children who had been exposed to nonviolent material (Bandura, Ross, & Ross, 1963).

Although an ingenious set of studies at the time, there are many problems with Bandura's findings; these are discussed in greater length in chapter 4. Certainly, the direct imitation theory of media effects has been substantially expanded since the 1960s, reflecting the changing nature of psychology as much as anything. After behaviourism, the task facing psychology involved an attempt to open up the "black box" postulated by behaviourists in place of the mind, or brain. Effects research subsequently developed along two separate paths. One approach was to regard the black box as a physical organ subject to electrical and chemical impulses, so measuring the physiological effects of media became the key issue. For example, when watching an exciting film, measures such as heart rate or galvanic skin response can be interpreted in terms of the effect the film has on the viewer's mood, emotional arousal, or degree of attention to the material (Lang, 1994).

The second approach was related to the "cognitive revolution" that took place in psychology during the 1960s, which followed the pioneering work carried out by Donald Broadbent and colleagues in Cambridge during the 1950s. Instead of filling the black box with cortical matter and studying the human brain as a biological organism, cognitive psychologists took a metaphorical approach, strongly influenced by contemporary developments in computer science, treating the brain as an information processor. The cognitive approach to media research, then, studied the effects of media on the thought processes of the individual, with specific attention paid to matters such as memory and comprehension (e.g., Reeves, Newhagen, Maibach, Basil, & Kurz, 1991).

Other researchers working in the same tradition attempted to integrate these approaches; for example, Dolf Zillmann, building on Schachter and Singer's (1962) two-factor model of emotion (which proposed that emotion consists of both cognitive and physiological components), advanced the theory of "excitation transfer" (Zillmann, Katcher, & Milavsky, 1972) as an explanation for the effects of violent media. This theory proposes that viewers become physiologically aroused by watching aggressive scenes and, if subsequently provoked, may respond in an inappropriately aggressive manner because they have misattributed the source of their arousal.

In later years, the effects tradition continued to diversify. Cognitive psychology exerted a much greater influence than behaviourism, so that the effects of media were increasingly seen to be moderated by individual thought processes (Berkowitz, 1984) and personality characteristics (Bushman, 1995). In addition to areas of public concern such as violence, effects researchers have studied the *prosocial* effects of educational and other media (e.g., Feshbach & Feshbach, 1997). Indeed, a glance at texts such as Bryant and Zillmann (1994) reveals a wide range of different approaches gathered beneath the "effects" banner.

In many areas of media studies, the "effects" tradition has acquired a bad name, bracketed with psychology in general, being charged with "individualizing" media concerns and ignoring wider social and cultural contexts (Ang, 1994; Hall, 1980). Although the criticism may be justified in many cases, something of a knee-jerk syndrome has evolved by which *all* psychological studies of media are dismissed as "effects" research, and media scholars lose interest at the mere use of the word *effects*. Sociologist David Gauntlett (1995) argued that the term *influences* is more appropriate, because it implies a complex interplay of social and environmental factors on behaviour of which media is one part, whereas the term *effects* suggests, perhaps erroneously, that the causal relationship between media and human behaviour can be studied in isolation. Nevertheless, to characterise all media effects research as crude behaviourism is a gross misrepresentation.

CULTIVATION RESEARCH

Criticism of effects research is not new by any means. As early as 1960, Joseph Klapper advocated a shift away from the behaviouristic effects approach toward a more contextual approach. Like Gauntlett 35 years later, Klapper preferred to talk of media *influence* rather than effects—seeing media as one element of a complex system of environmental and cultural factors. Today, as society becomes increasingly media saturated, it has become harder and harder to disentangle media from other modern social and cultural phenomena—no study of rock or pop music, for example, can ignore the role that media plays in almost every aspect of the subject. An embryonic band rehearsing in a garage will require press attention in order to attract record company interest; once the band is signed, successful, and undertaking international tours, media concerns continue to dominate, dictating to some extent the creative output (e.g., will it get played on the radio?) and the band's behaviour (hiding from paparazzi, avoiding reporters).

Klapper's concerns paved the way for a more global approach to media effects, which regards media as a key element in cultural socialization as a whole, looking at the way in which individuals grow up in a society in which media help shape our understanding of the world. This has been referred to as *cultivation theory*, or *cultivation analysis* (Signorielli & Morgan, 1990). This approach grew out of the work of George Gerbner, who carried out a series of content analyses of violent television during the 1970s (Gerbner & Gross, 1976). Gerbner's argument was that society and culture, of which the media are now an integral part, interact continuously in a dynamic process, creating a "symbolic environment" that we enter at the moment of birth (Gerbner, Gross, Morgan, & Signorielli, 1994).

Gerbner and colleagues argued that the most fundamental effect of media violence was not increased aggression in individual viewers but instead a more general climate of *fear*, characterised by a tendency to overestimate the amount of crime in viewers' own neighbourhoods. This was investigated through the development of a "mean world index" based on various factors, including education level and amount of television exposure (Signorielli & Morgan, 1990). This was applied in a variety of different cultural settings—such as Holland, the United Kingdom, and Australia—with varying success; for example, heavy viewers of violent U.S. films in Australia overestimated the amount of violent crime locally but *not* that of violence in the United States (Pingree & Hawkins, 1981).

Two key ideas in cultivation theory are *mainstreaming*—the idea that different cultural backgrounds and values gradually converge as a result of international TV culture—and *resonance*—in which media simply acts to reinforce people's real-life experiences (Potter, 1991). The concept of mainstreaming shares certain similarities with theories of cultural, or media, *imperialism* that argue that as a result of the vast export of U.S. television and films American cultural values have permeated the globe, with particularly strong effects in developing countries. This approach has been widely criticised, partly because developing countries' proportion of locally produced media has increased in recent years, but also because it seems to make the (possibly biased) assumption that American cultural values are uncritically absorbed wherever they are broadcast.

Most cultivation research uses viewing patterns as a key measure, comparing "heavy" and "light" viewers on various scales and questionnaires. Therefore, most of the research uses survey methods, such as questionnaires and diaries of media use. However, many researchers have argued that there are key factors that influence cultivation beyond viewing patterns (and these generally don't tell us much about *how* TV is watched) or the part that other media (e.g., newspapers) play in the process. One influential theory has been Greenberg's (1988) *drench* hypothesis. This argues that certain media figures and themes have far more impact than do others (e.g., a single celebrity endorsement of a product may have more impact than thousands of ingenious ads). "Drench" is sometimes discussed as an alternative to the usual "drip drip" approach of cultivation.

USES AND GRATIFICATIONS RESEARCH

Another strand of criticism of the traditional effects approach went in the opposite direction from cultivation theory, toward individual differences among viewers. This became known as the study of media uses and gratifications, which began in the early 1970s and became very popular in the 1980s. Like effects research, uses and gratifications (U&G) research draws on traditional psychological theory, but from the Maslow school of humanism rather than from behaviourism. In this approach, the viewer (or general media user) is in control, and rather than studying the person as a passive recipient of effects, U&G researchers look at the *motives* for using media and the *needs* that media use gratifies. A typical U&G subject is the isolated older adult who uses TV for companionship, and, increasingly, information about the outside world.

U&G research, above all else, studies how and why people use media in general. For example, Papachrissi and Rubin (2000) examined the factors that were most likely to predict people's use of the Internet. They identified five motives: interpersonal utility (online social interaction), a way of passing time, information seeking, convenience, and entertainment. Some Internet users used the medium as a *functional alternative* to social interaction, particularly those who had difficulties making friends and forming relationships in face-to-face communication.

Katz, Blumler, and Gurevitch (1974) identified five assumptions of U&G research:

- Media use is goal directed and purposive (after all, someone has to turn the TV *on*).
- Media is used to gratify wants and needs.
- Effects need to be studied through a filter of personality (individual differences) and environmental factors.
- There is competition between media use and other forms of communication (e.g., we choose to stay in and watch a video rather than go to the pub).
- Most of the time, the user is in control.

The U&G approach has spawned a number of interesting approaches. Chief among these is the media system *dependency theory* (Ball-Rokeach & DeFleur, 1976). In a media-saturated world, people have come to depend heavily on media outlets for information about all manner of topics. The most typical example of media dependency is the weather forecast (especially in changeable climates like the United Kingdom), although most of us will have a further level of dependency in that we will trust certain weather bulletins (e.g., BBC Radio 4) more than others (other BBC radio stations, or TV channels). Our dependency may be limited by other resources—for example, at the time of writing, football matches in the English Premiership are only screened live on Sky Sports (a cable or digital channel), so terrestrial television users must depend on a highlights package for their information.

DeFleur and Ball-Rokeach (1989) outlined three key ways in which individuals develop "dependency relations" with media. First, media provides information that enables us to *understand* the world, which at the level of "self-understanding" provides us with information about ourselves—it enables the creation of identities by allowing us to interpret our behaviour and compare ourselves with others. Second, we may depend on media for *orientation*, either in terms of action (deciding to go on a diet, or voting in an election) or interaction (how to deal with social situations). Some recent British research on children's discourse about television would seem to support this idea (Messenger Davies & Machin, 2000). Finally, media provides us with opportunities for *play* (either for solitary relaxation, or social activity like visiting the cinema). Dependency theory is more overtly psychological than many aspects of media theory in that it draws on several psychological theories, notably cognitive processes, symbolic interactionism, and ecological psychology.

Another U&G approach that has drawn heavily on psychological research is *expectancy-value theory* (Palmgreen, Wenner, & Rayburn, 1980). This approach has applied Ajzen and Fishbein's (1972) theory of reasoned action to explore media use and attitudes toward media. According to the expectancy-value model, we watch TV shows that we expect will fulfill our needs (e.g., watch a sitcom to be entertained), and also ones that we value highly (our friends recommend it). Then we weigh up how well those needs have been gratified (did we laugh? were we offended?) in order to make a decision to repeat the behaviour in the future. If our expectancies are always met, we establish patterns of habitual media use (perhaps we become "addicted" to a soap opera).

THE "ACTIVE AUDIENCE"

Although uses and gratifications research has helped to shift attention from passive to active media users, the approach has nevertheless been criticised—particularly by media scholars in the cultural studies tradition—for working at the level of the individual rather than focusing on the social and cultural context of media use. In media studies (as opposed to communication science), the preferred term is *audiences* (Ruddock, 2001; Tulloch,

2000). At the same time, there is much more interest in actual media content (as opposed to the detached, often artificial, media stimuli used in effects research). The focus is on *texts*, which have been examined in isolation for the cultural "representations" that they contain. One important influence derives from the work published in the journal *Screen* during the 1970s, in which film scholars drew heavily on psychoanalytic theory to investigate the way audiences identify with and respond to different representations and imagery in films. However, these studies lacked an important ingredient—the audience—because they consisted largely of theorists' readings of film "texts" rather than studies of audiences themselves.

Rather than treating the media user as an isolated television viewer locked into dependency relationships with media, audience theory sees media users as social groups that are strongly influenced by media, but—like U&G subjects—far from passive. Much audience research, particularly in the United Kingdom, has focused on the cultural *meanings* that users derive from media. However, even within this tradition there is considerable diversity. The role of the text in audience activity is contested—some researchers (e.g., Fiske, 1987) prefer to examine texts by themselves, although there is a growing awareness of the importance of empirical audience research alongside analyses of cultural material (Livingstone, 1998a; Ruddock, 2001).

The origins of audience research, certainly in Europe, can be traced to the establishment of the Birmingham Centre for Contemporary Cultural Studies by Stuart Hall and colleagues in the 1970s. "Cultural studies" is a disciplinary hybrid of literary theory, the arts, and social and political theory, strongly influenced by political thinkers such as Marx and Gramsci. One objective of the Birmingham Centre was to replace the two-step flow concept of communication (sender–message–receiver) as the dominant model of media research with a *circuit*, in which information is encoded (e.g., using television production codes) and then decoded by the audience (Hall, 1980). The idea behind this model was that concepts such as two-step flow and the "hypodermic needle" theory of media effects treat "messages" as fixed by the sender, and reception processes as determined by the message content. For example, a TV documentary criticising the IRA will be interpreted by viewers as critical, and will achieve the producer's desired intention of hardening viewers' attitudes against the IRA. In Hall's model, the documentary may be encoded so as to suggest criticism, but viewers may "read" it in a completely different way.

Hall suggested that there are three ways in which audiences could "decode" media messages: first, the *dominant* code, by which viewers select the "preferred reading" intended by the producers (e.g., anti-IRA); second, the *negotiated* code, by which audiences modify the message, perhaps on the basis of personal experience (e.g., thinking that some of the documentary's criticism is a little harsh); and third, the *oppositional* code, by which the message is treated with deep suspicion, as biased establishment propaganda (e.g., the reading of IRA sympathisers). These different encodings were put to the test in a major project by David Morley, who studied many different social groups and their "readings" of *Nationwide*, a BBC current affairs show from the late 1970s (Morley, 1980). He found that certain groups—trade union officials, for example—made very different readings than did others (e.g., housewives), thereby suggesting that the social and cultural characteristics of the audience partly dictate which form of encoding they will use.

Hall's circuit model has been enormously influential, particularly in Europe, and has in some ways created a body of audience research that is entirely different in nature to the communication science tradition. Much of this literature is openly hostile to the notion of communication as a science, criticising effects and gratifications research alike for their apolitical adherence to objectivity, and arguing that media research should be deeply embedded in political and cultural theory. However, within the audience literature there is much that is directly relevant to media psychology—naturally, because audiences are made up of *people*, whose activity constitutes *behaviour*, the two essential ingredients of any psychological theory.

One interesting departure from Hall's circuit model is the "active" audience tradition, which moves away from the overtly political approach of the Marxist cultural scholars and tends to treat audience members as passive victims of state oppression rather than as individuals or groups with critical interpretative freedom. In addition, certain features of Hall's model have been criticised; for example, Lewis (1991) argued that it is impossible to identify "preferred readings," and that the encoding/decoding process is not so great a departure from the two-step flow model of communication that it was set up to oppose. Other authors have asserted that the circuit model can perhaps be applied to news and current affairs media (because it was designed with this sort of material in mind), but offers inappropriate explanations for audience responses to popular cultural material, such as soap opera and pop music (Livingstone, 1998a).

Active audience research has been heavily influenced by postmodernist theory, which at its most extreme has argued for a dissolution of the concepts of audiences and texts altogether: "There is no text, there is no audience, there are only the processes of viewing" (Fiske, 1989, p. 57). Such a move leaves audiences to make what they like of cultural material; for example, one could reinterpret *Top Gun* as a gay film by attaching different meanings to communal male showering and other male bonding episodes (Ruddock, 2001). Inevitably, these developments have come in for criticism from traditional media researchers, but in areas like feminist research they have been seen as a crucial move away from media theories dominated and restricted by deterministic notions of social class (Ang, 1996).

The most exciting research carried out in the active audience tradition is closely examined in part V of the book (where important studies of soap opera, talk shows, and cartoons are discussed) along with work on fandom by the likes of Henry Jenkins (Jenkins, 1992a, 1992b). This work differs from much of the literature on media audiences because it credits the audience with much more interpretative power—here, media products are viewed not as political propaganda, disturbing imagery, or texts encoded to produce certain readings, but instead as cultural material from which viewers and readers can construct identities (as *Star Trek* fans, or whatever). This research sits uneasily within academia, partly because popular culture has been treated with immense suspicion by universities (and often in the media itself) as material unfit for intellectual investigation. However, it is vitally important that such snobbery is countered by academics in order for serious media psychological research to flourish.

THE WAY FORWARD?

It seems that, in terms of media theory and audiences, something of a crossroads has been reached (Livingstone, 1999). Within media studies, authors like Ruddock (2001) and Tulloch (2000) have begun to address the issue of *method*, which cultural scholars have preferred to ignore in their emphasis on excavating cultural meanings, "preferred readings," and the like. Media researchers are urged to support their textual analyses with empirical data collected from audiences themselves. Meanwhile, in psychology there has been an increased emphasis on the need for qualitative research (Giles, 2002), which leaves the way open for media psychology research that is more interpretative in nature. There is the exciting possibility, then, for convergence between the fields of media studies and psychology, with scholars on each side importing relevant theories, concepts, and methodologies from the other. Furthermore, the popularity of both psychology and media studies at the undergraduate level ensures a healthy academic base from which to integrate the most important work in the two disciplines.

Chapter **3**

Research Methods in Media Psychology

With such a diverse range of theoretical approaches to media research, it is not surprising that there is so little agreement on methodology. Whereas experiments and quantitative surveys have ruled the roost in North America, European scholars have tended to study media texts themselves. As two leading figures in media research put it, "Some of us are studying the texts of popular culture while others are studying their effects on audiences . . . the former don't know anything about the audience, and the latter don't know anything about the texts" (Katz & Liebes, 1986, cited in Gunter, 2000a, p. 9).

In this chapter I summarise the most important approaches and techniques that have dominated media research, and suggest some potential avenues for research in media psychology. The chapter is structured in much the same way as the previous one, in that it begins with a discussion of experimental techniques similar to those used in "effects" research, followed by survey- and questionnaire-based approaches such as those used in cultivation analysis and uses and gratifications research. The chapter concludes by looking at qualitative approaches such as ethnography and discourse analysis.

THE EXPERIMENTAL TRADITION

Drawing from the natural science approach of behaviourism, media effects research relied almost exclusively on experimental methods for many years. Scientific orthodoxy within psychology meant that research was only taken seriously if it adhered to the rigid controls of experimentation—complete control over "confounding" variables, random allocation of participants to treatment and control groups, scrupulous attention to the design of experimental materials, and so on. Rather less attention was paid to the nature of both the participants (invariably undergraduates, although increasingly schoolchildren were studied) and the generalizations made about the statistical results. However, one of the characteristics of the experimental psychology approach is that it is *nomothetic*—in other words, it seeks to explain human behaviour through the application of universal laws—so students, as a readily available subject pool, were deemed as good as any other group for examining these laws.

The classic "effects" study could be described as a *pretest/posttest* experimental design with one control group and one (or more) treatment group(s). This is the kind of design that has been used to study the effects of violent media. For example, the treatment group watches a film clip containing violent action whereas the control group watches a neutral clip. Because the researchers are interested in changes produced by the film, participants are tested on the same measure (perhaps a mood inventory, or physiological measure, or attitude scale) both before and after the screening. Then a statistical test is used to find out whether the film has produced a significant change in that measure for the treatment group. If so, this must be compared against the data for the control group; if there is no significant change for this group, the researchers could claim support for their "effects" hypothesis. Table 3.1 contains a hypothetical example of the kind of results for which the researchers would be aiming.

The most common way of testing whether such a result is significant is to carry out an *analysis of variance* (ANOVA). This kind of test examines the effect of different "factors," or independent variables, in an experiment, and aims to explain which factors account for most of the variance in the data. In this example, there are two factors: One is a between-subjects factor (which group the subjects are in), and the other is a within-subjects factor (the difference between the pre- and posttest measures). Obviously, we would expect both of these factors to explain the results, but individually they may not tell us much; what is important in this example is the *interac-*

TABLE 3.1
Hypothetical Data From an "Effects" Experiment

	Mean Score on Mood Inventory (High = Positive)	
	Before Film (Pretest)	*After Film (Posttest)*
Treatment group	35	18
Control group	33	34

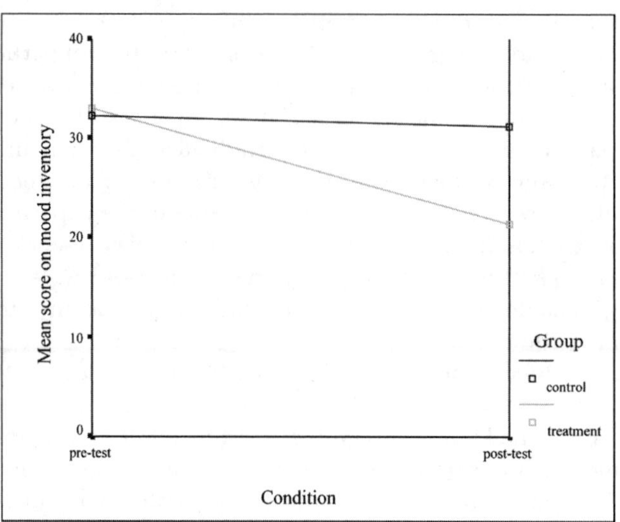

FIG. 3.1. Lineplot of means for hypothetical example.

tion between the factors; in other words, the pre-/posttest difference is only significant for one of the two groups (the treatment group). This effect is best illustrated using a lineplot (Fig. 3.1); if the lines are nonparallel, then an interaction has occurred.

This kind of research design is elegant and parsimonious—it is easy to follow, and produces convincing data. But there are two very important disadvantages of experiments of this kind, which place fairly rigid limitations on what we can conclude from such studies. These disadvantages concern external validity and statistical inference, which are addressed next.

External Validity

The term *external validity* refers to the application of the experimental findings to the behaviour we are hoping to study. One of the harshest criticisms of effects research is that most of the data, however convincing, are collected using students in artificial laboratory environments that bear no resemblance to real-life media experience. Furthermore, as ethics procedures began to tighten up in the 1970s following the controversy surrounding studies like Milgram's obedience experiments and Zimbardo's prison study, the measures of behaviours like "aggression" and "violence" became increasingly tame (see chap. 4).

These criticisms can been countered in two ways. First, it could be argued that the studies are not *meant* to be realistic, they are simply meant to demonstrate short-term effects under controlled conditions. Second, the use of student participants could be defended by the claim that responses to the stimuli are governed by universal behavioural laws, so the demographic characteristics of the sample are irrelevant. Furthermore, inferential statistical tests such as ANOVA take into account the size of the sample, so the significance of the result is based on conservative estimates of the probability of discovering this effect in the overall population.

Unfortunately, effects researchers have not always been so modest in the interpretation of their findings, often claiming that results of this nature demonstrate unquestionably a direct causal link between everyday media experience (e.g., television) and everyday behaviour (aggression, sexual offences, etc.). Much of the time it is simply extrapolation of actions performed on video in the laboratory as a shortcut to studying "television." Again, researchers might defend these measures by claiming that (a) the environment is not so artificial as is made out, and (b) people will display the same cognitive and affective responses under any conditions; therefore, any results obtained in the laboratory are likely to be an *underestimate* of what happens in the real world.

At this point, the argument relies on our faith in universal laws, and scientific rigour—a philosophical tradition known as *positivism.* This tradition underpins much of the research carried out in psychology, and indeed in science in general. Aviation engineers will point to the ecological validity of aircraft design, in which laboratory studies of flight and fuel capacity have been thoroughly supported by the aviation industry's ability to fly millions of people around the world every year. Can the same inferences be made for psychological data obtained in the laboratory?

Today, many experimental media researchers are sensitive to these issues, and attempt to design experiments using more realistic stimuli (e.g., whole shows rather than clips)—stimuli that are chosen by participants—to reflect individual preferences, and a wider range of samples beyond the undergraduate population (Ward & Greenfield, 1998).

Statistical Significance

A second problem with experimental data, indeed with any data that are analysed using inferential statistics, is that much of the time the outcome is determined by the design. To begin with, the whole research process may be driven by a desire to support a specific hypothesis; this is particularly the case with media violence research, in which political interests often may have pressured researchers into designing experiments to demonstrate direct effects (Ruddock, 2001). Furthermore, for a long time there has been a bias in psychological journals toward publishing only studies that report significant results (Peters & Ceci, 1982). One study demonstrating a significant media effect may be published at the expense of a dozen demonstrating null effects.

At the moment, one trend in (quantitative) psychology is toward the design of increasingly *powerful* studies. It has been argued that psychologists typically design "low-power" studies that reduce their chances of supporting their hypotheses. By selecting the right sample size for the size of effect you are hoping to demonstrate (based on previous research), you are much more likely to obtain significant findings.

One method that is frequently used to counter the problems of statistical inference is *meta-analysis,* which is a statistical technique designed to examine relationships between specific variables across a number of studies (Giles, 2002a). In meta-analysis, the data from the original studies is converted to a standard form, such as Cohen's d (a measure of effect size), thus ironing out most of the biases that result from flaws of individual studies. The work of Paik and Comstock (1994) and Wood, Wong, and Chachere (1991) are examples of meta-analyses examining the relationship between media violence and aggression. Meta-analysis has, however, been criticised for use with psychological variables, which are notoriously difficult to control, and—compared with, say, chemistry or microbiology—subject to wide variation in terms of stimuli, dependent measures, and study design. For the reasons outlined previously, these criticisms are particularly relevant for experimental research in media psychology.

Other Uses of Experiments in Media Psychology

Of course, experimentation is still an important method for media psychology. However, today scientists are perhaps more modest about the inferences they can draw from their results, and of the kind of psychological processes that are most suitable for the experimental method. Typically, experiments are used when researchers wish to examine physiological effects of media; for example, heart or pulse rate, brain activity such as EEG (electrical firing of neurons), and electrodermal measures such as skin conductance (Hopkins & Fletcher, 1995; Lang, 1994). Alternatively, researchers may wish to record overt behaviour—for instance, an "eyes on screen" measure of attention to television (Thorson, 1995). These kinds of data are useful because they provide a measure of continuous response, rather than relying on participants' self-reports after viewing. However, they usually require more sophisticated statistical analysis, such as time-series analysis (Watt, 1995).

Another area in which media psychologists make extensive use of experiments is the field of cognitive processing of media material, such as newspaper headlines or advertisements (Cameron & Frieske, 1995; Gunter, 2000a). Experimental measures have been used to examine participants' memory for differently structured narratives (Berry, Scheffler, & Goldstein, 1993), and recall for different types of news content (Gunter, Berry, & Clifford, 1981). Other experimental studies have investigated the importance of cognitive load on media processing; in these, secondary reaction-time measures (e.g., how long it takes a television viewer to respond to an audio tone or visual cue) have been employed as a way of monitoring viewers' attention to media material (Basil, 1995; Geiger & Reeves, 1993).

Possibly the most common class of media experiments are those deriving from the tradition of social psychology. Here, Reeves and Nass (1996) were particularly influential in devising experiments that effectively replicate those carried out in social psychology but are instead applied to users' interactions with media. Some of these concern perceptual responses; for example, faces seen in close-up are responded to more intensely than those seen in smaller scale (Reeves, Lombard, & Melwani, 1992). Others address the quality of media stimuli, such as gender, voice, evaluative criteria, and personality of media figures. There is also a tradition of experiments designed to assess issues such as gender stereotyping, through paired association of gender and particular behaviours, and through the use of attitude measures (Ward & Greenfield, 1998).

In addition to laboratory-based studies, media researchers have also used experimental designs to carry out fieldwork in "natural" settings; some of the well-known media violence studies in the 1970s were carried out using relatively controlled environments such as young offenders' institutions (Leyens, Camino, Parke, & Berkowitz, 1975). These studies are generally referred to as *field experiments*, not to be confused with *natural experiments* in which researchers use naturally occurring behaviour as the basis for statistical analysis. An example of the latter could be any number of studies that have observed the effects of the introduction of television into new environments, ranging from Himmelweit et al.'s early studies of television in the United Kingdom (Himmelweit, Oppenheim, & Vince, 1958) to a more recent project that looked at the introduction of television to the Atlantic island of St. Helena (Charlton, Gunter, & Lovemore, 1998). These designs lack the control of laboratory studies, but make up for this by their enhanced ecological validity; however, establishing causation is nearly impossible in natural settings, where there are so many confounding variables in operation.

SURVEY METHODS

Opportunities to carry out natural experiments are, of course, extremely rare, and restricted to unusual circumstances. If we are interested in studying everyday experiences of media we have to resort to more contrived methods of data collection (which typically involve asking people what media they use) and devising indirect measures of its effects or influences. Typically, such research is done as part of a large project using a variety of methods, known as a *survey*. Most people are familiar to some extent with the techniques employed in surveys, having been accosted at some point by market researchers wielding clipboards in shopping centres. Media researchers *do* occasionally use on-the-spot sampling techniques, usually to recruit potential interviewees, but they also employ a host of other methods.

The survey was the principal tool of cultivation research (see chap. 2), in which disillusionment had set in regarding the kinds of information gleaned through laboratory-based studies. George Gerbner has often been quoted as saying that, in media research, there is no such thing as a control group (Livingstone, 1998a), or, more specifically, if we are to divide television viewers into "light" and "heavy" viewing groups, the light group will always be contaminated by other media influences in addition to the number of hours spent in front of the set. This effectively rules out the use of independent variables manipulated by researchers and the kind of causal hypotheses employed in laboratory studies. In its place, the trend in audience research has moved toward *correlational* designs, in which researchers study associations, or relationships, among a number of measured (dependent) variables instead of studying the effects of one variable on another.

An example of this type of research at its most basic might be a questionnaire that measures demographic information about respondents (e.g., age, gender, and ethnicity) along with quantifiable information about media use (e.g., amount of television watched, number of magazines bought regularly, number of hours spent using the World Wide Web). These latter measures would then be related to the demographic measures. The basic measure here is the *correlation coefficient* (r), a value that measures the degree of association between two variables.[1] We might expect older adults to watch more television than younger adults; therefore, in an adult sample, we would expect a positive correlation between age and amount of television viewing ($r > 0$). A perfect correlation ($r = 1.0$) is extremely unlikely, and one would treat such a figure with deep suspicion, but even values as low as 0.1 might be statistically significant in very large samples. Conversely, we would expect younger adults to spend more time surfing the Web than older adults. In this case we would predict a negative correlation ($r < 0$). Again, a perfect negative correlation ($r = -1.0$) is unlikely, and the same sta-

---

[1]Note here that an *association* between two (or more) variables cannot be used to infer cause and effect. With complicated correlational designs (e.g., those used in structural equation modelling), there is some degree of control over potential confounding variables, albeit not as much control as in an experiment. Even so, whether such designs can be used to examine cause and effect is open to debate.

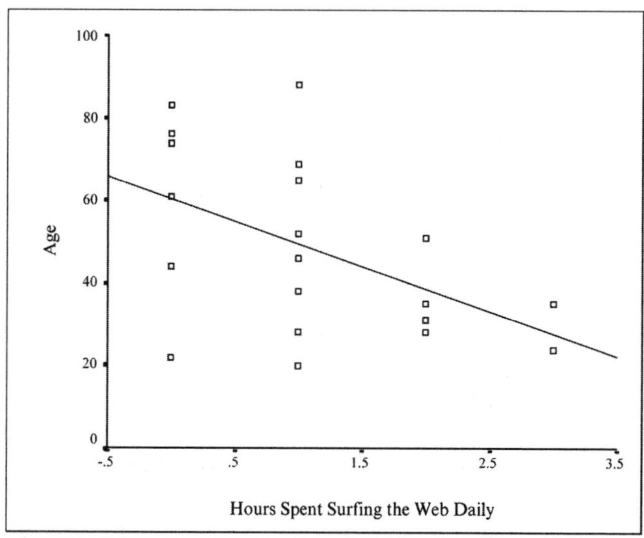

FIG. 3.2. Scatterplot of hypothetical negative association between age and Internet use.

tistical significance rules apply. Figure 3.2 depicts this association using a scatterplot with regression line.

The association between two variables is a useful starting point in an analysis, but bivariate correlations (as they are called) have a notorious habit of throwing up spurious relationships. For example, at the time of writing, the computational hardware required for Internet access is still relatively expensive, and it might be that the age/Web correlation could be attributed to the fact that younger adults are wealthier, or at least have more disposable income, than older ones. Therefore, we need to weight the age/Web correlation according to the correlations between both of these variables with income. This is called *partialling out* the effects of a third variable. We can calculate a new *partial correlation* between age and Web use that might be fairly close to zero (i.e., no association) because, with income taken into account, old and young adults do not differ significantly in their use of the Web. Figure 3.3 depicts this relationship by plotting the points on a three-dimensional scatterplot. Notice how, with the third variable introduced, the points cluster together in the centre of the plot, with only the occasional "outlier" (exceptional case).

This kind of partial correlational analysis provides the building blocks for a hugely influential statistical approach known as *multivariate* analysis. In recent years, psychologists and other social scientists have devised models of behaviour on the basis of many different variables, all entered into the same equation. The goal of such analyses is to examine the extent to which

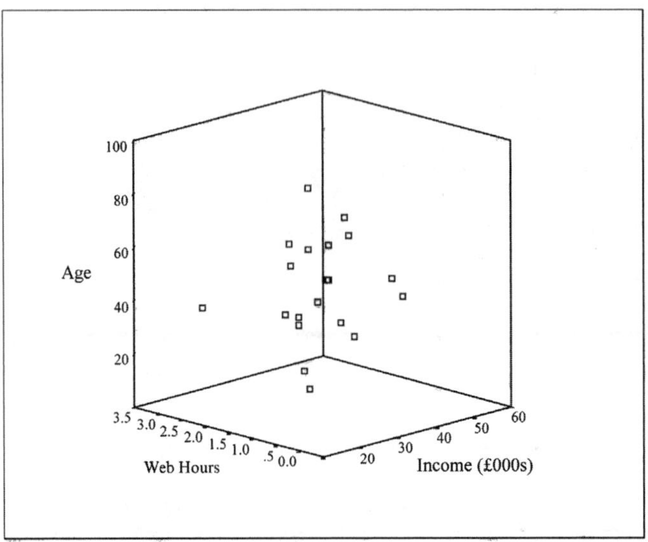

FIG. 3.3. Age, Web use, and income plotted in three-dimensional space.

variables predict one another, both individually and collectively. Therefore, in our hypothetical study, we might devise a model in which we can lump together all the demographic variables, measure their combined influence on all the media use variables, and portray this analysis by means of a path diagram (see chap. 7 in Giles, 2002a). Such analyses may seem horrendously complicated, but they have become a popular alternative to "reductionist" experimental designs, because they acknowledge the complexity of real-world media influence. Although rarely in use when Gerbner was developing his cultivation theory, such designs would seem ideally suited to the kind of questions that cultivation theorists were addressing.

Sample Selection in Survey Research

Because surveys are carried out in the real world, the choice of respondents is a highly important matter. We can no longer rely on student samples from which to generalise our results, unless we are studying a specific population (e.g., working-class African American women, or young Bangladeshi men in East London). The goal of a large-scale survey is usually to assemble a sample that is *representative* of the overall population. This may require stringent recruitment procedures.

In 1988, the British Film Institute conducted a project entitled *One Day in the Life of Television,* in which 22,000 U.K. viewers—recruited through press and TV advertisements, posters, and leaflets—wrote a diary about their television viewing on a single day (1 November). Three years later, the BFI began a 5-year Audience Tracking Study using a subsample of the original respondents, in which a number of "questionnaire diaries" were completed during the period. Gauntlett and Hill (1999), in an analysis of the data, described how the tracking study sample was determined. First, respondents in different age groups were recruited so that the sample reflected the age distribution in the U.K. population. Second, respondents from different types of households were recruited on a similar basis (to ensure representative numbers from single-person households, two-adult/two-children households, etc.). Third, roughly equal numbers of males and females were recruited.

The one major sampling omission in this study was the failure to document respondents' ethnic backgrounds. It might be argued that this was not the point of the study, or that any further restrictions would have drawn out the sampling process interminably. Whatever the case, it lessens the genuine "representativeness" of the sample for the U.K. population as a whole. This is another example of the difficulties inherent in attempting to generalise from sample to population. However, different surveys have different functions; in-depth studies with individual semi-structured interviews over a long time period may involve as few as 20 respondents (Hansen, Cottle, Negrine, & Newbold, 1999). Here, representativeness is sacrificed for the richness of the data.

Survey Materials

The bedrock of the survey is the questionnaire, although the term *questionnaire* covers a vast range of different instruments, from the kind of diaries used in the BFI tracking survey to tightly designed measures such as semantic differential scales (Livingstone, 1989). Of course, the choice of measure used depends entirely on the analysis you are intending to conduct. Surveys using interview data are likely to be analysed qualitatively, whereas scales and other psychometric measures are designed specifically with statistical analysis in mind. Giles (2002a) contains an overview of the different types of questionnaires and scales appropriate for this kind of research (see also Hansen et al., 1999; Robson, 1993).

An alternative approach to measuring audience activity is to track media use as and when it happens. The diaries used in the BFI tracking study are an example of this type of technique, but other, ingenious measures have also been used by audience researchers over the years. One such device is the "people meter," used from the 1980s onward to track television viewing activity. This is an electronic device that each viewer in a household activates as he or she begins and ends watching television. Other reactive measures include time-sampling techniques, in which the researcher telephones respondents at key moments during the study period to ask them questions about their media use, or sends messages using an electronic pager (for a discussion of the pros and cons of these different methods, see Gunter, 2000a). Again, the usefulness of these measures very much depends on the information required; people meters, for example, record very little apart from hours spent in front of the screen.

Although this kind of information may seem rather basic for media psychological research, it must be remembered that a lot of the archival data that media researchers rely on is collected in this manner—namely, audience "ratings" for television shows. These data are enormously influential in determining television companies' approaches to programming (we are all familiar with the term *ratings war*—for example, when BBC and ITV are competing for the prime-time viewing audience). Ratings have been criticised for their low reliability (notably by Ang, 1991)—if ever there was a case of generalising from sample to population, they are it. *I've* never been asked what shows *I* watch on television, so why should I believe the figures?

Other (more serious) criticisms of television ratings include the argument that electronic devices like people meters are problematic because viewers forget to switch them on and off, especially during long viewing periods (Gunter, 2000a). Diaries and other self-report techniques may be prone to rather selective data, possibly for social desirability factors; Ruddock (2001, p. 10) gave the example of a "45-year-old father of two who doesn't really want to admit that he religiously tunes in to *Baywatch.*" In defence of ratings, it could be argued that they have quite high test–retest reliability; audience estimates remain pretty consistent across channels and shows. If they were as unreliable as claimed, there would surely be much greater fluctuation in the figures. Furthermore, if there is a taboo surrounding the report of watching softcore shows like *Baywatch,* which already has quite healthy viewing figures, what on earth is their true popularity? Perhaps we are best off not knowing!

INTERVIEWING AND QUALITATIVE ANALYSIS

Qualitative research has gained in popularity over recent decades, particularly in media research, as the emphasis has shifted away from studying effects and texts and toward the study of natural audiences—"the actual unfolding of everyday interactions with media" (Lindlof, 1987, p. x). Qualitative research in psychology differs from quantitative research in that it is concerned with *understanding* human behaviour rather than trying to control and predict it. It is therefore particularly useful in media psychology if we are interested in the meanings that media hold for their users, both individuals and groups. Qualitative methods have had to struggle for acceptance in both psychology and communication science, but this is now changing rapidly.[2]

Qualitative researchers often talk of an "umbrella" of methods, or a "toolbox," that applies to both the overall approaches to research (e.g., ethnography, grounded theory) and the techniques used to analyse data. Other researchers demand that techniques be allied to philosophical positions, such as feminism or critical theory. Almost any qualitative approach or technique is applicable to media psychology, because the field covers research with both audiences and texts, and the latter may include visual data as well as verbal. Many people working on the boundary of psychology and media studies advocate using a blend of quantitative and qualitative methods, or switching from one to the other as the research question requires (Livingstone, 1998a).

Interviews are frequently used in order to collect qualitative data in psychology. We may use one-to-one interviews to gather data on individuals' media uses and experiences, or focus group discussions to investigate how people talk about media and their role in everyday life. Focus groups were initially used in media research as an alternative to conducting experiments, in order to study the effects of radio (Merton, Fiske, & Curtis, 1957). The method was later adopted by market researchers to study brand image, and by political researchers as a tool for evaluating electoral campaigns. Recently, with the increasing popularity of qualitative social science research, focus groups have come into vogue in media studies as well as psychology (Adams, 2000).

Focus groups have been used to discuss many different aspects of the media, from soap operas to children's television to political issues. Often, they are used in an exploratory fashion, to generate ideas and materials for large-scale data collection using questionnaires or scales. However, they are probably most useful where the goal of the study is to collect rich data that can be analysed from an interpretative perspective—that is, to examine the meanings that different media products hold for people, rather than inferring these from closed-response questionnaire items or controlled behaviour in the laboratory (Lunt & Livingstone, 1996).

Focus groups usually consist of enough people to generate a meaningful discussion, but not so many that individual contributors drop out of the conversation. The optimum number is generally regarded as between six and ten (Morgan, 1988). Groups are sometimes assembled so as to be rep-

---

[2]All the same, this acceptance is a slow process, and long-held prejudices are hard to break down. An example of the hard work that needs to be done can be seen in W. James Potter's (1999) book *On Media Violence*, which referred to "social scientists" and "qualitative researchers" as if these constitute mutually exclusive groups of academics.

resentative of a particular social group, but often researchers prefer to use readily available "interpretative communities"—for example, groups of people who watch television together on a regular basis (Ruddock, 2001). As with survey methods in general, the number of groups studied and the degree of representativeness depend on the scale of the project and the topic under investigation. Livingstone and Lunt's (1994) research into British audience responses to talk shows is an example of a large-scale representative survey of this type. They carried out 12 different focus group interviews of between 4 and 8 people each (69 in total); data collection was stopped when "comments and patterns began to repeat and little new material was generated" (p. 181).

Electronic focus groups are becoming increasingly common in Internet-based research. These are groups of Internet users who take part in an online discussion forum, either synchronous (in real time) or asynchronous, at a conference site to which participants can contribute when as and when they log on. There are many special issues surrounding the use of the Internet for research, and there are probably good reasons for reserving such methods to studies of Internet use per se (see chap. 16). An excellent source for those interested in online research is Mann and Stewart (2000).

There are a number of different qualitative techniques that can be used to analyse interview data, although generally these dictate the nature of the study itself. For example, conversation analysis (Hutchby & Wooffitt, 1998) and discourse analysis (Dickerson, 1996) are both useful techniques for examining audience constructions of media phenomena as well as other social aspects of media use. In a more general sense, grounded theory (described in Giles, 2002a) provides some analytical techniques that may be applied to interview data; for an application of this approach, see Lemish and Tidhar's (2001) study of Israeli interpretations of *Teletubbies.*

ETHNOGRAPHY AND OBSERVATION

The term *ethnographic* has been used rather loosely in audience research. For example, David Morley's (1986) study, in which he interviewed participants in their homes (rather than some neutral setting), is often referred to by media scholars as an ethnographic study. There is a tendency in European media research to confuse "ethnographic" with "empirical" in cases in which audience researchers have taken the unusual step (unusual, that is, in the cultural studies tradition) of venturing out into the field and studying people rather than texts.

True ethnographic research—at least within social science—involves more than conducting a few interviews or questionnaires. In a study of everyday media use, it may mean that the researcher actually sets up camp in a household to record as much observational data as possible about the activities of the household and the role of media in its everyday life. Two examples from media research include a study of the effects of family interaction on television viewing (Bryce & Leichter, 1983), in which Bryce lived in a home with each family for a month, and Lull's (1990) research on family viewing behaviour.

The ethnographic tradition derives from anthropological research (particularly the work of Malinowski), in which researchers would establish themselves within a social community for long periods, often several years, and amass vast quantities of fieldnotes, archival documents, and other materials. Modern-day ethnographers often work much closer to home, and for shorter periods. An example of a media-related study that follows in this tradition is Marie Gillespie's (1995) examination of media use in a Punjabi community in a west London suburb.

In the same way that survey research encompasses a variety of methods (interviewing, questionnaires, etc.), so may ethnography incorporate a number of specific techniques. The most important of these is participant observation, which is often confused with ethnography per se, although it is a specific method in its own right (a participant observation could consist of an hour spent in a pub, but you could hardly call such a study an ethnography). The important difference between participant observation and natural, or laboratory-based, forms of observation is that the researcher usually makes no attempt to disguise his or her identity, acknowledging the importance of being "in the thick of things" in order to carry out a thorough analysis of the phenomenon under investigation. Even when—for safety's sake[3]—the researcher is incognito, he or she will mingle with the people being observed, making covert fieldnotes whenever possible.

Interviews are also an important part of most ethnographic research, both formally and informally; sometimes, during observational fieldwork, it is important to ask questions of coparticipants and record their answers later. Obviously, such data will not be scrutinised in the same way as tape-recorded verbatim interviews, but they will add important detail to the fieldnotes. Finally, archival data—documents, textual materials, and so on—often form part of ethnographic research, where appropriate. (For further detail on ethnography, a valuable source is Hammersley & Atkinson, 1996.)

---

[3]An example of an undercover participant observation is the research into football hooliganism by Marsh, Rosser, and Harré (1978), during which, for obvious reasons, the researchers did not wish to make it known to their coparticipants that they were social scientists carrying out a study!

ANALYSIS OF MEDIA TEXTS

Research on media materials themselves has been an important—indeed, central—part of European media research. As with audience research, texts have been studied both quantitatively and qualitatively.

Content Analysis

Content analysis has a long history within media research, dating back to the work of Berelson (1952), who advocated a tightly systematic approach to the technique in order to combat the inevitable problem of subjectivity. Berelson suggested ways of quantifying the frequency of syntactic or semantic characteristics of verbal data or visual symbols, and argued that such codification should be comprehensive; *all* content needs to be included in the analysis, otherwise researchers can take the liberty of being selective in what they choose to study. Some authors have cast doubt on whether content analysis can ever be a truly objective method (Gunter, 2000; Hansen et al., 1999), but see Thomas (1994) for a defence of the technique.

Content analysis is most frequently used in media research in order to investigate the nature of media representations (see chap. 10). Typically, a researcher constructs a schedule based on the possible types of representation (e.g., ethnic groups on British television) and the different texts to be covered (e.g., different genres of television show). A good example of a content analysis in media psychology is Livingstone and Green's (1986) study of gender portrayals in U.K. television advertisements; an important consideration in this study was how to group together different types of ads (is it enough to create a category such as "advertisements for alcohol," or do you need to break this down into beers, wine, spirits, and so on?). Very often, such decisions are determined by the research question or hypothesis you are seeking to test. Usually, categories in content analysis are not determined until all the material has been coded. For example, Wilson, Nairn, Coverdale, and Panapa (2000) content-analysed children's cartoons for references to mental illness, but the different categories these references fell into could not have been predicted in advance.

Analysing data gathered through content analysis poses problems different from those encountered when analysing experimental or survey data, because they normally come in the form of category counts ("nominal" data). The most basic type of analysis for this kind of data is the chi-square test, which can be conducted with only a few categories. For example, suppose you have collected data on the simple appearance of men and women in beer and food advertisements. You might end up with data like those in Table 3.2, usually referred to as a *contingency table.*

TABLE 3.2
Hypothetical Content Data for Chi-Square Example

Type of Advertisement	*Men*	*Women*
Beer	68	49
Food	34	77

The first step in a chi-square test is to calculate the *expected value* for each cell in the table. This is done by multiplying the total of the relevant row by the total of the relevant column and then dividing this figure by the sum of all the cells in the table. So, for the first cell, this would be:

$$\frac{117 \times 102}{228} = 52.3$$

Therefore, we would expect, from the overall distribution of men and women, and the frequency of different ads, the number of men in beer commercials to be somewhat lower than our *observed value* of 68. If we carry out the same calculation for women appearing in beer ads, we find an expected value of 64.7. However, our observed value is somewhat lower. This pattern is reversed for the food advertisements. A chi-square statistic (χ^2) is calculated by adding together the discrepancies in the cells; generally speaking, a high value is considered significant, meaning that there is an unexpected amount of deviation in the table. This finding is interpreted in a similar fashion to the two-way interaction in the experimental example at the start of this chapter—in this example, we could say that our two factors, gender and type of advert, are interacting to a significant degree; it seems that beer ads favour male representations and food ads favour female representations.

Naturally, most content analyses are much more complex than this one. There are sophisticated techniques for dealing with larger contingency tables, known as *log-linear analysis* (Giles, 2002a). This works a little bit like the model approach to correlational data described in the section on survey research; you predict interactions between different factors and test these as a set of equations. That way you could examine the portrayal of gender in several different genres of advertising, and also look at the inclusion of children, and perhaps the effect of different screening times or programme genres.

Finally, there is no need for content analysis to be quantitative; often, the data we have is not suited to statistical testing, because either we prefer not to assign the data to inflexible categories or the category boundaries are blurred. When this is the case, we may use qualitative content analysis

(Berg, 1995) in order to build up a taxonomy of materials, or to demonstrate a process or theory that explains the data.

DISCOURSE ANALYSIS

A different approach to textual analysis altogether is to perform qualitative analysis of verbal or visual data. This is a useful approach if we are interested in the meaning of texts rather than in simply counting the frequency of occurrence. Our previous gender/advert type analysis may look interesting, but the figures alone do not possess any explanatory power; for that, we need some form of interpretative analysis.

Discourse analysis has become a popular qualitative approach in both psychology and media studies in recent years, particularly in the United Kingdom (see Giles, 2002a). There are two broad traditions of discourse analysis, influenced by different concerns and theoretical orientations. The first tradition derives from sociolinguistics and conversation analysis, and is primarily concerned with language use, which requires close attention to the linguistic features of texts. In media research it has been used to study the structure of news stories, with particular emphasis on narrative style (Fowler, 1991; van Dijk, 1988).

The second strand of discourse analysis hails from the critical social science tradition, in particular the work of Michel Foucault. Here, the emphasis is on the text as deeply embedded in a variety of social and discursive *practices* that together constitute a version of reality. With regard to media texts, we might use this form of analysis to investigate the way that formal realism is produced in a television show. This relates closely to Stuart Hall's (1980) circuit model of communication discussed in chapter 2, in which media texts are seen as the discursive product of various "encoding" practices (production techniques, etc.), and operate as various discourses that then need to be "decoded" by audiences.

A detailed example of this type of coding practice was presented by Fiske (1987), who examined at some length a scene from the 1980s husband-and-wife detective show *Hart to Hart.* One technique he analysed was the use of extreme close-ups, which were used much more often with respect to villains (in the "preferred reading" of this particular text) than to heroes. Fiske argued that this is related to the use of personal space; the invasion of this space by the extreme close-up conveys either intimacy or hostility, depending on the context, and also enables the viewer to "see through" the villain, giving us privileged access to his or her body language or physiological response (e.g., beads of sweat on the brow, a private smile). Other production features that Fiske identified include the use of lighting, music, casting (attractiveness, ethnicity, etc.), deviant subcultures, setting, costume, make-up, and dialogue.

Discourse analysis has been criticised for its subjectivity and lack of formal procedure. Indeed, analyses such as Fiske's are frequently conducted without any disclosure of methodology—such details are often considered stifling or even irrelevant by cultural scholars (Tulloch, 2000). In psychology, however, more formal procedures for conducting discourse analysis have been articulated, and there is a growing acceptance of this kind of research. Furthermore, discourse analysis feeds into related techniques such as rhetorical analysis, which has proved useful for studying the nature of advertising (Berger, 2000), and narrative analysis, which has been used to study both textual material (e.g., news stories) and interview data (identities, life stories; Alasuutari, 1995).

It is important to regard all the methods in this chapter as complementary: Experiments can tell us some useful things about media and psychology, but questionnaires, interviews, observations, and textual analysis (both quantitative and qualitative) are essential for full understanding. There seems little doubt that the convergence between methods and epistemologies will play an important part in shaping the field of media psychology.

Part II

PSYCHOLOGICAL EFFECTS AND INFLUENCES OF MEDIA

The next four chapters deal with the material that is most often brought to mind when one thinks of media psychology, and that have been investigated using the most common social scientific methods from the second half of the 20th century. First off, there is a chapter on media violence. There should be no surprise that this is one of the book's largest chapters, because it is this aspect of the mass media that has attracted the largest amount of research funding, particularly in North America. Here, the consensus view is that there is a clear causal link between media violence and antisocial behaviour. In Europe the evidence is treated with some caution, but only recently have there been attempts to explore the media violence issue from other social scientific perspectives.

The chapter on violence is followed by one on prosocial media; these differ in that they are designed specifically for their intended effects. They range from educational media such as children's programming to informational media such as public service announcements and health communication. Also, mainstream media may communicate prosocial effects in the same way as antisocial effects, although research into these has attracted rather less funding, perhaps because psychology (and science in general) tends to be problem-driven—reactive rather than proactive.

Chapter 6 examines the issues around the effects of pornography on consumers. These have been investigated using methods that are similar to those employed in research on violent media, but the issues are somewhat different—like prosocial media, pornography is largely designed with its psychological effects very much in mind. However, rather less attention in the social scientific research has been paid to the actual users of pornography. There are also moral and political issues surrounding pornography, which have attracted much research from a feminist perspective; here the arguments are sharply divided, largely on the issue of censorship. However, recent developments in online pornography may be challenging the argument that pornography is fundamentally male exploitation of women.

Finally, there is a chapter on advertising, which spawned its own psychology over the last century, but is closely connected with mass media. At present, there are several loose ends of research that this chapter attempts to knit together. First, the advertising industry uses psychological theory in its own research, aimed at a business-oriented readership. Second, there have been various studies of the cognitive effects of television advertising, mostly on children. Third, cultural scholars have examined rhetorical appeals in advertising and the practice of "reading" ads. What is now needed is some integration of these literatures; hopefully chapter 7 might act as a springboard for this.

Chapter 4

The Effects of Media Violence

In Britain, 1972, violence certainly seemed to be on the rise. The Troubles had finally exploded in Northern Ireland, the IRA's first mainland bombing had taken place, the Conservative government was involved in increasing conflict with the Trade Unions, football hooliganism was rampant, and police statistics showed rises in criminal activity. Into this atmosphere was pitched another element: film violence.

Ten years earlier, the novelist Anthony Burgess had written *A Clockwork Orange*, a novella about a teenage thug, Alex, and his behavioural therapy at the hands of the prison service aimed at correcting his violent tendencies. The novel's most noteworthy feature was its strange language (an invented, Russian-influenced argot), which Burgess used to present the narrative in the first person, enabling the narrator to describe his "ultraviolent" activity in chilling, detached terms. For a while, a film version had been discussed; Mick Jagger was rumoured to be interested in the part. Eventually, the successful director Stanley Kubrick stepped into the breach, and in 1971 delivered a cinematic interpretation that matched the stylised charisma of the book. Alex and his "droogs" were kitted out in white overalls, bovver boots, and bowler hats. Each wore a single false eyelash. The first 15 minutes of the film showed them breaking into various houses and raping, murdering, and robbing the occupants.

Although the remainder of the film (over 2 hours) dealt largely with Alex's aversive therapy and rehabilitation, the blue touch paper had been lit. Even before the film went on release, there was feverish press attention: One paper carried the headline "THE SHOCKER TO END THEM ALL." A Labour MP, invited to a prerelease screening, allegedly declared: "I believe that when *A Clockwork Orange* is generally released, it will lead to a Clockwork cult which will magnify teenage violence." Nevertheless, the British Board of Film Censors saw enough merit in the film to award it an "X" (over-18) certificate.

The doom-mongers were not disappointed, however, as the press found plenty of examples to bear witness to the "Clockwork cult": A tramp beaten to death by a 16-year-old in Oxfordshire who claimed to have been influenced by the film; various sightings of rowdy teenagers sporting the droogs' garb; and, eventually, the rape of a Dutch tourist in London by a group of teenagers singing "Singing in the Rain," in emulation of the film's most notorious scene. After this incident, Kubrick, fed up with constantly denying the link between film violence and criminal behaviour, withdrew the film from general release, where it remained until it was granted a certificate again in 2000, after Kubrick's death. Needless to say, the re-release of *A Clockwork Orange* was greeted with much media interest, but as yet there have been no reports of imitative violence by viewers.

Of course, movie violence had stirred up controversy long before 1972, notably Hollywood gangster films in the 1930s. Here, again, the fear concerned imitative behaviour; reportedly, during this period, a New Jersey 12-year-old returned home from seeing *The Secret Six* and shot another child through the head (Hoberman, 1998). This heralded a long line of controversial films whose content has been associated with real-life violence, the most recent being Oliver Stone's *Natural Born Killers*, which has been linked with 14 murders worldwide (Ruddock, 2001). Television has not been spared; concerns about the effects of watching violence on the small screen have been rife ever since the medium's introduction (Himmelweit et al., 1958).

Today, it seems that violence is an accepted part of television programming and filmmaking, grossly exaggerated in its prevalence, and glorified in digital clarity. Three major content analyses of television violence have been conducted in the United States. The first, by George Gerbner and colleagues, spanned 22 years from 1967 to 1989. This analysis found that 80% of all the shows in the study (mostly prime-time viewing) contained some element of physical violence (Potter, 1999), although their definition of violence was very broad ("physical force" might be more accurate a term). However, it was not as broad as that used by Bradley Greenberg and colleagues in the mid-1970s, whose definition included verbal aggression as well as other forms of antisocial behaviour. These researchers estimated that there are, on average, 14.6 violent acts an hour on American television (see Greenberg, 1980).

The third major content analysis was conducted during the 1990s—the National Television Violence Study, funded by the National Cable Television Association. This study used a more precise definition of (physical) violence and found such content in 60% of prime-time programming (Potter, 1999). It also examined the narrative contexts in which violence occurred. In most cases, violence was used for personal gain (30%); in 58% of cases, the victim was not shown suffering harm from the violence; and 37% of violent perpetrators were left unpunished at any point in the show. Thirty-nine percent of violent acts occurred in a humorous context, thereby—the authors argued—trivialising their impact. The physical outcome of violence is rather neglected, so there is relatively little blood and gore in prime-time television—in fact, the authors observed close-up footage of the aftermath in only 3% of cases (Wilson et al., 1997, 1998).

What is it about fictional violence that causes so much controversy? Are we really that impressionable? Is there a direct causative relationship between watching violence (or any other kinds of activity) onscreen and then behaving violently in subsequent real-life situations? These questions troubled media and communications researchers throughout the last century, and the putative effects of media violence remain a source of vehement disagreement in this one. Despite vast amounts of empirical data apparently showing a clear relationship between watching violence onscreen and behaving aggressively in real life, both sides of the media violence debate remain as entrenched as ever. To paraphrase Freedman (1986), how can two eminent psychologists look at the same set of data and draw completely opposite inferences from it? The fact is that the media violence debate is highly complex, tapping into many of the methodological and epistemological arguments outlined in the previous chapters, and it raises all manner of questions about the best ways to research media influence and what we can conclude from the findings.

There are numerous articles, chapters, and books documenting the many findings concerning media violence from experiments, surveys, and field studies over the last 40 years. I do not attempt to summarise this literature in full, but I do want to discuss a number of interesting features of the media violence debate allied to specific studies, and suggest a number of avenues that have yet to be fully explored. Interested readers who want a full range of findings should consult one of the following sources. Two meta-analyses—Wood et al. (1991) and Paik and Comstock (1994)—are the most convincing studies to argue a correspondence between media violence and "antisocial" behaviour. Freedman (1984) offered a sceptical review of this literature, highlighting methodological concerns; see also the subsequent exchange between Freedman (1986) and Friedrich-Cofer and Huston (1986). For a complete rejection of the empirical research evidence from a range of epistemological perspectives, see Gauntlett (1995), Barker and Petley (1997), and Fowles (1999). For a well-balanced discussion of the media violence debate, Gunter (1994) is probably the best source.

WHAT ARE THE IMMEDIATE EFFECTS OF WATCHING VIOLENT MEDIA?

Two particular explanations have been very influential throughout the media violence debate. They are role modelling, derived from social learning theory (Bandura, 1973); and excitation transfer, a cognitive/physiological response to watching dramatic entertainment (Zillmann, 1971). Both explanations seem rather dated now—they have either been considerably elaborated in recent decades, or discredited entirely, depending on which version of the debate you read. Nevertheless, they long ago filtered into lay discourse about media effects in general, perhaps most importantly in the "video nasty" debate that followed the murder of toddler James Bulger in the early 1990s (Vine, 1997).[1]

Imitation

The imitative modelling of media effects was studied in a series of experiments by Albert Bandura in the 1960s, widely known as the "Bobo doll" studies due to the use of an inflatable plastic doll that children were observed to strike more frequently after watching an adult perform the same activity on video (Bandura et al., 1963). These studies have become an obligatory reference point for the coverage of aggression in social psychology and developmental textbooks, although they have been criticised for their low external validity. Particular problems include the artificiality of the laboratory setting and the use of leading cues such as the juxtaposition of the doll and a mallet; there are even reports of child participants saying, "There's the doll we have to hit" (Gauntlett, 1995). Perhaps the most problematic aspect of all is the use of artificial stimuli (video footage of psychology students playing with toys), bearing scant resemblance to the material

---

[1]Space does not allow a full discussion of the Bulger debate here, although the supposed link between the murder and violent media has had an enormous impact (in the United Kingdom, at least) on public thinking about media effects. My media psychology students (at the outset of the module, that is!) routinely offer the Bulger murder as incontestable evidence of the effects of video nasties on impressionable youngsters, although the connection was only made by the British press following a casual comment by the Bulger trial judge about the sort of "culture" in which Bulger's killers may have been brought up. A copy of the *Child's Play 3* video was subsequently discovered in one of the boys' houses, although there is no evidence that either child had actually watched it (Barker, 1997).

children would have watched on television, and having arguably little to do with media at all.[2]

The work on imitation of media violence has been somewhat curtailed over the years through ethical consideration for child participants (although see Josephson, 1987), and has led to a switch to more naturalistic forms of enquiry, notably surveys and self-report measures. Clearly, these methods are less capable of testing causal hypotheses because they rely on observed patterns of stastical association, and cannot test hypotheses about direct effects of viewing. Nevertheless, Comstock and Scharrer (1999, p. 287) argued that meta-analyses of this work offer "incontestable documentation that empirically there is a positive association between exposure to television violence and antisocial behaviour." This may be, although that association is tempered by many other variables that are not consistently controlled in all studies.

Given some of the modest effect sizes in Paik and Comstock's (1994) study, some caution must be exercised, particularly because the smallest effects are those for "extremely violent criminal behaviour"—precisely the outcome of media violence about which there is most concern. Furthermore, there is a clear relationship between the artificiality of the measures and the strength of the media violence effect. Experiments provide the strongest effects, as do aggression measures of "simulated violence," whereas actual violent behaviour, and measures of actual media use, provide weaker effects. I return to the measurement issue shortly.

Proponents of the media violence/aggression link often point to the results of "natural experiments" as convincing evidence of the link. Phillips (1983) examined U.S. crime statistics for the 10-day period following televised heavyweight boxing matches, and discovered a significant rise in homicides during this period. No corresponding effect was found for Super Bowl contests. Also, the ethnic background of the homicide victims was consistent with that of the victor in these matches, suggesting that the murders were carried out to avenge the boxing results. Although these findings look convincing enough, there are other significant correlations within the same dataset that are less obviously explained. For instance, the significant rises in homicide were observed on the third, sixth, and ninth days of the period. Also, the effect was stronger for bouts taking place outside the United States and for those featured on network news.

Leaving aside the question of whether sport can be lumped together with other forms of violent media to produce identical effects, these rela-

---

[2]To be fair to Bandura, the primary objective of the Bobo doll (and later) studies was to observe the role that modelling and imitation played in the learning of aggression per se. As in much psychological research, the inclusion of a "media" condition in the experiments seems to have been a secondary consideration.

tionships remain spurious in the absence of any theoretical framework that can explain them. Similar doubts surround the retrospective study of Hennigan et al. (1982), who examined crime statistics around the time of the erratic introduction of television to the United States between 1949 and 1952, and found that the cities that received television at the start of this period showed an increase in crime relative to cities with delayed introduction. The biggest rise here concerned burglary, rather than violence, and can only be attributed to the introduction of television *in general*. One possibility is that commercial television stimulates materialistic envy among disadvantaged members of a society, although this would not explain a similar link between violent television and burglary found by Paik and Comstock (1994), except that most studies have noted a relationship between heavy viewing of violent television and viewing of all television.

Imitation of violent behaviour on television is likely to be influenced by the status of the aggressor. A common complaint is that media coverage of violence glamourises the behaviour. Certainly the fears concerning the effects of *A Clockwork Orange* were based partly on the popstarlike portrayal of Alex and his droogs, and the sharpest criticism of films like *Bonnie and Clyde* were that the casting of attractive young stars Faye Dunaway and Warren Beatty would make their violence acceptable (even desirable) among young fans. There is some evidence that the attractiveness of, and degree of identification with, aggressive models enhances the effects of media violence (Donnerstein & Smith, 1997; Huesmann, Lagerspetz, & Eron, 1984; Jo & Berkowitz, 1994). It is even argued that video game characters may act as violent role models for children (McDonald & Kim, 2001).

Excitation

Imitation is in the eye of the beholder; the researcher needs to make a judgment about whether or not a child has hit a Bobo doll in response to a televised stimulus. Physiological responses to the same stimuli are less ambiguous. Clearly, an exciting film will speed up heart rate and increase blood pressure and skin conductance; could violent film be an exceptionally exciting stimulus, whose effects carry over to subsequent activity? This was essentially the hypothesis advanced by Dolf Zillmann, who developed the concept of "excitation transfer" in line with Schachter and Singer's (1962) two-factor theory of emotion. The theory states that emotions are physiological responses to which we assign appropriate labels according to a variety of personal, social, and cultural factors. Excitation transfer takes place when the adrenalin produced by an exciting stimulus carries over to later activity and may be misidentified as a result. Thus, in the context of media violence, an exciting film produces an excess of adrenalin production in a viewer; the viewer then gets into an argument on the bus home that descends into physical conflict, unaware that his or her physiological excitation is the residue of the viewing experience rather than adrenalin produced by the argument itself.

This effect is rather easier to test experimentally than imitation, because it is, in terms of latency, a short-term response (its duration is another issue). It is also somewhat easier to measure, because overt physiological responses are involved. Perhaps most importantly, it is (partly) a low-level response that can be tested using artificial stimuli; this contrasts with imitation, which depends wholly on higher-level cognitive processes. Not surprisingly, then, there have been numerous experimental studies examining the short-term effects of viewing violence, and these have generally produced positive associations between violent media and subsequent aggressive behaviour (Paik & Comstock, 1994).

A typical excitation transfer experiment involves participants viewing films, or short clips from films, in different conditions; usually there is a control condition in which the film is neutral, or nonviolent, and at least one experimental condition in which the film is violent. Participants are then placed in a situation in which they can display aggression or hostility toward a stimulus figure (typically, a confederate of the experimenter). Initial excitation transfer studies (e.g., Zillmann, 1971) used Milgram's classic electric shock paradigm, where aggression is measured by the intensity of (simulated) shocks given by the participant to an actor masquerading as a participant in the context of a conditional learning task. Usually, participants in the violent condition display higher levels of physiological arousal during the viewing episode than do those in the control condition. They also display significantly higher levels of aggression in the subsequent task, particularly when anger or frustration has been induced (Freedman, 1986).

Is excitation transfer a good explanation for media-related violence? Much depends on the length of the effect; certainly, if the adrenalin produced by film violence wears off within 2 hours, it cannot explain the *Clockwork Orange*-related incidents, because the violence in that particular film is restricted to the first 15 minutes of a 136-minute epic. There is also remarkably little record of violence *during* film screening; the most famous examples of lawless cinema behaviour accompanied footage of (nonviolent) early rock 'n' roll performances, such as Bill Haley's "Rock Around The Clock." The misattribution effect in subsequent exchanges is an ingenious theory, and Zillmann and Weaver (1997) produced some interesting evidence in a study in which violent viewing led to the endorsement of force as a way of resolving conflict in a story-scenario study. However, the absence of a pre-viewing measure of aggressive conflict resolution makes it hard to establish causation in this particular study.

The measures of aggression themselves in excitation transfer studies do not provide much confidence for the application of the theory in real-world situations. Ethical considerations have greatly restrained the measures that can be used; indeed, if induced aggression due to excitation transfer is believed to persist well beyond the viewing episode, it is doubtful whether any such experiments are ethically acceptable unless participants are detained for some time afterward. Clearly, it would be unacceptable to put participants in a situation in which actual physical violence could be elicited, and even the manipulations used by Schachter and Singer (1962) would raise eyebrows at ethics panels today.

Increasingly, researchers have had to get creative. "Aggression" in a study might consist simply of a response to a questionnaire. Even studies with more naturalistic designs have used nonharmful measures, such as the delivery of blasts of loud noise toward opponents in a reaction time task (Anderson & Dill, 2000). One commonly used paradigm involves the use of a confederate of the researcher as a stimulus figure toward whom participants can display aggression. For example, Zillmann and Weaver (1999) had a research assistant deliver negative feedback on a pen-and-paper test in order to induce anger in participants, who were later informed that the assistant had been offered a permanent post in the university. They were then asked to indicate their impression of her suitability. Low scores were taken to indicate "hostility," and were highest for participants in both the "violent" and "negative feedback" conditions. But if the effect of media violence is merely to make employers a bit more fussy, is it worth all the money spent on research?

The biggest problem for excitation transfer theory, however, is the fact that violent media are not necessarily the most exciting stimuli to which viewers are exposed. This was evident in the original Zillmann (1971) study where, as a comparison condition, participants were shown a nonaggressive (indeed, "nonpassionate") erotic film with nudity and "tenderness." This stimulus not only produced higher physiological arousal than did the violent and control films, but also induced participants to give higher-intensity shocks to mock participants in the learning task. This finding clearly supports excitation transfer, but provides mixed evidence for a media violence effect; it should perhaps be pornography users who riot in the streets. In fact, studies that have used combinations of erotic and violent stimuli have produced the highest aggression measures of all (Paik & Comstock, 1994). Pornography, however, is a complex topic that requires a chapter of its own, and I leave the issue of sexually violent media for chapter 6.

Desensitisation

An important issue related to excitation transfer, or any physiological theory of media violence, is the effect of repeated exposure to violent material over a long period of time. Short-term effects induced in the laboratory are spectacular in themselves, but surely don't the effects wear off after sufficient time as habituation sets in? The result, it is argued, is *desensitisation* to violence, both on television and in real life. If such an effect occurs, might repeated exposure to violent media not blunt the effects of laboratory research on physiological responses? Friedrich-Cofer and Huston (1986) argued that because of such considerations, the media violence literature actually *under*estimates the real effects.

On the other hand, if exposure to violent media desensitises us to televised violence, its effects should be more pronounced for research participants who are unfamiliar with such material. However, large-scale analyses of media violence have consistently noted strong effects for males, who are much heavier consumers of violent media, and weaker effects for females—the reverse pattern of what might be expected from desensitisation theory (Freedman, 1984). Friedrich-Cofer and Huston (1986) dismissed this argument on the grounds that biological differences in aggression are sufficient explanation for any observed male/female differences in media effects. Nevertheless, even when boys have been studied separately, the amount of televised violence they have watched predicts their levels of aggression (Huesmann et al., 1984).

All in all, the direct effects of media violence offer something of a mixed bag of findings (Freedman, 1984; Gunter, 1994). Whether we accept the positive relationships found by researchers in experiments with numerous shortcomings may depend on what we are prepared to consider evidence of an effect. Do we allow a modicum of imperfection in our research designs? Is internal validity the most important feature of good science, or must we be able to generalise from all studies? Increasingly, researchers are moving away from "magic bullet" theories such as excitation transfer and modelling; even those theories' original authors have elaborated considerably on their ideas. Nevertheless, there are many other important factors that need to be taken into account when assessing the impact of media violence.

CHARACTERISTICS OF THE USERS OF VIOLENT MEDIA

A year before writing this book, on hearing that *A Clockwork Orange* was due for official general re-release, I headed for the cinema, eager to see what all the fuss was about. Some of my favourite films are extremely violent—

Scorsese's *GoodFellas* and *Casino*, for example, which, according to Comstock and Scharrer (1999), are liable to increase my use of aggressive language. Perhaps they have. I have certainly not hit anyone since watching these films, or other favourites such as *Pulp Fiction* and *Trainspotting*, all of which contain scenes of extreme violence. Furthermore, if the effects of media violence were universal, we should be most concerned about the film censors themselves, who watch endless scenes of graphic violence, some of them too disturbing to merit a certificate!

As a middle-class academic, it could be argued, I have developed a critical sensibility that allows me to enjoy such cultural fare without it interfering with my day-to-day behaviour. But we must beware of applying what has become known as the third-person effect with regard to media, which is particularly strong in relation to media violence and aggression (Hoffner et al., 2001). In this situation, the effects of media on other people are overestimated, especially on people of lower social class and educational level, and on members of outgroups. Conversely, the effects of media on the self, and on members of the same social group, tend to be *under*estimated (Duck, Hogg, & Terry, 1999). If violent media induce physiological effects, as excitation transfer theory would suggest, these should override individual differences in response. Nevertheless, gender has been found to moderate the effects of violent media considerably (Freedman, 1984). Perhaps other individual characteristics are important too.

In order to study individual differences rather than blanket responses, it is necessary to move from experimental designs to survey designs and the use of psychometric tests. This makes direct causation impossible to infer, but indicates a less reductionist approach to the problem, examining the effects of violent media on people with different personal histories and attributes, rather than as experimental subjects in a laboratory. It also prompts a shift from studying direct effects to actual media use. This has important implications for media psychology, because it means we can begin to consider the *functions* of watching violent media.

Personality Characteristics

What sorts of people are attracted to violent media, and what individual characteristics make some people more vulnerable to its effects than others? Personality, or dispositional, variables have been increasingly built into media violence research designs. Most obvious, perhaps, is the level of aggression exhibited by participants at the outset of a study. Brad Bushman (1995) assessed *trait aggression* (the biological tendency for an individual to display aggression) in a series of studies that examined both preferences for violent media and the amount of noise delivered against an opponent in a reaction-time task following exposure to violent film. High levels of aggression measured by a standard questionnaire predicted both a preference for violent films and the volume of the noise delivered in the reaction-time task.

Bushman (p. 950) interpreted these results as evidence for differential effects of media violence, quoting movie director Alan Pakula as saying that "movie violence is like eating salt. The more you eat, the more you need to eat to taste it." This is the desensitisation argument in a nutshell. It also suggests that individuals actively seek out violent stimuli to satisfy a craving. Krcmar and Greene (1999) developed this idea in their research relating violent media use to self-report measures of risk-taking and sensation-seeking behaviour. Like a lot of multivariate studies of media violence, their findings are mixed; the subscales of their instruments have different associations with different forms of media use. For example, disinhibition predicts viewing of cop shows and contact sports, but thrill seeking predicts noncontact sports alone! The authors admit that their data offer little support for any direct causative influence of these personality characteristics on violent media use.

Perhaps the biggest popular concern about violent media is that they may act as a trigger for dormant aggressive tendencies in certain viewers. Zillmann and Weaver (1997) examined the relationship between the effects of violent media (measured by a choice for violent solutions to conflict scenarios) and scores on the psychoticism scale of the Eysenck Personality Inventory. Although no overall relationship was found between psychoticism and preference for violent solutions, there was a strong association between these measures for males scoring in the upper half of the scale. This concurs with other findings in relation to gender and violent media, and Bushman's findings relating to trait aggression.

Studies of young offenders' media preferences, although thin on the ground, paint a different picture—not one of vulnerable psychopaths tipped over the edge by the antics of Arnold Schwarzenegger, but instead one of distinct social groups differing in their use of media. These individuals—the kind who elicit most concern in popular fears about media violence—display similar viewing habits to other young people except that they actually watch *less* television, and rarely watch films either at the cinema or on video (Gauntlett, 1995). These findings concur with Paik and Comstock's (1994) low levels of association between violent media and extremely violent criminal behaviour. Intuitively, we might suggest that teenage criminals spend their evenings out burgling and mugging, not staying in to watch video nasties.

McGuire (1986) claimed to have identified two subgroups of media users who buck the overall trend: One, "street fighting men," fit the previously described profile, displaying highly antisocial behaviour but little violent media use; the other, ironically labelled "wimps," watch large amounts of violent media but refrain from acting it out in real life. The street fighting pattern makes logical sense, but the wimps are surely a much more interesting bunch than McGuire's dismissive label might suggest, and warrant closer inspection.

Other personality attributes have been studied in relation to media violence, such as extraversion. It is hard to imagine low-arousal individuals being content to sit quietly and watch television for long stretches.[3] One study that directly related extraversion to media use found that adolescent extraverts showed a preference for action and adventure films (Aluja-Fabregat & Torrubia-Beltri, 1998). Conversely, Krcmar and Greene (1999) found that risk taking negatively predicted violent media use, also suggesting that perhaps individuals requiring high arousal find that media, however violent, fail to satisfy this need.

Motivations for Violent Media Use

Why do people watch violent films and television? The studies discussed so far seem to treat media violence as an unfortunate by-product of media use in general. The literature is full of content analyses detailing the prevalence and nature of violent scenes on television (Comstock & Scharrer, 1999; Gunter, 1985a; Signorielli, Gerbner, & Morgan, 1995), but there is relatively little data collected on people's reasons for actively selecting violent media in the first place. However, we cannot answer this question without taking a closer look at what actually constitutes violent media, a major problem with the literature.

The rape and murder scenes in *A Clockwork Orange* are indisputably violent. Thirty years on, however, their impact is considerably diminished by more relaxed attitudes of filmmakers and censors, and by technological innovations that have increased the graphic realism of screen depictions of violence. Nevertheless, one of the features of the media violence literature has been a tendency to ignore different genres of media to the effect that the category "violent media" can encompass such diverse material as Bugs Bunny, contact sports, adventure films, and snuff movies across several decades, and there is no distinction between the presentation of this material on grainy black-and-white movie reel and on DVD. One content analy-

[3]Environmental factors might override the effects of (inherited) personality; for example, heavy television viewing has been blamed for the inability "to sit quietly for several minutes" (Singer, Singer, & Rapaczynski, 1984, p. 87). However, other explanations for this finding might include cultural factors, family background, or even the idea that television has replaced "doing nothing" as a way of passing the time.

sis identified no fewer than 31 different types of violence in a range of popular media (Berger, 1995).

When we talk about violent media we must be precise about what we mean. Signorielli et al. (1995, p. 280) described television violence as "the overt expression of physical force . . . compelling action against one's will on pain of being hurt or killed or actually hurting or killing." Such a definition can suffice for a content analysis, but it is too broad to capture the type of media that is actively sought out for its violence. Simple content description also ignores the cultural value of the material; motivations for viewing a film like *A Clockwork Orange* will differ enormously between cinema or video users. Most films that receive certificates based on violent content are valued for other reasons, such as comic appeal or general artistic merit (e.g., *Pulp Fiction, GoodFellas*). In the purest sense, the term *violent media* refers to cultural material that has little to recommend it *apart* from its violent content—films that would be classified as "video nasties."

There are two fundamental reasons why an individual (or a group) might seek out violent media. The first is simple curiosity; the second is that violent media presents viewers with a challenge. Curiosity is aroused initially by the publicity surrounding violent movies. Audiences flock to the cinema to see what all the fuss is about, and are then drawn into a test of endurance as the drama unfolds.

Initial curiosity may be driven by the ratings that censors award to films. Although the aim of this system is to guide parents and protect children, some researchers have found that it may have the effect of turning adult material into "forbidden fruit" (Christensen, 1992). In an experiment involving undergraduates, Bushman and Stack (1996) found that warning labels positively influenced participants' choices of programs from a television guide. For adolescents, gender is a mediating factor; whereas the attraction of forbidden fruit increases boys' preference for material with warnings, girls tend to avoid potentially disturbing or inappropriate material (Sneegas & Plank, 1998). Gunter (2000b) argued that a ratings system based on age evolved because it was thought that viewers might avoid a film if explicit information were included in the warning (e.g., "contains scenes of graphic violence"). He proposed a system closer to that for children's toys, based more on age-appropriate information ("suitable for age 12 and upward").

The attraction of "forbidden fruit" for teenage boys is part of a broader rite-of-passage that is part of the preparation for adulthood (Johnston, 1995). Like smoking a first cigarette and tasting a first alcoholic drink, seeing an adult-only movie has become one of the targets of early adolescence. Goldstein (1998b), in an analysis of the attractions of violent entertainment throughout history, emphasised the importance of the group viewing context for the enjoyment of violent movies. Enduring a video nasty with your friends is a test of nerve. Open revulsion, or avoidance, are signs of failure; instead, adolescent boys distance themselves from the drama by marvelling at the special effects. This way, the effects of violence are rationalised, although displays of excitement are not uncommon, providing an acceptable outlet for emotional expression. Teenage girls are more likely to use romantic drama ("weepies") for this purpose.

Annette Hill (1997) studied the reactions of viewing violence by conducting focus group interviews with undergraduates. She found that the endurance test of adolescence appears to continue in adulthood, with "testing boundaries" emerging as a key theme in the interviews. Much of the time this involves a form of self-censorship—for example, a viewer may cover his or her eyes in anticipation of a grisly scene. However, these interviewees were articulate, educated adults discussing artistic fare such as *Reservoir Dogs*, where the violence itself is not the primary attraction of the film (although the surrounding controversy may act as a spur to potential viewers).

Catharsis

One long-held theory is that watching violence has a cathartic effect on the viewer, enabling them to discharge violent tendencies by acting them out vicariously through identification with fictional aggressors. This derives from Freudian theory, and the belief that humans enter the world programmed with a set of "primitive" impulses; civilized society, so the story goes, has developed ever-more elaborate outlets for releasing these impulses, including artistic expression (Freud, 1930). This is excitation transfer in *reverse*—viewers enter the cinema full of pent-up aggression and leave it sated and becalmed. In actual fact, this is probably just what *does* happen in the cinema, especially when lurid press reports of sensational violence attract groups of viewers bristling with the anticipation of a good bloodbath. The rarity of actual violence in the cinema provoked by onscreen violence suggests that this is a classic case of the expectancy-value effect (see chap. 2). Audiences are more likely to riot if the anticipated shocker turns out to be a frothy romance.

Note, however, that empirical research offers little support for the catharsis hypothesis, but this may reflect the fact that media violence in the laboratory tends to be unexpected, and not actively selected by participants. Few studies have been *designed* to investigate the cathartic effect of media violence, and it is not enough to reject the catharsis hypothesis on the evidence of excitation transfer studies. In the latter, baseline measures of excitation are carried out to ensure that participants are screened to make sure that they are not highly aroused prior to viewing the violent stimuli, and it is likely that highly aroused participants are excluded from any analyses (dropped as "outliers"). According to the catharsis theory, these are the people who are most likely to seek out violent fare. This is one area that would still benefit from further experimental study.

Studies of everyday violent media use are less common, but in a diary study of long-term media use, adult males were found to watch more violent media during periods of stress (Anderson, Collins, Schmitt, & Jacobvitz, 1996). One suggestion is that the cathartic effect of screen violence works at a symbolic level, particularly for children watching cartoons. In an unusual study observing children's facial expressions as they watched television, Lagerspetz, Waldroos, and Wendelin (1978) found that although adult aggression and violence were clearly disturbing, the children responded to the violent antics of cartoon characters with expressions of pure joy.

This finding is consistent with Bruno Bettelheim's (1976) theory (following Freud) that violent fairy tales perform a therapeutic function in childhood, purging children's primitive desires. However, Tatar (1998) suggested that the childhood appeal of violence lies more in the nature of its telling—children are responding with glee to the "surreal excess" of the narrative. Asbach (1994) argued that there is a symbolic aspect to such material, maintaining that the appeal of violent cartoons lies in children's identification with the underdogs as they are seen to triumph over physically more powerful aggressors (e.g., Jerry in *Tom and Jerry*, Road Runner and Tweety Pie). This identification works at a metaphorical level, with the sympathetic characters as children and their opponents adults. A similar framework underpins much adult-oriented media violence, particularly in the "Rambo," Clint Eastwood, and Arnold Schwarzenegger films that pit lone, essentially moral, figures against a cast of hostile aggressors (e.g., the *Terminator* films).

Does Media Violence Sell?

One other long-standing debate in media research concerns the attractions of violent media. A commonly held (and somewhat paradoxical) view is that "violence sells," and thus it is inserted into otherwise harmless television shows and films by unscrupulous producers intent on upping the ratings and box-office takings. How true is this? Diener and de Four (1978) conducted a study in which they compared students' ratings of favourite television shows with the amount of violence the shows contained. Not surprisingly, perhaps, there was no relationship between the two. Diener and de Four tested this experimentally by showing participants two versions of a cop show—one with violence inserted and one without—and found no significant association between enjoyment and inclusion of violent content.

Similar findings were obtained in a British study examining audience appreciation of programmes and the amount of violence they contained

(Wober, 1992). When respondents were asked directly about the aspects of shows that enhanced viewers' enjoyment, there were mixed findings. Some viewers enjoyed an episode more if the violence resulted in the baddies' comeuppance; for others, notably females, a negative relationship between violence and appreciation was found (Wober, 1997). These issues suggest that a key element in the media violence debate is the *meaning* of violence for viewers, which may differ sharply among individuals. This element has been largely neglected in the laboratory research.

COGNITIVE FACTORS IN MEDIA VIOLENCE

Cultivation theorists took a perspective on the media violence debate different from the effects researchers. For them, the primary concern was not that violence would be imitated, but instead that the prevalence of violence in the media resulted in a climate of fear in the population at large. This "mean world" effect was demonstrated in studies that found that heavy viewers of television were likely to overestimate the amount of violent crime that took place in the real world (Gerbner, Gross, Morgan, & Signorielli, 1980). Although this interpretation rests largely on an association between total viewing of television in general and estimates of crime, Gerbner and colleagues defended their argument by addressing their many profiles of mainstream television that found substantially higher levels of violence than real crime figures would predict (Gerbner et al., 1978).

Subsequent research in this vein has looked more closely at the precise link between media use and attitudes. For example, Reith (1999) argued that frequent viewers of crime dramas developed an authoritarian "aggression structure." Aggressive individuals are attracted to crime dramas, which tend to portray the defenders of law and order in a victorious light, and this channels their aggression into an authoritarian direction against lawbreakers. However, the data in Reith's study seem rather ill suited to test her hypothesis, consisting of 1976 U.S. election survey statistics that point to nothing more startling than a relationship between amount of crime drama viewing and positive attitudes toward the police and the military. Other studies have suggested that crime drama is popular because it has a reassuring effect on the viewer (Berkowitz, 1984; Zillmann & Wakshlag, 1985); however, the current popularity of more realistic crime programmes (such as ITV's *The Bill*), which often lack the "closure" of traditional cops-and-robbers shows, may require alternative explanations.[4]

---

[4]Indeed, *The Bill* is arguably a soap opera (see chap. 15), and its success has spawned many "warts and all" crime dramas on British television. Does the current diversity of this genre render most of the earlier theories redundant? Some follow-up studies would seem to be in order here.

Most public concern about media violence concerns the effects of films and entertainment in general. Cultivation theory forces us to look more broadly, particularly at the role that news bulletins and current affairs television play in perpetuating fear about crime. For example, memory for disturbing features of TV news tends to be more powerful than for other kinds of information (Newhagen, 1998; Newhagen & Reeves, 1992), thereby making crime and violence more salient to viewers. At an individual level, negative news bulletins have been found to intensify personal concerns, even when not directly related to the content of the programme (Johnston & Davey, 1997).

At a more general level, there is occasional concern about "copycat violence," particularly in relation to civil unrest. Outbreaks of street disturbances in different urban areas of the United Kingdom often cluster together in time, although it is difficult to determine how television coverage of the first incident has acted as a catalyst for subsequent disturbances in other areas of simmering tension. Esser and Brosius (1996) carried out a study of right-wing attacks on ethnic minorities in Germany, and found that there appeared to be a pattern relating to media coverage of previous attacks. As this correlation might be spurious, they further analysed the data in terms of the outcome of the attacks. During the first wave of violence, victims tended to be rehoused in foreign workers' hostels away from the area of the attack—presumably a desired outcome as far as the racist aggressors were concerned. During the second wave, this outcome was less common. The correlation between news reports and subsequent attacks was much stronger for the first wave, suggesting a "priming" effect whereby right-wingers were more likely to attack minorities if they heard of similar attacks that had resulted in victims' relocation.

Concerns about the effect of television news have, however, tended to be downplayed in relation to the effect of entertainment. This result perhaps stems from the opinion that news programmes are faithful reflections of reality, and that it is simply a matter of public interest to be informed about real-life violence.

Priming Effects

One way in which media violence might elicit aggressive behaviour in viewers over long periods of time (a lifetime, perhaps) is through *cognitive* processing rather than crude behavioural responses. Cognitive effects of media can be grouped into two very broad categories: They may elicit obtrusive thoughts (e.g., dreams, fantasies, or preoccupations about violence), or they may work at a more conscious level in that they stimulate *ideas* about how to behave. It is the latter mechanism that is thought to provide the basis for imitation of screen violence, rather than the simple learning and reinforcement process argued by behaviourists. In fact, Bandura has revised his earlier proposals considerably over recent decades into a more global social cognitive model of media effects (Bandura, 2001).

Another earlier theory of the effects of violent media has also been modified in recent decades. This is the *disinhibition* argument, which states that media violence causes viewers to shed their (supposedly natural) inhibitions about displaying aggression—for example, if violence is seen to be successful for a screen hero, according to the disinhibition argument we are likely to select a violent option for solving real-life problems. This theory was tested using movie footage of a fight and providing half the participants with a justification for the violence; those participants then responded more aggressively to a graduate assistant who subsequently angered them (Berkowitz & Rawlings, 1963). The problem with disinhibition theory is that it assumes that an individual is naturally predisposed to solve problems peaceably—fair enough in the sample of college students used in this study, but hardly true of the violent criminal offenders who pose a greater threat to society.

Berkowitz has since refined his theory into a more general cognitive–associationist approach to media violence, in which the key mechanism is *priming* (Berkowitz, 1984). According to this theory, implicit (or unconscious) memories of violent scenes can be reactivated if appropriate cues are provided. In one study, participants watched either a hostile or a neutral film, and were then presented with a series of incomplete sentences. Those in the hostile condition chose significantly more hostile words to complete the sentences (Jo & Berkowitz, 1994). These processes are thought to underly the effects produced in studies like Zillmann and Weaver (1999), in which target people are rated negatively after watching violent films, because the violence is said to have activated hostile thoughts and associations.

Similarly, when individuals are required to make decisions, the priming of violent stimuli may influence their choice. In one study, a group of children were shown a film containing either a fight scene or a boat ride, and the content of the film predicted whether they would subsequently choose to take part in a pie fight or a raft ride (Worchel, 1972). Another way in which media violence might prime subsequent behaviour is by activating certain patterns of cognition or behaviour that have become formulaic over time. Huesmann (1986) described this process as the learning of aggressive "schemas," or scripts, which are activated under certain conditions. For example, a young man confronted by an aggressive drunk in a bar might respond by throwing a series of punches in the style of a favourite film star, perhaps emulating a sample of videotape that he has watched repeatedly.

These findings suggest that the effects of media violence may well depend on the *meaning* that the violence has for the viewer. Research into children's attitudes to cartoon violence indicates that cartoons are generally not perceived as violent, particularly by boys (Aluja-Fabregat & Torrubia-Beltri, 1998). Perceptions of violence by adults also seem to depend on programme genre, and on specific aspects of the action. Gunter and Furnham (1984) found that British viewers rated violent scenes from British television as more violent than similar scenes from U.S. television, largely because the portrayals were believed to be more realistic. The type of violence was also important; many of the British victims were stabbed or beaten (i.e., scenes involving actual physical contact), whereas American victims tended to be shot (remote, long-distance violence). Interestingly, this trend was reversed among highly aggressive viewers, perhaps because they identified more closely with the use of firearms in real life.

If semantic characteristics of media violence are important, does violence actually have to be *viewed* to have an impact? A current area of concern, particularly in the United States, is the violent content of popular music lyrics, particularly in rap music. Artists like Eminem and 2 Live Crew have provoked much press controversy (no doubt with a bit of help from their publicists!) in recent years by reciting lyrics that are loaded with sexist, homophobic, and brutally violent words and imagery. Rubin, West, and Mitchell (2001) found that fans of rap and heavy metal music scored significantly higher on measures of aggression than did fans of other musical genres. Catharsis theory might suggest that loud, angry music serves as a tension release for aggressive listeners, but fans of this music also displayed less trust (toward people in general) than did fans of the other genres in this study. Rubin and colleagues hypothesised that rap music in particular is popular among disaffected youth, and questioned whether the appeal of violent lyrics can be explained by catharsis alone.

One recent study suggests that although violent rap lyrics may or may not prime aggressive cognitions, they may serve a negative purpose by contributing to stereotypes about minority groups. Johnson, Trawalter, and Davidio (2000) played participants either a violent or nonviolent rap track and then presented them with a list of scenarios in which the stimulus figure was either a Black or White man. In the "violent" condition, participants of both ethnic groups rated the Black figure as both dispositionally more violent and lower in IQ than the White figure.

CULTURAL AND IDEOLOGICAL ASPECTS OF THE MEDIA VIOLENCE DEBATE

Scientific evidence alone is not enough to convince sceptics of the association between media violence and real-life aggression. The debate is coloured by all manner of cultural and ideological issues, and even if the methodological flaws in the literature were to be ironed out, many academics would still be unwilling to acknowledge the relationship. Frustration engendered by the situation has led some proponents of the link to make ever-more ludicrous claims, such as Centerwall's (1993) comment that media violence is responsible for 10,000 homicides annually! Such hyperbole does not lend credibility to the scientific argument.

Many authors see the media as a scapegoat, cited by cultural commentators and politicians who are desperate to provide a simple explanation for what appears to be an uncontrollable rise in violent crime (Fowles, 1999; Gauntlett, 1995). Media influence also provides a good argument for a defence lawyer who wishes to present his or her client as the victim of uncontrollable psychological forces (indeed, one police officer at the time of the *Clockwork Orange* furore claimed that many youngsters were successfully citing the film as an excuse in order to reduce the length of their sentences). Ironically, the media themselves seem as keen as anyone to promote the link. The press frenzy surrounding the James Bulger murder trial in Britain in 1993 is a case in point. This was sparked by a report, written at a politician's request, by a child psychologist (whose research was not remotely connected with media psychology) about her concerns over the effects of violent video. The report was subsequently published in *The Psychologist* (Newson, 1994a).

Following a short radio interview about the report, press agencies informed the British national newspapers that, after years of denying the link, psychologists had changed their minds and were now eating their words. The following morning's headlines screamed: BOFFINS' U-TURN ON VIDEO NASTIES (or words to that effect). It was a fantastic opportunity for the media to bash academia, but why should the media be so eager to hurl blame at themselves? The answer may have something to do with the idea of a media hierarchy in which newspapers present themselves as arbiters of truth, whereas entertainment media are essentially vulgar and of little value. However, it is interesting to note that two crimes involving reenacted scenes from *Child's Play 3* occurred *after* the publicity explosion surrounding the video in question (which had been available for some time before the Bulger murder itself; Newson, 1994b). The prospect that ideas based on the film may have been actively "primed" by the tabloid coverage of the Bulger trial has been conveniently overlooked!

Cultural snobbery has been cited as a key factor in the media violence debate. Barker (1997) argued that fears about violent entertainment are part of a general attack on lower-class culture by the middle classes through history, pointing to numerous analogies in recent history. During the 1950s, comic books were the subject of similar concerns about the effects of depictions of violence on impressionable minds, and even as far back as the 19th century the same argument was used to condemn "penny dreadfuls"—the forerunners of tabloid newspapers.

Gunter (1994) argued that these concerns are part of the culture of uncertainty that accompanies the advent of each new medium, and so it is not surprising that the latest version of the media violence debate concerns the effects of video games. A much-publicised link between violent video games and real violence was made following the gun attack on fellow students by two boys at Columbine High School in 1999. Subsequent reports claimed that the boys were frequent players of "shoot-em-up" video games and that their penchant for these games must be linked to their crime (a link keenly pursued by other groups with interests in deflecting attention away from issues such as the availability of firearms).

Not surprisingly, the effects of video game violence have been researched to some extent by media academics and psychologists, typically drawing on the same experimental paradigm as the media violence literature of the 1960s and 1970s. The Bobo doll has even made a comeback, this time clad in a white karate-style robe (Schutte, Malouff, Post-Gorden, & Rodasta, 1988). However, it is not clear whether media violence methods (and findings) can be translated directly to the effects of video game play.

First, because video games are, above all else, *games* rather than entertainment media, the role of the user is notably different. The interactive nature of games such as *Tomb Raider* means that excitation transfer effects are likely to be greater, especially in the short term; video games may also have a greater role to play as cathartic activity. Second, individual differences are likely to be more salient for video game effects given the fact that the user plays a more active role in choosing to play a specific game than, say, the role of a television viewer who may simply watch whatever channel is on, or whatever show his or her parents are already viewing.

For a variety of reasons, the findings of research on the effects video game play are even more inconclusive than is the media violence literature in general (Griffiths, 1997). There is some evidence that trait aggression may enhance the negative effects of game play (Anderson & Dill, 2000), although this study was carried out using an adult sample, and its findings have not been replicated with adolescents (Warm, 2000). General increases in hostility were found in both studies, which suggests that there may be some excitation transfer, although these increases were evident for video game play in general, regardless of the violent content.

Violent games and toys of the nonelectronic variety—such as toy soldiers—have a long history, although these have inspired little psychological research into their adverse "effects." Goldstein (1998a) suggested that such predominantly masculine pastimes may serve, like media violence, as rites of passage in gender role acquisition. However, the function of video game violence may be closer to that of cartoon violence as far as children and adolescents are concerned. More research is needed on this topic, particularly from the uses and gratifications tradition.

FUTURE AVENUES IN MEDIA VIOLENCE RESEARCH

One path that researchers have taken is to treat scientific progress as a linear process—each new field of research yielding new information that can be added to the old to create ever-more comprehensive behavioural explanations. Hence, there has been a gradual appearance of what can only be described as "kitchen sink" theories, such as Anderson and Dill's (2000) General Affective Aggression Model (which was designed to explain the effects of playing violent video games) and Potter's (1999) lineation theory (which is less of an explanatory theory about media violence than a comprehensive synthesis of research findings).

Potter's work is important in that it addresses the limitations of the existing research, and is certainly more constructive than Eron's (and others') argument that there is no need for any further research on the media violence topic because its causal link to aggression is proven beyond doubt. However, the search for an all-encompassing model of media violence effects may ultimately prove a thankless task. An alternative is to explore certain aspects of media violence that have been neglected, perhaps due to the preference for experimental designs and quantitative surveys.

The study of the cultural meanings of violent media—and how these may determine the use of such media—has not been fully explored. Some work on this topic has been conducted in recent years in the United Kingdom using focus groups. In two separate studies of male and female groups discussing a range of media violence, Philip Schlesinger and colleagues found that their participants drew on their own disparate life experiences to understand the meaning of acts of violence. For example, viewers from violent backgrounds sometimes failed to interpret acts as "violent" that frightened those with a gentler upbringing (Schlesinger et al., 1998; Schlesinger, Dobash, Dobash, & Weaver, 1992).

Other studies have examined the importance of *context* for understanding media violence through conducting interviews with groups of viewers (Morrison, 1999). In one study, the discourse of viewers in response to isolated violent clips from the film *Natural Born Killers* was compared, using a group who were familiar with the film and a group who had not seen it. The former group were able to use their knowledge of the narrative to make sense of the clips, whereas to the latter group the scenes simply represented mindless acts of violence (Shaw, 2001). Shaw suggested that three contexts need to be considered in order to understand media violence. First, the *narrative* itself has a powerful influence on viewers' responses; by setting up a storyline and creating characters, viewers are able to interpret the violence, and through the use of social scripts may even be able to anticipate it (e.g., an arrest scene in a police drama). Second, the program or movie genre may determine viewers' anticipation. We would arrive at the screening of a gangster movie fully expecting bloodshed and would probably be disappointed if it failed to appear, whereas viewers of a period drama would be shocked if it suddenly descended into a shootout. Third, in accordance with Schlesinger's findings, viewers' own experiences—both of viewing violent media and of real-life violence—will have a moderating effect for their interpretation of and reaction to a violent incident on screen.

For too long, media effects research has utilised inappropriate stimuli; for example, equating research assistants performing acts on video with the rich cultural environment of children's television. It may be time to give the producers of violent entertainment some credit: How do they put this material together; how do *they* think it works? Understandably, many directors are reticent when it comes to discussing technique; Hitchcock, for instance, was notoriously coy when interviewed about the art of production, even when probed by a psychiatrist concerned about the effects of his films (Rebello, 1990).

It could be argued that it makes more sense to study violence in television series because they are subject to continuous evaluation on part of viewers and subsequent adjustment by producers. For example, the makers of one BBC police series were allegedly requested to "beef up" the violence quotient in order to boost flagging viewing figures (Wober, 1997). In either case, the view from the creative side of the fence would contribute valuable insight into the relationship between media culture and the psychology of the viewer.

CONCLUSION

Potter's brave attempt to construct a theory out of the existing research on media violence may be overoptimistic in its ambitions. Nevertheless, it is probably the right way to go. At present, there is something of a stalemate in the media violence debate. North American researchers in the field of communication science have effectively closed the book on psychology by moving on to the effectiveness of technological devices such as the V-chip. Meanwhile, European researchers from the cultural studies field are openly hostile toward "the effects tradition." Many of the shortcomings levelled at earlier "effects" research are no longer applicable to studies like the National Television Violence Study, in which, for example, narrative context was examined (albeit in a more restricted way than that advocated by qualitative researchers).

Both sides in the debate suffer, in my opinion, from an outdated view of psychology, in which the individual person is isolated from his or her social and cultural environment. Moving toward the study of natural viewing groups, and those who actively select violent entertainment, should help us begin to understand more about both the appeal and influence of media violence. Nor should we rule out the importance of history. There is no disputing the (often spectacular) effects of violent media that were demonstrated in the laboratories of the 1960s and 1970s, where adults (typically undergraduate students) responded aggressively to violent stimuli. But this was a point in history where television was relatively new, and contained scenes of violence that seem laughably unrealistic alongside the vivid digital horrors of modern cinema. Would these findings be replicated with modern-day audiences? It is perhaps time to brush some of the dust off those old studies and reexamine their impact on a different generation.

Chapter 5

Prosocial Effects of Media

Look in the subject index of any psychology textbook, and you will find no more than a smattering of entries for "media." Chances are that those entries will be associated with exclusively negative aspects of media. Here are three examples that I have plucked at random from the bookshelf. Hogg and Vaughan (1998), renowned European social psychology text, has the following entries under media: aggression, attitude formation, propaganda, sex role stereotypes, violence. Westen (1999), introductory psychology text, has only one: aggression. Hewstone and Stroebe (2001), renowned multi-author social psychology text, fails to list "media" at all, although a quick glance finds "television violence." Can media's influence on human behaviour really be all bad?

It is probably no surprise that the vast bulk of research examining the effects of media has concentrated on the supposed negative influence of television, films, and video games. In the same way that we only call the doctor when we are feeling ill, social scientists are increasingly called into action only to solve social problems. Some attempts to counter this trend have been made in the United States recently, as Martin Seligman and other psychologists have pioneered the field of "positive psychology," whose goal is to use scientific research to enhance social well-being and quality of life rather than to simply troubleshoot. Although there is no sign so far of media playing any role in this project, it may yet bring about a change in the way psychology views media in the long run.

If viewing media violence can be cited as a causal factor in aggressive or violent behaviour, then the reverse side of the coin should also hold true—viewing prosocial behaviour in the media should make us nicer to one another. For all the blood and bullets in mainstream cinema and television, there are probably more acts of kindness and affection, and certainly more comic moments. If, therefore, television has made society more violent, it should also have made us kinder and more cheerful. If cognitive "priming" is the main effect, then along with all the horrific ideas for violence and murder might mainstream television not pass on far more beneficial information on the whole? Tales of a teenage boy successfully giving mouth-to-mouth resuscitation to a drowning friend after watching a similar scene on *Baywatch* suggest ways of communicating socially useful material without dressing it up as education.

The largely negative attitude to media over the years means that much of the psychological literature on media is somewhat *reactive*; there are many studies of the effects of violent media, but relatively few examining the effects of other kinds of media, even though they should ostensibly share certain characteristics. At low levels, perceptual and cognitive responses to televisual stimuli should hold true whatever the programme content; at higher levels, processes such as identification and parasocial interaction with media figures, or comprehension of story lines and the "reading" of generic and formulaic media styles, should shape understandings and responses to all televised material.

One way of framing the question is to use the media violence research as a template for media psychological research in general. Take "priming" as an example: If aggressive behaviour can be "primed" by violent scenes, might altruism be similarly primed by acts of kindness? There is a body of literature on prosocial media effects that is not dissimilar to research on media violence in terms of theory and methodology, although—consistent with psychology's role as a reactive science—its findings have received far less attention than have those relating to violence. The first part of this chapter broadly reviews the findings of this research.

An important difference between the antisocial and prosocial effects of media is that the former are almost invariably accidental. The primary function of most violent media is *entertainment*. Filmmakers may set out to shock viewers as part of the entertainment process, but the media content itself is not designed to produce the effects that have been investigated by social scientists (i.e., long-term increases in viewer aggression). It is probably safe to say that no media producer has *ever* deliberately set out to produce such effects. On the other hand, media producers frequently set out to create material that will have positive long-term benefits on consumers, whether it be a soap opera storyline that informs viewers about health issues, or an educational programme for children. In this sense we can talk about "prosocial media," and the second part of the chapter examines attempts by the makers of television programmes and public service information to induce prosocial behaviour in the media audience.

Another approach to prosocial effects of media is to study the ways in which children come to understand the content of television and video. Parental mediation—by which parents actively participate in their child's viewing experiences—is of particular importance here.[1] This research is somewhat different to the first two types, because it deals with media material that is both pro- and antisocial. The implications are that children can learn how to deal with disturbing or violent material so long as they interpret it with a critical eye. This research is discussed in the final part of the chapter.

MEDIA AND PROSOCIAL BEHAVIOUR: THE "EFFECTS" TRADITION

Before discussing the research on prosocial effects of media, it is necessary to define what is meant by prosocial behaviour, and the best way of studying it. Whereas studies of media and *anti*social behaviour have concentrated on aggression and violence, studies of prosocial behaviour have been more diverse. Prosocial behaviour may be explicit; the most heavily researched behaviour is *altruism*, or helping (typically, going to the aid of another person in difficulty or distress). This type of behaviour is frequently studied using experimental methods, as in the bystander intervention tradition (e.g., Latané & Darley, 1970).

Less easily researched behaviours include *sharing* and *empathy*. Sharing behaviour might lend itself to an observational design—children in the playground, for instance. Empathy is a rather more elusive phenomenon, open to many differing interpretations. Zillmann (1991) regarded empathy as a complex experience operating on several different cognitive and behavioural levels, but essentially involving an affective response to another person whose emotional expression has a causal explanation. Typically, empathy has been researched using psychometric scales (Davis, 1980). These behaviours have universal application—they would generally be seen as prosocial in any society or historical period. Other prosocial behaviours are less observable and more culture specific, such as holding a nonracist or nonsexist attitude.

---

[1]It is, perhaps, unfortunate that the term *mediation* has been used to describe the effects of parental intervention. In quantitative (multivariate) social and clinical psychology, *mediation* refers to behaviour that *reinforces* the association between two other variables (here, media use and effects; Baron & Kenny, 1986). Although this might describe parental mediation in relation to *pro*social media content, for antisocial material the appropriate term would be *parental moderation*. Then again, it could be argued that *parental mediation* describes the *act* of intervention rather than its presumed effects (it may not always work). Either way, there is plenty of scope for confusion!

The earliest studies of media and prosocial behaviour were very much like studies of media and aggression. A typical example is the experiment reported by Baran, Chase, and Courtright (1979) in which three groups of 7- to 9-year-old children were shown different segments of *The Waltons,* containing "cooperative," "noncooperative," or "neutral" behaviour. Then an associate of the experimenter walked past the room and dropped a pile of books. The children's responses were recorded in terms of (a) whether they offered unprompted help, (b) how quickly, and (c) whether they helped if requested. Children who had watched the "cooperative" segment were more likely to offer help (81%) and did so more quickly than did those in the other groups. However, those in the "noncooperative" condition were also much keener to help than were those in the control condition.

An alternative approach is to observe prosocial behaviour in unconstrained social interaction. One example is the study of Sprafkin and Rubenstein (1979) that assessed children's viewing habits, rated the programmes for anti- and prosocial content, and then worked out an index for each child. The authors then asked children (and teachers) to rate their classmates on a series of items (e.g., "X does nice things," "X stays out of fights"). As with many antisocial media studies, the results were rather inconclusive: Gender, parents' education level, and academic performance all emerged as the most significant predictors of prosocial ratings. Viewing amount, and anti- and prosocial indexes came out much lower, although marginally significant. Even less conclusive results were obtained in a later Dutch study (Wiegman, Kuttschreuter, & Baarda, 1992). Although no meta-analytical studies on prosocial media have been published in the literature to date, it is likely that the pattern of antisocial media effects would be repeated but with smaller effect sizes (and, again, the experimental studies have tended to produce larger effects than have surveys).

Perhaps not surprisingly, studies of viewer empathy have produced a mixture of findings. Feshbach (1975) found that 3- to 5-year-old children were less scared by a televised scene in which a swarm of bees buzzed around a boy's head than were 9- and 10-year-olds. When the bees alone were presented, the younger children were scared; when the distressed boy was presented alone, only the older children reported negative feelings. In Piagetian terms, this could be explained as an egocentric response on behalf of the younger children; however, it could be related to age differences in reality perceptions of televised material.

Zillmann and Bryant (1975) examined children at two stages of moral development in a study of empathic responses to a televised fairy tale. In the story, a "good" prince is betrayed and banished by a "bad" prince, and subsequently returns to wreak his revenge. Three different endings were created for the story: In one, the revenge is overly mild and forgiving; in another, it matches the hurt bestowed by the initial wrong; in the third, it is unnecessarily brutal. Children at the earlier stage of moral development, where "expiatory retribution" is the only concept that can be grasped, displayed more facial joy as the revenge became harsher. Children at the later, "equitable retribution" stage displayed highest facial joy for the second ending; the harsh revenge produced as little joy as did the mild revenge. This finding suggests that empathy is strongly determined by character judgments, usually involving some degree of moral evaluation.

Zillmann (1991) argued that empathy is hard to establish given the fast pace of action adventure films and also of contemporary news media, where "an interview with a woman who has just lost her wife to a mine disaster is followed, without delay, by a report on union demands in a strike by auto workers" (p. 161). Although this format might blunt the immediate effects of empathy with the victims of accidents or crime, the accumulation of news reports both on television and in print media often results in extreme instances of public empathy for injured parties in high-profile stories. The anger that followed the murder of Liverpool toddler James Bulger in 1993 arose through empathy with his parents; similar public support was evident after the death of Essex teenager Leah Betts from an ecstasy tablet shortly afterward the Bulger murder. Increasingly, the relatives of victims of murder and other unlawful deaths are invited to give press conferences, because the police are well aware of the empathic impact of television, and the resultant increased likelihood of members of the public coming forward with useful information.

Thus far, the evidence for prosocial effects of media is mixed. One problem is that, as with violent content, prosocial content is usually embedded deep within the narrative context of a dramatic production. Attempts to classify a programme as "violent" or "prosocial" are misguided—for instance, within the same show (e.g., a soap), a fist fight might be followed by an act of kindness within a few minutes—so it is not surprising that attempts to classify research participants as viewers of either violent or prosocial media have been remarkably unsuccessful. Indeed, it seems that the main criterion that distinguishes among viewers is viewing *quantity* rather than viewing quality. In their sample, Wiegman et al. (1992) found a 0.9 correlation between the amount of anti- and prosocial TV watched.

An alternative is to examine viewing preferences for shows that have an abundance of either violent or prosocial content. Davis (1983) found that children who scored highly on an empathy scale tended to prefer prosocial programmes such as *The Waltons*. However, this relationship is at odds with the finding that a measure of "perspective taking" was inversely related to both pro- *and* antisocial viewing. We must be wary of treating overall media use as a causative variable by itself; heavy use may be determined by a third variable (education, social class, or whatever), which might also explain variation in the dependent variable (in this instance, perspective taking).

Once again, such findings underline the need for quantitative media research to analyse as much information as possible in complex multivariate designs.

THE EFFECTS OF "PROSOCIAL MEDIA"

If altruistic behaviour can be observed under laboratory conditions when participants are exposed to prosocial media content, what about real-world viewing of "prosocial media"—materials that are specifically designed to have positive effects?

Educational Media

By far the most research into educational media has focused on *Sesame Street,* the long-running U.S. children's television series first broadcast in 1969. *Sesame Street* was designed with deliberately prosocial aims in mind. It intended to educate preschool children from diverse socioeconomic backgrounds about the alphabet and the number system. After several years of civil unrest in the United States, it was also part of a drive within the media to promote racial harmony, and the series featured groups of children drawn from different ethnic backgrounds. It was also set firmly within the inner city, in an attempt to create an environment that would be recognisable to urban viewers. Finally, it encouraged parents to watch with their children by incorporating "adult" content, such as topical/satirical material, and characters with adult appeal, like Bert and Ernie.

Since its inception, there have been numerous attempts to evaluate the educational impact of the show (for a roundup of 30 years' research, see Fisch, Truglio, & Cole, 1999). Rice, Huston, Truglio, and Wright (1990) studied its effect on vocabulary acquisition and found that frequency of *Sesame Street* viewing was a good predictor of vocabulary knowledge at ages 3 and 5 (controlling for parental education, number of siblings, and gender). However, older children did not seem to benefit from watching; indeed, those still watching at ages 6 and 7 were more likely to be slow learners. The authors explained this in terms of "quick incidental learning," which is more effective with 3-year-olds than with 5-year-olds.

Other studies suggest that *Sesame Street* viewing is also a good predictor of children's later performance in science and mathematics, and of nonracist attitudes and behaviour (Christensen & Roberts, 1983; Huston & Wright, 1998). However, it is doubtful whether all of the original aims of the show have been met. For example, early reports suggest that, counter to the producers' objectives, it was children with higher socioeconomic status who benefited most from watching the show (Ball & Bogatz, 1970). This effect might be explained by the finding that parental mediation (discussion about the show's contents) enhances the effect of viewing, something more likely in educated, middle-class families (Cook et al., 1975).

Some authors have argued that viewing television is passive activity from which it is impossible for children to learn *anything*. Such beliefs have prevented greater use of television as an educational medium in British schools over the years (Gunter & McAleer, 1997). However, anyone who has observed young children for more than a few minutes can identify much verbal and gestural material that has its roots in television content, perhaps filtered through peer interaction. Even in front of the set, much activity is taking place, especially watching any show that involves musical content or dancing, or where a presenter directly addresses the viewer (Palmer, 1986).

A popular standpoint in the psychological literature on children and media is that however harmful media might be in the hands of television producers and Hollywood directors, they could nevertheless be immensely beneficial were they to be harnessed to educational ends. Greenfield (1984) argued that screen presentation of educational material can be highly successful if used in a supplementary context with printed texts, and has even been found to enhance reading comprehension.

There is also a popular belief—perhaps one that offers some consolation to concerned parents—that frequent video game play might sharpen cognitive skills. On the other side of the coin, following the Columbine High School shootings in 1999, a former colonel in the U.S. army warned about the dangers of "shoot-em-up" video games and argued that they trained children in the use of real firearms, a sentiment later reiterated by President Clinton. However, a recent study examined the abilities of players of the computer game *Tetris,* which involves the manipulation of complex shapes (Sims & Mayer, 2002). *Tetris* players demonstrated enhanced performance in mental rotation tasks involving shapes similar to the ones used in *Tetris,* but performed no differently from controls on tasks involving other kinds of shapes. This finding suggests that any cognitive skill sharpening resulting from repeated video game play is likely to be very localised.

Global Issue Awareness

Appeals in the world's media for charity have successfully raised money for needy causes, most notably famine relief. Undoubtedly the most famous of all charity events was the Live Aid appeal in the mid-1980s, which was estimated to have raised over $100 million for famine victims in Ethiopia. This campaign was set in motion late in 1984 by news reports of appalling conditions of drought in the area that, in a pretty spectacular example of a positive "media effect," inspired Irish pop star Bob Geldof to dream up the project of a multi-artist charity pop single.

Following the success of the single, a concert was organised for the following summer that was to be transmitted live throughout the world, accompanied by requests to viewers for monetary donations. Eventually, two concerts were screened—one in the United Kingdom and one in the United States—and together these attracted over a billion viewers in 170 countries. The money that was raised was spent on various projects in famine-affected areas of central Africa.

Interestingly, and humblingly, it is not always rich countries giving to poor ones. Harris (1999) reported an amazing case in which residents of a Malian village raised $66 to help victims (including, presumably, some wealthy businesses) of a Canadian ice storm after watching a news story about it on local television. Admittedly, the village had a reciprocal arrangement with a nearby Canadian town, and had received aid from them in the past, but the Canadians were 75 times better off in terms of income! Perhaps this is an effect of "exotic otherness," which we tend to think applies only to Westerners; in Mali, the very idea of an ice storm may be terrifying.

One of the fears that surround constant charity appeals via the media is that eventually public generosity will run dry, as "compassion fatigue" sets in. Certainly this appeared to be the case with charity pop singles in the United Kingdom. The Band Aid record sparked a number of similar projects during the late 1980s. Initially, these were almost as successful, such as one to aid victims of the *Marchioness* disaster (a pleasure cruiser that sank in the River Thames during the late 1980s), but later releases fared less well, as the novelty of the idea wore off. On the other hand, BBC television's annual charity event, Red Nose Day, which features an evening of specially produced comedy shows and short charity-information films, has become something of an institution in British media culture and raises millions of pounds each year for selected causes. The success of this venture suggests that the media has high potential for worthy causes, although these need to be carefully marketed.

Health Awareness

Whether or not media produce the psychological effects claimed by many social scientists, there is no doubt that they are invaluable means of communicating information. Periodically, state agencies as well as private businesses have harnessed the informational power of media in an attempt to promote desirable behaviour, such as road safety or care with handling fireworks. Media have also played an important role in the communication of health messages, including worldwide publicity about HIV/AIDS (Johnson, Flora, & Rimal, 1997), smoking cessation programmes (Korhonen, Uutela, Korhonen, & Puska, 1998), and warnings about skin cancer risk from sunbathing (Buller, Borland, & Burgoon, 1998).

How effective are such campaigns? A lot depends on the type of information that is being communicated. During 1999, the Australian state of Victoria ran a campaign via television, radio, and print media to try and encourage women to undertake screening for cervical cancer. The advertisements presented several popular excuses associated with cervical screening, such as "I'm too old to need a Pap smear," followed by the slogan "Don't make excuses, make an appointment." A research team later found that the media campaign had been effective in getting the information across, but that it had lowered self-efficacy among the women that were interviewed—in other words, they now identified more barriers to taking a Pap test (Fernbach, 2002). The author suggested that, as in a similar U.S. campaign for mammography screening (McCaul, Jacobson, & Martinson, 1998), the use of negative health messages had actually backfired; rather than shaming the public into changing their behaviour, it inadvertently provided them with a readily available set of excuses for *not* changing their behaviour!

This study raises a common problem with using psychology for health communication and other public service announcements—media material is often devised by educated, middle-class people whose idea of a persuasive message may not ring true with the public at large. In England in the 1980s, the government launched a poster campaign bearing the slogan "Heroin screws you up." One poster, featuring a hollow-cheeked, emaciated adolescent boy, kept disappearing from the billboards; it was turning up in the bedrooms of adolescent girls! The poster was swiftly withdrawn from the campaign.

Of course, there are instances in which health communication in the media has been at odds with other media representations of health behaviour. Smoking is possibly the best example there is of a true media effect. Its popularity, in the Western world at least, seems to have been determined exclusively by media trends. In the early years of Hollywood, rates of smoking increased dramatically, probably owing to the glamorising effect of actors and actresses smoking in films. Visits to the cinema were enormously influential in terms of audience behaviour; fashions in clothing explicitly followed the Hollywood agenda, and other social trends could be traced to its influence, among them smoking.

However, during the latter quarter of the 20th century, the health risks associated with smoking became a cause for major concern, and governments across the world became committed to reducing the incidence of smoking by their citizens. Although curbs on smoking in public and cigarette taxes have played an important part in achieving this effect, the media have also contributed. First, major restrictions have been placed on cigarette advertising across the globe. Second, public service announcements concerning the dangers of cigarette smoking have been screened on television in several countries.

Since the 1970s, there have also been substantial changes in the way that smoking is represented on television and in the cinema. Films from the 1960s featured glamorous actors and actresses puffing their way through packet after packet, but it is now regarded as unacceptable if a soap character lights a cigarette onscreen, unless the detrimental health effects of such behaviours are featured in the narrative.

Education Through Entertainment

In many parts of the world, information about social issues is embedded within popular drama. Prosocial soaps (also referred to as "entertainment-education" media) are hugely popular in parts of Asia, Africa, and Latin America (Sherry, 1998; Singhal & Rogers, 1999). These soaps follow the same broad structure as do soaps in Europe and North America, except that the storylines are explicitly prosocial, featuring issues ranging from local subjects (e.g., dowry in India, or agricultural information in Africa), to health issues (e.g., HIV prevention), to global issues (e.g., environmentalism). Even in the West, soaps often feature storylines that are intended to educate as much as entertain. These programmes, and the factors that may account for their success, are discussed in more detail in chapter 15.

There is always some doubt about the effectiveness of such shows—the success stories are numerous but, at the same time, long-standing attitudes may be resistant to change. Getting the message may require viewers to recognise the function of the characters and the storyline, described by Liebes and Katz (1990) as a "critical" reading of a media text. As we have seen with regard to health messages that backfire, audiences are often not as sophisticated as producers assume they are. In India, the series *Hum Log* ("We People") was broadcast during the 1980s with the aim of advancing the status of women. Although it produced numerous notable successes, at the same time many female viewers identified more with the traditional matriarchal female character rather than with her independent daughters (Brown & Cody, 1991).

The same problems occurred on both sides of the Atlantic during the 1970s, when sitcom writers attempted to challenge right-wing bigotry by making reactionary comic figures the butt of the jokes. Although the shows were highly regarded within the television industry as artistic creations, their psychological impact was perhaps less successful. In the U.S. sitcom *All in the Family*, "traditional" viewers actually identified with the bigoted Archie Bunker (Vidimar & Rokeach, 1974), and in the parallel U.K. show from the same period, *Till Death Us Do Part*, the racist right-wing protagonist Alf Garnett was upheld by some viewers as a hero. These examples clearly signal the need for media psychologists to study the *meanings* that media hold for audiences, rather than assuming (as with much media violence research) that their effects are homogeneous.

One of the advantages of deliberately constructed prosocial media, as opposed to prosocial content within media in general, is that producers can design unambiguous contexts for the "preferred" reading. Sanders, Montgomery, and Brechman-Toussaint (2000) reported on the success of an Australian study in which a series of videos were specifically designed with the intention of preventing child behaviour problems. A number of mothers were given these videos and asked to watch two per week over a 6-week period. At the end of this period, when compared to a control group, they reported a significant reduction in problem behaviour among their children, and had higher perceptions of parental competence. These effects remained unchanged in a 6-month follow-up study.

Of course, there are enormous differences between the parents in this study and parents consuming everyday media, and, as the authors themselves acknowledged, it is possible that the reported changes in disruptive behaviour may reflect changing parental perceptions (no independent observation was carried out, or any data collected from fathers). Nevertheless, the findings from global soap operas indicate that, when positive social messages are embedded in narrative texts, they can have a substantial impact, even if only on public awareness of important issues.

PARENTAL MEDIATION

In the previous sections I have described instances in which media "messages" are misinterpreted by audiences—or, at least, not interpreted the way their producers intended. Although it may be hard to force adult audiences to interpret material that challenges preexisting attitudes and beliefs, children's understanding of media may be shaped strongly by the surrounding social context. If a parent is on hand to explain some of the more difficult or disturbing scenes a child witnesses on television or video, this may help blunt any negative effects that occur during lone viewing. A growing body of literature on the topic of "parental mediation" has examined this parental contribution to children's media use.

What does parental mediation consist of? At its simplest, the parent is a coviewer; this is a contrast with the feared image of TV-as-babysitter, in which—at least in popular lore—the parent dumps the child in front of the set in order to be free to carry out household chores and other activities undisturbed. The concern here is that the child is left vulnerable to the unmediated influence of violence, sex, aggression, and other undesirable material, and after a certain age may be competent enough to actively select and operate "video nasties" left unattended on the shelf by the negligent parent. When the adult views television with the child, there is an opportunity to discuss and explain some of the more disturbing material, and to consolidate the prosocial or educational content.

How far should we be concerned about children's lone television use? A study by St. Peters, Fitch, Huston, Wright, and Eakins (1991) found that children below the age of seven watched around 75% of children's television by themselves, but this figure was notably lower for comedy, drama news, and sport programmes. Ironically, given the "video nasty" fears, children are much more likely to view adult material when coviewing with an adult; in other words, it is the adults who make the decisions about viewing material. However, it might be that coviewing tends to be incidental (e.g., children being allowed to stay up late especially to watch an adult programme with their parents).

Of course, the view of many parents is that the only way to prevent children from watching undesirable media is simply to prohibit viewing. St. Peters et al. found that, in their sample, restricted viewers generally saw less of everything—in other words, rather than controlling the quality of television their children watch, restrictive parents simply control the quantity ("One hour and no more!") There are several problems with blanket restrictions on viewing: Policing exposure to undesirable media is virtually impossible; even if preschool children can be protected from it, they are likely to find out eventually; and the "forbidden fruit" effect may be stronger for children whose media use is subject to such censure. Nevertheless, a 1988 Gallup poll in the United States found that adults were seven times more likely to change channel, or forbid viewing, rather than discuss undesirable content (Austin, 1993).

The significance of mediation was realised by the early creators of children's media at the BBC, where the radio schedule was entitled *Listen with Mother* and the corresponding television schedule *Watch with Mother.* The pattern of contemporary domestic media use is vastly different, of course, with so many young children owning their own television sets, and having the ability to operate video playback. Therefore, the need for parents and children to share viewing experiences assumes greater importance than in the past. Nor is simple coviewing the answer; Austin (1993) argued that effective mediation requires parents to discuss the programme content with the child, perhaps explain ambiguous or disturbing material, or follow up on concepts from the viewing session.

Not only has parental mediation been found to enhance the learning effect of *Sesame Street* (Rice et al., 1990); it is also possible to blunt the negative effects of television by discussing the relevant issues. Corder-Bolz (1980) examined attitudes toward gender roles following a sitcom in which the lead male and female characters were each shown performing nonstereotypical tasks. Both male and female mediators effected huge decreases in preschool children's stereotypical attitudes, whereas watching alone actually produced a small increase. With older children (aged 11 or 12), mediation still had a powerful effect, but there was also a decrease when viewing alone, suggesting that by this age children are able to process the prosocial messages without adult help. (Rosenkoetter, 1999, suggested that children as young as seven are able to understand quite complex moral messages contained in sitcom storylines.)

In a study of cartoon violence, Nathanson and Cantor (2000) asked children between the ages of 6 and 10 to consider the feelings of the victim in a cartoon that featured a substantial number of violent acts. Children who did not receive the mediation achieved significantly higher scores on a self-report measure of aggression immediately following viewing than did those in the mediation group, who also felt that the violence was less justified.

How does mediation work at a theoretical level? Austin, Roberts, and Nass (1990) studied over 600 children and 400 parents in California in their responses to questions about an episode of *The Cosby Show.* It was predicted that children who had the most discussion about television with parents would enhance the similarity of the television world with their own experience, and that this would lead to stronger wishful identification with that television world. The results of the study supported the authors' prediction.

On the face of it, these results seem to conflict with the idea that mediation might work by enhancing the difference between reality and fantasy (e.g., a parent telling the child that a shot man is not really dead, the blood is only tomato sauce, etc.). It may be that mediation works differently for different media effects, or for different viewing genres. Certainly, in this example, it is assumed that mediation enables children to absorb the *prosocial* messages from *The Cosby Show.*

However, the model lacks specificity regarding the precise effects; for example, the concept of "identification" was studied by asking children whether they would like to be part of the family in the show. Besides only tackling one aspect of identification, this measure fails to distinguish between the characters in the show; as the authors argued, parents may influence their children's identification processes by steering them away from certain characters (by saying things like "You don't want to be like that character"). There is no indication of how identification processes might be different *without* parental mediation.

Another possibility is that the focus on a specific television family may introduce confounding factors into the mediation process. The fact that mediation predicted a perceived similarity with the television world may reflect the fact that families with positive patterns of communication identified with the fully communicative (and possibly unrepresentative) Huxtable family. Children from families who rarely discuss television content, perhaps those of lower educational and socioeconomic status, may see fewer similarities between themselves and the Huxtables. Nevertheless, this model makes an important contribution toward a more complex analysis of mediation processes.

Not only might there be different styles of mediation for different material, but there may be differences between the mediators themselves. Valkenburg, Krcmar, Peeters, and Marseille (1999) identified three different mediation styles among parents: *social coviewing,* when parents and children watch together but do not discuss content; *restrictive mediation,* when parents prohibit watching certain material; and *instructive mediation,* which involves discussion and explanation. It could be argued that only the third style qualifies as mediation in the classic sense because, as Austin (1993) argued, simple coviewing and prohibitive viewing are largely ineffective means of modifying children's interpretation of television.

Austin, Bolls, Fujioka, and Engelbertson (1999) examined mediation in more depth in a telephone survey with 255 adults, and identified four mediation styles. *Nonmediators* are parents who might coview with children but never discuss content. *Optimists* are those whose mediation consists of mostly positive comments about the content, and who tend to be generally trusting of television (even using it as a "babysitter"). *Pessimists* make generally negative or sceptical comments to their children, and tend to be generally distrustful of television, watching less prime-time material. *Selectives* are mediators with a more or less equal balance of negative and positive contributions.

The nature of parent–child discussions about television are therefore likely to rely heavily on parental attitudes toward the media. They are also likely to rely on existing communication patterns within families and on general parenting style (Gunter & McAleer, 1997). Furthermore, we need to appreciate that adults may fail to pick up on the salience of much media content, particularly prosocial material. "Pessimists" may moderate the effects of media violence on their children but fail to compensate by not reinforcing prosocial messages.

CONCLUSION

Research on the prosocial effects of media is much more limited in its extent than is research on violent media, but it does illuminate some of the problems with the effects approach in general. Identifying and isolating prosocial content in standard media fare is much harder than coding acts of violence and aggression—not because it isn't there, but because it has to be understood and interpreted in its narrative context. Slowly, media violence researchers are appreciating that the same is true of violent content. A punch in the face does not mean the same thing in every media production, nor does it mean the same thing to every member of the media audience. The mixed success in communicating prosocial media messages—attempting to change negative aspects of health behaviour, or unacceptable attitudes—highlights the variety of "readings" that are open to media users, and indicates the need for more carefully targeted campaigns. Multiple readings exist for all forms of media message, not only the prosocial ones. That it has taken so long to appreciate this fact casts doubt on the wisdom of isolating specific aspects of media and studying their effects while neglecting the psychology of media use in general.

Chapter **6**

Pornography and Erotica

The word *pornography* derives from the Greek terms for "prostitute" and "to write." Literally translated, it means "depictions of acts of prostitutes" (Linz & Malamuth, 1993). There is no doubt that such depictions have existed in every communication medium throughout history; one of the first responses to any new form of technology is, it seems, to use it to create better sexual imagery. Probably no topic covered by this book excites more frenzied debate than pornography, and whatever I write in this chapter is bound to offend *somebody*. Does pornography incite men to rape women and children? Should we ban it, and if so, how do you draw the mark between gratuitous depictions of sex and artistic portrayals of lovemaking? Are the effects of using pornography universal, or specific to certain individuals such as paedophiles?

Many of the arguments and debates around pornography are very similar to those surrounding media violence, except that there are two crucial elements added to the mix: the issue of *taste*, in which *morality* is confused and used interchangeably with *decency* and *obscenity*; and the issue of *gender*. Some academics might argue that pornography is better studied under disciplines such as feminism and gender studies than under media studies or psychology, and they have a point, to which I return toward the end of the chapter. Nevertheless, psychologists have played a key role in legal cases involving pornography, many of which have turned on the potential harmful effects of the material. Sex and pornography are central to some of the more general theoretical issues involved in constructing a psychology of media. In addition, in the last 25 years or more, the media status of pornography has changed dramatically, and the advent of the Internet has begun to transform the industry in unexpected ways, some of which have implications for feminist theory.

DEFINITIONS OF PORNOGRAPHY AND EROTICA

The etymological origins of pornography notwithstanding, there are a multitude of definitions of the term as it relates to actual material. The debate surrounding definition is almost as complex as those about censorship and "effects," for a good reason—because we need to *know* what is supposed to cause what, and what to ban, if anything.

The word *pornography* is usually pejorative; it tends to be contrasted with *erotica,* which implies a degree of artistry or "good taste" in the depiction of sex and nudity. Because taste is a factor, and therefore introduces an element of *subjectivity* into the definition process, many researchers in the area have preferred other terms altogether, such as *sexually explicit materials* (Check & Guloine, 1989). There are problems, however, with casting the net too wide: Smith (1976), for instance, defined pornography as any "material that is sexually explicit in referring to or visually depicting male and female anatomy" (p. 16), which would include sex education manuals and erotic scenes in mainstream cinema. Within the media, there are various operational definitions—typically, the terms *softcore* and *hardcore* are used to distinguish between nonviolent erotica and sadomasochistic material and other "specialist" genres (including child pornography). The novelist and journalist Martin Amis (2001) reported on the contemporary U.S. market, in which the defining terms are *features* and *Gonzo*: The former indicates a standard film narrative, with plots, characters, and so on; the latter is used to describe material that is unstructured sexual activity, mostly involving anal and oral sex, or fetishism.

The definition of pornography is important because researchers are divided over the actual effects of different types of material. However, it is interesting that these issues have been more prominent in pornography research than in the "effects" literature on media violence, which is in many aspects a much more difficult topic to define. For a start, pornography, like prosocial media, is created for a specific reason. Some definitions of pornography use its effects as the key; in 1977, the Williams Committee on Pornography in the United Kingdom distinguished it from erotica on account of its "intention to arouse its audience sexually," whereas erotica "expresses sexual excitement rather than causes it . . . [and] may have other merit which cancels that effect" (cited in Einsiedel, 1988, p. 113). Such definitions require substantial assumptions about media effects, and thus it is no surprise that media psychologists have played an active role in court hearings of prosecution cases involving sexual material. Nevertheless, changing public standards in relation to art, obscenity, and media themselves suggest that any definitions restricted to the materials alone are constantly subject to revision.

Throughout this chapter I use *pornography* as a generic term first and foremost. We can speak of "the pornography industry" (various authors estimate its annual profits to be somewhere between $6 and $10 billion). *Erotica* is a much smaller concern, restricted to a number of films and series primarily made for mainstream television, as opposed to specialist subscription channels. Much of this material is designed to appeal to women as much as men, tends to prioritise foreplay and postcoital affection, and sets sex within the context of relationships.[1] Of course, explicit sex is frequently depicted in mainstream cinema and television. Harris (1999) used the term *media sex* to refer to such content, which seems adequate so long as it is distinguished from pornography and erotica. However, the main concern of this chapter is with pornography itself.

A BRIEF HISTORY OF PORNOGRAPHY

We have become so accustomed to the idea of pornography as a modern phenomenon that it is easy to forget its long artistic tradition. It is often argued that the first examples of pornographic literature were created by Italian author and engraver Pietro Aretino in the 16th century, in particular the dialogues between a sexually experienced woman and an innocent woman in *Ragionamenti* (1534–1536), and a series of sonnets used to accompany erotic engravings (Hunt, 2000). Aretino himself defended his work on the grounds that it was immoral to suppress thoughts about or depictions of the very act of creation. The rise of the printing industry meant that these writings became widely available, and by the 17th century a clear genre of pornographic literature had emerged across Europe. Samuel Pepys was a renowned consumer of this material. Often, these early writings were highly political; following Aretino's subversive aims, pornography was used as a weapon to attack the French aristocracy.

In the 18th century, the themes of modern pornography emerged in the writings of the Marquis de Sade, who "explored the ultimate logical possibility of pornography; the annihilation of the body, the very seat of pleasure, in the name of desire" (Hunt, 2000, p. 370). Of course, Sade was an exceptional figure for the time in that he actually lived out his fantasies of

---

[1]The belief that these concerns are principally *feminine* (i.e., women prefer sex as part of a relationship, whereas men are preoccupied with the physical act itself) makes all kinds of assumptions about gender that have their roots in biological determinism and evolutionary theory.

rape and murder. Nevertheless, his work broke every taboo possible, and—from the point of view of pornography as art—should effectively have closed down the genre. The fact that pornographic writing has continued, expanding into a colossal multimedia industry, suggests that "art" has little to do with it. Indeed, it is possible to view Sade as the cutoff point between pornography as literature and pornography as functional medium. After 1800, as Hunt (2000) argued, sexually explicit literature was only ever produced with the intention of sexual arousal.

Slade (1984) traced the origins of the media pornography industry to the early years of the 20th century, when the first sexually explicit films were made. Up to that point, black-and-white nudes could be glimpsed through Edison cabinets, and milder sexual material was freely available in "What the Butler Saw"-type seaside amusements. Early scenes of sexual intercourse were highly prized materials, watched by clandestine groups of men in clubs and fraternities. During the 1920s, as such material began to diversify, a split emerged between heterosexual audiences and both gay and fetishist audiences (the latter material consisting of films focusing on feet and other nongenital parts of the anatomy). The "straight" audience gathered momentum across the century, eventually infiltrating the mainstream cinema industry, with the first public screening of a hardcore feature film in 1968 in New York.

At this point, the pornography industry went into overdrive. In the early 1970s, films such as *Deep Throat* (1972), starring Linda Lovelace in repeated scenes of fellatio,[2] achieved worldwide fame, and the invention of the videocassette recorder in the late 1970s turned an increasingly profitable industry into a business with a higher gross national product than most countries. It also marked a change in viewing practices, because, until this point, audiences for pornographic films had been restricted to viewing films in public cinemas (Hebditch & Anning, 1988). The popularity of home pornography viewing is linked to the function of such material as an aid for masturbation; for years, the sex film audience was personified by the image of a "dirty old man" in a raincoat worn, even in hot weather, to conceal both the viewer's erection and any masturbatory activity during the film. With the advent of pornographic video, the raincoat business must have suffered a major slump.

Throughout the last century, particularly since the 1960s, there have been debates about the legalisation of pornography. The position in most countries until this time was that sexually explicit material of any kind

---

[2]Linda Lovelace (real name Linda Marchiano) claimed later that she had performed the acts in *Deep Throat* and other movies against her will, evidence that is often used by feminist antipornography campaigners to support their argument that women are routinely abused in the making of such material.

should be prohibited. A shift in attitude came with the lifting of restrictions on erotic literature, such as D. H. Lawrence's *Lady Chatterley's Lover* (which had been banned briefly in the United Kingdom under the Obscene Publications Act of 1959) and, later, the novels of Henry Miller. In 1969, the Danish government took the unprecedented step of decriminalising pornography; for a short while, Denmark became a hive of pornographic activity, with English filmmakers in particular swamping the market with increasingly violent material such as *Her Daughter Raped* (Slade, 1984). Despite fears about a possible connection between pornography and sexual violence against women, there was actually a reduction in sexual offences in Denmark in the years following decriminalisation (Kutchinsky, 1973, 1991).

During the 1970s, the British government came under pressure from both sides of the pornography argument. Whereas the Danish experience seemed a strong argument for decriminalisation, a number of antipornography campaigners voiced strident objections to what they saw as increasingly lax public standards toward the depiction of sex in the media. One organisation—the National Viewers and Listeners Association, led by former head teacher Mary Whitehouse—became particularly influential. Support for Whitehouse's campaign was weakened by the breadth of its scope. Pornography was merely the tip of the iceberg; concern focused on other "immoral" material, such as swearing and violence on mainstream television. A number of other high-profile obscenity trials also contributed to a certain ambivalence toward censorship in general, notably successful cases brought under the Obscene Publications Act against satirical magazine *Oz* and homosexual magazine *Gay News.*

In 1977, the Williams Committee investigated the case for further restrictions on pornography in Britain, relying to some extent on evidence collected by psychologists on media effects. These suggested that there was mixed evidence that pornography (or media violence) would produce harmful antisocial effects (Howitt & Cumberbatch, 1975), and consequently the Committee reported that, all in all, pornography represented no more than a minor nuisance to society. Nevertheless, in the following decade, under Margaret Thatcher's right-wing government, tighter restrictions were placed on the industry, deriving in part from an assumption that pornography was responsible for antisocial behaviour (Einsiedel, 1988).

The reverse situation occurred in the United States during the 1980s, when in 1986 the Attorney General's Commission on Pornography relied heavily on social scientific research that seemed to provide evidence for a "causal relationship between exposure to sexually violent material and aggressive behaviour towards women" (Einsiedel, 1988, p. 116). Although the Commission endorsed the experimental laboratory findings that suggested a causal relationship between violent pornography and aggressive behaviour toward women (including the acceptance of "rape myths"), the U.S. government has consistently refused to intervene on the legal front to restrict the production of such material, regarding it as a violation of free speech (Linz, Malamuth, & Beckett, 1992).

Gunter (2002) suggested that the treatment of the social scientific literature in the U.K. and U.S. enquiries reflects differences between research traditions in those countries. North American research on pornography has been largely carried out in the experimental social psychology tradition, whereas in the United Kingdom, research on pornography has been mainly confined to qualitative and theoretical work in disciplines like sociology and feminism. Gunter also pointed out that the "ill effects" of pornography seem to be confined to a small minority of users, so restricting its availability would curb the freedom of the majority of users. Furthermore, both Commissions highlighted a number of methodological problems in the experimental literature, which I discuss shortly. A Canadian enquiry (the Fraser Committee in 1985) was even more critical of the experimental research, preferring to endorse feminist objections to pornography.

A number of studies comparing the availability of pornography with the incidence of sex crime have found little association. Kutchinsky (1991) examined statistics for four countries and found that, during the 1970s and 1980s, in three of them (Denmark, Sweden, and West Germany) rape had increased slowly relative to other violent assaults. Given that the production and distribution of pornography expanded rapidly during the period under investigation, and that definitions of rape and a willingness by victims to report it became more prevalent, this seems like a pretty strong endorsement for the "no effects" position.

Nevertheless, it is often argued that the putative pornography/rape association is immaterial; pornography is still harmful to women, whether it causes men to assault them, or whether it simply contributes to male domination (Cameron & Frazer, 2000). With the rapid growth of Internet pornography there are also fears that children will be exposed to easily accessed pornographic websites, and there are calls for tighter regulation of online material.[3] Some of the most vigorous campaigners have called for what amounts to a war on pornography; writer Andrea Dworkin urged women to "take [pornography] from [men], to burn it, to rip it up, bomb it, raze their theatres and publishing houses to the ground" (2000, p. 43).

[3]Some of my students recently conducted a content analysis of the most widely used search engines by entering terms that schoolchildren were most likely to search for on the Web, such as *animals* and *toys*. A number of pornographic sites were thrown up by these searches, although the worst offender (www.excite.co.uk) has since ceased to exist, closing in December 2001.

THE "EFFECTS" OF PORNOGRAPHY

The history of psychological research into the effects of pornography should be familiar reading to anyone aware of the media violence debate; a rash of experimental findings during the 1970s, followed by entrenchment on both sides, and a curious détente on entry to the 21st century. The main difference between the violence and pornography literatures is that there is more disagreement between "effects" researchers themselves—partly due to the confounding factor of violence in pornography—and a near-absence of uses and gratifications research on the topic.

Experimental Findings

Experiments studying the effects of viewing pornography in the laboratory have produced mixed findings, largely because—as with media violence—the stimuli and measures are so varied. Early studies relied on erotic literature as stimuli, either in print form (Malamuth, Heim, & Feshbach, 1980) or presented on audiotape (Malamuth & Check, 1980). Increasingly, however, researchers have used visual material, usually commercially available pornographic films. Invariably the participants in the experiments are university undergraduates. Measures of response have included "penile tumescence," in which a strain gauge measures changes in penile circumference (Malamuth, Check, & Briere, 1986); aggression as measured by variations on the Milgram simulated electric shock paradigm (Donnerstein & Berkowitz, 1981); and various pen-and-paper measures of attitudes toward women, rape, mood, and sexual arousal.

The earliest study claiming to demonstrate a link between pornography and antisocial behaviour was Zillmann's (1971) original excitation transfer study, described in chapter 4. The main finding here was that, using Milgram's paradigm, participants gave highest-intensity "shocks" to learners after watching an erotic (although nonviolent) film. These were higher even than those given by participants in the "violent" condition. This finding suggests that the negative effect of pornography is simply a general increase in aggression, a simple physiological response.

Later research has studied the effects of specific types of material on cognitive responses to pornography, particularly attitudes toward rape. Using pornographic literature as stimuli, Malamuth et al. (1980) found that, generally, participants reported higher sexual arousal after listening to stories featuring consensual sex than those featuring coercive sex, although this effect is reduced if the female victim of coercive sex achieves an orgasm (a typical scenario in pornography). Similar findings were obtained by Donnerstein and Berkowitz (1981) using a Milgram-style shock paradigm.

A common theme in the literature is the effect of viewing pornography on the acceptance of "rape myths." A typical rape myth is that "only bad girls get raped" (i.e., the victim is partly responsible); others include "a woman can resist a rapist if she really wants to," "women cry rape when jilted," and "rapists are either sex-starved or insane" (Burt, 1980). These myths, it is argued, proliferate in pornography, and are a major contributing factor in predisposing men to consider rape as an acceptable behaviour (Russell, 2000). In a meta-analysis of 24 studies, Allen, Emmers, Gebhardt, and Giery (1995) found a positive association between exposure to pornography and the acceptance of such myths. However, the studies featured an enormous range of measures, and no effect at all was found for studies outside the laboratory (indeed, some nonexperimental studies have shown quite high *negative* correlations).

Using a more indirect measure, Zillmann and Bryant (1984) found that, after 5 days of viewing pornography, participants gave shorter prison sentences to rapists in a mock trial. Linz, Donnerstein, and Penrod (1984) found similar effects in a study comparing attitudes to the victim in a rape trial; however, the authors subsequently noted that the effect was replicated only for violent pornographic material (Linz & Donnerstein, 1988). This led them to suggest that many of the findings of laboratory research into pornography are the result of "demand characteristics" (i.e., participants conforming to the expectations of the experimenters). In one study, for instance, participants were told that the experiment gave them a rare opportunity "to say something *directly* to the government of Canada" (p. 183). However, it is not clear why this factor should affect only the experimental group in the study.

An important criticism of the experimental research on effects of pornography is that participants are often limited in terms of response options (Gunter, 2002). In many studies that have demonstrated a relationship between viewing pornography and antisocial behaviour, the only response open to participants is to behave aggressively. Milgram's simulated shock paradigm is a good example—group differences are measured on the strength of the shocks delivered to a fellow participant, not whether the participant has chosen to shock them in the first place. In a replication of an earlier (Malamuth & Donnerstein, 1982) study, Fisher and Grenier (1994) provided a nonaggressive option to participants and found that most of them selected this option, even those who had viewed violent sex scenes.

It is argued that an important effect of pornography, as with media violence, is *desensitisation*. Viewing sexually explicit material over a long period of time reinforces rape myths and instils an appetite for ever-more extreme material as viewers become bored with "softcore" content. In a way, this argument is similar to the "thin end of the wedge" argument surrounding drug use (i.e., that cannabis users will soon get used to its effects and seek out harder drugs, eventually getting hooked on cocaine and heroin). Zillmann and Bryant (1986) put this to the test in an experiment in which participants received an hour's exposure to pornography once a week for 6 weeks and were then left alone in a laboratory with a collection of videos to watch. Experimental participants chose significantly more "XXX" videos than did controls, leading the authors to conclude that the exposure had whetted their appetites for hardcore material.

A similar argument underlies studies that have examined the effects of viewing pornography on participants' attitudes toward their partners. Weaver, Masland, and Zillmann (1984) found that male participants who had viewed slides and videos of beautiful models gave lower ratings to their real-life partners than did those viewing slides of unattractive women. Zillmann and Bryant (1988), employing the same methodology as in their earlier-cited 1986 study, determined that both males and females reported lower sexual satisfaction with their partner after viewing 6 weeks of pornographic material.

Similar findings were reported in a study by Kenrick, Gutierres, and Goldberg (1989), although the authors interpreted the findings slightly differently; given other research that has found similar effects simply for beautiful *faces,* they argued that the findings "make less of a case for avoiding sexually arousing materials than they do for avoiding the popular media in general" (p. 166). In other words, exposure to highly attractive models, clothed or unclothed, is enough to make us dissatisfied with our own sexual partners. This effect is considered again in chapter 9, in relation to adolescents' perception of their own bodies.

Nonexperimental Findings

One of the major problems with the experimental research into the effects of pornography is that, even more than with media violence research, it is hard to generalise from the results to real-life uses of pornography. Media violence research has been criticised because the viewing conditions in the laboratory are so unlike those in real media use (Freedman, 1984). The same objection is even more pertinent in relation to pornography experiments, especially given the changing use of pornography in the 1980s and onward, in which, typically, viewers watch videos or read magazines at home alone, usually as masturbation accessories. Occasionally it is suggested that such use is *cathartic* in nature—pornography as a functional alternative to actual sex.

Although little U&G research has investigated this possibility, one approach is to examine pornography from an evolutionary perspective. Malamuth (1996), an experimentalist turned Darwinist, claimed that pornography works for men as a biological "trick." In masturbating over a nude model, a man may subconsciously think he has "scored," thereby providing a cathartic effect. There are many good things about such a trick—it avoids any likelihood of contracting sexual disease, there is no possibility of rejection, and it may be useful when resources are scarce and competition is high. Women, on the other hand, do not benefit from this type of trick in the same way as men, because it is only beneficial when following a short-term mating strategy. Therefore, they prefer erotica, in which male models demonstrate higher "investment" (i.e., suggesting they will be loyal partners and good parents).

Whether or not we accept the evolutionary argument in relation to gender, it seems fair to argue that there may be some positive benefits from pornography use. Given the astonishing financial success of the pornographic industry, it seems hard to imagine that its use is solely *deviant.* A number of authors have examined these benefits, from what Weaver (1991) referred to as the "sexual information" perspective. For example, marital counsellors and psychosexual therapists have argued that pornography may provide couples with stimulation, both physical and mental (in providing ideas), to recharge a flagging sexual relationship (Malamuth & Billings, 1984). It is often argued that pornography may play a valuable role in providing sexual information in general. Trostle (1993) found that although pornography was not listed very highly by undergraduates as a source of learning about sex in general, 50% of respondents cited it as an information source about oral and anal sex, and 43% cited it as an information source about foreplay. This is a surprising finding given the arguments that pornography tends to gloss over aspects of lovemaking other than the act of intercourse itself.

Despite the impression that typical pornography use involves a lone male in a bedroom with a box of Kleenex at his side, there has been hardly any research on the everyday uses of pornography. One rare example is a study by Demare, Lips, and Briere (1993), who asked 422 male students to complete questionnaires on pornography use. Eighty-six percent of this sample responded by claiming that they had used pornography at least once in the previous month. That is a very high number, bearing in mind that many of those students are likely to have been in romantic relationships! However, it goes some way to explaining the success of the industry. Disturbingly, in the same period, 25% had used pornography that depicted the rape of a woman, and 36% had used porn featuring forced sex against a woman.

The study then went on to examine the students' attitudes toward rape and their own history of "sexual coercion." The figures here were also disturbing: 28% were likely to use "some force" to achieve intercourse, and 11% admitted that they were capable of carrying out an actual rape. In terms of past sexual behaviour, 16% had used "coercion" to achieve intercourse, and 12% had used force (in all likelihood the same subgroup that admitted to being potential rapists—i.e., they *were* rapists). These data were entered into a model to see which factors were the best predictors of rape; interestingly, use of violent pornography was a significant predictor ($r = .15$, still quite low), but nonviolent pornography failed to show a significant association with attitudes to rape ($r = .08$).

It is of course impossible, on ethical grounds, to test empirically the causal hypothesis relating pornography to sexual assault. One solution is to test the hypothesis in reverse, by examining pornography use among convicted sex offenders. Shortly before his execution in 1989, the U.S. serial killer Ted Bundy blamed pornography for his crimes, arguing that he had started out merely as a "peeping Tom" but, through his addictive obsession with pornographic material, worked his way up to becoming a murderer. Cameron and Frazer (2000) identified a number of problems with the "addiction" model of pornography, not least the fact that it gives offenders an opportunity to disclaim responsibility for their acts. In this respect, pornography plays a similar role to media violence as a scapegoat for aggressive behaviour.

Studies of sex offenders in general find little support for the pornography/rape model. Groth (1979) actually discerned a negative relationship between the two, whereas Howitt (1995) argued that sex offenders tend to be exposed to pornography later in life than are most people. Both authors agreed that a fundamental error in the pornography/rape argument is to equate rape with sexual arousal; essentially, rape is violent crime, and is therefore more likely to occur as a result of viewing violent media in general, regardless of sexual content (although the priming argument would suggest that sexual content is necessary to provide potential rapists with ideas). Nevertheless, feminist antipornography writers argue that it is the sexual climate produced by pornography that results in abuse against women, rather than there being a simple cause-and-effect relationship (Cameron & Frazer, 2000).

Gender Issues

Overwhelmingly it is *men* rather than women who use pornography, and in recent years the debate has focused on this anomaly. Feminist critics maintain that pornography is just a tool that men have used over the centuries to subordinate women ("Woman-hatred underlies all pornography"—Itzin, 1992, p. 34), but oddly enough the levelling out of gender inequalities in the last half of the 20th century failed to kill off the pornography industry—on the contrary, the relationship has been inverse, with more and more produced every year! Some of that pornography (although more typically, erotica) is aimed deliberately at women, but women still remain very much the minority in terms of consumption. As for the actual *use* of pornography, very little research exists, although it would seem from anecdotal evidence that although men tend to use pornography in private, as a masturbatory aid, for women using pornography may be more of a group "bonding" exercise, like attending a strip show.

Malamuth's (1996) evolutionary argument, although convincing as an explanation for male use of pornography, fails to account for the fact that *some* women enjoy the same sort of pornography as men, even the extreme material. Walsh (1999) asserted that female consumption can be explained by the individual's developmental history. In this study, women who admitted to reading pornographic magazines (27 out of 109 students, pretty much the opposite pattern from men), were more likely to have parents who had divorced, to have been divorced themselves, to have less positive attachment to their parents (probably explained by the divorce), and to have twice as much sex as nonporn users. This is the opposite of the argument that pornography is used as a (cathartic) substitute for real sex, as is assumed with male users.

In a rare example of qualitative research on pornography, Boynton (1999) examined the talk of women who were discussing pornographic images in magazines aimed at male and female readers. The women found male nudes a source of humour, although this could be attributed to the group situation. Female nudes were either pitied (as uncomfortable, cold, bored), or despised (for being unattractive, old, "unnatural," or unpleasant—"She looks a right cow"). In some cases, the more attractive models were envied ("If I had a body like that, I might show it off"), but less attractive models acted as a source of comfort ("It's not just me, she's got pubes down to her knees as well"). Interestingly, there was little concern that these images might incite men to attack or rape a woman—far more worrying was the idea that their own male partners might find such pitiful material stimulating!

One frequently voiced feminist objection to pornography is that its very creation involves the sexual abuse of women. This is an issue that has provoked intense debate within feminist circles, because it runs the risk of simply portraying women as "victims," incapable of acting out of their own free will. It takes an extreme position to argue otherwise; Andrea Dworkin (2000) who, like Itzin, considers pornography to be an inevitable outcome (as well as a cause) of misogyny, argued that any scene portraying sexual coercion must be regarded as equivalent to a real rape, although it would be protected legally under the right to freedom of speech. This version of media as "magic window" poses problems at a theoretical level, and it is compounded by the relatively small number of charges brought against pornographic moviemakers by women who have been "exploited" in the movies' making.

Mackinnon (2000) argued that this is not surprising, because most women become involved in pornography either as a result of poverty or as a consequence of childhood sexual abuse. The same arguments are often voiced in defence of women involved in prostitution, and, as Boynton (1999) noted, there is a case for regarding prostitution and pornography as two components of the more general "sex industry," and their personnel as "sex workers." This definition affords higher status to the women involved in making pornography, as well as giving credibility to their profession as a whole.

Recent developments in the world of Internet pornography look set to further enhance the status of women in the profession. Increasingly, female models are seizing control of their own careers by moving away from the video market and setting up their own websites (Podlas, 2000). The Channel 5 show *www.sex* recently claimed that there are now more websites devoted to pornography stars than to mainstream movie actors and actresses; one example is Jenna Jameson. Already a millionaire through pornographic films and videos, Jameson has set up her own online business that features her own roster of models; the website has recorded as many as 2 million hits in a single day. Another porn star, Bridget "the Midget" Powerz, became fed up with exploitation from filmmakers and set up her own website through which she records movies on demand. Internet pornography also enables performers to prolong their careers. At an age where many (female) stars are forced to take early retirement, the 39-year-old Teri Weigel has set up a successful site where she is filmed constantly by 18 webcams set up around her flat, and spends an hour a day communicating with fans by e-mail.

Ultimately, the future of pornography may well lie with the Internet. One commentator has claimed that the video market will be dead by the year 2005. In the meantime, ease of access to Internet technology means that more and more "amateurs" are entering the fray, with the effect that before long the ownership of the pornography industry may become increasingly fragmented, along with fewer opportunities for the exploitation of female performers.

EFFECTS AND USES OF CHILD PORNOGRAPHY

Over recent years, concerns about pornography have shifted slightly, away from the exploitation of women (hard to prove, hard to find claimants) and toward the exploitation of children, the nature of which is rarely within doubt when it comes to pornographic activity. Although the Internet offers liberating possibilities for women in the sex industry, it has also brought about expansion in the demand and production of child pornography. There have been an increasing number of high-profile legal cases concerning this section of the market in recent years.

The illegal nature of child pornography has meant that not only is prosecution a possibility for the makers of such material, but possession also brings with it the risk of imprisonment. In 1999 this was highlighted in spectacular fashion in the United Kingdom, when 1970s pop star Gary Glitter (real name Paul Gadd) was convicted of the possession of over 4,000 indecent images of children on the hard drive of his portable laptop computer, and sentenced to 4 months of jail time (he was released after 2 months, as is customary with British law). The case highlighted the seriousness of child pornography use, because Gadd's disturbing collection came to light only after he carelessly left his computer in the hands of a repair engineer with the instructions not to look at anything on the hard disk. Ignoring the request, the engineer then discovered material that was so offensive (including scenes of rape and torture) that he felt he had no option but to involve the police. After his conviction, Gadd/Glitter became something of a hate object in the British tabloid press, was smuggled out of prison following death threats, and is believed to have "begun a new life" in Cuba.

The Gary Glitter affair is somewhat unusual in relation to the possession of pornographic material over the Internet involving children, except that he fits the profile of the typical offender: middle-aged professional male with some computer expertise (although evidently not a lot). Most are in denial about the seriousness of the offence, failing to see it as harmful, and receive no harsher punishment than 80 hours community services. Ostensibly, the outcome of the Glitter trial was severe because of the media attention surrounding the case and the fear of a public outcry that would have undoubtedly greeted a lenient sentence, thus undermining the procedure for less high-profile equivalent offences.

Quite apart from simply following the letter of the law, how far should we be concerned about the protection of children from adults who simply download obscene images of them? The pornography/rape argument rears its head again: Are individuals driven to attack children as a result of viewing explicit sexual imagery? This is a very important question, although answering it involves confronting some very uncomfortable issues. In one study, Quinsey, Steinman, Bergersen, and Holmes (1975) measured penile circumference while exposing both convicted child abusers and "normal" participants to sexual images of both adults and children. Normal men were found to be 50% more aroused while viewing pictures of naked pubescent and prepubescent girls than while viewing pictures of adult women.[4] Other similar studies have found numerous misclassifications of "paedophile" among supposedly normal men (Howitt, 1998).

Part of the problem is that heterosexual male desire often sits on a knife edge between a preference for neonate facial features in women (clear skin, large eyes, high cheekbones) and an intense revulsion toward paedophilia. It could be argued that the ferocity of assaults on convicted (child) sex offenders and the mob violence often enacted against rehabilitating child abusers are driven partly by the need for heterosexual men to have clear boundaries between what is acceptable sexual desire (i.e., the youngest, healthiest fertile female) and what is not (legally protected children). If a subgroup of men can be clearly identified and labelled, it reduces the uncertainty surrounding their own borderline desires for young-looking women. It may also partly explain the sexual significance of large female breasts for heterosexual men, which in the same context act as a reassuring sign that a woman is a legitimate target of sexual desire.

There are many other grey areas to consider in the case of paedophilia and pornography. Howitt (1995) argued that a crucial omission in the literature on pornography concerns the role of *fantasy*—of particular relevance to paedophilia—for which it was harder to gain access to appropriate material before the advent of the Internet. Howitt asserted that many convicted child abusers actually have an aversion to pornography in general. Access to children is of course the major factor, and experience of child abuse is almost always a factor as well. Instead of pornography, paedophiles are likely to use "harmless" media as fantasy material, such as clothing and toy catalogues, scout magazines, and programmes featuring fully clad children such as *Grange Hill*. In addition, Howitt also claimed that, for many paedophiles, genital contact is not necessarily the objective; quite often they are aroused merely by cuddling or touching.

These findings flag up numerous concerns with simplistic pornography/rape theories. Although we may feel disgust at the cognitions and behaviour of such people, is anyone ever likely to suggest a ban on *Grange Hill* as a means of combatting sex crime?

MEANINGS OF PORNOGRAPHY AND EROTICA

The topic of fantasy provoked by research on paedophilia raises an important issue for pornography in general. Considering alternatives to models

---

[4]Although immensely valuable to scientific research, it is hard to imagine a modern-day ethics panel allowing such a study to proceed! Apart from anything else, given the current climate in the United Kingdom concerning child abuse and the sex offenders' register, one can imagine all kinds of pressure being placed on the researchers to reveal details of the "aroused" participants to police and social services.

of the "effects" of pornography, the question of meaning and interpretation of media content seems relevant. Cameron and Frazer (2000) argued that pornography should be considered as a text like any other media product—our attention should be on the particular "reading" made by the audience rather than trying to pass judgment on pornographic material as merely "stimuli" to which viewers may be "exposed."

Howitt (1998) offered an interesting example of a scene from a pornographic movie on which he was required to make a judgment about its potential harm to a viewer. The scene was listed as one of extreme violence and degradation in which a female performer had a broom handle inserted into her anus. Although hardly claiming that such an act is desirable or healthy in any way, Howitt challenged the interpretation of the scene as "violent and painful." For one thing, the actress was positioned in order to receive said instrument; for another, the person doing the "inserting" was another woman, and the object appeared to be received with pleasure. In recasting the scene in such apparently innocuous terms, Howitt argued, many of the lurid claims by antipornographers appear problematic and reductionist.

Ross (2000) made a similar point in relation to much gay and lesbian pornography (hitherto ignored in this chapter, but highly relevant to the debate). She also found herself defending pornographic material in a court case, this time the "erotic lesbian fantasy magazine" *Bad Attitude*, which was seized by Canadian plainclothes police in 1991, leading to the prosecution of both bookseller and publisher. The trial featured two leading media psychologists, Neil Malamuth (against) and Jonathan Freedman (for). In neither case had the experts actually conducted any research into gay and lesbian pornography, which Ross maintained is radically different from heterosexual porn ("The whole meaning, context and significance of the images has changed"—Ross, 2000, p. 265). The argument in favour of gay and lesbian pornography essentially rests on the idea that it subverts straight imagery, playing with it in a largely ironic fashion. Because its consumers read the imagery as ironic, it is less likely to lead to antisocial behaviour than is heterosexual pornography.

It could also be argued that the same is true for pornography in general. Isolating and decontextualising the components, then presenting them to experimental subjects under artificial conditions, tells us nothing about the meaning and significance pornography holds for casual, everyday users of such material. This is an area badly in need of further research.

CONCLUSION

I have concentrated on pornography in this chapter rather than sex per se; clearly, the issues surrounding sex as a secondary characteristic of films and television (e.g., short erotic scenes embedded in a feature film) are somewhat different. Gunter (2002) is an excellent source for literature on all forms of sex in the media. Pornography itself is a *functional* genre, produced solely for sexual gratification. This makes it more like prosocial media than like media violence. Despite this, there has been very little research into the actual use of pornography, and most of the social scientific research has low ecological validity—the participants are typically male students, watching (often extreme) pornography in alien surroundings. Unlike extreme violence, which can erupt without warning in an adult-rated movie, exposure to extreme pornography on film and video—and even on the Internet—is tightly controlled. People usually *choose* to purchase such fare, or to subscribe to adult cable channels or "specialist" websites. Therefore, future research should concentrate on those people, however hard they may be to find.

Chapter 7

Advertising

In a recent British study (McKee, 2002), children were asked the question: "What are adverts for?" One child, clearly wise beyond his years, replied: "To glue the programmes together." We might smile at the blissful naïveté of the 6-year-old mind, and the Piagetians among us might record the statement as "preoperational," but the kid has a point. Even as far back as 1974, the cultural theorist Raymond Williams remarked that commercial television seemed like a string of ads occasionally interrupted by programmes. If it weren't for the commercials, there wouldn't be nearly as much television.

But advertising is about much more than television. However much we try and avoid its gaze, the call to consume follows us wherever we go. A bus rumbles past, and a slogan flashes across our visual field; we look up from the road and a famous brand name reactivates stored memories; even the act of picking up a tin of beans may consolidate our relationship with a brand. Some advertising has (almost) become dissociated with its products. Promotional pop videos are now seen as a stand-alone art form, although their primary function is to sell CDs. Seen in this light, MTV and its offshoots are 24-hour-a-day commercials.

However, most advertising, particularly advertising we encounter in the media, is somewhat less successful in blurring the boundary between manufacturer and marketer. Commercial breaks on television are a good opportunity to put the kettle on, or visit the toilet. Internet pop-ups are batted down again in the time it takes to click the mouse. Few of us actually invite advertising into our lives, organise our viewing patterns around the commercials, or complain about the amount of news that clogs up the ads in the colour supplements. So advertisers have had to become ingenious. Think of advertorials—those naughty ads that look just like magazine features. Until we have spotted the disclaimer in the corner, we read an advertorial as if it were, say, a feature on garden tools. When we *do* eventually notice the disclaimer (perhaps, after a couple of paragraphs) we turn the page rapidly, feeling cheated.

Why do we react in this way? After all, if the copy had been penned by a journalist, how could we tell whether the writer wasn't as "neutral" or "objective" as he or she claimed? How do we know that the writer hasn't been slipped a crafty backhander by the manufacturer to plug their wares? The same uncertainty dogs all our media consumption. Has someone paid extra for the cigarette that our favourite actor lights during a film scene? Is the film really just a glorified vehicle for flogging toys to pestered parents? Am I drinking this brown fizzy liquid just because the manufacturer sponsors the cinema in which I am sitting?

Psychology has been at the heart of advertising since its invention, although, academically, advertising and psychology have long since gone their separate ways. For advertisers, the ability to manipulate consumer impressions and decision making has been the key to success. If product sales increase following a carefully orchestrated campaign, the persuasive tactics have evidently worked, although as with any natural experiment it is hard to establish cause and effect due to the lack of control over confounding variables.

Nevertheless, there are numerous advertising campaigns over the years whose success can be traced confidently to advertising factors. Take, for instance, the Levi's 501 television commercial from the mid-1980s in which model Nick Kamen stripped to his boxer shorts in a launderette. This ad had multiple effects on consumer behaviour in and outside Britain for years to come, some of them (presumably) unforeseen by Levi's or the advertising agency. To begin with, the primary sales objective was met spectacularly: In the year following the ad's introduction, sales of 501s increased by 800%. Furthermore, the music playing in the ad (Marvin Gaye's 1960s hit "I Heard It Through the Grapevine") was re-released and went to number one in the singles charts, sparking off a succession of re-released "oldies" (and, eventually, original compositions) that were catapulted to the top of the charts through exposure as advertising soundtracks. Nick Kamen himself became a major celebrity for a short while, also releasing a hit single. To top it all, boxer shorts were rejuvenated as essential underwear for all young males.

For media users, advertising will undoubtedly have an effect on their lives in the same way as other media, but—even more than with sex and violence—we try desperately to avoid being influenced, or to deny it, perhaps through the "third person effect." This is because advertising, unlike media violence or even pornography, is founded on a theory of media effects. It exists *only* to dupe and persuade, and if it fails to dupe and persuade, it fails completely.[1] Increasingly, the secret of successful advertising has been the extent to which the advertiser can disguise the ad, or at least disguise the elements of the ad that achieve the intended psychological effects.

This is testimony to our stubbornness as media consumers *not* to be influenced by information that we perceive as vulgar, low culture, and over which we have no control. It is also testimony to the way in which media literacy develops over time among increasingly sophisticated generations of users. The ability to "read" a Silk Cut billboard ad—in which neither the name nor the product are in view but instead are represented instead by a strip of purple fabric—suggests that the cleverness and ingenuity of advertising is rubbing off on the public at large.

ADVERTISING THROUGH HISTORY

Gillian Dyer (1982) traced the birth of advertising back to the 17th century with the development of newssheets, or "mercuries," that provided traders with financial information. These publications, the forerunners of local papers (particularly freesheets, which are probably the best example of a media product that exists solely as an advertising vehicle), also carried publicity for local fairs and markets, and formed the model for the first newspapers to emerge at the start of the 18th century. Ten years after the launch of the first British newspaper, the *Daily Courier*, in 1702, the government instigated a tax on advertising that effectively killed off many fledgling publications. This was not lifted until 1853, by which time billboard advertising and handbills (distributed, e.g., to theatre audiences) had become prevalent. Meanwhile, in the United States, the absence of a similar tax resulted in the rapid growth of the press. Newspaper owners found that the revenue gained through selling advertising space allowed them to lower the price of their product, so that some publications devoted as much as 50% of their space to advertisers.

Initially, newspapers created advertisements themselves from the information supplied by the client. In the 1880s, however, the creative teams declared independence from media outlets to receive direct payment from manufacturers. Newspapers were obliged to publicise their circulation figures so that advertisers could select appropriate targets, and relax some of the creative restrictions they had previously placed on advertising (the

[1]Admittedly, people who work in advertising lost sight of this objective many years ago, and see their work as "art." However, in the same way that the TV channels would not exist without the commercials, so the art of advertising would not exist without the clients' beliefs about its ability to dupe and persuade!

amount of space occupied by a single ad, the use of specific typefaces, etc.). Advertising began to develop its own industry, demanding more and more sites for its products: Eventually, billboards began to appear throughout the environment, on buildings and railway stations. Suddenly, advertising had become a medium of its own.

As advertising expanded, the nature of the advertisements themselves began to change. Early ads employed little visual material, consisting solely of verbal claims for the product along with factual information such as price. By the late 19th century, the big soap manufacturers took advertising down a different route. In 1886, A & F Pears purchased a painting from a successful contemporary artist, Sir John Everett Millais, of an angelic-looking small boy gazing at two bubbles floating through the air. The advertisers simply inserted a bar of Pears soap in the scene and sold the picture to numerous outlets.

The success of "Bubbles," as the Pears boy became known, sparked a debate in the English *Times* newspaper about the appropriateness of mixing commerce with culture, a debate that remains pertinent to media psychology to this day. Modern advertising is indisputably an art form; agencies employ "creative directors," and ads win prizes on the basis of artistic criteria rather than sales effectiveness. Recently, the U.K. television network Channel 4 asked viewers to vote for the 100 best television commercials of all time. The winner was a Guinness commercial ("Surfers") in which galloping white horses were morphed with Polynesian surfers via state-of-the-art computer technology. The question of whether or not it increased sales of Guinness seems strangely irrelevant.

THE ROLE OF PSYCHOLOGY IN ADVERTISING

Psychology and advertising have grown hand in hand across the last century, but although there is a clear "psychology of advertising" you are unlikely to find much reference to it in mainstream psychology textbooks. As with other aspects of media, the general consensus seems to be that psychology will only address the issue of advertising when it becomes too much of a problem to ignore, as in the case of advertising aimed at children. However, academic psychology owes some of its history to the interests of advertisers; the topic of *persuasion*, for a start, only entered into psychological discourse during the 1920s following the needs of marketing (Danziger, 1997). It has since spawned a vast theoretical literature in social psychology.

At the start of the 20th century, early advertisers were quick to seize on the scientific credibility of psychology, and psychological ideas manifested themselves in many early ads. Perhaps the most obvious use of psychology can be seen in propaganda advertising, notably war recruitment posters. In the United Kingdom and United States, conscription was advertised using a figure (Lord Kitchener and Uncle Sam, respectively) pointing at the viewers of the poster and addressing them directly ("Your country needs YOU!"/ "I want YOU for U.S. army"). In these, the principal tactic of persuasion is direct eye gaze, along with the finger point, creating in the viewers an illusion that the figure in the poster is making contact with them.

There is little doubt that such images make an explicit appeal to the individual viewer, and it is hard to imagine a similar campaign working today (imagine the U.K. prime minister or U.S. president in such a pose!). It is not surprising that advertisers quickly realised the importance of developing more subtle methods of persuasion. Freudian theory and studies of subconscious awareness in general gave advertisers an excellent opportunity to sneak their appeals in through the psychological backdoor. An early example of an ad that used associationism along with guilt creation as its persuasive tactics is the famous World War I recruitment poster whose text reads "Daddy, what did YOU do in the Great War?" In the picture, the father sits in his armchair staring sadly into the distance while his son plays soldiers on the floor and his daughter, to whom we attribute the question, sits on his knee. In this ad, the viewer is invited to identify with the father as a feared "possible self" (Markus & Nurius, 1986). These tactics are still in frequent use, particularly in the field of health promotion.

As early as 1908, a distinct "psychology of advertising" had begun to emerge in the United States, with a series of books by Walter Dill Scott and other authors. Visual perception, memory, comprehension, and credibility were among the topics studied, and psychological tactics became increasingly attractive to advertisers during the depression of the 1930s (Maloney, 1994). The earliest academic research on advertising studied either the effectiveness of advertising from the marketing perspective (i.e., how to bolster the impact of ads), or the impact of advertising on the general public. The latter was closely bound up with research into the effects of propaganda. Many early studies of the psychology of radio (e.g., Cantril & Allport, 1935) were concerned that the medium would be abused for political ends, and in some respects they may have been right—the continuous barrage of advertising for luxury goods ever since could well be regarded as propaganda for the glories of capitalism.

After World War II, as advertising developed a science of its own, its link with academic psychology became increasingly remote. Advertising agencies recruited their own research teams, importing scientific methodology and creating their own scientific jargon. For example, the term *brand image,* which has crept into the popular consciousness, was first coined in a 1955 paper by Gardner and Levy. This concept marked a growing awareness that the study of advertising should not be confined to the short-term effects of buying behaviour but on longer-term effects of impression building, and the elements of ads that shape it. Although advertising research teams have often been held back from advancing academic research by the short-term demands of their clients (e.g., stifling data that fail to show their products in the best light), the expansion of marketing and business science has allowed research to flourish. Today, academic journals such as the *Journal of Advertising* and the *Journal of Advertising Research* carry scientific papers on all aspects of the discipline, although they are aimed more at the business analyst than at the psychologist.

COGNITIVE AND BEHAVIOURAL EFFECTS OF ADVERTISING

Academic research into the effects of advertising tends to fall into two groups of effects produced by ads: *perceptual* effects, such as low camera angles to make the speaker seem authoritative (a tactic now abandoned by political advertisers); and *attitudinal* effects, which examine the short- and long-term impact of an ad on the consumer's impression of the brand and product. More generally, research has focused on the *effectiveness* of ads in shaping consumer behaviour. This is a somewhat different approach to media effects from the research discussed so far in this section of the book, largely because the research is driven more by the interests of businesses than by the interests of the state. Compared to research on sex and violence in the media, most research on advertising rarely queries the cumulative effects of continuously viewing ads on human behaviour (although see Comstock & Scharrer, 1999; Condry, 1989).

Perceptual Effects

Most of the research on perceptual effects of advertising have drawn on the information-processing approach of the 1950s that tended to view memory and attention as discrete cognitive processes, leading to something of a debate about their relative importance (Olshavsky, 1994). Condry (1989) argued that attention is the key issue for television advertising, because it is in the sponsors' best interests that viewers are glued to the screen so that they will not miss the advertisers' messages. Although this may seem an obvious point, the nature of attention is complex, and there are more subtle factors mediating between attentional processes and the effectiveness of advertising. McGuire (1985) attempted to create a model of advertising effectiveness that explains this process in terms of a hierarchy of cognitive effects. This is a classic information-processing model presenting cognition as a linear process, with early attention essential for later processing. The "message" is unambiguous—nowhere is "interpretation" included in the process, so it appears to be a simple case of absorbing and understanding a clear statement about the world.

The idea that advertising may work at a level below full consciousness has long been a feature of mainstream psychology itself. Most psychology graduates will have encountered the concept of *subliminal advertising*, perhaps in relation to the study of iconic memory (Sperling, 1960). *Iconic memory* is the term given to the storage of a fleeting visual stimulus, typically a grid of nine letters presented on a screen for a brief period (50 milliseconds or so). Experimental research has suggested that our retention of such displays is better than we realise; when asked to recall a specific line from the display at random, we are able to recall more than we consciously perceive.

These findings would seem to support the belief, still widely held in the business world, that advertising messages can be injected into the memory through exposing audiences to brief snatches of persuasive text in the middle of television or cinema programming. Most authors trace the origins of subliminal advertising to a 1950s study by advertising expert James Vicary (reported in *Life* magazine) in which he claimed to have flashed the messages "eat popcorn" and "drink Coca-Cola" onto a cinema screen for 1/3000th of a second every 5 seconds during film showings. Over 6 weeks this led, it was claimed, to an 18% increase in sales of popcorn and over 50% increase in sales of Coke at that particular cinema. As a result of this report, the American government outlawed the practice of subliminal messages in advertising, and the ban has remained in place ever since. However, there has never been any evidence that the original study actually took place as reported, and there certainly has been no confirmation of the findings (Condry, 1989).

Despite the lack of scientific evidence, the concept of subliminal advertising has stuck within modern culture. Four books by the author W.B. Key in the 1970s and 1980s castigated the advertising industry for using such underhand techniques, involving much covert sexual imagery in shadows and reflections (Key, 1989). Evidence for the effectiveness of such imagery is decidedly mixed (Messaris, 1997).[2] The willingness of the public to accept the myth about subliminal advertising may simply be an effect of general suspicion and distrust surrounding advertising (and media in general). However, there is evidence that subliminal-type effects may occur with material that is not directly perceived by viewers. Eagle, Wolitzky, and Klein (1966) carried out a study in which some participants were exposed to slides, one of which had the outline of a duck embedded in a tree trunk. When asked subse-

[2]However, if we consider product placement as subliminal advertising, the success rate is somewhat higher—for a concrete example, in the 3 months after the child protagonists in *E.T.* had been seen eating Reese's Pieces candy, sales of the product rose by two thirds (Messaris, 1997).

quently to list the animals pictured in the slides, no participants listed ducks. However, when asked to write a story about a farmyard, a significant number of participants in the "duck" condition introduced ducks into their stories. More recently, tightly controlled laboratory studies using brief presentation of hidden (masked) words have allowed researchers to demonstrate unconscious activation of semantic processing (Draine & Greenwald, 1998).

These results suggest that, if subliminal advertising is capable of influencing consumer behaviour, it is probably through the process of cognitive *priming* (see chap. 4 for a discussion of priming as a possible explanation of media violence effects). But this has not held back a brisk trade in audiotapes promising "subliminal learning," in which listeners can hear nothing but music or "nature noise" (waves breaking, birdsong, etc.). The manufacturers claim that just by listening to such tapes one can pick up unconscious information, sometimes while asleep, and use this information to master a new language, enhance memory ability, lose weight, quit smoking, boost self-esteem, or even reduce anxiety.

Needless to say, there is scant scientific evidence for anything other than placebo effects for such techniques, although in the case of psychological issues, such as self-esteem, one might argue that placebo effects are sufficient by themselves. Greenwald, Spangenberg, Pratkanis, and Eskenazi (1991) tested the claims of memory and self-esteem enhancement tapes in a double-blind experiment in which participants were unaware of the nature of the material on the tape (half were given memory-enhancing material and half self-esteem material). The manufacturers' claims were not supported by the results. Memory scores were not improved after several weeks of listening to memory material, nor did self-esteem material significantly increase self-esteem scores. Nevertheless, participants who *thought* they were listening to self-esteem material believed themselves to have increased in self-esteem (and the same effect occurred for memory participants).

Subliminal advertising is a contentious area, although it seems certain that some of the success of advertising must, given the third-person effect, be attributed to unconscious processing. We can do little about our memory for advertising jingles and slogans, which is usually a function of simple exposure (Condry, 1989). If we hear a jingle enough times on television or radio it will inevitably seep into our unconscious through the reactivation of neuronal firing patterns. Furthermore, our exposure to ads is rarely governed by conscious, deliberate attention. This was demonstrated in a study by Bogart and Tolley (1988), who measured the behaviour and brain activity of 10 women as they read a newspaper. Ads were glimpsed only by accident; only a fraction of them were remembered, and then only if salient for the individual reader. Furthermore, processing of ads was unconnected to reading of the paper's editorial content.

Television and cinema advertising have been hugely successful because the ads have a captive audience, particularly in the cinema. Television audiences have rather more options open to them: According to one study, 80% of viewers are likely to leave the room during commercial breaks, and most people watching prerecorded material on video will fast-forward through them (Comstock & Scharrer, 1999). The increasing sophistication of television advertising over the years reflects the need to compete with programming for entertainment value. Nevertheless, research in this area suggests that programme genre has a strong effect on cognitive processing of commercials. Both violent and humorous programmes have been linked with low recall of advertising material (Bushman, 1998; Furnham, Gunter, & Walsh, 1998). In both cases it seems that emotional response blunts the degree of attention that viewers can pay to advertising, although Bushman only measured self-reported anger (overlooking the possibility that viewers might actually take pleasure from watching violent material!).

The latest challenge for advertisers is how to maximise the effectiveness of advertising over the Internet. Nearly $1 billion was spent on online advertising in 1997—a threefold increase since 1995—and yet the lack of standardised measures of online advertising effectiveness means that this outlay is something of a gamble (Drèze & Zufryden, 1999). One problem is how to identify unique site visitors, because most programs only record the number of times a page is accessed, not who accesses it; whether that visitor has actually *read* the ad is even more doubtful. Nevertheless, businesses continue to shell out for Internet advertising because it is relatively cheap and can allow the provision of detailed product information (Leong, Huang, & Stanners, 1998).

From a cognitive perspective, Internet advertising is never likely to be as effective as cinema and television advertising because of the user control over the medium. Interactive advertising (in which the user can dismiss the ad at the click of a button) cannot use many of the persuasive tactics of traditional advertising—ads interrupt shows or films and have time to develop storylines and characters, or they sit on a page, slowly sinking into the subconscious while the reader peruses the story alongside. If the Internet has more value as an information medium rather than as an entertainment medium, advertising may eventually return to the hard-sell, product-oriented approach, away from the soft-sell, image-conscious trend of the late 20th century.

Attitudinal Effects

Theories of subliminal advertising work on the assumption that attention and perception are sufficient motivation for consumers to buy products, as though shopping is an activity conducted by solitary individuals in a state of trance. Most consumer decisions, however, are made on a largely rational basis, and many take place in a social context. In the history of advertising, advertisers soon felt the need to look beyond perception and memory toward socially oriented behaviour, particularly the study of consumer attitudes.

Attitude research has a long history in psychology, based largely on the use of psychometric instruments such as the Likert scale (for which respondents are asked to agree or disagree with a series of statements by selecting a point on a continuum). This kind of research methodology has proved useful to advertisers in providing information about public impressions of products and brands. Increasingly, the "effectiveness" of an ad is measured by whether consumers *like* the product on offer and the advertisement itself, rather than whether the ad has actually inspired them to purchase the product. Instead of studying perceptual effects of ads, there has been increased interest in their emotional appeals, and the use of music and humour as effective devices. Although the incidence of these is lower than commonly imagined,[3] there is some experimental evidence suggesting that music can enhance the popularity of an advertisement and its product (Middlestadt, Fishbein, & Chan, 1994).

One of the most heavily researched areas in the psychology of persuasion concerns the degree of personal *involvement* with the issue or product concerned, a term first coined by Herbert Krugman (1965). Petty and Cacioppo (1981) developed this idea in their Elaboration Likelihood Model of persuasion, in which they argued that if consumers are highly involved with a product (e.g., it means a lot to them, such as a car), they will devote more thought ("elaboration") to the message contained in the advertisement. Johnson and Eagly (1989) attempted to distinguish between value-relevant involvement (where the involvement concerns deep-rooted values and beliefs) and outcome-relevant involvement (concerning more immediate concerns, like passing a college exam). However, their distinction seems to be determined by the stimuli used in the literature, which in "value-relevant" studies tended to concern actual political and social issues rather than artificial scenarios. Petty and Cacioppo (1990) argued that the degree of involvement is likely to vary among individual consumers rather than among the products or issues themselves.

The focus on the role of advertising in self-concept and identity construction has shifted the emphasis in advertising away from product-oriented ads toward consumer-oriented ads, with a corresponding shift from perceptual features of ads toward discursive and narrative features

[3]According to Comstock and Scharrer (1999), only 40% of televised ads are accompanied by music, and only 10% of ads contain humour.

(sometimes characterised as the distinction between "hard sell" and "soft sell"). The effect of this contrast on the individual consumer was examined in a study by Snyder and de Bono (1985). They found that the hard sell and soft sell approaches had different effects on different people. Consumers who scored highly on a test of "self-monitoring"—in other words, those who are socially more self-conscious, and likely to adapt their behaviour according to the situation—had more favourable attitudes toward soft-sell ads. This happens, the authors maintained, because such consumers are more image conscious and thus respond better to advertising eliciting moods and associations rather than to hard-sell advertising with more factual information about a product. Low self-monitors, on the other hand, prefer hard-sell ads that describe the benefits of the product; such consumers take a more pragmatic approach to life, and are less concerned with image.

This study demonstrates how different groups of consumers respond differently to the same ads, even though the difference between the groups was simply their scores on a psychometric test. When we compare real social groups such as those differentiated on the basis of gender, ethnicity, or age, we find equally important differences in response to advertising. For some time, businesses have based their marketing strategies around consumer profiles—it is standard practice to select the target audience on the basis of demographic characteristics before deciding what sort of ad to commission. In advertising, such profiling is known as *psychographics*—a picture is built up of the typical consumer, and the ad is designed to appeal to his or her assumed personality characteristics (Condry, 1989).

This means that all kinds of assumptions are poured into advertising—about the best way to appeal to men rather than women, older rather than younger adults, or different ethnic groups. As Jhally (1990) asserted, advertising is less about how people are acting than about how they are dreaming: It reflects the *aspirations* of the consumer rather than his or her current situation. This is sometimes expressed as the difference between one's current sense of self and an "ideal self," which is one of a number of "possible selves" that a person might generate at any given time (Markus & Nurius, 1986). Therefore, an ad for life insurance aimed at married couples might invite viewers to identify with a happily married couple in a comfortable and stylish home, surrounded by attractive children, a contented family pet, and so on. This situation represents the ideal future selves of the people who are most likely to take out a substantial insurance premium. The World War I conscription ad with the slogan "What did YOU do in the Great War, Daddy?" represents the *negative* future self of the guilt-ridden conscientious objector, an equally powerful persuasive tactic.

Appealing to consumers' sense of self requires a good deal of speculation, perhaps drawing on psychodynamic theories of selfhood and fantasy, but there is evidence to suggest that the role of consumer goods in modern life is more central to our psychological life than is sometimes assumed in psychology. In one remarkable study, 248 American adults were asked to grade items on a continuum from "self" to "not self": Male respondents ranked cars higher than their own bodily organs and their religion in relation to "self" (Cook, 1992). The salience of such items for the way we construct our identity (and, perhaps, our psychological well-being) cannot be overestimated.

Like cognitive/perceptual approaches to advertising, attitudinal studies of advertising can only speculate about its *effectiveness*. Rather than measuring participants' memory for commercials, or awareness of specific features, attitudinal studies rely on measures of liking for ads, liking for products, how much money participants might be willing to spend on the advertised product, or how likely they think the ad might affect their consumer behaviour. All these measures are indirectly related to *actual* consumer behaviour. Indeed, even the sales response to a specific advertising campaign tells us little about the behaviour of the individual consumer. It might be possible to study this through ethnographic research (observing buying behaviour over a period of time), or perhaps through a diary study in which the respondent lists all the programmes he or she watches, newspapers and magazines he or she reads, and every product he or she buys over a period. Such studies would be cumbersome and subject to inaccuracies, but they might tell us more about the psychological effects of advertising in real-world settings.

RHETORICAL EFFECTS OF ADVERTISING

A third approach to research on the effects of advertising is to ignore the consumer altogether and focus on the way advertising is created, particularly the use of *rhetoric*. Such research is frequently regarded as nonpsychological because it does not involve real participants. In the long run, this is a fair comment, because it makes little sense to discuss the effects of an ad without actually examining those effects on consumers. Media scholars have begun to appreciate this point and are increasingly taking an ethnographic approach to studying audiences (Ruddock, 2001). Nevertheless, we need to understand the materials before we can examine their effects. One of the biggest flaws in the psychological study of advertising is the use of artificial stimuli (often quite unlike real advertising) and of findings obtained using these stimuli to generate theories about real-life behaviour.

Early advertising relied on a very simple strategy of persuading the consumer: It provided information about the product in simple language. Figure 7.1 contains an advertisement from a 19th century magazine for a "re-

FIG. 7.1. Advertisement for revolving refrigerators from *Harper's Weekly*, 14 April, 1860. Reproduced with permission from HarpWeek L.L.C. from the website http://advertising.harpweek.com

volving refrigerator" (an ingenious piece of 19th-century technology from the days before dry ice and CFCs). There is a picture of this fascinating product and a lengthy description of its attributes. Such a useful, and undoubtedly expensive,[4] product required very little soft sell. Indeed, were it

[4]The price of this item is conspicuous by its absence, heralding a rhetorical strategy that has been used ever since! By contrast, the "pain paint" ad in Fig. 7.3 contains far more pricing information than a reader would possibly need, in keeping with many 19th-century ads that were often little more than long lists of prices.

A HUNDRED YEARS AGO

There were no Railroads—
Not even a Horse-Car;
Only one Church in Brooklyn;
Ferry-Boats not running:
Wall Street, New York, a Slave-Market;
Not a Telegraph Wire;
Not even WOLCOTT'S PAIN PAINT;
New York *Herald* not printed;
Harper's Weekly unknown;
Grant had not smoked a cigar;
Horace Greeley and Jeff. Davis unborn;
No President to Impeach;
Dr. WOLCOTT, 170 Chatham Square,
Did not remove Pain free of cost.

Times have changed wonderfully. Bleeding, Blistering, and Mercury are played out. Burning Liniments made of Turpentine and Cayenne Pepper lie on the shelves unsold; not even fools can be induced to purchase them. Pills are mouldering for want of customers, although coated with sugar. People know better than dose the stomach with physic and pukes. This practice was worse than brutish, for even a beast would not swallow such heathenish nostrums. WOLCOTT'S PAIN PAINT cools Inflammation, Heat, and Fever without a smart or stain, and every body knows they can prove it free of cost at 170 Chatham Square, New York. PAINT is all the go at every drug store, and is a hundred years ahead of the worn-out nostrums formerly used. PAIN PAINT is sold every where at 25c., 50c., $1, $3, $5, and $8 per Bottle. $8 Bottles hold sixteen $1 Bottles, or one quart of PAINT, and is sent, free of express charges, to any part of the country, on receipt of the money.

FIG. 7.2. Advertisement for "pain paint" from *Harper's Weekly*, 2 May, 1868. Reproduced with permission from HarpWeek L.L.C. from the website http://advertising.harpweek.com

not for the manufacturers' details, this copy could have passed for a short feature article.

Contrast that ad with another from the same period, for an equally exotic product known as Wolcott's "pain paint" (Fig. 7.2). This has AD stamped all over it, opening (like many ads of the time) with a piece of blank verse, followed by prose, slowly building a consumer "need." The product itself is introduced midway through the verse without elaboration, and a full description is delayed by a series of barbs aimed at rival products until the reader is practically begging for information.

Medical advertising has always been something of a conundrum. On the one hand, the public are invited to trust their doctors and the findings of medical science, yet drug companies and other manufacturers need to push their wares too, especially those for minor ailments that do not require sufferers to contact their physicians.[5] Thus, cures for headaches, colds, and indigestion still proliferate on commercial television. These ads usually feature appeals to science, and phrases such as "clinically proven to . . ." and "tests show that . . ." are employed along with other signifiers such as white lab coats and test tubes. Increasingly, ads for consumer goods such as certain foods, toothpaste, and washing powder also draw on the discourse and imagery of science.

Outright deceit in advertising has long been regulated by the state; in the United Kingdom the Trades Descriptions Act was passed by the British government in 1968. One way for advertisers to avoid legal action is to issue *disclaimers*, usually as unobtrusively as possible. Indeed, many television commercials contain little text other than a disclaimer. This usually takes the form of small print at the bottom of the screen toward the end of the ad, such as "Can only aid slimming as part of a calorie-controlled diet" or "Offers apply only to. . . ." The fact that the product does not by itself deliver the promises it claims or seems to claim is rendered irrelevant when the information appears, by which time the rhetorical force of the ad has done its work. This is particularly true for ads targeted toward children, who may not notice or even understand the disclaimer; according to Harris (1999) this applies to 36% of children's ads.

Much of the research on advertising rhetoric has restricted itself to the analysis of verbal appeals to consumers. However, ads differ tremendously in the amount of verbal information they contain: A magazine ad will contain more text than a television ad; a billboard on a railway station or in a train will contain more text than a billboard by a roadside, simply because of the time most viewers have to read it. Increasingly, advertisers work in a visual domain, and so studies of rhetoric have had to examine the manipulation of nonverbal information. Naturally, this is harder to determine, because visual rhetoric is more reliant on analysts' interpretative skills.

In the 1960s, French theorist Jacques Durand was one of the first authorities to carry out a systematic study of visual rhetoric in advertising. He identified four types of rhetorical figure that might be present in an ad: figures of addition, suppression, substitution, and exchange (Dyer, 1982). An example of addition might be using several pictures of the same product to create different effects; an example of suppression is a missing element, such as the product itself; a figure of substitution is likely to involve a meta-

[5]During the advertising explosion in the United States in the 1920s and 1930s, the market was flooded with purported cures for all manner of mysterious ailments such as "vacation knee" and "ashtray breath"; as Dyer commented, "The public were taught through the ads that they could consume their way out of any trouble or misfortune, real or invented" (1982, p. 45). Today, the same could be said for cosmetic surgery advertising, which can be found in great profusion on the World Wide Web.

phor or visual pun; whereas a figure of exchange is often an ironic juxtaposition or paradox. Durand argued that almost all these figures (22 in total) could be used to describe the rhetorical effect of an ad, and that this demonstrated a *lack* of creativity involved in advertising, although this argument may only be relevant to ads in the historical period in which his typology was put together.

Product Endorsement

Advertising rhetoric can only be taken so far before consumer cynicism sets in. Although appeals to the authority of science can persuade a reader that a particular cold remedy or even a brand of toothpaste is worth buying, many products require a little extra recommendation. Most of us might buy a product on the recommendation of a friend, and advertisers have increasingly drawn on ready-made friendships to promote their goods: "parasocial" relationships between the public and well-known celebrities (Alperstein, 1991; Giles, 2002b)

The use of celebrities to promote advertised goods is known as *product endorsement.* In 1990, 22% of magazine ads used celebrity endorsements, along with 20% of television commercials (Fowles, 1996). Typically, the celebrity performs a dual function: On the one hand, as a familiar face, he or she is seen as a *reliable* source of information, so we use the trust built up through our existing parasocial relationship with that person to evaluate the product; on the other hand, the celebrity is seen as a neutral and *objective* source of information. Celebrities have an existence beyond that of the commercial itself, or the financial lure of the manufacturer, and so perform the function of rubber-stamping the advertisers' claims. Thus, in one study, a viewer described how she had bought baby food on the advice of Joan Lunden, a former host of *Good Morning America* (Alperstein, 1991).

Does celebrity endorsement work? The previous example would seem to suggest that it does, albeit for certain products allied to certain celebrities. At a more general level, the results are mixed. In a study of the "persuasiveness" of over 5,000 television commercials, celebrity endorsement was not found to enhance the communication of the advertising message (Hume, 1992). Indeed, the presence of a familiar face may overwhelm the message itself; when American footballer Joe Montana appeared in a commercial during television coverage of the Super Bowl, 70% of a viewer sample correctly recognised the star but only 18% recalled that he was promoting Diet Pepsi (Fowles, 1996). The star–product connection may need to be established over the course of more sustained advertising campaigns, such as the Walker's crisps commercials on U.K. television starring former England soccer star Gary Lineker.

One way in which celebrity endorsement may work is to transform the image of the product through its association with the star. Walker, Langmeyer, and Langmeyer (1992) examined viewer associations with a number of products that were advertised using different celebrity endorsers. They asked participants to rate the products along a number of "semantic differential" scales (good–bad, kind–cruel, etc.), and found that the same participants rated the same products differently according to the celebrity promoting them—hence the product VCR was evaluated differently when Madonna promoted it than when Christie Brinkley promoted it. Fowles (1996) interpreted this effect as a "flow of meaning" from endorser to product.

When there are no celebrities willing or available to endorse a product, advertisers may decide simply to create a new character, whose persona is permanently associated with the product. Such examples abound in television advertising, from the Energizer Bunny to Kellogg's Tony the Tiger and, perhaps most infamously of all, cigarette-smoking icon Joe Camel. These characters can carry the message of the advertisement far beyond the confines of the original text.

Intertextuality and Brand Awareness

Experimental research on the effects of advertising tends to rely on responses to isolated commercials, typically involving imaginary or unfamiliar products. These studies tell us how much information might be attended to, or remembered, in the first moments of a campaign for a brand-new product from a new manufacturer, but can tell us little about the influence of advertising in general. An advertisement is not a single, independent event; it is a text woven into the cultural fabric, cueing memories of other advertising and product characteristics. Brand awareness is built up through years of viewing and interpretation, and advertising goes way beyond the mass media, into our homes and other immediate environments (e.g., designer-label clothing). The message contained in a specific advertisement is therefore hard to isolate from the everyday experiences of the consumer.

Links between advertising can be seen as a form of *intertextuality* (Kristeva, 1980). This has the effect of stretching the meaning of an ad into other textual forms, so campaigns can build up meaning through different media. A recent example in Britain was a campaign to promote pet insurance by the insurance group Royal & Sun Alliance, who launched a fly-poster campaign featuring a crude black-and-white photograph of an Airedale/collie cross under the slogan "Where's Lucky?" There was no mention of the manufacturers' name, let alone any product information; the posters were designed to simulate, in large scale, private handbills for lost pets.

Shortly afterward a television commercial appeared with full company information, enabling viewers to complete the puzzle.[6]

One might argue that such a link is so tenuous as to be pointless. If it is so hard to decode an advertisement, why do clients spend so much money on the campaign? Goldman (1992) maintained that advertisers actually see the intellectual effort involved in interpreting complex advertising as a selling point. The original "Where's Lucky?" posters were remembered *because* of, not in spite of, their lack of information. Linking them up with the subsequent television commercials requires extra cognitive work that eventually pays off in terms of recall and recognition. This relates to Cacioppo and Petty's (1982) "need for cognition" theory, which stipulates that differential effects of advertising are associated with individual preferences for "thinking." From this perspective, armchair philosophers are more susceptible to peripheral (subtle) routes to persuasion because they are prepared to invest more cognitive effort in processing the material (Cacioppo, Petty, Kao, & Rodriguez, 1986).

The same logic can be applied to the long-running billboard campaign for Benson and Hedges' Silk Cut cigarettes. United Kingdom restrictions on cigarette advertising in the early 1990s persuaded the tobacco company to employ more subtle suggestion in their posters. The company replaced depictions of the product with symbols, such as ripples of purple silk, often juxtaposed with cutting instruments. The only verbal text was the obligatory government health warning. Such visual texts would be indecipherable if studied in isolation, but we use our brand awareness, and our media sophistication, to make sense of them. Although Freudian semioticians may speculate about the luxurious imagery triggering unconscious desires, the function of the Silk Cut campaign seems to be more about defiance in the face of advertising restrictions than about encouraging people to smoke.

One other form of intertextual advertising is *product placement,* by which manufacturers pay large sums to television or film companies so that their products can be visible during a show or movie. Thus, a leading star becomes a celebrity endorser by swigging from a specific can of lager; at the same time, the visibility of contemporary consumer goods enhances the realism of the movie. One experimental study of product placement studied attitudes toward smoking following exposure to a clip from the film *Die Hard* (Gibson & Maurer, 2000). In one condition, the film's star Bruce Willis was seen smoking; viewers in this condition liked the character more if they were smokers themselves, but less if they were nonsmokers. Thus, the product placement had little effect in this case but to reinforce existing be-

---

[6]Not all viewers, it seems; shortly after the poster campaign, *The Independent* newspaper reported that the Advertising Standards Agency had received a number of complaints from parents of distressed children who thought that a real dog had become lost!

haviour patterns. Once again, it seems unlikely that exposure to one single instance of a product will have much impact on long-term behaviour.

ADVERTISING AND CHILDREN

Although children watch television at various times, the programming that they view alone tends to be specifically aimed at children. In the United States particularly, most of the advertising during this segment consists of ads for food, particularly sugared food (Harris, 1999). During the run up to Christmas, increasing numbers of ads concern toys and games. Such practices are believed to put pressure on parents to yield to what the media have dubbed "pester power." This has led to calls for legislation to regulate advertising in Europe and the United States. Indeed, the Swedish government has outlawed television advertising of products aimed at children under 12, and recently in the United States 50 psychologists signed a petition calling for a ban on the advertising of children's goods.

The practice of advertising to children has been hotly debated by psychologists, media and communication experts, and the advertising industry itself, and researchers are sharply divided over some of the issues involved. Critics of advertising to children argue that children have not developed the cognitive sophistication that enables them to tell advertising apart from other forms of programming, and that even children as old as 12 may misunderstand the nature and function of advertising.[7] Others maintain that children are more sophisticated than cognitive psychologists sometimes think, and that a ban on television commercials is unlikely to have much effect against other forces promoting relentless consumption in contemporary society.

Stage Theory of Consumer Development

Valkenburg and Cantor (2001) identified four stages that children pass through in their development as consumers. During infancy (0–2 years), children become interested in brightly coloured television programming (which includes commercials), and by 18 months start asking for products they have seen advertised on television. In one Dutch study, 40% of parents of 2-year-olds claimed that their children had recognised an advertised product in a store display.

[7]There is some doubt over the validity of the Swedish research that motivated the government's decision to ban advertising to children under 12. Allegedly, the study's author claimed that the policy was based on a misinterpretation of his data, and that he suggested only that *some* 12-year-olds did not understand advertising (Oates, Blades, & Gunter, 2002).

During the preschool period (2–5 years), children are at their most vulnerable to television advertising. They still have a largely literal understanding of television, believing that objects depicted on television are real. They find it hard to resist tempting products, which leads to tantrums in stores when parents decline to yield to their requests (the feared "pester power"); in this study, 70% of parents of 5-year-olds reported experiencing conflict over such issues.[8]

In the third phase (5–8 years), children become more sophisticated consumers of media and have developed strategies for negotiation with parents over purchasing. By the end of this phase, they have begun to display independence in terms of purchasing. This independence increases during the final phase (9–12 years), as children become more critical media users and are attracted toward more adult forms of entertainment. At this stage, peer influence is more important than individual media use, and adult styles of consumption such as brand loyalty, begin to appear.

This model is loosely based on Piagetian notions of cognitive maturation, in which child development is determined by the growing brain rather than by social interaction. There are several issues that remain contentious within this cognitive approach. The first concerns children's ability to discriminate between advertising and other forms of programming. Valkenburg and Cantor argued that discrimination does not take place until the third phase, although some years ago research by Hodge and Tripp (1986) suggested that commercials were the first television genre to be successfully identified, at around the age of 3, and other researchers have found that children at that age were able to distinguish advertising from the surrounding programming (Butter, Popovich, Stackhouse, & Garner, 1981; Levin, Petros, & Petrella, 1982).

A second bone of contention concerns children's ability to understand the nature and function of advertising. The cognitivist argument is based on research conducted on television processing in general, which portrays children's understanding of television as a simple matter of distinguishing between events on television as "fantasy" and events in the immediate environment as "reality." However, most of the research on children's understanding of advertising has focused on their ability to understand the economic principles involved in advertising itself, rather than semantic aspects of individual commercials. Young (1990) coined the term *advertising literacy*, defining "understanding" as both the recognition that advertising has a

---

[8]Using a different approach (a 4-week diary study), data collected by Isler, Popper, and Ward (1987) suggest that instances of pester power may be exaggerated. In this study, parents reported very few instances of their children placing undue pressure on them to buy goods, either inside or outside stores. (It could be significant that this study was published in the *Journal of Advertising Research* rather than a psychology publication, and it would be interesting to see a contemporary replication.)

specific source distinct from other television programming, and a recognition of advertising's persuasive intent. A meta-analysis of studies (Martin, 1997) demonstrated a clear positive correlation between age and comprehension of persuasive intent, although this was less clear when ads were isolated from surrounding programming, suggesting an inability even among older children to identify "advertising" as a genre distinct from television itself (a study by Kunkel, 1988, also shows that children are confused by intertextual devices like celebrity endorsement).

How much "understanding" do children need to display before they are considered mature enough to cope with the wiles of advertisers? Goldstein (1999) asserted that there is no "magic age" at which such understanding can be said truly to take place, and that in many cases adults would fail the tasks that researchers give to children. For one thing, there is no "reality"of advertised products that can be distinguished from the claims made by advertisers. Lay consumers of all ages are unable to tell whether 8 out of 10 owners say their cats prefer Whiskas, unless they are researchers equipped with cat food sales preference data.

Arguments that cognitive maturation is the main determinant of advertising awareness also fail to explain how young children differ in terms of the products they request. If the effects of advertising are a simple matter of automatic responses to stimuli, why don't boys ask for Barbie dolls (Goldstein, 1999)? Evidently, young children are identifying with protagonists in commercials, if only on superficial characteristics such as gender. But this indicates the selective processing of advertisements, a task well beyond what Valkenburg and Cantor have predicted for 2- to 5-year-olds.

Clearly, cognitive maturation plays a part in children's media interaction, inasmuch as children have to develop the perceptual skills to identify formal features of television. However, children rarely watch all television alone; a parent or sibling is never far away from the screen, and the interaction between coviewers will have considerable impact on how children respond to advertising.

"Pester Power" and Modern-Day Consumption

As mentioned earlier, a particular worry among parents in recent years is the phenomenon of "pester power," by which repeated appeals on television lead children to make prolonged demands on parents for products that the parents may not be able to afford. In conditions of real poverty, as in most of India, parents are simply unable to give in to such demands, with the result that many children actively resent advertising for falsely raising expectations (Unnikrishnan & Bajpai, 1996).

The effectiveness of advertising to children was examined by Pine and Nash (2001), in a study relating television use and gift requests to Father

Christmas. They found that the amount of commercial television that children watched predicted the number of goods on the children's list; the more time spent watching TV, the more gifts were requested, particularly the number of branded goods. This was strongest in children who watched television alone, suggesting an effect of parental mediation. Little correspondence was noted, however, between specific ads and gift requests, except for established toys like Barbie and Action Man. The authors concluded that the effect is probably more general, producing a consumer-oriented, materialistic culture among children. To reinforce this view, a comparison was carried out with data collected in Sweden, where advertising to children is banned, and letters to Santa contained significantly fewer requests for branded goods.

Although such data may point to a clear advertising/pestering link, one must bear in mind the possibility that consumer demand culture in a specific family may be linked to the amount and nature of television viewing. As with media violence, we can never rule out motives for viewing the material in the first place. Another factor is peer influence; parents may be familiar with their children's viewing patterns but not with the conversations they have with their friends, and thus overestimate the influence of television (Goldstein, 1999). At the same time, much peer talk may be related back to media; it is almost impossible to disentangle the two influences.

This points to a difficulty with studying at a purely individual level the effects of advertising to children. Historical and social factors are essential considerations for a developmental media psychology. Gunter and Furnham (1998) and Turow (2001) identified a number of factors related to the changing nature of family interaction that have important implications for the children and advertising debate.

First, children do not demand only children's products, such as sweets and toys. A ban on advertising such goods would not rule out children's influence over parental purchases of family goods, such as holiday destinations and the family car. Modern-day children occupy a different position in the family regarding decision making—they have more power over parental choice.

Second, as Turow (2001) pointed out, modern homes and technologies have led to something of a splintering of the family; children spend increasing amounts of time alone, and these boundaries are exploited by advertisers, who emphasise the differences between members of the family rather than the similarities. Important issues here concern the disclosure practices of the family, and other communication patterns. Do children discuss media with their parents? The proliferation of media makes parental mediation difficult to actually practice.

A third issue relating to modern-day consumption concerns the dynamics of modern families. Modern parents have fewer children and more spending power, so the number of products bought per child is continually rising. One only needs to witness the mountain of consumer goods that accumulates at Christmas and on birthdays to appreciate the way the child enters a continuous cycle of consumption. This is often exacerbated by the breakup of families, so that the children of divorced parents are often bought twice the usual number of presents, and estranged parents may invest yet more money in presents to compensate for their absence.

FUTURE DIRECTIONS IN ADVERTISING

Clearly it is time for psychologists to move away from the 30-second television commercial as the main source of study. McKee (2002) examined children's responses to print advertising, and found this medium to be even more subtle in its influence—at least in terms of the amount of information recalled and children's inability to identify ads from surrounding material. In one publication, a comic strip advertising Kellogg's Coco Pops was indistinguishable from an original strip on the opposite page. Like advertorials, such devices fool adults as well as children.

The mechanisms of advertising are so established in contemporary society that it is hard to see what a ban on advertising could achieve; in terms of chilren's programming, it is more likely to harm children's television by forcing specialist commercial channels out of business. Furthermore, it is difficult to regulate advertising because the links between media content and merchandising are too close. The BBC is an ostensibly noncommercial state channel paid for by viewing licences, yet shows such as *Teletubbies* and *Bob the Builder* generate substantial income for the Corporation from marketing to children in the United Kingdom and beyond.

On commercial television, some shows are even more blatantly created solely for the purpose of merchandising. One early example, *He-Man: Master of the Universe,* was a show that was specifically designed to market Mattel's He-Man toys in the 1980s. Invariably, modern feature films aimed at children are vehicles for toy manufacturers to market their products, a fact borne out by the arrival of official merchandise in the toyshops concurrent with such films' general release. Rather than waiting for the film to generate the demand for associated goods, the marketing opportunities are exploited as early as possible, so that a visit to the cinema is merely the first step in a chain of related purchases. Although a ban on advertising to children might send out a moral message, it is only the tip of the marketing iceberg.

As media technologies evolve, advertising will be forced to adapt. As suggested earlier, there are severe limitations for advertising on the World Wide Web, and it is likely that these limitations will force closer links between television and the Internet, perhaps leading to a fusion between text-based services and the Web (this has already started happening on digital interactive television services). Advertisers will attempt to use more intrusive means of contacting consumers; recent concerns have been voiced over the use of "spam" text messaging on mobile phones, by which advertisers got hold of private numbers and sent out commercial messages to individual consumers. Such practices are costly, are currently seen as invasive, and in the short run are likely to do more harm than good to brand image.

One other form of advertising that will undoubtedly increase as television becomes more interactive is the kind of "whole industry" marketing that is associated with lifestyle television. In this, television programming serves to increase demand for certain types of good—such as gardening tools, cookery implements, and even houses—rather than specific brands or products. This type of programming will be discussed in more detail in chapter 14.

CONCLUSION

Research on the psychology of advertising has been handicapped by its concentration on the effects of 30-second television commercials as being representative of the effects of all advertising. Today, as new forms of market penetration have taken root, commercials now represent merely the tip of the advertising iceberg. The study of the psychological influences of advertising cannot be confined to the laboratory; it is also essential that psychologists study the processes of interpreting advertising, because this remains a grey area, particularly for children.

Advertising is problematic as a media psychology topic because, like politics, it spills beyond the limits that we set for "media" (unless we are following McLuhan to the letter). Is a billboard a medium? A pair of trainers? A bottle of tomato sauce? Can a theory of advertising effects derived from media psychology be successfully applied to all instances of advertising? The answer perhaps lies in our concept of media; here is a clear instance of the need to study media as forms of *culture* as much as technology. If a theory of advertising is to be useful in psychology as a whole, it needs to transcend the tin boxes, wires, and plugs that bring it to the consumer.

Part III

DEVELOPMENTAL ISSUES IN MEDIA PSYCHOLOGY

Chapter **8**

Young Children and Television

One of the most popular shows in the history of children's television in the United Kingdom is *The Sooty Show,* in which an adult presenter interacts with a small group of glove puppets. Star of the show is Sooty, a yellow bear, whose sole form of communication is to whisper into the ear of his handler (and occasionally Soo, one of the other puppets), who then repeats verbally what Sooty is supposed to have said. Despite never having uttered a word throughout his 50-year history, Sooty's popularity with children below the age of 5 or so has continued unabated, outliving both his original handler, Harry Corbett, and his son Matthew, who took up the role after his father suffered a heart attack in 1976.

In two ingenious studies, Australian-based academics Michael Emmison and Laurence Goldman (1996, 1997) demonstrated what a remarkable phenomenon *The Sooty Show* is. First, they analysed the way Sooty's apparent communication difficulties are resolved by the pattern of interaction involving the presenter and the other puppets, particularly given that Sooty's co-star Sweep is a dog who cannot speak either but merely squeaks his contributions. Second, Emmison and Goldman examined the extraordinary complexity of *pretence* that young children need to negotiate in order to appreciate the show: They need to believe that Sooty has a supernatural ability to communicate with certain other figures; they need to understand that the puppets represent animals (but also, in their relation to the presenter and their general discourse and behaviour, the puppets represent children); they need to believe that the puppets have animation; and they need to develop the pretence further when the characters themselves are pretending to be adults (e.g., Sooty as a waiter in a make-believe restaurant).

Despite this complexity, even the youngest children seem to understand and enjoy the show.

These studies are important for media psychology because they show how sophisticated young children's processing of media can be, and because they present innumerable problems for the crude behaviourism that still underpins much research on children and television. For many years, the "effects" of media, invariably television, on children have been studied with negligible regard to content; in studies of media violence, as noted in chapter 4, *Bugs Bunny* has been lumped together with *Driller Killer* as potentially harmful entertainment. It has generally been assumed that the only possible positive role that television might have is of formal education, as with *Sesame Street.* In this chapter, I discuss the cognitive development of children in relation to media use (arguing that media now teach children much more than simple arithmetic), and address how developments in psychology might be usefully applied to future research in this area.

FANTASY VERSUS REALITY: A SIMPLE CHOICE?

The construction of make-believe worlds, full of imaginary characters and implausible plots, has taxed human creative powers since the beginnings of civilization. Historian Julian Jaynes (1976) maintained that the brain's hemispheres were once unconnected, so that many imaginative processes, such as future planning, were experienced as hallucinations, giving rise to an intense experience that might account for the origins of mysticism and religion. Certainly the power to invent parallel universes and credible fictional representations of people is among one of the most prized human gifts, whether in the act of producing the *Aeneid, King Lear,* or *Coronation Street.*

Yet the esteem in which fiction has been held has often turned to worry when contemplating its influence on young children. Even Plato was concerned that the Greek poets were seducing children with lies: "A child cannot distinguish the allegorical sense from the literal, and the ideas he takes in at that age are likely to become indelibly fixed; hence the great importance of seeing that the first stories he hears shall be designed to produce the best possible effect on his character" (*The Republic,* cited in Hodge & Tripp, 1986, p. 101). It hardly seems worth pointing out the differences in the cultural life of children in ancient Greece and those in 21st century Greece; nonetheless, these sentiments are echoed in much contemporary writing about children and fictional media.

Two broad lines of argument are often advanced in relation to the harmful effects of television on children. The first corresponds to the "magic window" approach—the idea that television is a faithful reflection of reality and that children need to be protected from its harsh truths. A parental strategy that might seem to follow from this position is prohibitive, or restrictive, viewing, even of *Bugs Bunny.* The second approach is that all television is artificial (and, by implication, worthless trash), and that too much television will simply rot children's brains. The parental strategy here would be to continually point out that events on TV are "pretend" and have no real-life equivalence. From this position, *Bugs Bunny* is harmless entertainment.

Why *would* a child use a cartoon rabbit as a model for behaviour? The answer would seem to imply a failure of understanding, or a failure to discriminate between symbolic representations (Bugs Bunny) and naturalistic representations (a soap character, say). This consideration has led many researchers to investigate the cognitive processes by which young children learn to distinguish between fantasy and reality, with occasional regard to media (mainly television). However, as I try to demonstrate in this chapter, there are problems with the idea of a simple dichotomy between what is real and what is fantasy, and the role of television in this transition is far from clear. Of course, most people will find themselves on a continuum somewhere between these two extremes, and accept that although some television is real much is fantasy. Therefore, the important issue—as far as child development is concerned—is *discrimination.* Successful development requires an awareness of which bits are real and which bits are fantasy.

The Development of Children's Understanding of the Fantasy–Reality Distinction in Television

Most researchers agree that the fantasy–reality distinction is made via a three-stage process (Jaglom & Gardner, 1981; Wright, Huston, Reitz, & Piemyat, 1994). At the first stage (2 to 3 years of age), children fail to make a fantasy/reality distinction. Until they are 3 years old, children fail to imitate actions presented on video, although they have no trouble imitating the same actions when they are presented by a live actor (Barr & Hayne, 1999). Does this indicate an inability to understand representation (particularly without the third dimension) with a reduced stimulus size (particularly in relation to test stimuli), or is it an attentional failure? More work needs to be conducted with this age group, especially because some children's television shows are aimed at them (*Barney and Friends*—1 year; *Teletubbies*—2 years).

The second stage occurs around the ages of 4 and 5, and consists of a flat denial of reality status for anything on television. Jaglom and Gardner (1981) wrote of an "impermeable membrane" during this period. For example, violence is generally dismissed as "acting," blood as "ketchup," and so on (Hodge & Tripp, 1986). It is not clear whether children are simply overgeneralising about the artificial nature of television, or whether, as Buckingham (2000) suggested, this is part of the growing child's desire to be seen as more mature, and distancing himself or herself from childish notions of television as directly representational. Interview data with children aged 4 and younger seems to suggest a literalness in their perception of television content—in one study, 3-year-olds claimed that a bowl of popcorn would spill if the television turned upside down (Flavell, Flavell, Green, & Korfmacher, 1990); in another, children of the same age believed that little television people were lowered into the set via a rope (Gunter & McAleer, 1997).

Awareness that some programmes are real and others are fantasy seems to arrive at some point between 6 and 7 years (like all stage theories, there are substantial individual differences). Many researchers attribute this awareness to the onset of "tele-literacy" (Bianculli, 1992), the process by which children learn to "read" media "texts." The clearest way this happens is through the identification of television genres—ads are identified first, at between 3 and 4 years of age, then cartoons, then news programmes—and eventually being able to distinguish children's from adult's programmes, and more subtle genres (e.g., the difference between a soap and a sitcom).

One of the problems inherent in studying children's understanding of the difference between fantasy and reality is methodological in nature. Young children are notoriously unreliable interviewees. In a well-known study, Hughes and Grieve (1980) asked 5- to 7-year-old children nonsense questions, such as "Is milk bigger than water?" Many children made serious attempts to answer such questions, such as "Milk is bigger because it's got a colour." Such findings raise doubts about the evidence for many developmental theories that are based largely on verbal data. Many interview questions may be too abstract for young children to give sensible answers; for example, Dorr, Graves, and Phelps (1980) found that children under the age of 10 were unable to explain how cartoon characters "moved," and took this to imply that the children were simply crediting cartoon figures with a degree of autonomy. However, other data suggest that even very young children are fully aware of the artificial nature of cartoons and of television as a whole (Hodge & Tripp, 1986).

Unpacking "Reality"

The problem with so much of the literature on children's understanding of the fantasy–reality distinction in relation to media content is that it is always assumed that the distinction is a clear one, and that adults have no difficulty in identifying it themselves. Even if the distinction *is* clear, adults do not always behave that way. Very often, soap actors and actresses complain that the viewing public is unable to see beyond the characters they portray; for instance, one *EastEnders* actress explained on a television chat show how she received abuse from a London taxi driver for the way her character was behaving in the show. Television companies frequently receive mail from the public that is addressed to the characters in soaps and other dramas. It is reported that over the course of 5 years, Robert Young (the actor who played the title role in the series *Marcus Welby M.D.*) received over a quarter of a million letters, mostly asking for medical advice (Gunter & McAleer, 1997).

Even with a genre like news media, the fantasy–reality distinction is blurred. We often display an inherent trust in the veracity of stories that we read in newspapers and hear about on television news bulletins, yet even pictorial evidence may be "doctored," and subtle nuances in presentation may distort the way we perceive the truth about the world. Nevertheless, we attach great importance to children's growing realisation that the news constitutes reality and cartoons and drama are fantasy—one is to be taken seriously and the other is to be dismissed as mere entertainment. It could be argued that the developmental path to distinguishing fantasy from reality represents nothing more cognitively sophisticated than an indoctrination into adult ways of perceiving the world.

Messaris (1987) identified three different types of mother–child discussion about fantasy and reality in relation to television. The first type of interaction concerns "magic window" thinking by the child. For example, the mother comforts a tearful child by pointing out that the scenes he or she has witnessed are "only pretend," that the blood is really tomato ketchup, that Tom and Jerry are just drawings, or that the scary witch in *The Wizard of Oz* is "that woman off the coffee ad." These comments are intended primarily to *protect* the child, to reinforce the fantasy–reality distinction. The second type of interaction concerns the realism of fictional portrayals: A child viewer, envious of idyllic children's drama *The Brady Bunch,* asks his mother why she isn't more like Mrs Brady, to which she replies, "That only happens on TV." The third type of interaction is used to reinforce realistic media, making comments like "that's what happens when you take drugs."

These exchanges, which are not restricted to specific groups of individuals but often occur at different points during viewing by the same mothers, suggest that the fantasy–reality distinction is a useful mediational resource for parents. They also suggest that children's developing awareness of the distinction may be as much a function of language development as one of maturing cognitive architecture. The assumption in most of the research on fantasy and reality in media is that age-related changes occur simply as a result of brain maturation. However, it has long been realised that cognitive development is inextricably linked with language development, and that social interaction plays a crucial part in the process (Bruner, 1990; Vygotsky, 1978).

Moreover, many adult responses to media are profoundly irrational; like the viewers who hoped that Marcus Welby, M.D., could tell them what to take for their chilblains, we perform a host of emotional behaviours in response to (clearly fantastical) media. We cry at the climax of a sad film; we are sexually aroused by erotica; we make person judgments about soap characters. Perhaps the most important media-related behaviour children learn from adults is that, contrary to what the adults say, much of what they watch on television is deeply important, and therefore highly "real," even if, in the cold light of rationality, they know that it is "only acting" or "only a game."

Types of Realism

If media socialisation principally involves the acquisition of teleliteracy and identifying different genres, perhaps the reality of news programmes is simply a reflection of production techniques, usually referred to as the "formal features" of television. Hodge and Tripp (1986) took an innovative approach to this topic, looking at television reception from the tradition of *semiotics*—the study of signs and symbols in communication. They argued that the *modality* (apparent reality) of a message is either strengthened or weakened by certain characteristics of that message. For example, "canned" laughter in a sitcom weakens the modality of the drama (makes it more unreal), whereas a serious voice-over or commentary will strengthen it.

In Messenger Davies' (1997) study of reality judgments, most 6-year-olds were able to identify messages with weak modality—for example, the *Sesame Street* character Big Bird was seen as implausibly large and yellow, and clearly a human being wearing a costume. Older children, however, were able to impute motives for weak modality—such as the creation of an entertaining character, or to make viewers laugh. In one scene in *Sesame Street,* a character attempted to play the piano but was constantly thwarted by the doorbell. This was seen by the older children as a clear fictional device.

Broadly speaking, we can conceive television content on a sliding scale of realism, with live events (e.g., sport) at the real end and cartoons at the other end. Within this scale, there are ambiguities, like drama, itself on a sliding scale from naturalism (e.g., *EastEnders*) to abstract theatre.[1] Wright et al. (1994) suggested that there are two properties of reality that children learn to identify: *factuality* (e.g., Barbara Windsor[2] is not a pub landlady in real life), and *social realism* (the Queen Vic[3] is just like a real pub). The latter

[1]It is worth noting that communist playwright Bertolt Brecht deliberately chose to make his drama as "unnaturalistic" as possible, in the belief that weak modality results in lower emotional involvement, thus reinforcing the ideological "message" contained in the plays.

[2]A British actress who plays landlady Peggy Mitchell in *EastEnders.*

[3]The *Queen Victoria* pub, around which much of the action takes place in *EastEnders.*

point extends to the perception of both real television people (presenters, etc.) and fictional characters. In one study, older children (age 8/9) provided more complex descriptions of fictional characters (dispositions, traits, motives) than of real people in their lives (Babrow, O'Keefe, Swanson, Meyers, & Murphy, 1988). In some ways, this is not surprising, because television sheds light on those aspects of characters that are hidden in real life (such as a protagonist's true motive for action). This proposition will be explored more fully in chapter 11.

It has been suggested that, in later childhood, the more realistic the medium is the more emotionally involved will children become. Hodge and Tripp (1986) argued that this explains why, as children grow older, their preferences shift from cartoon characters toward real people. Table 8.1 shows the maturational trend from naming cartoon characters as favourites to preferring fictional human characters, although we must remember that these figures can only be interpreted within their specific context (i.e., Australia in the mid-1980s).

Huston et al. (1995) put the modality–emotionality hypothesis to an experimental test and found that, when 9- to 11-year-old children were shown a fictional drama in three different guises (as documentary, as naturalistic drama, or as sensationalist drama), reality status had very little impact on emotional response. In each condition, children responded with appropriate emotion (sadness in line with protagonist's sadness, etc.), but neither self-reported affect nor facial expressiveness were enhanced by the information that the scenes in the show were "real." If anything, there was a slight advantage for the naturalistic condition.

Although in isolation these findings cannot tell us much about the development of emotional response (replications with younger and older children are awaited!), they nonetheless suggest that whatever reality biases emerge around the age of 5, they are soon forgotten as children develop empathic awareness and are able to draw analogies between fiction and real life. They also demonstrate the importance of using behavioural measures with children rather than relying on verbal data. Most of all, however, they cause problems for Hodge and Tripp's modality theory.

TABLE 8.1
Breakdown, by Percentage, of Children's Favourite Television Characters, by Age and Genre (from Hodge & Tripp, 1986)

Age Group	*Cartoon*	*Drama*	*"Stars" (Celebrities)*	*"Real Life" (Personalities)**
6–8	7	13	11	0
9–12	28	58	9	5

*The distinction between "stars" and "real life" seems to be based largely on celebrities' activities ("stars" are those drawn from the world of entertainment or show business, whereas "real-life" figures are general television personalities, such as presenters and newsreaders).

In recent years, one of the most popular programmes across the world has been *The Simpsons,* a cartoon that at a textual level shares more in common with traditional sitcoms than with other cartoons. There are reports even of adults displaying strong attachments to the characters in this show, which is indisputably low in terms of modality (even the human characters do not resemble humans because they are bright yellow, with elongated heads, and—in the case of Marge Simpson—have blue hair). The modality theory is convincing if we consider only the visual mode. *The Simpsons* provides evidence that the power of the text, and of character creation, can override low modality markers, an effect that should prove even more powerful for soaps and other naturalistic dramas.

SCRIPT AND SCHEMA EXPLANATIONS

Not all research into children's understanding of media has focused on the fantasy–reality distinction. Other studies have looked at children's processing of television narratives, and memory for television stories (Lorch, Bellack, & Augsbach, 1987; Low & Durkin, 2000; van den Broeck, Lorch, & Thurlow, 1996). These suggest that children's recall of television narratives is similar to that of stories presented in other media, such as pictures (Shapiro & Hudson, 1991). When narratives are jumbled up in an unpredictable, illogical fashion, children below the age of 9 tend to make errors based on logical inferences—in other words, they fall back on familiar narrative routines. By the age of 9, however, children are just as good at recalling the mixed-up narratives (Low & Durkin, 2000).

These findings suggest that young children are happier when events fall into place in a familiar manner that echoes their limited previous experience. This might explain why children are so captivated by television advertising, where ads repeat ad nauseam, and children often respond by joining in with jingles or slogans (Palmer, 1986). It also explains why children enjoy repetitive programme segments such as title sequences, and the drawn-out scenes in *Thunderbirds* where the characters board their engines, and the swimming pool and palm trees of Tracy Island give way as the rockets emerge and take off. Silverstone (1993) argued that television acts as a form of lifelong transitional object (such as a "comfort blanket") right through adulthood; in early childhood, such repetitive sequences offer a sense of reassurance and stability, and the illusion of control—you *know* what is coming next.

It may not be too much of a conceptual leap to argue that *all* television, and maybe all experience, is understood in the context of narratives, or scripts. This would explain young children's understanding of *The Sooty*

Show, as discussed at the start of this chapter. Emmison and Goldman's (1997) analysis demonstrated how the puppets in this show are "linguistically constituted as children" through their interaction with the presenter. This effect may take place because the activities in which they participate resemble the kinds of games and interactions between children and parents; typically, the puppets/children indulge in mischief, which gets them into trouble with the presenter/parent. The situations are highly familiar to those in which children find themselves, and it does not matter that the protagonists are puppets representing animals, two of whom cannot speak; the "mischief-trouble" script overrides the low modality every time.

Hodge and Tripp (1986) argued that far from filling children's minds with worthless or harmful junk, television gives them experience of a rich variety of discursive and narrative forms. This is important for the development of "transformational power"—in effect, the ability to apply concepts to different situations. One example is the identification of a character type, such as the ordinary individual who gains special powers that enable him or her to perform superhuman feats. The repetition of this particular fictional device throughout children's fictional media allows viewers to equate Superman, Batman, the Incredible Hulk, and Wonder Woman as exemplars of a character type. Hodge and Tripp maintained that this kind of cognitive activity explains children's demand for the most challenging material available for their age group, why primary school children are quick to discard preschool media as "baby stuff"; and maybe how the "forbidden fruit" effect emerges during adolescence.

Maire Messenger Davies, another media scholar who has studied children's use of television, put forward a similar argument. She suggested that children develop knowledge structures about the world that she called "schemata" in the time-honoured tradition of cognitive psychology. These set up certain expectations about cause and effect, or what will happen next (Messenger Davies, 1997). One way in which such schemata may work is in the development of understanding the notion of taxonomies. This can clearly be seen in the collection of Pókemon cards, on which different creatures are depicted along with information about their unique attributes. Children (particularly boys) catalogue and discuss such information in the way they might discuss the venomous properties of different snakes, or even the elements in the periodic table. The same device can be seen throughout children's media wherever there are classification systems available (e.g., the properties of the different engines in *Thunderbirds*). It could be argued that these schemata may have some benefit in setting children up for the type of knowledge-building activities they will encounter in later education.

CHILDREN'S SOCIALISATION THROUGH MEDIA

If television might aid in the development of abstract cognitive structures (or narrative scripts), it may also teach children more directly about how to behave and respond in social situations. Of course, such thinking underpins the modelling theories of harmful media influence, and although I have tried to maintain an optimistic note throughout this chapter, we cannot necessarily be complacent about children's media socialisation. Nevertheless, it could be argued that socialisation involves much more than simply copying behaviour viewed on screen, especially when the behaviour is strikingly inappropriate (as in cartoons or obvious fantasy shows like *Superman*).

One of the most interesting, although underresearched, questions about children and media concerns the way in which children come to identify media characters as analogous to people they know in real life. It may be supposed that such awareness develops in tandem with their real-life person knowledge. Bretherton and Beeghly (1982) found that children as young as 28 months were able to offer descriptive terms about real people based on personality traits such as "nice," "bad," "naughty," and so on. The development of more complex character judgments is the subject of a wide literature on childhood cognitive and social development (Yuill, 1992).

Some limited research has been conducted on children's use of trait terms to describe media figures. Reeves and Greenberg (1977) and Reeves and Lometti (1979) used multidimensional scaling techniques to show how children from 7 to 11 years of age evaluate characters on the basis of typical human personality dimensions, but it is not known at what stage, and how, children come to equate the huge variety of anthropomorphic and human figures on television with the people around them in real life, and attribute consistent behavioural patterns and personality traits to them.

Bearison, Bain, and Daniele (1982) examined developmental changes in children's understanding of people on television with reference to Piaget's theory of cognitive development. For Piaget, the key concept was perspective. Young children are largely egocentric because they do not consider that others might see the world differently; this was famously demonstrated using a model of three mountains and a doll placed on the side of the model opposite from the child. When children under 5 were asked to say what the doll was looking at, they overwhelmingly chose their own visual perspective; it was not until later that they appreciated that the doll might have a different perspective (Piaget & Inhelder, 1969).

Bearison et al. applied this theory to children's perspective of television characters. They showed a short clip from a daytime television drama to 5- and 6-year-olds, 7- through 10-year-olds, and 11- through 14-year-olds. These age groups corresponded roughly to Piaget's three key stages: preoperational (egocentric), concrete operational (reasoning based only on personal experience), and formal operational (ability to reason using abstract premises). As predicted, the preoperational children were only able to describe the physical settings and superficial aspects of interpersonal behaviour, whereas children at the concrete operational stage were able to go beyond the appearance of social interaction and actually make some inferences regarding characters' thoughts and feelings, and how these helped to shape the interaction. Similar findings were also obtained in a study by Hoffner and Cantor (1985).

The Bearison et al. study could be criticised on a number of grounds, largely because the material used in the film seems to be wholly inappropriate for child participants, dealing largely with adult relationships. It may not be surprising that younger children were unable to follow the subtle psychological complexities of the plot. Furthermore, there were substantial differences between the number of statements the different age groups generated when asked to describe the film, suggesting that linguistic development may explain the findings. Few differences were found between concrete and formal operational children, which the authors took to indicate that "viewers do not on their own attribute complex psychological qualities to television characters" (Bearison et al., 1982, p. 142).

The argument that viewers, even very young viewers, do not automatically attribute psychological qualities to television characters seems highly unlikely given the depth of the discussions that they have at school about real and fictional people on television. Nevertheless, Bearison et al. did make the point that these attributions may be a joint production between viewers. It may be that characters on television spring to life only when viewers compare notes—otherwise, they remain two-dimensional images on a screen. The solitary viewer needs the assurance that he or she is not being overly fanciful in making these attributions to mere televisual images, so when two people meet up and discuss the motives of a soap character they are effectively promoting that character to the status of a real person.

Nevertheless, in a study by Babrow et al. (1988), children actually produced more abstract psychological descriptions of child characters on television than of their own peers, although the overall number of concrete behavioural attributes was greater for real children. One explanation for this finding, which is explored in more detail in the chapters on soaps and "reality TV" later in the book, is that television provides viewers with unique insights into aspects of human character that remain inaccessible in real life. A character in a drama (think of Hamlet, even) is depicted in solitude, articulating his or her own private thoughts, revealing "true" motives for his or her behaviour. Indeed these motives are sewn neatly into the plot—for example, in a "whodunnit" mystery, we treat each utterance as significant, and skilled writing binds these motives into explanations for the behaviour.

Children's exposure to a vast array of human and nonhuman figures on television makes the media an important agent of socialisation, much underrated in the developmental literature. Inevitably the focus has been on the harm that depictions of unsavoury figures might cause children, but there are clear indications that exposure to a broad range of television people may actually promote a more positive view of different ethnic groups and nationalities. This was demonstrated in a study of Alaskan children during the first few years that they were able to receive television. Lonner, Thorndike, Forbes, and Ashworth (1985) measured their attitudes to people from different ethnic groups before and a few years after the introduction of television, and found that although the groups' attitudes to White Americans changed little in that period, their attitudes toward Black Americans (with whom they had little or no contact in real life) improved significantly.

In some respects this is a surprising finding, given the argument that television tends to portray minority groups in a stereotypical, unflattering light (see chap. 10). However, it may be explained by what is sometimes referred to as the "mere exposure effect"—the idea that familiarity breeds content rather than contempt, and before television reached Alaska the children there had little knowledge of Black Americans or people of African descent in general. Furthermore, this effect may be reinforced through coming to know Black *characters* rather than simply seeing Black people in general, even though those characters were not always positive portrayals. Gillespie (1995) obtained similar findings when asking Punjabi adolescents in west London about their viewing of Australian soap *Neighbours*; some interviewees claimed that the show fostered a more positive attitude toward White people than did their actual social encounters in London. Such findings have rarely been obtained with adult samples, however, suggesting that early childhood viewing of characters from different ethnic groups has a more positive effect even than explicitly antiracist material aimed at older viewers (Messaris, 1997).

IMAGINATION, PRETENCE, AND THEORY OF MIND

Although we can credit media with some degree of importance with regard to socialisation, it is impossible to disentangle social development from cognitive development, and much psychological research in recent years has explored how our understanding of how the world emerges in our early years. One of the most important areas of developmental psychology at present is the literature on *theory of mind,* which is the ability to impute mental states to others and use this information to predict their behaviour (Premack & Woodruff, 1978). Clearly this research is highly relevant to the findings discussed earlier about descriptions of television characters, although media research has yet to make an explicit link. This is undoubtedly an area worthy of further exploration.

Theory of mind (ToM) has been studied using a variety of (mostly) experimental methods. The most commonly used experiments are the *appearance–reality distinction*, and the *false belief task*. The appearance–reality distinction is tested using a common object that assumes the form of another object, typically a sponge shaped like a rock. Children below the age of 4 are more likely to describe the object as a sponge that looks like a sponge (Flavell, Flavell, & Green, 1983). The false belief experiment (often referred to as either the "Maxi" or "Sally-Ann" task) typically involves two puppets, one of whom leaves the room while the other is seen to move an object (say, a marble) from Location A to Location B. When the other puppet returns, the child is asked where it will look for the marble (Wimmer & Perner, 1983). Children below the age of 4 are more likely to nominate Location B. Essentially this is the same skill as Piaget's mountains task, except that the explanations for failure go beyond merely describing the child as "egocentric."

Although ToM is a *social* cognitive skill, most of the research on the topic has treated it as a property that derives solely from cognitive maturation. In other words, ToM is seen as a biologically "hard-wired" behaviour that emerges of its own accord as the human brain matures. This is surprising, because ToM is clearly about *other people* and it is therefore hard to imagine that the social environment plays no part in its development.[4] However, there is some evidence for an important contribution of social experience to ToM development. Dunn, Brown, Slomkowski, Tesla, and Youngblade (1991) found superior ToM ability in children whose conversations with their mothers contained more abstract psychological descriptions of people and attributed internal motives to behaviour. This provides support for the argument that cognitive development takes place simultaneously with language development and that the two are inextricably linked.

However, it is unlikely that language alone, or cognitive maturation, can enable children to impute mental states to others; the benefit of experience must not be underrated. In one study, Perner, Ruffman, and Leekam (1994) discerned a positive correlation between ToM ability and the number of siblings a child had. These findings suggest that the more opportunities children have to learn about "other minds"—whether through talk or

---

[4]Impossible to test, of course, because there are no instances of children growing up alone, except in the most traumatic abuse cases or exceptional circumstances such as "wolf children." Perhaps the focus on ToM as a naturally emerging property of the individual mind can be attributed to the fact that much of the research has been concerned with *autism*—there is, understandably, a reluctance to grant too much importance to environmental factors in ToM development, if only to avoid reopening the "parental neglect" debate.

play—the sooner a theory of mind develops. Feldman (1992) argued that ToM is best seen as a two-way interaction between the child and his or her social and cultural environment, which is where media enter the picture.

It is certainly possible that television provides preschool children with another opportunity to learn about other minds. Children's television contains much rich interaction between clearly defined characters. Even in the most basic of shows, such as *Teletubbies*, the characters have strong identities, and even 2-year-old viewers are able to differentiate between them. Furthermore, shows such as *The Tweenies* and *Bob the Builder* (both shown regularly on British television at the time of writing) involve their characters in quite sophisticated social interaction during which many ToM themes are involved, such as appearance–reality distinction and false belief. Familiarity with this material (particularly reinforced through the availability of video recordings) means that children who are regular viewers of these shows will encounter many situations requiring ToM skills in addition to those that occur during family interaction.

Although no research has yet examined ToM directly in the light of media use, a study by Rosen, Schwebel, and Singer (1997) produced some interesting findings when they used *Barney and Friends* to explored the links between ToM and pretense. The clip from the show involved a group of children sitting on a bench, pretending to be travelling on a plane. The authors asserted that children would need a theory of mind if they were to recognise the children's activities as pretense; indeed, this was found to be the case, with the best performers on ToM tasks being those who could infer the mental states of the children in the show.

However, the most interesting aspect of Rosen et al.'s study was their use of a novel false belief task in which children were shown a clip of *The Pink Panther* cartoon in which a hunter chases a bird, and the bird hides in a cave (so children were asked "Where will the hunter look for the bird?"). Performance on this task far outstripped that on conventional ToM tasks, as displayed in Table 8.2.

Almost half the 3-year-olds were able to pass the false belief task when it involved familiar characters and situations, and nearly all the 5-year-olds. This finding has important implications both for media psychology and de-

TABLE 8.2
Percentages of Children in Three Age Groups Passing Different Theory of Mind Tasks (from Rosen, Schwebel, & Singer, 1997)

	3-Year-Olds	*4-Year-Olds*	*5-Year-Olds*
Appearance–reality distinction	14	40	42
Doll false belief	19	55	44
Cartoon false belief	44	63	94

velopmental psychology. First, it provides substantial evidence that children as young as age 3 are able to make complex psychological judgments about characters and plots depicted in cartoons.

Second, it reinforces some of the doubts about the validity of laboratory-based false belief tasks as measures of ToM. Elsewhere it has been argued that tasks such as the Maxi and Sally-Ann experiments may be too difficult for 4-year-olds to pass, not because of their lack of cognitive sophistication but because their verbal abilities are not equipped to deal with the abstract nature of the questions they are asked (Bloom & German, 2000). However, the young children's success on Rosen et al.'s Pink Panther task suggests that, under more "natural" conditions (compared with strange psychologists moving strange puppets about), children are capable of dealing with false belief questions, maybe because the events they are asked to describe are more meaningful and interesting.

Rosen et al.'s experiment is not the only study to explore the link between ToM and pretense. A number of researchers have attempted to explain the cognitive mechanisms behind the understanding of pretense; for example, Leslie (1987) argued that the same "meta-representational" development underpins both ToM and the ability to pretend. However, when studied in naturalistic conditions, the pretence/ToM association is not necessarily as clearcut as it might seem. Astington and Jenkins (1995) studied the play activity of a group of 3- to 5-year-olds recorded on video (to avoid the prospect of the researchers affecting the children's behaviour), and recorded the amount of pretend play in which the children engaged. They then tested the same children's ability on false belief tasks. False belief performance showed only a small (nonsignificant) correlation with pretend play; however, it was a strong predictor of language ability ($r = 0.66$), supporting the claims that it is the verbal aspect of the tasks that trip up younger children.

Lillard (1993) claimed that children see pretence not as a mental activity but instead as an *action*. In other words, when a child pretends to brush his or her teeth using a finger as a toothbrush, he or she is simply reenacting a familiar behavioural routine—no abstract analogy between fingers and toothbrushes is necessary, nor is the notion of pretense. Harris (1994) made a similar point: A 2-year-old is capable of understanding a pretend routine in which an adult pretends to give teddy a bath by twiddling his or her thumbs (turning on taps) and simulating the act of towelling teddy dry. It seems logical to argue that the activities of brushing teeth and having a bath—both familiar childhood routines—can be described as scripts. This which brings us back to the earlier discussion of children's understanding of televised narratives, which could account for their ability to negotiate the many layers of pretense involved in *The Sooty Show.*

Finally, there has been some research on the connection between television and imagination that has a bearing on this literature. It is sometimes argued that media spoil children's imaginative abilities by providing them with too much stimulating visual material. A number of studies have explored the link between overall television viewing and fantasy play, which provide little evidence to suggest that television use has a detrimental effect on the amount of fantasy play (Valkenburg & van der Voort, 1995). However, there does appear to be a link between television content and the type of play—for example, educational television can stimulate play involving props and materials (Comstock & Scharrer, 1999). Taylor and Carlson (1997) examined the link among fantasy play, ToM, and television use, arguing that overall amount of television use negatively predicted ToM ability and fantasy play. However, without a breakdown of that use and more demographic information (social class, IQ, language ability), the precise nature of the relationship is not clear.

Valkenburg and van der Voort (1995) studied the television/imagination link by focusing on the activity of *daydreaming*. Again, the amount of television watched has little effect, but the content of that viewing strongly influences the nature of the daydreaming. For example, a preference for violent television shows is associated with "aggressive-heroic" daydreaming, although—as with much of the media violence literature—it is not possible to establish cause and effect using such data. Overall, it seems that television cannot either stimulate or suppress imagination, although it may help shape the nature of childhood fantasies.

CONCLUSION

Children's television has become an important part of our cultural heritage, although this would not be clear from a survey of the developmental psychology literature, which seems to have deliberately avoided any mention of media. Meanwhile, media research on children's television has not always drawn on contemporary theories from child psychology. This is a rift that developmental science badly needs to heal. A possible starting point would be the literature on parental mediation discussed in chapter 5, which has highlighted the need to consider family interaction and parenting style as key factors in shaping children's understanding and interpretation of media content. We might also benefit from less concern with protecting children's "innocence" and instead studying the child as an active meaning-maker of cultural material who does not necessarily take the material's fantastical nature at face value.

Chapter 9

Media and Adolescence

It is quite possible that, without the mass media, we might not be discussing adolescence as an important stage in human development. Historically, the invention of "the teenager" is simultaneous with the rise of the adolescent as consumer and the cultural revolution of the 1950s, through which the mass introduction of television and the commercialisation of popular music led to the emergence of rock'n'roll as the first youth-oriented cultural phenomenon. The worldwide changes that this period effected are hard to contemplate without standing back and imagining a world without 24-hour music television, designer training shoes, jeans, nightclubs, and pop stars. As the original rock'n'roll generation reaches retirement age, what has happened to youth culture?

Strangely enough, not very much has changed in the last 50 years: Young people seemingly grow up faster, learn more about the world than we would sometimes like, and continue to rebel against authority wherever possible. Of course technological advances make today's teenage bedroom look like a space-age multimedia laboratory compared to the relatively frugal 1950s home environment. When your granddad is a rock'n'roll fan, however, rebellion needs to become more imaginative, and for 50 years youth culture has continued to circulate fashions and ways of speaking that are unintelligible to adults, and therefore treated with the deepest suspicion. As a result, much of the research on adolescent media use has (like most media research) focused on its negative aspects—the "effects" of modelling bad celebrity behaviour and listening to aggressive music.

And yet adolescence *is* important, arguably the most significant period of the life span when it comes to media psychology. Young children's media use consists largely of television and video (and, increasingly, video games); by adolescence they have begun to use personal computers (and, therefore, the Internet) and mobile phones. Moreover, their media use becomes more solitary, particularly in families that own more than one television or video recorder. Peer influence becomes increasingly more important than parental influence, and much of this involves media content. Finally, adolescence is a period during which individuals are actively involved in constructing a coherent identity, and media may play a large part in supplying the cultural materials for this use.

MEDIA USE IN ADOLESCENCE

One of the problems with any academic study of contemporary cultural life is that culture itself is constantly in flux. Given the snail's pace of academic research, studies of media use are invariably out of date long before they ever make it to publication. A good example of this is the European survey of children's media use carried out during 1997 (Livingstone & Bovill, 1999). This is an extensive summary of media use in 12 different European countries conducted by a large team of researchers, yet it coincided with a massive rise in the ownership and use of mobile phones throughout the world, and with huge expansion of Internet availability. As the largest and most important study of its kind, I draw on its findings throughout this chapter; however, it is important to remember that the data may already be of little more than historical value (e.g., its figure for teenage mobile phone use in the United Kingdom stands at a mere 4%!)

Television

By far the most highly used media among preadolescent children, television continues to be popular with teenagers. This is true not only in Europe but throughout the world. In a substantial survey of adolescents' leisure time in various countries worldwide, Larson and Verma (1999) found that viewing times are remarkably consistent across cultures, mostly averaging between 1 and 3 hours a night (highest were the United Kingdom and United States with 2.8 hours; lowest was Italy with 1.1 hours). In the West, viewing time decreases across adolescence, probably because teenagers spend increasingly more time outside the family home, although the reverse has been found in Japan, a more family-centred culture.

Television is pretty much a universal activity: In the United Kingdom, 95% of children watch it, and in the Netherlands, 99% (van der Voort et al., 1998). At the time of the van der Voort et al. study, this slight difference could be attributed to differences in the number of channels available. However, with the increased use of satellite and cable television in Britain since the study was conducted, even the figure of 95% may be an underestimate. A notable difference between the British and Dutch samples in this study was that British children were twice as likely to have their own personal television set, usually located in a private bedroom, and four times as many British children had a video recorder in their room. Notable differences were also found between France and Flanders (the Flemish-speaking part of Belgium), where one in four children had a personal television set, and Italy and Sweden (one in two; Pasquier, Buzzi, d'Haenens, & Sjöberg, 1998). These differences may have important implications for both viewing content and context, as discussed later in this chapter. Even in countries without massive television ownership, television is a prized activity; Larson and Verma found that a third of "impoverished street children" in India had access to television and watched on a daily basis.

Typically, adolescents watch television as a form of relaxation, especially as a means of relieving boredom. This finding has remained consistent across the 20th century, from Himmelweit et al.'s famous 1958 survey up to Larson and Verma's worldwide study in the 1990s. Some of the critics of television have pointed to this as a negative effect, although as the daydreaming studies reported in chapter 8 suggest, watching television does not seem to have stunted children's imagination in the ways that early critics feared. In the United Kingdom in particular, parents are often grateful that their children are at home, even if only in front of the set, rather than playing outside where they may be prey for paedophiles and serial killers. Although such a "mean world" effect may be attributed partly to the lurid sensationalism of British tabloid journalism, the European study also suggests that British adolescents have fewer outside leisure options than do their peers in other countries, and that the television on offer tends to be of higher quality than elsewhere (van der Voort et al., 1998).

As children grow older, their tastes in television content change; boys become increasingly interested in sport, whereas girls become increasingly interested in soaps (Livingstone & Bovill, 1999). At the same time, patterns of viewing change too. Although parents are more likely to share the same taste in television with their children (i.e., children begin to watch more "adult" shows), the tendency for children to have their own television means that, in dual-ownership households, adolescents watch increasing amounts in isolation (Pasquier et al., 1998). Of course, this is a problem for parents who wish to regulate the content of their children's viewing, although increasingly there are technological options for this, such as the V-chip, which was introduced in the United States as a way of enabling parents to block certain shows identified by television stations as having content inappropriate for children.[1]

One of the greatest concerns about adolescent viewing is that television is a largely sedentary activity that may have detrimental effects for teenage health. For example, Dietz (1990) claimed to have found a link between television use and obesity, giving rise to the image of the "couch potato"—the adolescent slumped in front of the television rather than being outdoors taking in lungfuls of fresh air. However, a recent Belgian study suggests that this may not be attributed to television viewing per se but instead to the habit of snacking while viewing (van den Bulck, 2000). But this is really only a problem for heavy users (those viewing, on average, over 4 hours a day), for whom television is a likely alternative to other leisure pursuits.

Music

Some researchers (e.g., Strasburger, 1995) have argued that, during adolescence, listening to music—either on the radio or on a CD—takes over from television as the preferred leisure medium. Certainly it has long been thought that popular music has a profound impact on adolescent socialisation (Lull, 1987). However, it is not clear whether this is due to the music itself, or through identification with different subcultural groups associated with different kinds of music. As Willis (1990) noted, "By expressing affiliation to particular taste groups, popular music becomes one of the principal means by which young people define themselves" (p. 69).

One important difference between watching television and listening to music is that although television is not always the *primary* activity during viewing hours, music is even less likely to be so. Larson and Verma found that, as a primary activity, listening to music occupied only 15 minutes per day. However, as Strasburger maintained, hours spent listening to music may rival television use if treated as a *secondary* activity; for example, listening to the radio while getting ready for school in the morning, or listening to a personal stereo while travelling to school. As Williams (2001) noted, in a study of young people and popular music in Southern England, music has a less profound influence in terms of identity development than is sometimes asserted. Indeed, she argued that her participants "did not seem to be as passionate or excited about popular music as I expected them to be" (p. 228).

---

[1]The adoption of the V-chip has not been without its problems, however; broadcasters have been reluctant to label shows for fear of losing viewers (Comstock & Scharrer, 1999), and because the chips need to be installed in TV sets during manufacture, a family has to purchase a brand new set in order to benefit from the device.

Williams' findings may, however, reflect cultural changes at the start of the 21st century.[2] In the previous 2 decades, popular music has become increasingly generic and compartmentalised (even in the traditionally pluralist United Kingdom), and perhaps offering less for the average teenager; during the same period, television has become more youth oriented. Data from van der Voort et al. (1998) suggest that compared with studies carried out 2 decades earlier, older adolescents were more likely to choose television for "excitement" (previously, this tendency had been found to decrease across adolescence). Today's television offers young people far more entertainment than it did previously, with some channels (e.g., Trouble, E4) dedicated solely to teen-oriented programming. Presenters have become younger and more streetwise, often with strong regional accents, and many soaps feature young characters, such as Channel Four's *Hollyoaks,* aimed squarely at the teenage and younger adult market.

These shifts in media culture have important implications for youth culture in general. As Livingstone and Bovill (1999) found, interest in music tends to be largely a stepping-off point for an interest in fashion, consumerism, romance, and sex. It starts somewhat earlier for girls (around the age of 10 or 11), but when boys become interested in music it is more likely to remain their primary interest, because boys are less likely to use it to explore other areas of socialisation. A number of studies have examined the popularity of heavy metal (HM) music in adolescence (a particular area of parental concern): Strasburger (1995) reported higher rates of drug abuse and risk taking among adolescent HM fans, although he acknowledged the lack of any cause-and-effect evidence.

Roe (1995) argued that teenagers may use HM as part of creating an anti-establishment identity or a "media delinquency"; as Strasburger suggested, music plays an essential part in dividing the cultural world into "teenage" and "adult" domains. Each generation since World War II has had its anti-establishment subculture—from rock'n'roll in the 1950s to punk in the 1970s and rap in the 1980s and 1990s—and each genre has met with the same set of complaints from concerned adults, that the music breeds incivility, aggressiveness, and disrespect. As time-honoured teenage virtues, it might be argued that these are essential properties of youth culture. Rock music and rap in particular *need* to be offensive to adults; this is part of their *raison d'être.* Nevertheless, this effect decreases as adult and adolescent tastes converge; rebellion itself has become stylised almost to a

---

[2]Williams actually interpreted her data in the light of "individualistic" explanations of previous media findings, which, she argued, overemphasise the importance of music in everyday life. I would rejoin that, if anything, media research has continually underestimated the importance of music (for certain groups, at least) in adolescence. Williams' research suffers from her treatment of popular music as homogeneous cultural material rather than as a dynamic cultural form.

point of meaninglessness, which suggests that music probably has less to offer today's teenagers than it did earlier groups of teens.

One aspect of pop that can still raise adult alarm is lyrical content. Rap artists in recent years have specialised in increasingly offensive material, much of it homophobic and misogynistic; at the time of this writing, the most notorious figure in this department is Eminem, an American rapper with a troubled past who is uncompromising in his use of violent and sexist imagery. Eminem has attracted vast amounts of publicity at the start of the 21st century, much of it driven by concern for his material's effect on younger listeners (as a best-selling artist, his music is featured extensively on MTV and other pop channels). Nevertheless, Eminem has many adult fans who are quite happy to "read" his offensive lyrics in context, and it could be argued that younger fans are equally able to interpret the material from a detached perspective.

Indeed, concern over the effects of the lyrical content of pop music may well be misplaced. In one study (Greenfield et al., 1987), teenagers could recall only 30% of their favourite lyrics, which suggests that they are hardly committed to verbatim memory (although it is not disclosed whether they simply recalled the salacious lines!). Furthermore, the *interpretation* of lyrics is very different for teenagers and adults: In one study, the same set of lyrics was described as being about "sex, drugs and violence" by adults, but about "love, friendship, hassles, fun and teenage life" by teenagers (Prinsky & Rosenbaum, 1987). There may also be marked cultural differences in the interpretation of pop lyrics and videos: A study of Madonna's *Papa Don't Preach* video found that Black viewers interpreted the song as about father and daughter relationships, whereas White viewers interpreted it as a song about teenage pregnancy (Brown & Schulze, 1990). Whether these findings can be applied to the lyrics of Eminem and his even more outrageous peers has yet to be investigated.

"New Media"

Very little data has so far been collected on adolescent use of new media, with the exception of the big European study mentioned earlier. In this, Livingstone and Bovill (1999) discerned that up to 43% of 12- to 14-year-olds used "TV-linked games machines" (e.g., PlayStation). This figure dipped later in adolescence, but very few had Internet access. Updates would—one imagines—reveal a much higher level of Internet use. In the United States, Larson and Verma (1999) reported, 9- to 12-year-old boys used the Internet for an average of 80 minutes a day (girls of the same age used it for 45 minutes). Livingstone and Bovill suggested that the United

Kingdom lags behind other European countries for Internet use (at least in 1997), but has a much higher rate of "screen entertainment media" use (i.e., games). Although a number of homes had PCs, these were often broken, or their use was very limited (as a consequence of missing the right software, etc.).

Other European samples suggest quite large differences among countries. Finnish children were much more adept and confident in using PCs than were Spanish children; this may be explained by the fact that, at the time of the study, Finland had the highest number of Internet connections per capita in the world (Suess et al., 1998). Most children there were using computers by the ages of 6 or 7, whereas in Spain children as old as 9 or 10 "still need[ed] help to load the games from their parents and older siblings" (p. 527). Other cultural differences persist; in Switzerland, for example, kindergarten children are discouraged from using electronic media in general in an effort to try and foster a print culture.

In the United Kingdom, one of the factors affecting adolescent computer use is that whereas most children have a television of their own, in most households there is only one PC (if any), so its use tends to be shared among members of the family. Those British children who *do* have Internet access, however, spend more time with their PC than do Dutch children (van der Voort et al., 1998). Social class may also be a factor; British PC-owning adolescents are typically middle class, a suggestion borne out by the figure that 30% of them use the Internet "to learn about things" compared with only 4% of the Dutch. Again, as with bedroom-based television, parental concern over private Internet use has focused on its negative aspects, such as the easy access to pornography, as well as the more obvious issues relating to cost. Most Web providers now come with their own equivalent of the V-chip—a blocking facility that screens potentially unsavoury content.

THE ROLE OF MEDIA FIGURES DURING ADOLESCENCE

One of the most important functions of media in adolescence is that they provide young people with a host of adult figures who play an increasingly important role in their lives. Traditionally, adolescence is a period when children seek out figures from beyond their immediate social environment who can act as heroes, idols, or role models. Theories of adolescent development have argued that adult figures from outside the family play an important function in guiding children toward adult life. Erikson (1968) referred to such relationships as *secondary attachments*, marking the transition between primary attachment to parents, and adult attachments (e.g., intimate, romantic/sexual). In Erikson's model this phase is necessary for the acquisition of adult values, and so it is perhaps not surprising that adults often worry that the heroes their children adopt do not always appear to share the same values as themselves.

Greene and Adams-Price (1990) found that these secondary attachments fell into two broad groups, either *romantic* attachments (e.g., having a crush on a pop star) or *identification* attachments (e.g., admiring a footballer). For teenage girls in particular, this first type of attachment may act as a kind of rehearsal for the development of intimate relationships in adolescence. The author of a study of Elvis Presley fans concluded that their attachment to the celebrity had helped girls "resolve the confusions of adolescent sexuality, allowing it full (imaginary) expression while keeping the fantasizer from having to enact the fantasy with nearby (and often unpredictable) boys" (Hinerman, 1992, p. 121). At the same time, an excess of preoccupation with teenage idols may be related to later difficulties in relationship formation (Cassidy & Waugh, 1997).

The second type of attachment is more related to the process of role modelling, especially if the media figure completes a link to the world of adult work and occupations. A budding footballer may well model himself on a professional star; a character in a soap might even act as a career model for a watching youngster. Role models tend to be most useful when the qualities they offer are attainable (Lockwood & Kunda, 1999), which raises concerns for adolescents who attach to glamorous, inaccessible show business stars. Ultimately, if the glamour of a star can only be attained through superficial means, role models may do more harm than good. Heilman (1998) reported the case of "Kara" who, at 14, amid some domestic unrest, latched onto fashion model Kate Moss ("so cool, I wanted to be like her, under control"). By dieting, she strove to emulate Moss's figure but as with so many developing girls, it was not possible to remain healthy on such a diet and she was eventually diagnosed as anorexic.

Adolescents' choice of role models is determined partly by broader cultural values. This was demonstrated in an interesting study by Yue and Cheung (2000), who compared a Westernised urban (Hong Kong) sample of teenagers with an Eastern urban sample (Nanjing in mainland China). They asked respondents to name three "idols" and "models." Over half of the Hong Kong sample named a pop singer as an idol, compared to 22% in Nanjing; as a model, the respective percentages dropped to 18% and 3%. More Nanjing respondents named a politician as an idol (23%), compared with 8% in Hong Kong, but this figure increased for both groups when naming a politician as a model (45% and 31%, respectively). The authors concluded that these differences reflect different Communist and Capitalist values, and that the Chinese government had promoted "appropriate" role models to teenagers at the expense of corrupt Western superstars.

If celebrities and other media figures act as a bridge between childhood parental attachments and adult relationships, these secondary attachments may be related to the processes of emotional *autonomy* in middle adolescence. One of the features of this stage in the life span is that children begin to see their parents as "real people" performing other roles beside parental functions, and this leads to a decline in their heroic status (Steinberg & Silverberg, 1986). Although to children their parents may seem omniscient and omnipotent, when the children reach adolescence their parents' human fallibilities become all too apparent, and may pale by comparison with the apparent virtues of adult figures in the media. Also during this period, stronger attachments are formed toward peers and romantic partners (Coleman & Hendry, 1990; Patterson, Field, & Pryor, 1994).

CULTURAL FUNCTIONS OF MEDIA USE

An interesting aspect of Livingstone and Bovill's (1999) report is the role of the private bedroom in adolescent media use. The private bedroom is an important site in adolescence, particularly if it is not shared by a sibling; 72% of adolescents in the Livingstone and Bovill study had their own bedroom. It is a private space that separates the teenager from his or her parents (and siblings) but—through a shared media culture, and use of communications technology—connects him or her to peers.

The private bedroom is a site where much creative work may be conducted—writing a diary, drawing, even just daydreaming—but these functions may be compromised if teenagers have to share space with a sibling and thus compete for personal space (Giles & Naylor, 2000a). Research into the historical development of individualism has cited the growth of urbanisation, and particularly the emergence of private spaces within the home, as commensurate with the emergence of the private self (Tuan, 1982). Indeed, it is claimed (Ariès, 1962) that prior to the 17th century, privacy as we know it today was never experienced, and even in the late 20th century there were quite different notions of privacy throughout the world, both inside and outside the home (see Altman, 1975). Nevertheless, in modern Europe and North America the need for a private space is seen as a basic human right.

Most important, the private bedroom is a space that teenagers can use to present their emerging identity through the employment of posters, music, photographs, original art work, and favourite toys, such as dolls and puppets.[3] Researchers Jane Brown and Jeanne Steele have conducted extensive

[3]Brown and Steele preferred the term "stuffed animals," which may be more accurate in some respects, but conjures up images of taxidermy.

research on what they term "room culture," in which teenage participants take them on guided tours of their own bedrooms and describe the meanings and functions of their contents (a methodological technique known as "autodriving"). Brown and Steele have found that the use of bedroom objects changes through adolescence, as media become increasingly integrated into the individual's sense of identity (Steele & Brown, 1995).

In addition, there are interesting differences between groups of girls in relation to sexuality; media material figures more highly among girls who are sexually active earlier in adolescence, with many pictures displayed of movie stars and pop stars. Nevertheless, puppets are still in evidence, albeit pushed to the background, where they serve as reminders of an earlier identity (Brown, Dykers, Steele, & White, 1994). There are also gender differences in room culture. In late adolescence, 27% of girls say that they spend most of their time in their room (compared with 14% of boys, who perhaps see bedroom confinement as social incompetence). Girls are more likely than boys to have a single best friend, and are more likely to spend time with that friend in the bedroom, typically engaged in media use (Livingstone & Bovill, 1999).

The use of media materials in constructing adolescent identities has been termed "patchwork identity" by some European researchers (see Suess et al., 1998). Media may be seen to offer young people such a range of lifestyle and consumer choices that they are able to construct a unique identity by mixing different styles. This contrasts markedly with youth subcultures in earlier decades. In the 1950s, when the distinction between children and adults was sharper, simply to be a "teenager" constituted a powerful identity. In the 1970s, teenage subcultures proliferated, and group membership was a key objective—one could choose to be a skinhead, punk, mod, headbanger, or soul boy, but the appearance and musical preferences of those groups were clearly defined, and hybrids were sternly frowned on. Modern youth culture, however, has moved away from such polarisation, and today's media offer the adolescent a cultural toolbox for identity construction. Suess et al. (1998) cited one of their participants as saying: "I'm a Homeboy. I wear these extra large clothes . . . and I'm a raver, because I like techno music. . . . And I'm a sportsman. I don't have any idol" (p. 533).

Some cultural scholars have seen this as an increasing trend toward individualism of life worlds and lifestyles (Beck, 1992), which is itself part of a gradual merging of public and private spheres (Livingstone, 1998b). Where this is most evident is in the use of the Internet as a means of connecting individuals across geographical and cultural boundaries; for example, Suess et al. (1998) described the case of a boy from a small town with a particular interest in Japanese *Manga* comic books, who found nobody in his area to share his enthusiasm but located many soul mates on the Internet.

MEDIA INFLUENCES ON ADOLESCENT BODY IMAGE

One of the most feared effects of the media on adolescents is that they promote body shapes that are unrealistic and unattainable, encouraging girls in particular to adopt unhealthy diets, in many cases with pathological consequences. This is especially problematic during adolescence, both physically and psychologically. The last thing a growing body needs is a drastic reduction in nutritional intake, and adolescent identity, a fragile thing in the best of circumstances, is made more complicated by societal demands for thinness and physical beauty.

Most studies of body image support the argument that the modern Western ideal of the super-slim, low waist-to-hip ratio female figure is the result of cultural changes rather than a biological imperative (Thompson, Heinberg, Altabe, & Tantleff-Dunn, 1999). It is often argued that the thin ideal reflects the economic independence of the modern woman, for whom childbirth is an option rather than a prerogative, whereas the maternal figure ("child-bearing hips") was more popular in less affluent times. Inevitably the media have been strongly associated with promoting the contemporary ideal; indeed this is one of the few areas in psychology in which culture and media are treated as synonymous, with most researchers favouring a version of cultivation theory. It is the cumulative effect of images of thin women in magazines, television, films, and the fashion industry that is said to promote body image dissatisfaction and eating disorders among teenage girls (Heilman, 1998; Henderson-King & Henderson-King, 1997). Indeed, so worried are policymakers by these apparent media effects that, in the United Kingdom, both the government and the British Medical Association have in recent times campaigned for media outlets and modelling agencies to use a wider range of female body sizes, although with no apparent success.

Several studies of media over time lend weight to the argument that the ideal female figure is becoming thinner. Garner, Garfinkel, Schwartz, and Thompson (1980) carried out an analysis of Miss America winners and *Playboy* centrefolds from 1959 to 1978 and found a significant trend toward thinner, lighter models, despite overall increases in the weight of American women in this period. The study was replicated 10 years later and the trend appeared to be consistent through the 1980s as well (Wiseman, Gray, Mosimann, & Ahrens, 1990). No equivalent data exists for the ideal male figure, although content analyses of television have suggested that far more female characters could be described as "thin" (69%) than could male characters (less than 18%; Silverstein, Perdue, Peterson, & Kelly, 1986).

This proliferation of thin female images has been blamed for rises in eating disorders and general body dissatisfaction in adult women; in one survey, the vast majority of American women wished they could be thinner (Thompson et al., 1999). But the desire for thinness is most problematic during adolescence, when the body is still growing. It is ironic that, at the age of 15, when crises of identity and anxieties about attractiveness are at their most acute, girls typically experience an increase in the distribution of fat around their hips and thighs, taking them further away from the contemporary cultural ideal (Dittmar et al., 2000). Consequently, low-fat dieting is an attractive option for teenage girls, a practice that is greatly encouraged by magazine advertising and feature articles (Andersen & Di-Domenico, 1992). In addition, teenage girls' magazines frequently convey information about slimming and binge eating, and other tactics used to counter the inevitable accumulation of body fat. Even where those articles may raise awareness of the dangers of these behaviours, they may inadvertently provide useful ideas for desperate readers.

Although it is generally agreed that by adulthood a healthy female should have 22% to 25% body fat, many celebrities and models have as little as 10% (Heilman, 1998). This does not stop them from being self-critical about their weight, however, and magazines often carry stories about celebrities' dissatisfaction with parts of their bodies. Indeed expensive cosmetic surgery among Hollywood actresses has become practically *de rigueur* at the start of the 21st century. If celebrities, with all their high-profile diets and beauty treatments, cannot find self-fulfilment through weight loss, then what chance does the ordinary teenager stand?

Methods and Findings

Research into media effects on body dissatisfaction and eating disorders shows a pattern similar to that on other topics. Laboratory studies are popular, in which participants are exposed to a series of slides of thin or neutral models and are then asked to rate their satisfaction with their own bodies. As with most laboratory studies of media effects, the results are mixed, partly because of the variety of different measures and participants used; Myers and Biocca (1992) failed to find any increase in negative body image, whereas Hamilton and Waller (1993) found that women with eating disorders overestimated their own body size after viewing thin models. Lavine, Sweeney, and Wagner (1999) discerned similar results for undergraduate women viewing advertisements in which women were portrayed as "sex objects," suggesting that there may be factors other than body size that produce negative body image for media users.

In addition to the experimental research there are numerous studies using correlational designs that have also produced mixed results. Again, the variety of measures may be a contributing factor. When overall media use is recorded, typically in terms of total viewing time, there is usually little association with measures of body dissatisfaction, even among adolescent samples (e.g., Borzekowski, Robinson, & Killen, 2000). However, studies that have employed more specific measures of media use suggest that preferred content may be important. Harrison and Cantor (1997) found that magazine reading was the best predictor of body dissatisfaction among undergraduate women, whereas Tiggemann and Pickering (1996) noted that the best predictors for adolescent girls were magazine reading, soap opera viewing, and music video viewing. Borzekowski et al. (2000) also discerned a small effect for video viewing, which may reflect either higher instances of sexist portrayals in music videos or the fact that adolescent interest in music often acts as a springboard for a more general interest in fashion (Livingstone & Bovill, 1999).

Theoretical Issues

Two of the most important theoretical approaches that have been used to account for media effects on adolescent body dissatisfaction are *social comparison theory* (SCT) (Festinger, 1954) and identification. SCT occurs for media users when they compare themselves with images of people on screen or in the pages of print media. Heinberg and Thompson (1992) found that undergraduate females experienced greater body dissatisfaction in a laboratory study in which they were explicitly requested to compare themselves with thin celebrities. In a more general sense it could be argued that social comparisons are at their most problematic when there is a large discrepancy between the person's actual (or perceived) self and his or her ideal self, resulting in efforts being made to attempt to close the gap (Wood, 1989). It has been found that adolescent females begin to compare themselves with models in advertising by the age of 12 or 13 (Martin & Kennedy, 1993), the period when eating disorders are most likely to start appearing.

Given the disproportionate number of thin women on television and in magazines, constant comparison is likely to have an insidious effect. This is cultivation theory in action. However, as Botta (2000) argued, cultivation theory does not explain all media effects. The limited number of significant associations found between overall media use and body dissatisfaction have mostly been obtained in studies of White females, whereas studies of African American females have not established such an effect. Indeed, in general, African American women have much lower levels of body dissatisfaction, and less desire to be thin, despite being on average heavier than White women (Abrams, Allen, & Gray, 1993). Although in the past this might be attributed to differences in the body sizes of different ethnic groups in the media, Cusumano and Thompson (1997) noted a parallel increase in the number of very thin non-White models and actresses over time. Where body dissatisfaction does occur among African American women, it tends to affect those who identify most strongly with White culture (Makkar & Strube, 1995). This would seem to support SCT if not cultivation theory, with Black adolescents creating a wider gap by comparison with White images.

Wilcox and Laird (2000) attempted to explain the effect of SCT by looking at individual differences in response to idealised thin imagery. They found differences in the amount of body dissatisfaction between women who rely on personal cues to account for self-perception and those who use situational cues. Cues were elicited by asking participants to smile and then say how happy this made them feel, or frown and say how angry this made them feel. Those who used personal cues (i.e., felt happiest when smiling) were more negatively affected by thin images; those who relied on situational cues (i.e., felt least happy when smiling) actually found that the thin images created more positive feelings about their own bodies. The authors maintained that this finding might explain the mixed results typically obtained in laboratory studies of media effects on body dissatisfaction. However, the methodology makes it hard to establish the extent to which self-perception is really a predictor of body image, except that it might involve a degree of emotional control that is important for dealing with external media influence (rather like self-monitoring, as discussed in chap. 7 in relation to advertising).

One of the problems with the studies relying on SCT is that they fail to consider the meanings that thin celebrities might hold for media users. Heilman's (1998) example of Kara the Kate Moss fan (discussed earlier in the chapter) shows how influential adolescents' selection of specific media figures may be in producing a desire for excessive thinness. Harrison (1997) measured undergraduate women's attraction toward celebrities of differing size, and found that an attraction toward thin celebrities predicted a number of eating disorder symptoms, including bulimia, anorexia, and general body dissatisfaction. However, the reverse effect was not found for heavier celebrities; the author suggested that many heavy television characters are generally less likeable and popular, older, and less stylish. Women who identify positively with thin characters seem to be those who are most influenced by their body shape.

One of the most difficult aspects of the media/body image association is that although studies continue to associate body dissatisfaction with various kinds of media use, there is no according decline in the popularity of those media. Indeed, the proliferation of dieting ads and thin celebrities seems to be reinforced by magazine sales, creating something of a two-way effect. Wilcox and Laird (2000) explained this in terms of individual differences—*some* readers are turned off (those who rely on personal cues), whereas others continue to support the media circus. However, their study lacks any information on participants' actual media use, so this hypothesis remains untested.

An alternative explanation is that adolescent females may not attribute their body dissatisfaction to the media at all, instead blaming their own biological make-up, their parents' genes, or specific instances of rejection or unrequited love. Thus they continue to read articles about thin celebrities, convinced that it is simply fate that prevents them from looking like those celebrities. However, there is a powerful current of opinion within the media as a whole that teenage magazines and, in particular, fashion models are responsible for the prominence of dieting fads and eating disorders. Nevertheless, even the belief that media effects are negative does not seem to dent the enthusiasm for such media among adolescents.

Family Factors?

Although there seems to be plenty of evidence supporting a media/body image link, the general consensus is that media play a supporting role among numerous other factors behind the rise in eating disorders. Chief among these is peer influence, which is usually cited as the most important factor. But what influences peer influence? Livingstone and Bovill (1999) found that 44% of 12- to 14-year-olds discuss magazine content with their friends. Much of that content involves fashion, appearance, dieting, and ultra-thin celebrities. Therefore, "peer influence" cannot be treated as entirely separate from media use. Also, some TV and video is watched with peers at this age, and thus joint consumption may need to be taken into account.

Another important factor in the media/body image debate is the interaction between family environment and media use. Studies of family influence on adolescent eating behaviour suggests that healthier diets are observed when families eat meals together, when parents and children have more positive relationships, and even when they shop together (de Bourdeauhuij & van Oost, 2000). As reported earlier, there is a growing trend for adolescents to spend much time alone in their private bedrooms, watching their own personal television sets, reading magazines, perhaps even surfing the Web, or just daydreaming about having an ideal body and attracting the most desirable partner. It is hard to control intake of fatty foods at the family meal table, where social forces operate to bind children into adult-oriented eating practices (Wiggins, Potter, & Wildsmith, 2001). When children eat alone, and are concerned by weight gain, they are much more likely to snack rather than eat full meals, and thus conceal their poor dietary intake from others.

CONCLUSION

Over the years, research on adolescents' uses of media has been patchy, to say the least. This may be just as well; concerns over the lyrical excesses of rap and heavy metal are part of an age-old tradition of disapproval, whereby adults have continually fretted over the suitability of youth culture whereas adolescents continually invent new ways to shock them. Being misunderstood by parents is part of youth's rallying cry, but being understood by them is worse. Roe's (1995) suggestion that schools incorporate youth culture into the curriculum is likely to lead to even more extreme forms of rebellion. However, there is a fine line between shocking parents by swearing or colouring your hair pink and starving yourself to death. Media probably have more to answer for in their contribution to eating disorders than to any of the negative effects that have been attributed to them, but the processes by which young people incorporate cultural material into their growing sense of identity are still far from clear.

Part IV

THE SOCIAL PSYCHOLOGY OF THE MEDIA

Chapter 10

Representations of Social Groups

It has been estimated (Gerbner, 1997) that the average U.S. child encounters over 350 different characters in television drama each week. Never before have people been exposed to such a huge variety of different types of human beings, and often television is the first (and maybe only) time we encounter certain social and occupational groups. In chapter 7, we saw how the mere presence of different ethnic groups on television might foster more positive attitudes among viewers; however, the reverse effect may also be present, which is that our dependency on media representations of those groups may, in some circumstances, force us to rely on stereotypes.

Along with exposing us to unfamiliar cultural and ethnic groups, media—and television drama in particular—provide us with memorable images of professional groups that we are unlikely to encounter in real life. In the United Kingdom, many of our ideas about prison life, and the behaviour and activity of prisoners, is derived from watching the 1970s sitcom *Porridge*; our contemporary ideas about life in the police force are likely to be drawn from the police soap *The Bill.* Many students enrolled on psychology courses in the United Kingdom after seeing the drama *Cracker,* in which actor Robbie Coltrane portrayed a tough, glamorous forensic psychologist who takes a key role in solving crimes and framing villains.

Although initially helpful in raising the profile of such professionals, media representations of occupational groups are frequently criticised by members of those groups for being unrealistic. Criminological psychologists (especially those teaching starry-eyed psychology students) have criticised *Cracker* for distorting and sensationalising the role of the forensic psychologist; in reality, most stay well away from the action, poring over crime statistics or liasing with police committees. Does this distortion of reality mean in this case that *Cracker* is flawed? In all other aspects it is riveting drama, brilliantly acted and scripted. On the other side of the coin, professional groups have sometimes complained about portrayals that are seen as unflattering or negative. Several schoolteachers complained about the Channel 4 series *Teachers*, in which members of their profession were portrayed as drug taking, hard drinking, and sexually promiscuous. Others, on the other hand, saw the series as essentially humanising, creating interesting and credible characters and dispelling some of the stereotypes about "stuffy" teachers.

There is an underlying assumption that television has a moral obligation to portray social groups as accurately as possible. Although this may be a reasonable assumption in the case of news media and current affairs programming, in terms of fictional drama the price of distortion may need to be weighed against the artistic freedom credited to the writers and producers. Nevertheless, inaccurate or stigmatising media representation is more contentious when it involves broader social groups, notably those defined in terms of age, gender, ethnicity, culture, sexual preference, or health status.

One of the chief concerns about the portrayal of different social groups in the media is that the groups will be *under*represented. In 1999, the U.K. charity Age Concern found that despite the fact that older adults comprised 21% of the British population, they accounted for only 7% of people seen on TV (Age Concern, 1999). Not only that, but within this televised group, men outnumbered women by two to one, the reverse of the real-world ratio. Similar underrepresentation has been found with ethnic minority groups; recent research in Southern California found that 86% of the people in depicted television advertising in this region were White, but only 1% were Latino and 2% Asian American. In reality, these last two groups together make up a third of the population in that region (Coltrane & Messineo, 2000).

However, underrepresentation is only one way in which minority groups may receive a raw deal from the media. A more pressing concern, perhaps, is that when members of the group are present in the media they suffer from *mis*representation. In the Coltrane and Messineo study, the authors determined that White characters in the ads were twice as likely to be (portrayed as) married as African American characters, and that African American men were more likely than other groups to be portrayed as aggressive. This is a problem not only for Black men but for society as a whole, because it is a stereotype that inevitably leads to racial prejudice—for example, White police may take defensive (perhaps violent) measures sooner when dealing with Black suspects if they believe that those suspects are more likely to respond violently.

Stereotypes need not be negative in order to perpetuate prejudice; racist beliefs may be circulated through representations that appear positive on the surface (Hall, 1981; Hoberman, 1997). One such representation is the African as "natural athlete," which reinforces other, less positive notions about racial differences in human ability (the obvious complement being the representation of the European as "intellectual"). Even when media products explicitly tackle racism as an issue they can end up unwittingly casting the ethnic minority group as the root of the problem through the way the issue is framed in the narrative (for more on this, see chap. 12).

In this chapter I take a close look at the way in which a number of social groups are portrayed in the media. The vast majority of studies on media representations have focused on gender (typically, women) and ethnicity. Because this material is well documented in the literature, I have concentrated here on some slightly less well-researched groups, whose portrayals act as examples of media representations in general. In the section on gender, I concentrate on representations of men and masculinity; for minority representations, I focus on mental health and disability, two controversial areas for media producers.

GENDER REPRESENTATION IN THE MEDIA

Studies of the representation of women in the media appear regularly in the communication science and gender psychology literature (Glascock, 2001; Gunter, 1995; Meyers, 1999; Signorielli, 1989a; Signorielli & Bache, 1999). The general picture sketched by this literature is that, after several decades of chronic underrepresentation and stereotyping of women, things are gradually improving, if only slowly. The overwhelming surplus of male characters in prime-time 1970s television was described by one author as "the symbolic annihilation of women" (Tuchman, 1978). Over the years 1973 through 1993, 68.5% of all characters in prime-time U.S. television were male, with only a fairly small decline over that period from 72% to 65% (Gerbner, 1997).

Not only were women still underrepresented in 1980s prime-time television, they continued to be represented by traditional stereotypes. Women were more likely to be married with children, or younger, and portrayed in a romantic or overtly sexual context. They were also more likely to be cast in traditionally "feminine" occupations such as nursing and waitressing. More worrying still, heavy television viewers were more likely to agree with sexist statements about women, even with demographic variables accounted for (Signorielli, 1989a).

Other analyses of media content have unearthed other issues that may compound the perpetuation of traditionally sexist portrayals of women. For example, Tuchman (1978) and others noted that women tended to be portrayed as passive victims waiting to be rescued by heroic male figures (e.g., Lois Lane by Clark Kent's Superman). Goffman's famous (1979) study of gender in advertising examined subtle ways in which women were cast in submissive roles by certain photographic angles and the use of passive postures. More often than men, female models were seen to be lying down, touching objects, or gesturing submissively toward a male model.

Glascock (2001) carried out a content analysis of prime-time television in the late 1990s and found that the underrepresentation disparity continued to lessen, although at a fairly sluggish rate, with women appearing as main characters in fiction 40% of the time (compared with the 28% reported in Tedesco, 1974). There were more notable gains, however, in the *ways* in which women were portrayed in 1990s television. The range of professional roles was much broader than in earlier analyses; like men, the most common role was that of a police officer, and notable numbers of female lawyers, journalists, and doctors were recorded. Female characters were displaying less traditionally "feminine" behaviours too; indeed, they made significantly more negative comments than did male characters, although this figure may reflect the large number of sitcoms, in which female characters traditionally hold the upper hand over males.

MEDIA REPRESENTATIONS OF MEN

Men have received rather less attention than women in terms of their media representations over the years. This is largely because the underrepresentation of women on television—particularly older, lower-class, and ethnic minority women—has traditionally provided the impetus for research on gender representations.

Furthermore, it has long been assumed that the typical viewer of media products is male. As film critic Laura Mulvey (1975) argued, the cinema has traditionally been based around the perspective of the "male gaze," and thus most cinematic content has been designed in terms of what is most likely to appeal to men, particularly heterosexual men. It is only recently that the male body has been overtly eroticised in the media. The same argument could be made for advertising, where until recently only household and domestic products were aimed at women; now the employment situation has changed, and with women playing a major role as consumers, advertising is aimed at them almost as much as at men.

Nevertheless, the rise of feminism, and the changing role of women, have brought about an interest in the ways that men are represented in the media, and in contemporary images of masculinity. Connell (1995) provided a useful breakdown of three different types of masculinities that are present in modern Western culture. They are *hegemonic masculinity, conservative masculinity,* and *subordinated masculinity,* and are described in the sections that follow.

Hegemonic Masculinity

This form of masculinity is based on the political idea of *hegemony* (Gramsci, 1985), which contends that the dominant culture in any society is based on the values of the ruling class. Because—in most societies across time and space—men have tended to have an unequally large share of political and economic power, their values are likely to have been more culturally influential than have those of women. A further characteristic of hegemony is that the dominant culture serves as a vehicle for reinforcing the power of the ruling class; thus, in terms of gender, this category refers to masculinity that is intended to *dominate* (either men dominating women, or men dominating other men). Hegenomic masculinity manifests itself in a hierarchy of men based on the "hypermasculine ideal" of strength and toughness. The men who are most admired are those who are most capable of dominating others.

In media terms, this type of masculinity is most obviously represented in the form of Superman. His name itself suggests that the character is an embodiment of the hypermasculine ideal, and Superman represents power, control, success, strength, and aggression—all the attributes that are associated with men who are high in the hierarchy. A further quality of high-status men is that they are sexually attractive to women; the notion of hierarchy is strongly reinforced in the Superman series by the fact that plain, reliable Clark Kent cannot attract the attention of Lois Lane until donning the identity of the all-powerful, charismatic outsider. The hegemonic function of Superman is most explicit in the original 1940s comic strip, where he is claimed to promote "truth, justice and the American way." Ultimately, hegemonic males are to be taken seriously; for instance, we do not see them represented in comedy.

Conservative Masculinity

Although Superman may represent "the American way," other figures represent a form of middle-class masculinity—perhaps as teachers or artists, or as political or philanthropic figures. Connell used the stereotype of the "new man" as an example of conservative masculinity. The "new man" was a 1980s cultural icon that represented notions of changing masculinities, moving from the hegemonic virtues of toughness and strength to a sensitive, nurturing ideal, embodied by images of men engaged in childcare or overt displays of emotion (e.g., weeping). Connell saw the "new man" as symptomatic of 1980s "therapy culture," in which stressed workers were encouraged to release their frustration through tree hugging, primal screaming, and other acts of emotional abandonment. The thinking man was portrayed as intellectually superior, possibly to women, and certainly to lower-class men.

Subordinated Masculinity

This is a kind of alternative or outcast masculinity that is generally seen as negative. Homosexuality is an example; traditionally, gay men in the media have been the subjects of derision, or presented as a problem for straight men to solve (e.g., how to deal with a friend who comes out). However, this is a very "straight" reading of gay representations; queer theorists, for example, might prefer to see this type of masculinity as "resistant." A pejorative representation of masculinity that would be universally seen as negative would be the "underclass" or "trailer trash" stereotype, epitomised in British television by the Harry Enfield comic character Wayne Slob, a shell-suit-wearing monosyllabic oaf, slumped permanently in front of a television set surrounded by empty beer cans and takeaway packaging (also see the character Onslow in the social-climbing sitcom *Keeping Up Appearances*). A counterexample here might the Glaswegian comic character Rab C. Nesbitt, who has all the surface characteristics of subordinated masculinity but whose rapier wit recasts him as an urban philosopher.

Representations of Men in Beer Ads

Media representations research has employed both quantitative (content analysis) and qualitative analysis, although the emphasis has been on the latter. Rather than counting categories and instances, the study of representations is more to do with the *cultural meanings* that these representations hold for us. Perhaps a good place to investigate male representation is in advertisements for beer. Given that men are the main consumers of beer, and that beer consumption is a hugely popular male leisure activity, it would seem that beer advertisers will represent men in a way that is specifically designed to appeal to a wide variety of them. Strate (1992) looked at five distinct aspects of men in American beer ads:

Activity. "Work hard, play hard," is the message conveyed in beer ads. Men are mostly portrayed engaged in rugged activities, as workers (labourers, cowboys, etc.), as enjoying healthy outdoor leisure (sport, fishing, etc.), or as engaging anything involving risk or mastery. The message is that beer is a reward for hard work, either as a transition to leisure at the end of the working day or as refreshment between bouts of strenuous leisure activity.

What is interesting about these representations is that they are markedly *un*representative of male beer consumption in reality; inevitably, most alcohol is consumed in distinctly unhealthy settings. Instead, the representations convey the impression that advertisers feel will most appeal to male drinkers—that beer drinking is a rugged, healthy, masculine thing to do. The one exception to this rule is, curiously, ads in which men are portrayed watching televised sport. Perhaps these reflect advertisers' occasional attempts to target consumption at realistic settings rather than ideal, romanticised ones.

Settings. The settings for males drinking beer in ads reflects a similar pattern, presumably dictated to some extent by the characters' activity. Therefore, most beer ads are set either outdoors, or in a bar, or in a living room with the television on.

Rite of Passage. Beer drinking, and its associated bar culture are portrayed in ads as part of acquiring an adult lifestyle, so young drinkers are depicted as being initiated into these rituals.

Male–Male Interaction. Beer drinking is overwhelmingly portrayed as a group activity, reinforcing many male stereotypes: nonemotional, nonaffectionate, humorous, irresponsible masculine bonding. Getting your round in is, Strate suggested, a substitute for (female-associated) displays of affection. Again it is notable that unacceptable—albeit common—images of alcohol consumption are avoided, such as lone drinking.

Male–Female Interaction. When this happens—and it does not happen very often in beer ads—such interaction is purely sexual. At one time, if women were portrayed drinking beer, it was a green light for men to "chance their arm," although, for obvious reasons, such portrayals have died out. However, the presence of women in beer ads is still used as an opportunity for men to display their sexual attractiveness.

Men as Buddies/Pals

From the same text as Strate's analysis comes a study of male friendships in the media (Spangler, 1992). This analysis looks at archetypal masculinities and how men have coped with intimacy; generally there is a feeling that the lack of emotional intimacy in men's friendships stems from a fear of homosexuality (one argument is that sport is a substitute; e.g., hugging and kissing goal scorers in football).

Men in popular culture and the media tend to fall into three types: *loners,* who are often powerful, charismatic figures—Superman, as previously described, or Clint Eastwood as the "stranger in town" (spaghetti westerns, e.g., *The Good, The Bad and The Ugly*); *close pals,* but not equals; here we could cite Lone Ranger and Tonto as an example, in which the cowboy is clearly the hero, although, despite his title, is constantly in the company of his saviour and friend (just like Batman and Robin); and *duos*—notably Laurel and Hardy, or Starsky and Hutch.

The Family Man

In a very thorough content analysis, Kaufman (1999) looked at the portrayal of men and women with children in TV ads. She compared ads in which children were present with those in which the person was alone, across different viewing periods. Generally, men were hardly ever portrayed with children without the mother also being present, although this pattern reversed slightly for ads shown during American football games (during which ads for sports equipment or games are most likely to be screened, and are more likely to show dad playing ball with the kids in the garden).

The most interesting data from Kaufman's study concern the ages of the children who are depicted with their parents, and the activities in which they are involved. The male role in parent–child interaction changes as the children get older. Men are much more likely to be seen engaging in child care with infants than with school-age children, and not one instance was found of a male caring for a teenager. Table 10.1 displays the overall comparisons, but further analysis revealed that male child care in ads was invariably directed toward boys (the reverse is true for female child care). Men are also more likely than women to be engaged in educational activity with children, and also in eating and play, typically described as "quality time" (i.e., parents derive as much pleasure from the interaction as the children). Play was found to be a particular feature of father–child ads. A recent ad for Eurodisney showing on U.K. television at the time of this writing exemplifies this finding nicely: A father is displayed taking his two sons around the theme park; in the final scene, it is dad who is whizzing around on a ride while his sons look on.

TABLE 10.1
Parent–Child Interaction in Ads, by Gender of Parent and Nature of Activity; Figures Are Percentages of Each Age Group (from Kaufman, 1999)

Activity Portrayed	*Male Parent*			*Female Parent*		
	Infants	*Children*	*Teens*	*Infants*	*Children*	*Teens*
Child care	33	7	—	37	27	6
Education	11	29	22	5	10	6
Eating	—	35	44	—	22	19
Playing	56	37	22	58	22	13

These data suggest that although men are more likely to be portrayed with their families than in previous historical periods, their activities are restricted mainly to "quality time" and education. Perhaps it is a case of advertisers trying to convey the message that parenting can be fun. However, the "new man" of popular lore has not yet made it into the ads; "the father baking cookies is literally 1 in 1000" (Kaufman, 1999, p. 456). Women are still left to do all the dirty, less obviously appealing aspects of bringing up children.

THE EFFECTS OF CHANGING MEDIA REPRESENTATIONS OF MEN

Although the research just discussed suggests that the arrival of the "new man" made less of an impact on media representations than sometimes thought, there do appear to be some trends away from the "hypermasculine ideal." Wernick (1987) claimed that the male image in advertising had "softened" since World War II ended, notably in the tendency for men to be presented as family members rather than peer group members, and more frequently as the object of desire (the "sexual gaze"). Even where male images are embedded in traditional roles, there has been an increasing feminisation of certain aspects of masculinity; Denski and Scholle (1992) cited the example of heavy metal musicians—hypermasculine in many respects (the term "cock rock" has been frequently applied to the genre) but notably feminine in others, such as their long, coiffured, teased hairstyles and ostentatious displays of jewellery.

Although in most respects positive, for many authors the "feminisation" of men has had its downside in that it has led to traditionally female activities being undermined or trivialised. Segal (1990) and Harrower (1995) both cited examples of Hollywood films in which men take on traditionally female roles, such as *Three Men and a Baby*, in which three flat-sharing male friends suddenly find themselves responsible for bringing up an infant; *Junior*, in which—thanks to a gynaecological miracle—Arnold Schwarzenegger's character gives birth; and *Mrs. Doubtfire*, in which Robin Williams' exiled father returns to care for his children in the guise of a nanny. The authors maintained that in each of these films childbirth and child care are portrayed as relatively easy tasks for males to accomplish given their apparent adaptive and transferable life skills.

A significant trend in the British media during the 1990s has been the development of a profitable market for men's magazines (see Stevenson, Jackson, & Brooks, 2000). Initially, titles like *GQ*, *Arena*, and *Esquire* were targeted at the smart, professional, educated, middle-class man; then along came *Loaded* and the alleged "dumbing down" of the genre as its success began to influence the content of its rivals (notably *FHM* and *Maxim*). These later magazines presented a new representation—the "new lad" (which can actually be traced back as far as a *City Limits* article in 1989). The "new lad" was originally conceived as a backlash against the "new man" and the growing influence of feminism; Stevenson et al. interpreted this as a "fear of the feminine"—certainly the content of modern men's magazines invokes something of a "men's club" atmosphere, complete with the ambiguous cover of irony (although *Loaded*'s editors deny that they are employing irony; perhaps they are being ironic in doing so. . .).

What are the *effects* of these changing representations of men in the media? Representations literature has often been criticised for making grand assumptions solely on the basis of content, rather than actually addressing audience response (Livingstone, 1998a). However, there is an increasing pressure on media scholars to investigate empirically the impact of media content on their audiences. In one recent study, Gill, McLean, and Henwood (2000) interviewed groups of men about their reaction to ads and magazine articles that featured eroticised male images or idealised male bodies. The authors discovered a wide range of responses; many interviewees saw such bodies as entirely unrealistic but also as threatening; others deemed them worthy of emulation; in some cases, even heterosexual males admitted to finding the images arousing.

Are media images a reflection of reality, or do they help shape it? This frequently asked question rests at the centre of media psychology, but really relies on how we define "reality," and how much influence with which we can really credit the media. Essentially, the question is a rerun of the "effects" debate around sex and violence, except that where issues such as gender and ethnicity are concerned the images are multiple and pervasive, almost impossible to avoid without opting out of media consumption altogether. Indeed, Craig (1992) argued that such is our dependency on media that the question is not whether media representations reflect reality, but whether they themselves *constitute* reality. Britain may not be full of men with rippling torsos and six-packs, but if we read enough magazines and watch enough ads, we may begin to feel that it is, and adjust our beliefs and behaviours accordingly.

REPRESENTATIONS OF MINORITY GROUPS IN THE MEDIA

Although the media image of men may have changed somewhat in the last 50 years, it is hard to imagine a social group consisting roughly of half the population ever being constrained by a single stereotype. When dealing with smaller and smaller social groups, however, it becomes increasingly likely that media representations are dominated by an all-encompassing image. The less visible a group is in the media, the more likely it will be represented by a stereotype.

The majority of studies of minority representations in the media have focused on issues of ethnicity and sexuality. Clark (1969) was the first to devise a catchall model that would explain how minority groups are portrayed over time. Clearly the first stage is that of *exclusion* or nonrecognition (either the group is not identified, or it is deliberately suppressed). Clark suggested that the initial stages of representation usually involve *ridicule* (e.g., racist portrayals of African Americans in the immediate post-World War II period), followed by *regulation*, in which pressure groups insist on minority representation in a range of portrayals (e.g., the presence of Black actors in positions of authority during the 1960s and 1970s), before full *respect* is paid, and the group are represented in the full range of roles, both positive and negative.

Clark's model does not seem to have stood the test of time. It may go some way to explaining how African American representations changed between World War II and the 1970s, but in doing so it is highly context bound; the social history of that (indeed, any) particular ethnic group is unique. The distinction between regulation and respect has become increasingly blurred over the ensuing decades; it is very hard to identify a point at which any group can be entirely free of regulated portrayal. The regulation–respect progression might prove to be a good account of minority representation in media areas such as newscasting and presentation, but the world of entertainment is far too complex for the model to work. Two instances serve to illustrate this complexity. The first is the Shakespearian role of Othello. Until fairly recently, the theatrical tradition was for White actors to play Othello in blackface. Increasingly, actors of African descent have played the role. There are a few instances of White actors playing Othello without blacking up, which may be treated simply as another case of "modern dress," although it renders much of the text meaningless. However Othello is portrayed, the ethnicity issue cannot be ducked, and any modern drama in which ethnicity is central to the plot will necessarily fall outside the scope of Clark's stage model.

The second instance concerns postmodernity and the ironic depiction of ethnicity (and other minority concerns) in the media. *Hypertextuality* is the term given to media that makes reference to itself, and such knowing awareness leads inevitably to a blurring of the boundaries between regulation and respect. The BBC comedy sketch show *Goodness Gracious Me* transcends many of the theories of minority representation. Its cast consists of four actors of Asian descent who portray a wide range of characters, some of them explicitly evoking White-origin stereotypes of Asians. Indeed, the show's title is taken from a Peter Sellers record from 1960 in which he portrayed an Indian doctor treating an attractive female patient, drawing on all the characteristics of the period stereotype. Is GGM an example of respect, or merely a case of minority programming (regulation)?

It is difficult to determine whether such respect is earned through quantity of representations or quality. Ultimately, although respect may have appeared to Clark as a satisfactory endpoint in terms of minority portrayal, there is yet one further step for minority groups to take—to assume positions of *power* within the media. The issue of how different groups are portrayed in different roles within media may tell us something about how they are seen by the majority, but full respect can never be earned until those groups are pulling the strings and making the programming decisions themselves (Tulloch, 1990).

The other problem with Clark's stage model is that it assumes a certain degree of homogeneity within the minority group itself. Ethnic groups are clearly diverse, but tend to be defined on basic characteristics such as skin colour or religious beliefs. Sexual minorities are defined solely on the basis of their gender and the gender of their sexual preference. Although these groups obviously incorporate wide fluctuations in degrees of skin colour, say, or how prominently sexual preference figures for individual identities, they are still more homogeneous than are groups such as the disabled, in which *disability* can refer to a huge variety of characteristics that are shared by small numbers of people. In the next section I discuss how problematic representations of such a diverse group can be.

MEDIA REPRESENTATIONS OF DISABILITY

Surprisingly little research has been done on media representations of disability, perhaps because of disabled persons' heterogeneity. Nevertheless, disability is an important social construct in contemporary society, and it is often felt that the umbrella label actually serves to empower people who otherwise risk being seen as isolated or unusual cases, and in danger of being excluded entirely from media representation.

Cumberbatch and Negrine (1992) examined 6 weeks of British television during 1988, concluding that people with disabilities were clearly underrepresented in British TV. Compared with an estimate of 14.2% of people in the real world, only 1.4% of people on television had an obvious disability (although the real-world figure falls somewhat, to 7%, when adjusted for age). Certain disabilities were represented more than others, notably locomotor problems (i.e., need of a wheelchair, stick, or crutch) and disfigurement, but also the category "behaviour," which seems to be a bit of a ragbag category possibly including mental illness (a separate topic of study). Conversely, communication problems and incontinence were underrepresented, the latter perhaps for obvious reasons! Disabled individuals were least common in light entertainment (e.g., comedies), and in the period studied not a single game show contestant had a disability. Representations of disability were most likely in local news, although typically they were the focus of the stories was on medical innovations or health policy (so the story was about the medics or academics rather than the people with the disability).

Balter (1999) developed a taxonomy of stereotypes of disability in the media, some of which are reflected in the Cumberbatch study. The *superhero* is the least common image, and typically involves a middle-aged man in a wheelchair—the 1970s television character Ironside is the classic example. The *sweet innocent* is usually a child, or perhaps an adult (e.g., Dustin Hoffman's autistic character Raymond Babbitt in *Rain Man*). The *sage* is the person whose disability seems to be compensated for by an intuitive ability (e.g. solving crimes). Finally, the *obsessive avenger* is a character who blames society for his or her disability and seeks revenge. Richard Dreyfuss' character Ken Harrison in *Whose Life Is It Anyway?* is a good example of this category. Harrison is a sculptor who becomes paralysed as a result of a road accident, thus losing the ability to produce his art. Marooned in his hospital bed, Harrison requests that his life be terminated. Although the play and film have tended to be seen as framing the issues pertinent to the euthanasia debate, they also raise important questions about disability and quality of life. "Obsessive avenger" portrayals often involve characters whose disability is acquired at some point after birth, and who have an acute sense of *loss.* This theme is central to the portrayal of Ken Harrison. It is interesting to compare such figures with those whose disability is congenital, particularly in relation to their identity as a disabled person.

What is the effect on media consumers of these representations of disability? Cumberbatch and Negrine (1992) conducted an interesting series of discussions with a broad sample of the viewing public, including both disabled and nondisabled people. Seventy-four percent of nondisabled viewers claimed not to be embarrassed at representations of disability on television, although 37% claimed that some disabilities were "too disturbing" to be broadcast. There was general agreement from both groups that disability was *under*represented on television but, as discussed in relation to ethnic minority groups, the question of positive representation (or respect) is not simply a matter of bumping up the numbers but of casting disabled actors in more empowering roles. Balter (1999) cited the example of the character Kerry Weaver in *ER*, whose disability (she needs to walk with the aid of a crutch) is not a major feature of the character or plots, so on the surface appears to be a positive portrayal of disability. However, Balter argued, the actress has not been taught how to use the crutch properly, and the role itself is somewhat "unidimensional"; thus, it seems that the character is purely tokenistic.

How can the problem of stereotyping and underrepresentation be tackled? Balter suggested a number of possibilities, mostly involving disabled people as consultants, actors, media personnel, and so on, or through education (e.g., raising awareness of media students). Why, for instance, did the producers of *ER* not get a disabled actor to play the part of Weaver? Most of Balter's suggestions are realistic, although psychologists and other academics have little power to influence media content unless directly invited to by producers.

Mainstream television is a competitive market; even state-owned networks like the BBC need to joust with commercial rivals for viewers. There is, therefore, a reluctance to take decisions that might result in a reduction in the viewing figures. The disability issue may be part of a much larger issue involved with the representation of *people* in the media in general, relating back to the issues discussed in chapter 9 regarding thin female celebrities. People who meet normative cultural standards of physical attraction are vastly overrepresented in mainstream television. This trend needs to be altered fundamentally before tackling separate issues of representation. If ordinary-looking actors struggle to appear on TV, what chance do disfigured actors stand? Harris (1999) described the case of a Brazilian soap that introduced a character who was deaf, played by a deaf actor. On the surface this appears to strike a blow for positive representation. At the same time, however, the actor is also described as "ruggedly handsome and sexy"; the popularity of the character, Harris claimed, inspired great public interest in learning sign language! It could be argued that, in this instance, overcoming one stereotype (deafness) simply served to reinforce another (attractiveness).

MEDIA REPRESENTATIONS OF MENTAL HEALTH

If the disabled represent a highly heterogeneous minority group, then the same could also be said of the mentally ill. Indeed, mental health is even more fragile a social construct than is disability in that it requires the identification of consistent patterns of behaviour, usually on one single classification system (the American Psychological Association's *Diagnostic and Statistical Manual of Mental Disorders*), and the nature of certain "syndromes" is often disputed. Furthermore, most psychiatric conditions are largely gross exaggerations of "normal" behaviour, much of which is considered highly entertaining in a fictional context. Shooting to kill and punching to maim are stock fare in Hollywood films, but are frequently upheld as evidence of psychopathy in courts and other legal situations.

There is much debate in the social sciences about the appropriateness of the medical model for the diagnosis and treatment of psychological distress (for an alternative perspective, see Parker, Georgaca, Harper, McLaughlin, & Stowell-Smith, 1995). In popular culture and media entertainment, the division between abnormality and pathology is often deliberately blurred. For example, the popular term *psycho*, short for *psychopath*, seems to derive from the Hitchcock film of the same name. This is a clear example of the media perpetuating popular stereotypes: The Norman Bates "unstable loner" figure has since become a powerful icon of mental illness, resulting in much public ignorance and bigotry. Nevertheless, *Psycho* remains a cinematic masterpiece, and need not be held responsible by itself for stereotypical representations in newspapers and current affairs programming.

Despite sensitivity to the issues, negative stereotypes of mental illness still abound in popular entertainment. In one study, Signorielli (1989b) found that three quarters of mentally ill characters were either violent or victims of violence, well in excess of other characters (42%–45%). The difference was particularly exaggerated for female characters. Hardly any mentally ill characters appeared in light or comic roles. Signorielli's conclusion was that "the presentation of a character as mentally ill is a decision that is made to serve very specific dramatic needs" (p. 329). Alas, these needs "result in overemphasizing the negative and stigmatized images of the mentally ill, such as violence, bizarre behaviour, and failure" (p. 329).

Rose (1998), in an analysis of newspaper representations of mental illness, argued that a big change took place in the United Kingdom during the 1990s in the reporting of crimes committed by former psychiatric patients receiving care in the community. Her argument is that the emphasis moved toward blaming "the system" (e.g., government policy) for failing to control the behaviour of former psychiatric patients, creating an impression of violent madmen roaming the streets. This representation can be traced back to a particular news story in 1992, when Christopher Clunis, diagnosed with paranoid schizophrenia, murdered a musician (Jonathan Zito) on a London tube station platform. This case was blown up into a "failure of community care" story, and all subsequent stories of this type seem to have followed the same basic narrative script: the straightforward report of a violent crime, followed by details of professional mismanagement, a damning appraisal of the health authority by a mental health "expert," and the conclusion of a lay judgment of the system itself. Invariably the quick-fix media solution is "lock 'em up"—but who, on what grounds?

An alternative approach to studying media representations of mental illness is to examine media content. Wilson, Nairn, Coverdale, and Panapa

(2000) chose to look at children's television, notably cartoons, for themes relating to mental illness. They found that almost half of the programmes made at least one reference to mental illness, typically using terms such as *crazy*, *mad*, or *losing your mind* to label characters, ideas, or actions as illogical or unreasonable, or to indicate wild spontaneity or passion. Other terms included *nuts*, *cuckoo*, and *loony*, and in several cases madness was depicted by "motions to the head and rolling eyes." Only six characters (all cartoons) were actually depicted as mentally ill; three had comic functions, and the others were "evil" villains, complete with stereotypical physical features.[1]

Wilson et al. admitted that they had not collected any data from children about their understanding of mental health, but argued that the overwhelmingly negative portrayal of mental illness "invites the viewer to generalise from the depictions to all mentally ill individuals" (p. 442). Although there is something slightly disturbing about the findings of this study, there are several problems with research of this type. First, such studies assume that mental illness is itself an unproblematic topic, and that to label someone (or his or her actions) as "crazy" is demeaning. But demeaning to whom? Genuinely "crazy" people? People with a mental health diagnosis, who may deeply resent the idea that they are "crazy"? Terms like *mad*, as applied to everyday activity, are very much older than DSM diagnoses of psychiatric disorders.

Two other problems are addressed in the work of the Glasgow Media Group (Philo & The Glasgow Media Group, 1996), which conducted an extensive study into media representations of mental illness. These are problems to do with media representations in general, but they are usually missed in simple content analyses of media material.

First, the Group took the unusual step of actually talking to programme makers about the content, rather than criticising from afar. What emerges in their interviews is the dilemma that producers face when trying to balance sympathetic portrayals with the need to make "good television." This is particularly difficult with mental illness, because the images of recovery and positive behaviour are far less interesting and dramatic than are the spectacular negative aspects of the condition. One television chief was reported as demanding that "the switchboard should be jammed" following a documentary about a psychiatric hospital—not because the patients' conditions were outrageous, but because the story would generate publicity for the channel. Similarly, positive news stories about mental health do not receive

---

[1]Remarkably, the physical characteristics of cartoon "villains" often hark back to Victorian theories of "criminal inheritance," notably Lombroso's taxonomy of physiognomic characteristics that he claimed were typical of criminals, demonstrating genetic inheritance for criminality. Lombroso's work had quite an impact on legal and scientific thinking in the 1800s, and perhaps existing stereotypes are themselves "inherited" from previous cultural products, such as literature and cartoons.

anything like the high priority accorded to murders and other sensational crime stories.

A second important point made by the Glasgow Media Group is that media representations are very often self-perpetuating. The Group reported a *Coronation Street* storyline involving a babysitter (Carmel) who developed an obsession with her employer. Carmel was portrayed as suffering from a mental illness that caused her to behave in a dangerous and illogical fashion toward her employer(s). The producers described this as "panto syndrome," a very successful dramatic technique in which the audience is more aware of the situation than most of the cast (a kind of "he's behind you!" situation). Therefore, the portrayal of the character was more about "audience pleasure" than highlighting a real social issue. Most revealing of all was the producers' revelation that Carmel's character was based not on a well-researched psychological study of obsessive behaviour but instead on a *Vanity Fair* article on "erotomania"[2] and the film *Fatal Attraction*!

FURTHER ISSUES

In a discussion of racist humour, Hall (1981) speculated that there may yet be a time when blacks and whites can tell jokes about each other without reproducing racial categories. But how will we know when this happens? Do the jokes aimed at White people by the Asian comics in *Goodness Gracious Me* meet this criterion? It is tempting to say that such an atmosphere needs to exist in society as a whole before the media can absolve itself of any part in the circulation of racist ideology. Broader representation of ethnic minorities and people with disabilities at production level is undoubtedly the answer (Tulloch, 1990).

One cloud on the horizon, however, is market segmentation (see chap. 7). Increasingly, decisions at the media production level are based on financial considerations rather than political ones; for example, the British tabloid *The Sun* only eliminated racist spins on news stories during the 1980s after it realised that a significant proportion of its readership was Black (Chippindale & Horrie, 1998). In advertising, target marketing may mean that positive images of different ethnic groups are lost on other groups, so that there is no effect of reversing harmful stereo-

[2]Erotomania is an extremely unusual (although highly dramatic) psychiatric syndrome, in which the patient genuinely believes that his or her love for another person (often a remote figure such as a celebrity) is reciprocated by that person (Franzini & Grossberg, 1995). Typically, erotomania involves the interpretation of incidental behaviours (e.g., you are the inspiration for a pop star's love song). The most famous example is the case of John Hinckley, Jr., who shot and wounded U.S. president Ronald Reagan in 1980 in order to demonstrate his love for actress Jodie Foster.

types. Indeed, other ethnic groups may simply disappear from the screen if they are not perceived as central to the marketing strategies of advertisers (Coltrane & Messineo, 2000). A more likely outcome, however, lies in further expansion of the television networks, with increasing numbers of minority channels that have their own advertising agendas. Whether such a move will prove beneficial for cultural harmony in society as a whole is open to question.

I conclude this chapter by returning to the notion of "stereotypes," which has dominated most of the literature on media representations. In the psychological literature there is some debate about whether stereotyping is *in itself* a problem, or whether it is simply an organising principle used by people to simplify the world or a lapse into cliché when there is an absence of information. The problem, in effect, is *prejudice,* not stereotyping, although the latter may be held as a cause of the former in any given situation.

Perhaps the reason why stereotyping refuses to go away is that it is impossible to completely alter the way people think about the world. Dyer (1993) pointed to a distinction between the stereotype[3] and the more multifaceted "novelistic character." He argued that the latter construction is somewhat unusual in cultural products across the world, being largely a peculiarity of Western literature. At the same time, it is important not to make stereotyping seem so natural and normal that its negative manifestations can be justified by recourse to a kind of cognitive determinism.

Perhaps the main problem with stereotypical media representations lies with their use as a way of reinforcing sharp divisions between people and behaviours (e.g., masculine/feminine, or social drinking/alcoholism). Dyer suggested that stereotypes are used to reinforce divisions where blurred boundaries cause a problem for those in power; for example, it is easier to see drug users as helpless addicts if we want to communicate a message that drug use is unacceptable. A portrayal of controlled drug use might dilute this message and lessen its impact. Another contemporary example is the representation of child abusers as subhuman paedophiles. Media representations of paedophiles as unstable loners shelters us from the uncomfortable fact that much (perhaps most?) child sexual abuse is perpetrated by parents.

At the same time, stereotypes can serve a useful purpose in countering prejudice in society. Writer Johnny Speight attacked racist bigotry in the 1970s sitcom *Till Death Us Do Part* by creating a stereotype of a White, working-class Londoner in Alf Garnett. Indeed it is almost impossible to think of a comic character in the media that does not reproduce a stereotype in some way. Popular culture is infused with symbols; without some degree of

[3]It strikes me here that Dyer may (also) have misinterpreted the term *stereotype* by confusing it with *caricature,* although the two terms are, of course, related.

stereotyping, we would never be able to recognise its analogy of the social world.

CONCLUSION

In this chapter I have not attempted to provide a comprehensive overview of the literature on media representations. Instead, I have concentrated on the representation of less well-researched social groups. One reason for shying away from full coverage of this literature is that there is something fundamentally unsatisfactory about the notion of "media representations" that relates back to the generally negative attitude toward media in academic research (content analyses of media are conducted only when there are *concerns* about their content).

The concept of media representations is, for a start, predicated on the assumption that there is a preexisting social reality, entirely independent of the media, that is capable of being misrepresented by them. However, media penetrate so far into our psychological life that their content irrevocably shapes our understanding of the phenomena they communicate. Men may understand themselves through the representations of masculinity in the media; media representations of men are then based on previous media representations of men, and so on. Although category-counting may provide useful data about social groups that are underrepresented in the media, *mis*representation is a much more complex issue.

Chapter **11**

The Psychology of the Media Audience

In many respects, this chapter is central to the study of media psychology. It ties together the loose ends from the earlier chapters and suggests some broad theories about the way that people process media material in a social context. In doing so, it explores the concept of the "active audience" that has proved popular with media scholars on both sides of the Atlantic—from the uses and gratifications tradition in North America to European "reception" studies and the analysis of the text–reader relationship.

The notion of "the audience" is of particular importance to media psychology because much of the time psychology attempts to deal with universal processes, designing studies in which the sample of participants is supposedly representative of an overall "population." In many cases, particularly in cognitive and physiological psychology, the population is no less than the human race itself, and the goal of research is to discover the cognitive and biological processes that explain all human behaviour. Studies of the "effects" of media have often followed in this tradition, working on the broad assumption that if random human beings watch, say, a violent act on a television screen, they will respond identically irrespective of history, culture, social environment, or media genre. Of course, most media and psychological researchers will argue that this is a gross simplification of their theoretical stance, and that they always attempt to factor in these potentially "confounding variables" when they are relevant.

Increasingly, social psychologists—particularly in Europe—are moving away from such "reductionist" models of human behaviour. The importance of social, cultural, and historical context on behaviour is becoming ever more a feature of psychological research, and has promoted an interest in qualitative methodologies as well as more user-oriented research paradigms. In media psychology this equates to a gradual shift from studying "the viewer" as a random human subject whose responses to stimuli can be easily measured and aggregated with other subject responses, toward understanding "audiences" and the variety of meanings with which they invest media texts. This shift is appropriate for the 21st century because, more than ever before, the influence and effects of media can no longer be isolated (say, by presenting audiences with a clip of film in a laboratory), and because of such wide cultural variations even within the same broad social group.

The idea that viewers perform their own readings of media texts has important implications for the work on children's understanding of television (chap. 8), where the sender-message-receiver ("two-step") model of communication still dominates the field. As I suggested in that chapter, children may well understand television texts at a different level than that supposed by the simple reality/fantasy dichotomy. But the same may also be true of audiences in general. David Morley's (1980) study of the *Nationwide* audience in the United Kingdom marked one of the earliest attempts to demonstrate the diverse readings of media material—in this case a current affairs television show. He compared the responses of three groups—apprentice engineers, trade union (TU) officials, and Afro-Caribbean students—to the show.

The engineers supported the message of the show more than the other groups did, identifying with the presenters and endorsing their views as "common sense." The TU officials were broadly critical of the message, failing to recognise themselves as part of the same "we" spoken of by presenters. These findings were largely predictable; both groups were producing a preferred reading of the media text, although one group took an oppositional stance to it. What surprised Morley, and caused problems for the two-step model of communication when applied to media, was that the students simply refused to produce any kind of reading of the text at all. This group failed to connect with the discourse of *Nationwide*; the show was "boring," politics was "rubbish," and the cultural framework of the show was virtually meaningless.

These findings, among others, led European media scholars to question the whole concept of messages that could be easily and unambiguously deciphered by readers, resulting in a more user-led approach that focused on the meaning of the text for the individual viewer. However, cultural studies and sociology's natural resistance to individual psychology[1] has led them to

[1]One exception here is the Swedish media scholar Birgitta Höijer, who urged the use of "socio-cognitive structures" to supplement audience research (e.g., Höijer, 1992) making the important point that "without cognitive processes there can be no reception at all" (p. 584).

frame the activity of reading in broader social groups (e.g., women, gay men, ethnic and cultural groups). This development gave a strong voice to feminist researchers, who sought to challenge some of the "masculinist" assumptions about culture and communication. Some of these authors used this position to reappraise popular genres that had long been dismissed as vulgar "trash," such as romance literature and soap opera. I discuss this work in more detail in chapter 15.

"THE AUDIENCE" IN MEDIA RESEARCH

McQuail (1997) identified a number of different ways in which the audience has been conceptualised in media and communication research. An important distinction concerns the source of the audience, depending on whether the audience is believed to exist before the medium, or whether the medium creates the audience. In the first instance, the audience is conceived as a pre-established social group—for example, the population of an entire country—that is reconceptualised as an audience for the purposes of media research. Such a perspective is adopted when we make the distinction between the general public and media figures (important for audience participation media, as discussed in chap. 14). Alternatively, the audience may be thought of as a "gratification set," for whom media serve to satisfy fundamental human requirements. In this case, the audience is still viewed as a social group whose existence precedes the medium; this functional approach to media works on the assumption that if the needs of the group are not met by the medium, then the medium will fail to become established.

The other potential source for audiences is the medium itself. McQuail distinguished between "channel" or "medium" audiences on the one hand, and special interest audiences on the other. The former type of audience is one that springs up in response to a new medium—for instance, the Internet audience—and consists solely of users of that particular medium. Special interest audiences are comprised of people whose media consumption is concentrated on specific content; we might talk of the *EastEnders* audience, or a group of fans of a particular star or show. Both types of audience are believed to form *after* the initial introduction of the medium and its content, although with many specialist audiences the content predates the medium (e.g., the audience for televised sport).

The distinction between social and media audiences is important, because it addresses the question of how much power a medium has to create its own audience. We could argue, from a media-audience perspective, that televised sport has created vast numbers of "armchair" sports fans who never attend live games, and who might lose interest in sport altogether were it to disappear from our screens. Or we might see the televised sport audience as feeding back into live sport by creating interest for sport in general. A social-audience perspective, on the other hand, views televised sport as the result of a basic human need for entertainment (for cathartic purposes, or whatever), whose popularity reflects how well it satisfies that need. Such perspectives are perhaps most useful for the media industry in developing new services. They consider the audience as a collection of individuals whose media consumption is determined by personality factors and long-held attitudes. This perspective on audiences has been evident in the use of viewing figures and advertising segmentation.

The "gratification set" perspective on the audience is perhaps best articulated in the uses and gratifications (U&G) work of North American communication researchers (Katz et al., 1974). The basic idea of U&G research was that rather than studying media audiences as passive recipients of stimuli or information, the focus should be on how audiences *use* media. A television set has an on/off switch, and somebody has to make a decision to press it. What motivates this decision?

McGuire (1974) was one of the first to devise a model of media gratifications based on theories of human motivation. Motivation can be either *cognitive* or *affective* (e.g., "I watch this show out of habit," or "I watch this show because I want to be able to discuss it with my friends"), and either *active* or *passive* ("I watch TV to keep me informed" or "I watch TV because there's nothing else to do"). Within these categories there are other forms of motivation. Active/passive modes can be either *internal* or *external*. If we take as an example watching television when there's nothing else to do, an internal motivation would be boredom whereas an external one could be lack of company. These motivational theories have inspired a good deal of research into people's uses of media, but they are complemented by theories of gratifications, which are built on the concept of basic human *needs*. Although basic needs (e.g., stimulation) may provide motivation for using media, the behaviour will not be repeated subsequently unless we have found the experience gratifying. Hence, in addition to reasons for watching a specific programme, we need to determine whether the programme has satisfied those initial needs.

The two sternest criticisms of U&G research are that first it is strongly individualist (or even "too psychological"), and that second it fails to reflect the influence of the overall media environment. The individualism claims have mostly been levelled by cultural scholars who prefer to study audiences en masse, with the individual user treated simply as an axis around which a variety of cultural and media influences circulate (Elliott, 1974). From a psychological perspective, however, it is entirely appropriate to focus on the individual user, who brings to each media event a host of unique life experiences (albeit within a wider social context) that collectively influence the uses of media and the gratifications derived from it, and that also determine the meaning of media content and the way in which texts are read.

The latter criticism is probably more difficult to be reconciled, especially as the media environment becomes ever-more complex. The U&G approach can only account for specific media at any given time—for example, why a television show is watched—so that it fails to capture the overall influence of media on behaviour. In the remainder of this chapter I address this problem by reference to a specific topic, namely *parasocial interaction*—the complex web of relationships between individual media users and the people (or "figures"), both real and imaginary, who populate the media environment.

WHAT IS PARASOCIAL INTERACTION?

Parasocial interaction (PSI) occurs when we respond to a media figure as though he/she/it were a real person. Media figures come in many shapes and forms. They may be presenters or newsreaders, or general personalities whose identity is unproblematic; as far as we are concerned, they represent themselves within the media. They may also be fictional characters whose identity is more ambiguous. Are we responding to the character itself, or to the actor? They may not even exist in human form. Cartoon characters are clearly not real, and yet we may still respond to them in the same way as we do toward fictional (human) characters.

PSI may take many forms. To make a statement about a media figure that implies some acquaintance with him or her is a mild form of PSI. Thus, for example, we might proclaim our undying love for a film star, or gossip with friends about one star's marriage to another film star, how long it will last, and so on. These discussions may involve making quite complex psychological attributions about the figure, as many people did when discussing the breakup of the marriage between Prince Charles and Diana, Princess of Wales. What effect would it have on the children? Who was more to blame? All these speculations refer to people we have never met but whom feel we "know" through our use, and our friends and neighbours' use, of various media. In some cases we may actively incorporate aspects of media figures into our behaviour (see chap. 9 for examples of adolescents modelling themselves on celebrities, e.g. a teenage girl dieting to look like Kate Moss). Even simply yelling abuse at a villain in a soap, or saying hello to a newsreader, fall into the realm of PSI.

Parasocial Interaction: The Research Literature

The term *para-social* (or *parasocial*, as it's now known) *interaction* was coined in a paper in the journal *Psychiatry* by Horton and Wohl (1956). This paper discussed ways in which the interaction between users of mass media and representations of humans appearing in the media can produce a form of parasocial *relationship*, to which the user responds as though in a typical social relationship. The authors concluded by suggesting that social psychologists "learn in detail how these para-social interactions are integrated into the matrix of usual social activity" (p. 225), although this task has yet to be fully accomplished.

The concept of PSI did not resurface until the U&G tradition brought it back to life as an explanation for the gratifications users receive from interacting with people onscreen. In a study of a British television audience, McQuail, Blumler, and Brown (1972) found many of the phenomena described by Horton and Wohl appearing in viewer responses to early soap operas. Following a car crash in *Coronation Street*, a viewer commented: "You feel as if they had been in a real road accident and you'd like to do something for them" (p. 157). The authors identified two essential functions of PSI: first, companionship; and second, personal identity. Soap characters frequently reminded viewers of people they knew, and viewers used characters' situations and behaviour as ways of understanding their own lives.

In a typology of audience–media figure relations, Rosengren and Windahl (1972) argued that PSI could be identified when a viewer interacted with—but did not identify with—a media figure. This is an important distinction, because *identification* has a longer history than PSI, and has typically been regarded as the central psychological process by film researchers drawing on psychoanalytic theory (e.g., Lapsley & Westlake, 1988; Tudor, 1974). For Rosengren and Windahl, PSI's most important function was as a source of alternative companionship, resulting from "deficiencies" in social life and dependency on television (i.e., as compensation for loneliness).

The next major development in PSI research took place in North America, with Mark Levy's (1979) important study of older adults and local television news. Levy conducted a number of focus group interviews concerning, among other things, viewers' PSI with newscasters. He then used this data to construct a 42-item psychometric scale to measure strength of PSI with local newscasters. This scale was correlated with a number of demographic variables in a sample of viewers in a broader age band. Among the items most strongly agreed with were, "I compare my own ideas with those of newscasters" and "When the newscasters joke around with each other it makes the program[me] easier to watch." These findings also have implications for the reception of news and current affairs, and are returned to in chapter 12.

What was most interesting in relation to PSI was that viewers became so attached to their local newscasters that they reported feeling "upset" when their regular newscaster was absent (ill, or on holiday). A later study by Alperstein (1991) echoed some of these views—one interviewee described Joan Lunden, presenter of *Good Morning America*, as a "trusted friend"; another claimed that she "suffered through her pregnancies" and bought baby food on Lunden's recommendation. Such is the importance of PSI that it can dictate the fortunes of a show; in the United Kingdom, Channel Four's *The Big Breakfast* was a news and current affairs show that was hugely popular—particularly with students[2]—when fronted by Johnny Vaughan. When Vaughan left the show, viewing figures plummeted.

Rubin, Perse, and Powell (1985) took PSI research further by creating a PSI scale that measures the strength of PSI with a specific media figure; later studies have used variations on this scale to measure PSI with soap characters (Rubin & Perse, 1987), comedians (Auter, 1992), TV shopping hosts (Grant, Guthrie, & Ball-Rokeach, 1991), and favorite television personalities of any type (Rubin & McHugh, 1987; Turner, 1993). Studies using the PSI scale have found that perceived realism and attraction to the media figure were highly correlated with PSI, which suggests that media users evaluate media figures along criteria similar to that they apply to people they encounter in the flesh. More recently, Auter and Palmgreen (2000) developed the basic idea of the PSI scale into an Audience–Persona Interaction (API) Scale, which taps four characteristics of audience activity: identification with a favorite character, interest in a favorite character, interaction with a group of favorite characters (e.g., a sitcom family), and a favorite character's problem-solving abilities.

Similarities Between Social and Parasocial Relationships

If we are to use the term *relationship* to describe the feeling that we know a media figure, there should be some concordance between the way we experience our relationships with real others and the way we experience our attachments to celebrities and fictional characters. Several studies have examined this by applying theories of actual relationships to relationships with media figures. For example, uncertainty reduction theory (URT) states that the more contact we have with someone, the more predictable they become and the more we like them (Berger & Calabrese, 1975). Perse and Rubin (1989) applied URT to the development of parasocial relationships, and found that higher levels of reduced uncertainty were associated with greater "parasocial complexity" measured by descriptions of favorite and disliked soap opera characters. Turner (1993) noted that similarity ("homophily") was an important factor in the strength of the parasocial relationship, particularly in relation to attitudes, appearance, and background. However,

---

[2]In a study by Giles, Naylor, and Sutton (2000), the PSI scale was completed by two sets of undergraduates who were asked to identify a "favourite television personality." Johnny Vaughan was a clear winner in this category, although admittedly one group was tested in mid-morning and may have been watching the show just before the test, exhibiting a recency effect.

these effects varied according to the type of media figure. Finally, Cole and Leets (1999) applied a measure of adult attachment to PSI and discerned a similar pattern of response to attachment in intimate relationships.

These findings suggest that if we examine social relationships at a cognitive level (i.e., how a single individual perceives other people), there is no reason why we should not treat parasocial relationships within the same framework. However, if a theory of relationships requires a true relationship to have an element of *reciprocity*, then PSI takes on a different character—the media figure does not answer back when we yell abuse at him or her. The waters are further muddied by consideration of *cyberrelationships*, in which people enter into intense interaction with remote respondents whose identity may be entirely false, or may conceivably consist of a group of individuals all using the same identification (Turkle, 1995). These aspects of identity are explored more fully in chapter 16, but they are important for PSI theory because they expose the shortcomings of traditional theories of relationships.

What's Missing From the Parasocial Interaction Literature?

Although many aspects of PSI have been explored in the media and communications research, an equal number of important questions remain unanswered. First, is PSI a phenomenon that is peculiar to mass communications, or is it an adaptation of a much longer-established aspect of human behaviour? The existing research tends to explain it solely in relation to needs and gratifications (e.g., company for lonely viewers), although some of the strongest PSI exists between groups of viewers and celebrities or soap characters. One of the most important functions of PSI, it seems, is to supply material for *gossip* in offices and bars.

Caughey (1984) discussed PSI in terms of "imaginary social relationships," and claimed that these relationships are a feature of all human societies, in which they act as a kind of shared knowledge structure. You may recall in the opening chapter that I described a whole hour at a party in which various guests and I discussed people with whom we were all familiar, although none of us had ever met them. In traditional societies such conversations might concern gods or spirits, knowledge of whom is necessary to be accepted as a member of society; we hear of many occasions (particularly among schoolchildren) when people feel excluded from a conversational group because they do not watch television, or watch the wrong shows.

The second unanswered question in the PSI literature concerns the breadth of the phenomenon. Most studies have focused on PSI with a single figure (e.g., a favourite personality) or a genre of media figure (newsreaders). However, at any given time an individual media user will have hundreds of parasocial relationships, some positive, some negative, with a whole host of media figures. Can we really equate PSI with a newsreader and PSI with a cartoon character? Furthermore, most PSI studies have conceived it as activity that takes place *during* the viewing episode (e.g., saying goodnight to the newsreader). I would argue that parasocial relationships stretch much further than this, taking in a multitude of interactions, from viewing television to listening to radio, reading newspapers and magazines, listening to CDs, and watching videos or DVDs. The strongest relationships are those built up over time with individuals appearing in a variety of media and possibly a variety of guises (e.g., film stars playing different roles).

Finally, in line with the critiques of the "individualism" of U&G research, PSI is not always an individual phenomenon. Although we may become strongly attached to media figures while interacting with media in our own rooms as teenagers, much of our media use, particularly in adulthood, is a joint activity shared with partners, friends, or families. PSI was initially envisaged as compensatory activity engaged in by lonely viewers, but it is clear that this does not embrace the responses of a group of house-sharing students arguing over the attributes of soap characters, or their postviewing gossip about those characters.

PSI has sometimes been criticised for "pathologising" media relationships (Picirillo, 1986). This stems from theories such as the "media equation" that treat the activity as irrational and illogical, or maladaptive. It makes it all the more important to return to Horton and Wohl's original call to integrate PSI as an extension of normal social activity; the model described in the next section is an attempt to do this.

A Model of Parasocial Interaction

This section describes a model (Giles, 2002b) that I have formulated in an attempt to deal with some of the criticisms of PSI research to date. It consists of two parts: a matrix of social and parasocial encounters, and a flow diagram indicating the processes in forming a parasocial relationship.

Table 11.1 contains the matrix of encounters that suggests some important ways in which parasocial relationships differ (and are similar to) social relationships. From top to bottom there is a continuum of "parasociability" suggesting that, the more remote interactants are from one another, the more features their relationship shares with a parasocial one. It also suggests that one of the important properties of any social encounter is its relationship possibilities. This enables us to identify three different levels of PSI, ranging from Level 1 PSI, at which the interaction is with a media figure who represents him- or herself (e.g., a presenter or newsreader); to Level 2 PSI, at which a human actor represents a fictional character (e.g., a soap star); to Level 3 PSI, at which the figure is nonhuman (e.g., a cartoon character). With each successive level, a social relationship with the media

TABLE 11.1
Dimensions of "Parasociability" (from Giles, 2002a)

Encounter	Location	Constraints: Formal	Constraints: Informal	Potential Relationship: Formal	Potential Relationship: Informal
			Social		
Dyadic	Proximate	Interview	Conversation	Work colleague	Close friend
	Distant	e-mail message	e-mail message	Future associate	Cyberfriend
Small group	Proximate	Working group	Friendship group	Colleague	Friend (within group?)
Large group	Proximate	Board meeting	Party	Future colleague	Future friend
	Distant	Lecture (re lecturer)	Lecture (re another student)	Semi-parasocial	Future friend/colleague
Encounter with media figure	Proximate	Fan club convention	Chance meeting	Dyadic, but role bound	As normal dyad?
	Distant	Phone-in show	"Personal" letter	Dyadic, but role bound	Semi-parasocial
First-order PSI	Distant	News broadcast	—	Parasocial, but chance of contact	—
Second-order PSI	Distant	Soap character	—	Parasocial, can only make contact at representative level (i.e., with actor)	—
Third-order PSI	Distant	Cartoon figure	—	Purely parasocial, no chance of contact	—
			Parasocial		

figure becomes less of a possibility. We may contact our favourite newsreader; we may meet him or her; we might even end up marrying him or her. At Level 2, the possibilities are limited to a relationship with the representative of the character (who may be nothing like the character). At Level 3, of course, no actual relationship is possible.

The matrix also deals with a number of other relevant properties of social encounters, such as the difference between formal and informal encounters. Parasocial encounters are necessarily formal because of the role of media, but what about actual encounters between ordinary media users and celebrities? If we bump into a celebrity on the street whom we "know" from television, how different is this from bumping into a complete stranger? The difference lies in the information the two interactants bring to the encounter: I may feel I know the intimate details of the celebrity's sex life, what he eats for breakfast, what his favourite colour is, and his entire life history, but to him I am a mere stranger plucked out of an anonymous sea of faces.

Sometimes people react to the concept of PSI as if it is determined by the medium alone, wrongly attributing e-mail communication between two strangers as a parasocial encounter. Although such encounters share some of the characteristics of PSI in that they are not directly reciprocal (i.e., nonsynchronous) and require some degree of imagination (we may have a mental picture of the other computer user), the nature of e-mail is entirely different. A newsreader, for example, is broadcasting to hundreds, perhaps millions, of viewers and receives no feedback from any of them; an e-mail exchange is fundamentally an intimate dyadic encounter, no matter who the interactants are, and falls well within the scope of traditional social interaction (albeit with some informational variations).

The second part of the model is an attempt to explicate the processes involved in the development of a parasocial relationship. The top part of Fig. 11.1 concerns the psychological activity engaged in by an individual during media use (e.g., watching a television show). The immediate response to an onscreen character involves making judgments about that person (e.g., "Do I like/dislike him/her," or even "Does this person have sufficient motive to commit such a ghastly crime?") In most cases we may actually carry over some person knowledge from previous encounters with the media figure (e.g., "Judging by his/her behaviour two weeks ago, this person is certainly capable of committing such a ghastly crime"). Two broad responses are possible here that have implications for the development of a relationship: We may *identify* with the figure ("Hmm, perhaps I would do the same in a similar situation"), or we may simply interact with him or her ("Oh, don't do that, for heaven's sake!").

In cases where we identify with the figure, we may go on to incorporate some of that figure's behaviour into our own. One of Alperstein's (1991, p.

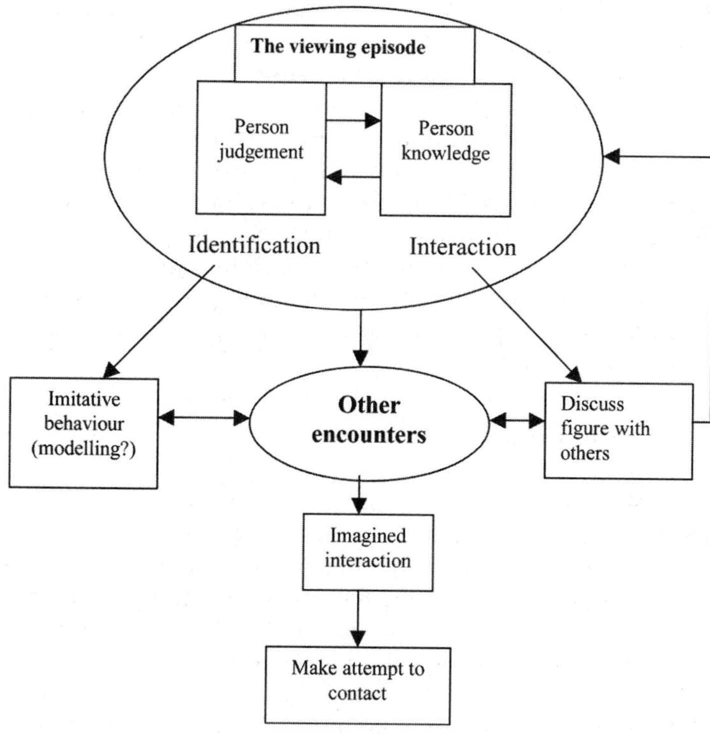

FIG. 11.1. Stages in the development of a parasocial relationship (from Giles, 2002a).

53) participants said of the actor Bill Cosby: "I try very hard to make my own character like him. . . . I feel that Cosby and I share that characteristic of trying to be different." Alternatively, we may simply develop our relationship in social interaction, by discussing or gossiping about the figure with others. The arrow in the top right of Fig. 11.1 allows for the possibility of this process taking place during viewing itself, when it may well transform our person judgments in the activity of viewing: Imagine a teenage girl who begins the show as an admirer of a character, but whose friends' reaction to that character is so negative that she completely revises her opinion by the end of the show. In either case, the identification or interaction will be strengthened in further media encounters with that figure. The teenage girl may, when viewing alone, revert to her original admiration for the character, or we may feel we have wrongly judged a celebrity through his or her television appearance after reading a newspaper story in which that person has been involved in a charitable act.

The arrows at the bottom of Fig. 11.1 allow for the possibility of making contact with media figures, although an important mechanism connects PSI itself to the attempt to contact the figure. This is *imagined interaction* (Honeycutt & Wiemann, 1999)—cognitive activity that seems to accompany our actual social relationships, in which we plan what we will say even to (perhaps especially to) our most intimate acquaintances. In order to turn a parasocial relationship into a social relationship we would need to imagine ourselves being acquainted with the media figure to spur us into making the effort to contact him or her. Such imagined interaction may take place very early on in the process, however, particularly when media figures elicit a sexual response. Indeed, a degree of PSI may underpin our responses to pornography.

Extreme Forms of Parasocial Interaction

Although one of the purposes of the model just discussed is to depathologise PSI and situate it as part of normal social activity, it is clear that in some cases our responses to media figures *are* irrational, and potentially harmful for both ourselves and the figures. In the most extreme scenario, attempts to contact celebrities may be fruitless, in which case desperate individuals may resort to stalking behaviours in order to force their way into the celebrity's life. One such example is Jona McDonald, who sat on the steps of Abbey Road studios in London for 110 days in order to meet her idol Chris Hughes, then-drummer with 1980s pop act Adam and the Ants (Giles, 2000). In most cases, stalking behaviour is treated as illegal activity (in 1990, California became the first U.S. state to adopt an antistalking statute) but, to confuse matters, there are frequent reports of celebrities who end up forming romantic relationships with fans.

Making contact with celebrities need not involve physical encounters: Many fans are content simply to write letters. Dietz et al. (1991) analysed a large sample of letters sent to celebrities and attempted to identify which factors best predicted attempts to contact celebrities face to face. The two best predictors were the mention of specific times and dates (e.g., "I will come and visit your house on Tuesday at 10 o'clock") and an attempt to obscure the letter writer's whereabouts. Surprisingly, threats to harm the celebrity were not a good predictor of attempts to contact. It seems that for many letter writers sending a threatening or offensive letter performs a cathartic function. Probably the most fascinating feature of the Dietz et al. study is the nature of the "enclosures," or items accompanying the letters to celebrities. Some of these items were largely innocuous, such as business cards or media clippings; some were predictably offensive (a syringe of blood, animal faeces); others were simply bizarre, including a toy submarine, a half-eaten candy bar, and a disposable razor!

Most of the time, media fandom is a harmless activity. In the next section, I discuss the growing literature in this field and the implications this work has for a more general theory of the active audience.

FANS AND FANDOM

By far the most influential work on fans and fandom has been conducted by Henry Jenkins, an American academic and avowed *Star Trek* fan. In his work *Textual Poachers* (Jenkins, 1992a), he argued that media fans are deeply misunderstood by both the public and academics, who frequently pathologise them as potentially dangerous obsessives and stalkers. Nonsense, said Jenkins; media fans are simply doing what creative, intelligent people have always done—they latch onto cultural material and recycle it to meet their own interests. There are historical precedents to fan culture; as Braudy (1997) described, the world's great religious texts emerged out of constant rewriting and reinterpretation by generations of holy men and hermits. Indeed, the word *fan* comes from the Latin *fanaticus*—literally, "of the temple." (There are many religious parallels to be drawn with fandom, to which I return later.) It was only with the establishment of publishing companies that the idea of the individual author emerged, with clearly determined meanings and intentions—even Shakespeare lifted all his plots from earlier sources.

Jenkins went on to describe the various activities that *Star Trek* fans engage in, such as "filking" (writing and performing songs about the show and its characters), composing novels about *Star Trek* characters that go way beyond the shows and furnish the characters with histories and alternative destinies, splicing video footage to create new stories, and even producing homoerotic texts depicting Kirk and Spock as gay lovers. He proposed a model of fandom based on four ideas (Jenkins, 1992b):

- *Fans adopt a distinctive mode of reception.* Their media consumption is not casual, to fill in dead time, but instead is selective and directed—certain programmes are viewed regularly, videoed, discussed, and taken beyond the individual viewing episode to "some more permanent and material form of meaning-production" (p. 210).
- *Fandom constitutes a particular interpretive community.* In other words, fandom is fundamentally a social pursuit, understood at an institutional level in clubs, conventions, fanzines, debates, and shared cultural knowledge.
- *Fandom constitutes a particular Art World,* with its own aesthetic standards, conventions, critical evaluation, and so on. But it differs from

the established art world in that the materials are recycled, and therefore acts more like a counterculture.

- *Fandom constitutes an alternative social community*, and is therefore attractive to minority groups, and individuals whose interests are otherwise pursued in isolation.

It may be that Jenkins' Trekkies are somewhat unrepresentative of most media fans, who are more likely to focus on an individual figure. When we look at other types of fans, the motivations and gratifications appear somewhat different. Parasocial interaction clearly plays an important role. A classic example was given by Hinerman (1992) in his study of Elvis Presley fans. He described the case of Vanessa, who as a teenager in the 1960s used to daydream that she and Elvis were friends; later, when she married, she fantasised that she, her husband, and Elvis were friends. Around the time of Elvis' death, Vanessa's stepsister (to whom she was close) also died, and in her depressed state Vanessa held imaginary conversations with Elvis that assisted in her recovery. Then her husband designed a computer program that enabled her to hold "conversations" with Elvis that made her feel "that he really does talk to me . . . through the computer" (p. 121).

This is a case of exceptionally strong parasocial attachment, and there are plenty more cases in Hinerman's paper. Fantasy figures have always played an important role, particularly in adolescence, as noted in chapter 9 when I discussed secondary attachments to adult figures other than parents as an important part of the passage to adulthood. Many people, particularly women, can recall teenage fantasies about pop stars. Fred and Judy Vermorel (1985), in a well-known book (*Starlust*), gathered together numerous letters and anecdotes from fans. Of course, when the parasocial relationship begins to interfere with normal social interaction, it is a cause for concern.

Religious Parallels

Many authors have drawn parallels between fan behaviour and religious devotion. The history of scripture, as suggested earlier, is a key example. However, there are many other similarities: the communal nature of devotion, the reverence toward relics, and the sense of intimacy (in some respects, prayer is another form of parasocial interaction). Jindra (1994) carried out an analysis of *Star Trek* fans' behaviour and argued that it satisfied enough criteria to be classed as a "civil religion," rather like L. Ron Hubbard's Church of Scientology—there existed an organisation, dogmas (including a ST "canon"), and a form of recruitment system. In addition, many ST rituals are clearly modelled on religious activities, including one case of a baby being baptized into a "Temple of Trek!"

In a remarkable paper, Frow (1998) claimed that fan worship of celebrities may often be "a cult of the dead" (p. 205). His argument is that once pop stars have preserved their voices on tape (or film stars their images on video) they have become disembodied, especially if it is their recorded output that is worshipped. Whenever a Hollywood legend dies (say, at a ripe old age), it is common to hear people say: "I thought he/she'd been dead for years!" Before Rock Hudson died, a tabloid paper placed pictures of his AIDS-ravaged body alongside promotional Hollywood shots of Hudson in his prime, but this gesture was partly redundant, because to most of the audience the "star" had already passed on. "The star is always already dead; by the same token, however, the star lives forever" (Frow, 1998, p. 206). I advanced a similar argument in my book *Illusions of Immortality* (Giles, 2000), citing this phenomenon as a possible explanation for the insatiable desire for fame.

A CASE STUDY: WHEN CELEBRITIES DIE

I end this chapter with a brief discussion of an unusual phenomenon that could be described as "parasocial bereavement." This occurs following the death of a celebrity or media figure, eliciting behaviour in fans that mimics the grief we experience from the death of a close friend or relative. Two notable celebrity deaths at the end of the 20th century were those of Diana, Princess of Wales, and Jill Dando, a BBC television presenter (see Fig. 11.2). Following their deaths, a large number of tributes were placed on the BBC website (http://www.bbc.co.uk/politics97/diana and http://news.bbc.co.uk/hi/english/uk/newsid_328000/328861.stm). These tributes were analysed for themes relating to aspects of the parasocial relationships that the posters had experienced with Diana and Jill (Giles & Naylor, 2000b).

First, identification played an important role in many cases. One poster wrote of Diana:

> I remember seeing the sadness begin to seep within Diana, you see once we reached are (*sic*) early thirties we had developed our personalities and began to gain independence. Our husbands forgot how to nurture us and give us the love and friendship that we both wanted so desperately to achieve. We were both divorced within six months of each other and began to spread our wings and live life again, we both have recently met gentlemen who are more like us and have become our lovers and best friends.

Another poster described how her friendship group had collectively formed a parasocial relationship with Jill Dando: "Jill Dando was somebody we all admired, she seemed always to be so full of life and vitality, she brought you with her on her holiday programmes. We admired her clothes, how nice she was, we all read how she was getting married in Hello magazine and how we hoped it would go well for her."

Many posters wrote about how they felt they had come to "know" Diana and Jill even though they had never met: "We didn't know her, and unfortunately never had the honour of meeting her. Yet her passing is as if we did. She touched all our hearts because unlike many others in the world spotlight, she came across as genuine and showed her emotions, particularly her sadder ones."

The most interesting reactions, however, came from posters who were taken aback by their strength of feeling at the death. It seemed as though Diana and Jill's deaths not only demonstrated the mortality of the celebrities (reinforcing their status as real people), but also brought home to their fans the degree to which they had formed attachments:

> I did not realise how much she meant to me, only now do I realise she was more than just a photo she was a friend.
>
> It is so difficult to describe my feelings. I never met Diana or even saw her in person, but feel like I have.

The following tributes capture the sense of confusion that media users face when confronted by the irrational nature of their PSI:

> I was taken by surprise at my depth of feeling for her on hearing of her death. . . . I would say that I am a fairly hard-nosed cynic, but tears came despite that and I am still finding it hard to take in that she is gone. She is an immense loss to the world as a whole, but more important and revealing is the feeling of so very many people that they have lost a personal friend.
>
> As a happy, well-adjusted woman, I was stunned by the emotions I felt and of the tears that flowed from my eyes all day Saturday as I watched the most moving and the most beautiful funeral I have ever seen. It rocked my soul. . . . I couldn't stop crying and I didn't know why.

It is interesting that both posters felt it necessary to issue a disclaimer ("I am a . . . hard-nosed cynic"/"As a happy, well-adjusted woman"), which seems to be an attempt to rationalise their grief in a context in which they feel slightly foolish at having been so moved by what is effectively a media event rather than a "true" life event. I would suggest that such a reaction is typical of most people, and is strongly related to the "third-person effect"—we always imagine that it is other people who are influenced by the media rather than ourselves, and yet, when we find ourselves grieving for someone we only know through our media interaction, we find it impossible to account for our behaviour in rational terms.

CONCLUSION

In this chapter I have addressed some of the issues that cause a problem for traditional psychological theories of media. It is perhaps fair to say that such problems stem from an adherence to a social-audience perspective in which the audience is regarded as a social group that exists prior to the introduction of a given medium. From this perspective, parasocial relationships with soap stars are seen as peculiar, even pathological, behaviours that can only be interpreted according to individual abnormalities. In the process, media consumers are stigmatised as irrational, perhaps even insane. My argument here is that psychology would benefit from viewing audiences as determined, albeit only to an extent, by the media themselves. Although parasocial relationships with both real and imaginary figures have always existed up to a point, it is historically absurd to compare the pre-20th-century experiences of novel readers with contemporary media users, who interact with a huge cast of real and imaginary figures in a media environment in which fantasy and reality continually overlap and invite all manner of irrational responses. The realism of contemporary soaps has no historical parallel and it is meaningless to search for one. In studying our responses to such phenomena, media psychology has the potential to take psychology itself into new territory.

Part V

GENRES

Chapter 12

News and Current Affairs

What is reality? For Kant, realism had two forms: empirical and transcendental. Empirical realism contends that I can only believe in the existence of something if I see it with my own eyes. To cite an old adage, if a tree falls in the wood it only makes a sound if a hearing person or animal is in earshot. Transcendental realism contends that the falling tree will produce a sound regardless of anything being able to hear it, because sound exists independently of hearing, as physical perturbation of the atmosphere. In the psychology of news and other so-called "factual media," it is essential that we consider the ways in which media act simultaneously as "windows on the world" and as vehicles for propaganda.

Let us suppose a rally is held in a London park to protest about current government policy. How many people have attended this rally? A TV news bulletin covers the story in a typically world-weary kind of way, offering us two figures: the organisers' estimate of 100,000 and the police estimate of 20,000. According to the bulletin, the organisers claimed the protest was a huge success, although police report a few arrests for "minor offences." However, the front page of a newspaper the next morning carries a photo of a blood-stained officer, accompanied by the headline "PROTEST RALLY TURNS UGLY," and the accompanying article describes a violent scuffle between protestors and police, along with organisers' comments that the rally passed peacefully for the most part, and that the incident was due to a "minority of troublemakers."

Now let us apply the empirical/transcendental distinction to this situation. You are a fairly liberal-thinking citizen, not actively involved in politics, and depend on the TV news and your morning paper for current affairs information. Although you didn't have sufficient time or interest to attend the rally, you quietly support the organisers' sentiments and have a vague interest in the event. You don't know anyone who attended it either. How do you know (a) it actually took place, (b) how many people were there, and (c) the extent of any trouble?

You don't want to spend your life "reading between the lines"—you have a job to do and a family to care for, and time is a precious commodity. Empirical reality, for you, is out of the question; therefore, you rely on your news sources as bastions of truth and objectivity to provide some transcendental realism. You satisfy your curiosity with the following set of answers: (a) The event took place because the TV news and morning paper both said so; (b) the two figures are clearly both biased, one in favour of the organisers and the other, probably, in favour of the government, so the real figure will be somewhere midway; and (c) the camera never lies, so the front page photo clearly indicates some sort of trouble, but evidently not severe enough to merit mention on TV and seemingly an isolated incident.

With news media, it seems, we are all transcendental realists, otherwise we would not bother with any of it. Indeed we rely on news media to enlighten us about things that we are unable to see with our own eyes, but it is quite clear that we cannot rely on any one source; our confidence in the existence of events can only be built up by consulting several. But what are these sources, and from where do *they* come?

SOURCES OF NEWS

Newspapers—the original source of news about politics and current affairs for the general public in the modern age—evolved hand in hand with advertising, as has been discussed already in chapter 7. Hence political interest has always to some extent been tied up with commercial interests, meaning that, traditionally, a newspaper has tended to have an explicit political identity reflecting its owners' agenda. In the United Kingdom, there has been an attempt to buck this trend with *The Independent*, which has marketed itself as a politically neutral mouthpiece (as far as the major parties are concerned), although most British papers tend to be strongly identified with their owners. The best-known example of this is the News International group of publications owned by Australian tycoon Rupert Murdoch, whose political influence has been immense in the United Kingdom and elsewhere, reflected by papers' shifting allegiances between the major parties. Notably *The Sun*, a staunchly working-class tabloid newspaper, began life as a Labour-supporting paper in the 1960s, swung toward the Conservatives before their successful 1979 election campaign, and then reverted to Labour in 1997 to cheer Tony Blair home.

The arrival of new media technologies is invariably accompanied by fears that traditional news sources will become redundant, but newspapers have remained popular, perhaps because they perform functions different than those of television and online news. When BBC radio began broadcasting in the 1920s, its news coverage was severely restricted by newspaper owners for fear of losing sales, until it became the state corporation (Scannell & Cardiff, 1991). Even then, news bulletins were still brief, lasting no more than 15 minutes (including the weather forecast).

Over time, news broadcasting has expanded to include many more types of stories, especially those with "human interest" themes, and, notably, coverage of serious crimes. With the advent of cable and satellite broadcasting, specialist news channels have been created that provide news 24 hours a day; the most well known of these is Cable News Network (CNN), a U.S. channel that achieved worldwide fame through its groundbreaking coverage of the Gulf War in the early 1990s. Today, the Internet also acts as a source of news, through both online interactive websites and newsgroups. For some years now, analog television has carried news information through services such as Teletext and Ceefax.

Certainly newspapers are favoured by people with a general interest in political issues, and studies of current affairs knowledge have found that newspapers are a better predictor than television. Indeed, Robinson and Davis (1990) found that the more television news people watch, the worse their comprehension of it becomes! Similarly, Wober, Brosius, and Weinmann (1996) found that people's television use was inversely related to their knowledge of issues in the 1989 European elections. Despite this, people generally regard television as being more trustworthy when it comes to the accuracy of news bulletins (Gunter, 1985b); this may simply reflect the explicit bias of newspapers, with most people interested in current affairs often choosing to read more than one daily paper. Typically, television news has remained neutral, preferring to present itself as a "window on the world" rather than as simply another television show put together by a producer with a vested interest. This may yet change, with increasing numbers of specialist news channels, each needing to offer unique services to ensnare viewers.

Certainly, television news is much less effective at conveying semantic information than is newsprint (Gunter, 1997). First, there is simply less time to present more than the essential facts concerning a story, unless a decision is made to concentrate on the lead story, as happens occasionally with disasters or major political events. However, on such occasions, newspapers still respond by devoting several pages to the story. Second, news programming is sequential, so viewers have to wait until the end of one story before proceeding to the next item; therefore, a story that we find less interesting may result in a lapse in attention, or even cause us to switch off the set or begin a secondary activity. The lack of obvious markers for stories means that we cannot return to the bulletin at a set time to catch up on a story we *are* interested in (with print, we can easily skim forward to an eye-catching headline). Third, until recently there has been no facility in television news to refresh our memory of the facts surrounding a story; as a result, we may find ourselves losing the thread. With newspapers we can scan back and reread earlier parts of stories, thus continually updating our absorption of information.

These differences are crucial, not simply in terms of information processing but with respect to the uses of the respective media. The highly visual nature of television news puts a different gloss on the stories than those of newspapers and radio. Crigler, Just, and Neuman (1994) compared two groups of participants on their recall and comprehension of reports of a South African riot, one receiving information in the form of a televised bulletin with audio and visual content, the other receiving identical audio content but no visuals. The former group made much more of the violence in the footage, particularly the brutality of the police, interpreting the riot as the result of establishment oppression rather than a random outbreak of mindless violence.

Whichever medium we prefer, there is no doubt that news media play an integral role in everyday life. Gauntlett and Hill's (1999) analysis of television viewing found that many viewers actually structure their television use—and their daily routines—around news bulletins. This is particularly important for more isolated viewers such as older adults and people with restricted mobility, for whom the news is perceived as a way of staying in touch with the outside world. One viewer even compared his news viewing to an addiction. Although for some people, especially working mothers, news is more of a luxury to be fitted in among essential professional and domestic chores, when important world events occur, such as the September 11 tragedy and its aftermath, even casual news-followers can assume the appearance of addicts.

CONTENT-BASED APPROACHES TO NEWS MEDIA

Broadly speaking, there are two approaches that have been adopted with reference to news in media and communications research. The first concerns the content of the news itself, whereas the second examines the impact of news on the viewer or reader.

Content-based approaches examine the way the news is put together by journalists and broadcasters to achieve certain effects. They are therefore the opposite of the "magic window" theory of media that argues that, for example, television news is simply a reflection of what's really happening in the world. One popular content-based approach is referred to as *agenda-setting* (e.g., McCombs, 1994). This approach views news as the reflection of the interests of media owners; in chapter 7 I discussed an example of this in relation to stories in Rupert Murdoch-owned publications that were (allegedly) cunningly disguised adverts for shows on Murdoch's own Sky channel.

Agenda-setting may take place in a broader context too, where news sources in general are driven by a collective sense of what constitutes "news." A national election will usually dominate the bulletins for a number of weeks during the campaign, but a major disaster would take precedence, if only for a short while. However, on the day of the election itself, the disaster may receive less coverage (although the odds of the two events coinciding are extremely short!). At other times, priority tends to be given to "home" news ahead of foreign news. If a plane crashes in the United Kingdom and 30 people are killed, this will certainly take precedence in British news over a similar incident in, say, Mozambique. Obviously, the situation would be reversed in Mozambique. "Newsworthiness" also fluctuates across time; in the days following a major plane crash, an aerial near-miss is likely to receive a higher news profile than usual.

The most overt form of agenda-setting concerns the *censorship* of news, whereby sensitive information is suppressed in the interests of the owners of the news source. When the owners happen to be the country's government, this can lead to direct political engineering by the ruling party; notably, one of the first gestures by citizens during the fall of Communism in Eastern Europe during the late 1980s was to seize control of the local media. In the United Kingdom, the BBC has occasionally fallen prey to political propaganda by the government; the most remarkable example came during the Conservative government's reign in the 1980s, when Margaret Thatcher insisted that representatives of the IRA should not be given airtime, and thus news producers were forced to substitute with actors' voices (a fact that the BBC lost no opportunity in pointing out to viewers!).

Agenda-setting can be studied with regard to all kinds of news, not just politics. Stories concerning celebrities, for instance, are carefully engineered by public relations firms, often to tie in with the launch of commercial products (e.g., a new record or film). The public relations (PR) industry owes much to the pioneering work of circus promoter P. T. Barnum in the 19th century, whose aggressive promotional strategies laid the foundations for news generation ever since. One of his most notorious scams involved publicity for a new "exhibit" at a fair, a woman who claimed to be 161 years old.[1] As the initial crowds dwindled, Barnum wrote an anonymous let-

[1]This was, in fact, an African American woman named Joice Seth, a former slave whose age at death was estimated to be a mere 80.

ter to leading American newspapers claiming that the woman was a fake, not human at all but an ingenious piece of machinery. Public interest was rekindled, and the crowds returned to take another look (Gamson, 1994). The spirit of Barnum lives on in the work of PR gurus such as Max Clifford, whose machinations have secured high-profile news coverage, particularly in the British tabloid newspapers, for many modern-day celebrities.

On other occasions, large sums of money pass between hands to secure "exclusives," or even to compensate for running scurrilous gossip. These sweeteners keep the stars happy, even if their reputations appear to be tarnished. For a brilliant exposé of the way the tabloid press works, see Chippindale and Horrie's *Stick It Up Your Punter!* (1992), a highly readable history of *The Sun*, with some hilarious and shocking anecdotes.

News Discourse

One of the most popular approaches to news research is to study the language itself and wider forms of textual expression, such as the use of visual rhetoric (including camera angles, photographs, and newspaper headlines). Very often this research is conducted using *discourse analysis* (DA), the study of talk and text. DA comes in many forms: Some versions examine language primarily as a toolkit for constructing the world and adopting positions in argument, others prefer a definition of discourse that incorporates broader cultural practices, and some adopt explicit ideological positions. Wetherell, Taylor, and Yates (2001a, 2001b) provided good sources for detailed coverage of all the different varieties of DA currently in use.

The form that has been applied mostly to news discourse is *critical discourse analysis* (CDA; Fairclough, 2001). CDA is rooted in "semiosis" (meaning making), by which it is necessary to study more than language itself. A newspaper article needs to be understood within its context, which means taking into account the remainder of the newspaper; the position of the article within the newspaper; the use of visual information such as headlines, photography, and photo captions; and even perhaps the relevance of neighbouring material (such as a strategically placed advertisement). Unlike some forms of DA, CDA does not begin with the text itself; it regards any text as an account of a real issue that exists beyond the text.[2] As its name

[2]This is important, because some forms of DA prefer to take a pure "relativist" slant, arguing that "reality" is entirely constructed through language and thus we should not regard texts (necessarily) as representative of some external reality (see Edwards, 1996; Edwards & Potter, 1992; Potter, 1996). For instance, the phenomenon of "road rage" only exists as a media construct; the category of behaviour described by the phrase *road rage* did not exist until a journalist or commentator coined the phrase, even though there may have been numerous instances of motorists behaving aggressively toward one another. Although this approach to DA has

suggests, it takes a critical stance on these issues, with a broad commitment to "progressive social change."

Ultimately, media discourse may shape the way we understand the political sphere. One example of this is the phenomenon of "New Labour." Traditionally, the British Labour party has been associated with socialist ideology, the emancipation of the working class, and the interests of the trade unions. When Tony Blair became its leader in the mid-1990s he continued a process of reform (otherwise referred to as "modernisation") that had been initiated by his predecessors. Through the use of CDA, Fairclough (2000) demonstrated how the phenomenon of New Labour has been constructed through both the media and official Labour party documents such as press releases, which are effectively "boundary genres" between institutions and media. The organisation and focus of these documents dictates what will be reported, and how, and the documents themselves use language to achieve particular rhetorical effects, such as terms like *work, partnership,* and *welfare dependence.*

Related to DA is *narrative analysis,* by which texts are understood in terms of their overall structure. Some writers have argued that the use of the term *story* to describe a news item is quite appropriate, for news tends to be expressed in the narrative form common to stories. For example, the sentence "Today, a plane exploded above the Atlantic Ocean, killing all 300 people on board" establishes time, place, and personae; "Terrorist involvement has not been ruled out" then establishes a possible motive. In fact, the narrative structure may continue across several broadcasts, allowing a complex story to unfold—indeed this may well heighten public interest, especially if it has a whodunnit-style plot. The Bill Clinton/Monica Lewinsky story is a classic example. By contrast, the narrative structure of a weather forecast is much looser—consisting of 32 unconnected statements (Gunter, 1987).

Conversely, some have argued that most news stories do not follow traditional narrative structure at all—in fact, they "abandon narrative" by presenting the resolution first, which "is like being told the punchline before the joke" (Lewis, 1991, p. 131). This is, however, a rather overliteral application of the idea of "narrative," which should encapsulate all manner of storytelling (jokes are, themselves, a rather unusual example of story form).

---

proved very useful in shaking up psychology as a discipline, it has obvious limitations for media discourse. Unless we have access to unlimited media material, we can never trace the origins of road rage and thus we have to treat each instance of the term as somehow related to wider discursive practices (i.e., go beyond the text). Researchers at the other end of the DA continuum adopt the perspective that media discourse can only be understood as part of wider cultural (or ideological) practice. I recommend steering a course between these two extremes, acknowledging the contribution of wider discursive practices to media texts, but studying the texts themselves as unique products of specific media.

Other studies have looked closely at the precise language used in news stories. As Fairclough (1995) argued, choice of words is not accidental; texts are built from a series of *optional* terms and expressions within a given vocabulary or grammar. He cited a Radio 4 item about "cheap" Russian fish being "dumped" on the British market as an example of the way that language can subtly frame a news story without making explicit the producers' ideological position. Such subtleties even extend to grammatical details. There is a difference, for example, between the use of an active tone ("Police shoot dead 11 protestors during riot") and a passive tone ("11 protestors shot dead after police fire on rioting crowd"). In the former headline, the police are more likely to be seen as culpable, perhaps opening fire on purpose; in the latter, the implication is that the shooting was simply crowd control that got out of hand.

This kind of textual analysis can also show us how news texts position readers through the use of personal and possessive pronouns, e.g. *we* and *our.* Such seemingly trivial details can have profound implications for the construction of identities—for example, if a British newspaper used *we* to refer to the English football team, this might change the way a Scottish reader felt about the paper (e.g., that reader would feel that he or she didn't belong to the readership). Other, seemingly innocuous descriptions can also have surprising effects (see van Dijk, 1998).

The problem with discursive approaches (and content-based approaches in general) is that although they reveal some interesting linguistic and rhetorical devices, they do not attempt to specify what effect these devices have on readers and viewers. The impact of rhetoric is assumed rather than demonstrated. It may be that nobody is fooled by "New Labour"; their success in the 2001 election suggests they are doing something right, but is it through action rather than discourse that they have survived in power?

INFORMATION-PROCESSING APPROACHES TO NEWS RECEPTION

The study of *news reception* (how readers and viewers actually understand and interpret news) has followed two broad theoretical approaches: the short-term cognitive approach, whereby memory for news material is measured in laboratory-type settings; and the cultivation approach, which looks at people's general media use and their understanding of news content. Gunter (1987) argued that, in general, our memory for news is not particularly good, even for news programmes on television. Partly this is due to distracting visual footage that does not always tally perfectly with the verbal material. One way in which news producers have dealt with this problem is to delay showing pictures until the details of the story have been read out. Research by Newhagen and Reeves (1992) suggested that this only works if the visual images induce a positive or neutral mood in the viewer. In fact, if the images shown are negative, it would be better to present them upfront, because they inhibit the recall of the preceding verbal material and enhance recall of subsequent verbal material. This may be because the emotive pictures heighten viewers' attention (Taylor & Thompson, 1982).

Indeed, much news production practice seems to be based on faulty psychology. As Schlesinger (1978) pointed out, news producers have long organised bulletins in clusters of stories based on thematic similarity (e.g., home news, foreign news, sport, etc.). This practice has evolved partly as a result of newspaper practice and partly in the belief that viewers and listeners find such story packaging easier to follow and recall. However, research by Mundorf and Zillmann (1991) indicated entirely the opposite. When a single item of foreign news was embedded in a series of home news items it was better remembered than when it was embedded in a series of foreign news items (and vice versa). There are also powerful effects of memorable or spectacular single items, which distract viewers or listeners from remembering neighbouring items that are rather less spectacular.

News Framing

One criticism of this research is that, like much "effects" research, it deals with memory for artificial stimuli displayed in laboratory conditions. In actual news reception, our recall for events needs to be examined in the light of our understanding of those events through broader frameworks of knowledge. Much of the news washes over us because we have missed, or not understood, key elements in understanding the story. For example, a cabinet reshuffle would be better recalled if we had some idea of who was originally occupying the posts. Similarly, a foreign election story would be meaningless if we had no idea who was presently in power.

Some of these processes relate back to standard theories of text comprehension—notably, the "framing" theory of Bransford and Johnson (1972), which suggests that learning is futile without a properly understood context. The authors demonstrated this effect by reading out a series of sentences that related to a bizarre picture. Participants who were able to see the picture recalled significantly more of the material than did those who only heard the sentences, suggesting that the context of the picture provided them with a frame to aid comprehension. Anderson and Pichert (1978) took this idea yet further, by providing participants in a story comprehension experiment with a particular perspective. One group was asked to read a description of a house from the perspective of a potential home buyer, whereas the other group was asked to read it from the perspective of a potential burglar. The perspective in each case determined which aspects of the story that participants recalled.

These theories are particularly relevant to our memory for political or international affairs. People generally recall news information much better if they are familiar with all the issues and personalities involved, because news producers often assume prior knowledge on the part of the audience. This may be due to time constraints, but research indicates that no matter how much time is devoted to a particular issue, if viewers have neither the interest nor the expertise they are likely to switch off, either actually or metaphorically (Wober et al., 1996). If viewers are interested in the issues, then they will benefit from increased coverage. Cairns, Hunter, and Herring (1980) noted that local children's awareness of "the Troubles" in Northern Ireland was positively correlated with the amount of television news they viewed, an unexpected finding, perhaps, given their proximity to the action. However, this effect was not found in a group of similar-aged Scottish children, for whom television would be their most likely source of information about Northern Irish current affairs.

The framing of news has become the subject of much research into media bias, because the frame of reference adopted by the audience can be influenced by the way that news producers choose to highlight certain features of the material. This was demonstrated in a remarkable study by Entman (1991), who examined U.S. media coverage of two similar incidents during the 1980s. In the first incident, in 1983, a Korean Airlines (KAL) passenger plane was shot down by a Soviet fighter plane, killing 269 passengers and crew. In the second, 5 years later, an Iran Air (IA) passenger plane was shot down by a U.S. Navy ship—again, all (290) on board were killed. Entman's study used material from *Time, Newsweek, The New York Times, The Washington Post,* and CBS evening news bulletins. He argued that there were four salient aspects of the text that created a frame for interpretation:

- *Agency.* Who was responsible for the incident? Coverage of the KAL disaster left little doubt in readers' minds of who the culprits were. *Newsweek*'s cover page screamed: "MURDER IN THE AIR," and *Time*'s cover read "SHOOTING TO KILL." In the text, the perpetrators were referred to as "Moscow," or "the Soviets." The IA disaster was accompanied by soul searching and questioning. "WHY IT HAPPENED" was *Newsweek*'s cover line, whereas *Time* relegated the incident to a small flap in the corner of the cover, reading "What went wrong in the Gulf." In short, the KAL incident was framed as deliberate sabotage by a nation—an act of war—whereas the IA incident was framed as a tragic mistake.

- *Identification.* With whom is the audience invited to identify? Entman argued that this could be interpreted from the pictorial coverage of the two incidents. In the KAL incident, the damage to the plane was evident—indeed, *Newsweek* carried a full-page photo of it exploding—whereas there was little graphic coverage of the IA plane. KAL victims were named, along with many horrific descriptions of the emotions that they would have experienced. However, the IA victims were not named, and after the IA incident most of the detail in the reports referred to the technical aspects surrounding the "mistake."
- *Categorisation.* Entman recorded the number of attributions that interviewees made in the five news sources, namely whether the incident was treated as "deliberate" or a "mistake." He found that the various sources interviewed largely labelled the KAL incident as deliberate and the IA incident as a mistake. Notably, the 16 *Washington Post* attributions of "mistake" in the KAL case were all Soviet sources, and most of the attributions of "deliberate" in the IA case were Iranian sources.
- *Generalisation.* Where did the blame lie for the incident—with an individual or a nation? Overwhelmingly, the KAL incident was blamed not on individual error but on the Soviet government, or even the Soviet Union as a nation, whereas the IA incident was treated as human error—certainly no wider than the *USS Vicennes* (the gunboat itself), or the U.S. Navy.

Taken individually, these fragments of emphasis might be explained by key differences between the two cases—perhaps there was a more obvious technical explanation for the IA disaster—or even as the bias of a specific news organ, perhaps reflecting its owner's political agenda. But Entman examined five of the most prestigious news outlets in the world and found that the framing was similar in all of them, reproducing long-held biases that had evolved through the Cold War. The words and images in the stories evoked different sets of ideas, such that the KAL incident became part of a *moral discourse* whereas the IA incident became part of a *technical discourse.* Of course, the positions held by the various members of the audience will ultimately determine how effective those discourses are in shaping public opinion.

An Integrated Model

The dynamic news processing model of Kepplinger and Daschmann (1997) goes some way to account for the role of prior knowledge. In this model, a "steering unit" monitors incoming information. This will differ for each person, determining how much attention we pay to a story and what prior knowledge structures we bring to bear on understanding. Media coverage is said to enter a filter through which some information is lost, and information continues to be lost throughout the process. At the end, some of the information retained feeds back into the steering unit for subsequent processing. This way we build up a "running memory" of current affairs.

Kepplinger and Daschmann tested their model by asking TV viewers questions about the day's news, and requesting elaboration on some points; they found that over 90% of participants added information that had not been broadcast on the news bulletins they had been watching. This suggests poor "source monitoring" for news information. The authors were also interested in the way that schemas are formed from a mixture of "real" and mediated experience. They noted that schemas for *negative* issues tended to be drawn from real life; for instance, people were quick to generate crime examples from their neighbourhood to back up media material. Other research has found, unsurprisingly, that people were more affected by negative news items when they related to personally experienced issues (Johnston & Davey, 1997).

Finally, one important consideration in terms of news reception is the role of the television newsreader. As discussed in chapter 11, Levy's (1979) study of parasocial interaction between viewers and newscasters demonstrated the importance of the human news source, certainly in terms of keeping the viewers watching. It is very important that we find this news source credible, so newsreaders need to communicate a sense of *trust*, especially given the finding that television is considered a more trustworthy source of news than newspapers. Interestingly, despite growing cynicism about media impartiality, there has been an increase in the proportion of British viewers who believe newsreaders to tell the truth, from 63% in 1983 to 79% 10 years later (Gauntlett & Hill, 1999).

However, newsreaders may influence the audience interpretation of the material in ways of which they themselves may be unaware. Mullen et al. (1986) explored the possibility that even the facial expressions of newsreaders may bias a viewer's response to the information being reported. They studied news coverage of the 1984 U.S. presidential campaign in which Ronald Reagan was reelected, beating his opponent Walter Mondale. Mullen et al. got students to rate the facial expressions of various network newscasters without hearing their voices, and found that one newsreader—ABC's Peter Jennings—displayed significantly more positive facial expressions than his rivals did when reporting on Reagan's campaign. A telephone survey later revealed that significantly more ABC viewers intended to vote for Reagan. Although this finding might reflect the bias of the ABC network itself, the authors found no other indicators of bias—indeed, the polls carried out by ABC were slightly more favourable to Mondale than were polls conducted by rival stations.

Although we expect our newsreaders to be trustworthy and impartial, we nevertheless prefer them to display human qualities. Levy (1979) found that a lot of his participants agreed with the statement "I like it when the newscasters joke around with each other." One interviewee explained that the newsreaders' banter was reassuring, especially when the news was bad; if they could find time to share a joke, it meant that life goes on regardless despite the awful events in the rest of the world. This reassurance provides *continuity* for viewers, a function of media that Silverstone (1993), drawing on the psychoanalytic theory of Winnicott, described as a "transitional object," like a comfort blanket, to which we cling for reassurance that all is well with the world. It shows how much the media exist as a framework for everyday life; one of the first things many of us do after returning from a foreign holiday is to switch on the television or consult teletext, just to see "what's been going on while we've been away." If we were to return to find our regular television channels closed down, or our favourite news source replaced with another show, it might well induce a sense of unease, even if only temporarily.

This explains why we find coverage of traumatic events, such as the September 11 tragedy, so harrowing; apart from our concern at the obvious human suffering and fears about what will happen next, even our comfort blanket has been wrenched out of our grasp. In societies with relatively few news sources, or media outlets in general, this feeling will be exacerbated. Thus, when major channels are filled with the horrors of war and destruction, it is comforting to be able to turn to cable channels where cartoons, music videos, and 1970s repeats continue merrily, seemingly oblivious to world events.

BAD NEWS AND SERIOUS NEWS

During the mid-1990s, a debate took place in the British media after BBC newsreader Martyn Lewis spoke out about the possible ill effects of bad news. He argued that the seemingly constant tide of negative news stories was bad for national morale and created for many media users the frequent impression that "the entire world is falling apart" (Lewis, 1994, p. 157). At the time he was roundly criticised for his stance by fellow media commentators, who regarded this as political naïveté (e.g., the events in Bosnia should be reported as graphically as possible in order to show viewers how serious the situation is and perhaps galvanise them into action).

However, Lewis's position raises a number of important questions about news media regarding the status of particular topics and stories, and the way these are changing gradually over time. As recently as 1980, Dorothy Hobson reported that many women regarded the news as a predominantly *masculine* domain and confessed that they found the content "boring" and "depressing." In the following 2 decades, there has been a notable increase in "human interest" stories in news bulletins that have often detracted significantly from the leading political news of the day. Probably the most spectacular example in British news in the 1990s were the murders of James Bulger, Rachel Nickell, and Sarah Payne, which all occupied the newspapers and television news bulletins for several weeks as events unfolded (the latter two murders occurred during the summer, a period traditionally devoid of major political material while parliament is inactive). Although these stories concerned members of the public rather than political figures, it is notable that many "human interest" stories are just as gloomy and depressing as most political affairs. It seems that whatever the source we simply find bad news more *interesting* than good news.

One argument is that the appeal of bad news might be rooted in evolutionary psychology (Shoemaker, 1996). Shoemaker maintained that news media perform a "surveillance function" for readers and viewers, and that we use this as a way of monitoring threats in our immediate environment. If we hear about a rape or murder that has taken place in the alley at the bottom of the road, we know to avoid using that alley in future. This can be equated with the drop in foreign holiday bookings that tends to follow news reports of tourist abductions or civil unrest in those countries. Shoemaker's argument suggested there is a basic *fascination* with bad news, which accounts for increased sales of newspapers after tragic events. One experimental study supported this idea: When confronted by disgusting news images, participants backed away from the screen on which they were displayed; when the images induced anger or fear, people actually moved closer, to get a better look (Newhagen, 1998).

The shift toward human interest stories at the expense of "hard" political news has been widely condemned as part of a more general process of "dumbing down" in the media (and perhaps in society at large). The argument tends to be that in order to increase sales of newspapers and raise television viewing figures, media are now aimed at the lowest common denominator: Informed and expert readers will continue to buy their traditional newspaper because they depend on it as a news source, but now have to wade through lots of showbiz/human interest material in order to reach the "real news." This viewpoint carries with it a lot of snobbery, and a lot of assumptions about the sort of information that we should find interesting and important; it is notable that the term is *dumb down*, which could be interpreted as "incorporating working class values."

Another, related argument is that the increase in human interest news media has come about through a more general "information explosion," whereby there is simply *more* news, and we are more selective about which bits we follow. This is clearly related to the expansion in televised news following CNN's coverage of the Gulf War. This expansion has not occurred due to consumer demand; it is simply a business war fought among cable and satellite companies (Ruddock, 2001). Because there is now more news, there is inevitably a larger proportion of trivia, but because, for most readers and viewers, the trivia is intrinsically more interesting than the "real news," it has started to infiltrate the coverage of the real news, too.

Today, it is almost impossible to disentangle "serious" political news from tittle-tattle and gossip. It is no surprise that some of the biggest news stories in the last decade have involved politicians and other key figures as objects of scandal, usually salacious. The Bill Clinton/Monica Lewinsky affair made headlines around the world, although, unlike many other scandals involving politicians through history, it had a negligible effect on issues of policy. For most British citizens, their overriding memory of former cabinet minister David Mellor is that he reportedly made love wearing a Chelsea football strip and enjoyed having his toes sucked.[3] Very few will remember the political details of his ministerial career (especially as he has arguably become better known as a radio presenter).

Corner (2000) noted that major political figures operate today in three overlapping "spheres of action": an institutional sphere (their political work/career); a private sphere (domestic life); and a public/popular sphere, in which their activities are visible to all through the eyes of the media. Clearly, public and institutional spheres overlap at election time, when candidates are evaluated on many visual criteria, from the appropriateness of their appearance to minute gestures that are captured by the camera (Rees, 1992). Electioneering is very much a *performance*. All three spheres come into play when a politician is involved in a scandal, especially one of a sexual nature. Corner cited the example of the British Conservative politician Jeffrey Archer, who was forced to resign as chair of the party during the mid-1980s following revelations that he had paid a prostitute £2000 to keep quiet about an alleged affair. Archer subsequently won a libel case against the newspaper that had made the original allegations, and a key figure in the trial was his wife Mary, who not only gave her husband her public support, but also influenced the judge's eventual verdict.[4]

CONCLUSION

Philip Schlesinger's 1978 study of news production was entitled *Putting Reality Together*, which rather neatly sums up the relationship between the de-

[3]This information became public following disclosures to a tabloid newspaper by Antonia de Sancha, a minor actress with whom Mellor had allegedly had an affair.

[4]The judge argued that a man was unlikely to seek the services of a prostitute when his wife had such "fragrance."

livery of news and the nature of its content. We do not know what is happening in "the world" unless we are part of it; even then we may have little more than a sketchy understanding of who did what, why, and what the consequences will be. News producers have to piece all this information together, often speculating wildly and misinterpreting what is said and done in search of a story that is not only coherent but also interesting. When rival news organs are competing against each other for readers and viewers, what price does the "truth" carry? In some respects, this chapter should be considered in relation to chapter 10 (on media representations): News producers have hours, sometimes minutes, to choose how to portray a perpetrator, a victim, or repercussions relating to a recent incident. Inevitably they will draw on stereotypes and other myths from the public domain to frame the story, and this frame may in turn influence how the audience interprets the story, or even whether they decide to buy the newspaper in the first place.

Chapter 13

Sport

This chapter begins, like the last, with a plausible scenario. You return home having just watched your favourite football team scrape by with a victory against their opponents; a reasonable game, largely unmemorable save for a controversial refereeing decision. Indeed, you have forgotten all about it as you walk through the door and head for the fridge to pour yourself a drink, mind focused on your plans for this evening. Your partner appears in the room and you prepare to relay the score and a pat comment about it being a run-of-the-mill victory. But before you can open your mouth s/he remarks: "I heard all about the match!"

"Yeah?" You pour your drink and wonder what the excitement is about.

"It was the lead item on the news," s/he continues. "I knew I should have come too."

Still perplexed, you ask: "What did they say?"

"Oh, well, the guy who started it is looking at a 6-month ban at least, and the referee may never recover."

"Guy who started *what*?"

"The punch-up in the tunnel after the game. Don't tell me you missed it."

"I didn't miss it. I was *there*."

"Still sounds like you missed it, though. Perhaps you should have stayed in and watched it on TV. . . ."

Nowhere is the distinction between media and "reality" more problematic than in the case of sport. We tend to think of the relationship between media and sport as fairly parasitic: Sport existed before mass communications, surely, and the media have just come along and corrupted it. In some cases this is a fair assessment, particularly in sports whose rules have changed to suit television companies and advertisers. Sport performers certainly see it that way; they are plying an honest trade and the media are a necessary evil, pouring money into their game while berating them for their on-field errors. However, for the majority of the viewing public, media shape sport in such a way that the games themselves are effectively a backdrop for a constantly unfolding drama with personalities, incidents, moral issues, feuds, heroism, betrayal, heartache, and elation. For this reason, some media scholars prefer to distinguish between sports in the pure sense and "MediaSport" (Wenner, 1998), literally a different ball game altogether.

Where do sports end and MediaSport begin? One way is to see sport as a media construction in itself; if the media present a game as a sport, it is a sport. Therefore, darts is a sport rather than a mere leisure pursuit, whereas tenpin bowling (competitive activity requiring a similar level of physical skill) is rarely classified as sport. Note the clear hierarchy suggested by *sport*; the label deems certain activities to be serious and worthwhile pursuits, whereas the labels *games* and *pastimes* denote mere idle pleasures. There is a clear distinction to be made between sports and games in terms of the seriousness with which they are taken by the media. Cooper-Chen (1994) examined this distinction in the light of gender, arguing that sports are elevated above game shows largely because they are enjoyed by men. I return to her argument shortly, but for the time being it is worth elaborating the point that valued activities are often determined by local culture to a degree that may appear purely arbitrary.

The intricacies of MediaSport are perhaps best understood by examining the impact of the media on specific sports. The most popular sport on a global scale is football (soccer); it is estimated that over a billion people watch the World Cup final every 4 years, and advertising generates phenomenal revenue throughout the world for rights to international and domestic competition. In the United Kingdom, after a slump in both attendances and viewing figures during the 1980s, public interest in the sport has been regenerated following the sale of exclusive rights to live domestic coverage to British Sky Broadcasting in the early 1990s. Football has managed to resist various attempts by the media to make it even more media friendly. For example, when the World Cup finals were held in the United States in 1994, the world governing body (FIFA) came under intense pressure from local television channels to widen the goals, in an attempt to raise the number of successful strikes to a level comparable to basketball or American football. Luckily the sport held out in favour of its traditions.

Although football has managed to avoid any major rule changes that might transform it as a spectacle, media influence has probably crept in via less obvious entry points. Advertising was once confined to the boards around the pitch, but now in most countries the leading clubs are obliged to wear their sponsors' name and logo on players' jerseys. In the United Kingdom and many European countries, the weekly football timetable, including the kickoff times of matches transmitted live, is dictated by the interests of the television companies, rendering the sporting calendar unrecognisable from earlier times. In England, club matches have traditionally been held on Saturday afternoons, but now Saturday Premiership programmes often feature as few as half the week's games. Half-time intervals of televised matches are strictly regulated in order to squeeze in the requisite number of ads.

One of the most profound effects of media coverage in recent years has involved the use of technology to settle issues in sport. For some years now, line calls in tennis have been made by an electronic device known as Cyclops. In cricket, technological innovation has considerably undermined the authority of the match officials. For many years, the availability of slow-motion replays have led commentators to question umpiring decisions, and much resentment has been felt by aggrieved players when television footage subsequently reveals the error. In 1992, during a tense match at Headingley, the England captain Graham Gooch was given "not out" by the umpire when the Pakistani fielders appealed for a run out, although the TV replay showed him to be well short of the mark. Gooch went on to complete a match-winning century and level the series. Later that year, the South Africa versus India series heralded the use of a "third umpire" who presided over run-out and stumping decisions by watching television replays off the field, a practice that has already become part of the modern game's tradition.[1]

The prying eyes of the television camera have done more than increase the need for pinpoint accuracy by officials. One of the most irritating developments in mediated sport, as far as performers are concerned, is that their every on-field gesture is now under scrutiny from a variety of camera angles. In football this has resulted in much post-hoc disciplinary action, in which match referees have "missed" off-the-ball incidents and the miscreants have been punished subsequently by administrative committees (it has also worked the other way round, with erroneous decisions being overturned). From an audience perspective, this scrutiny heightens the level of parasocial interaction with the players; now we are all armchair psychologists—inferring thoughts, motives, and intentions; studying body language; and drawing our own conclusions about "character," "temperament," personality, and even mental health.

These speculations form an integral part of the narrative structure of mediated sport, from the buildup to the events, the match commentary (of-

[1]The recent introduction, by both Sky and Channel 4, of software that is capable of predicting LBW (leg before wicket) decisions may further disempower on-field officials, although this particular means of dismissal will always contain an element of doubt.

ten superfluous, especially in individual sports like tennis) to the post-hoc analysis, much of it relayed by pundits (ex-performers), thus lending continuity and a sense of "sporting community" (Blain, Boyle, & O'Donnell, 1993). The personality characteristics of certain stars become part of the shared knowledge of the sport. Much discussion revolves around players who appear to lack emotional control and frequently incur the wrath of the match officials,[2] or players who seem to lack the moral fibre to compete consistently at the top level.[3] In team sport, attention is often focused as much on the coaches or team management, with frequent close-up camera shots in the dugout at tense moments.

It is psychological speculation about sports performers that usually pushes sport from its specialist role (typically referred to as "the back pages") to mainstream current affairs coverage. A good example of this occurred at the 1990 football World Cup in Italy, when star player Paul Gascoigne received a yellow card during the semi-final against (West) Germany. Gascoigne had emerged during the tournament as a favourite with both live and television audiences, but the referee's punishment meant that he would be suspended from the final if England were to win the present game.[4] Shortly after the award of the card, England captain Gary Lineker could be seen to be gesturing toward the team coach, pointing first at Gascoigne and then at his own eye. The camera then zoomed in on Gascoigne, visibly in tears, overcome at the disappointing prospect of missing the final. The British media had a field day; overnight, "Gazza" was transformed from a very good player into a legendary figure, familiar to the whole British public and beyond. This rare sight of a rugged masculine figure succumbing to such an overt emotional display struck a chord with

---

[2]Ian Wright, the former Arsenal and Crystal Palace striker (now a presenter of TV game shows), was frequently described as a player with a short fuse, who was reported to have taken a course in anger management during the latter stages of his career. However, much of the punditry surrounding Wright tended to query whether curbing his aggression might adversely affect his game. The assumption was that it was Wright's "innate" aggression that drove him as a player. A counterexample is the former Manchester United captain Eric Cantona, suspended for 6 months after kicking a spectator during the mid-1990s, whose long lay-off and penitence led to speculation that he would have to "behave" on his return and therefore tone down his aggression. This indeed happened, but Cantona appeared to benefit from a more responsible approach to the game, and led his team to the Premiership title that season.

[3]Another example from English football concerns mercurial striker Stan Collymore, whose career spanned several major clubs as he attempted to settle into a secure team place. A string of spectacular goals left nobody in any doubt as to his talent, but regular incidents involving teammates, managers, and romantic partners built up a picture of Collymore as a troubled soul, which seemed for the media to be confirmed when he eventually underwent stress therapy. Although Ian Wright tended to receive sympathy for his bursts of temper, Collymore has rather been held in contempt by the media—"awkward" rather than "fiery," and much less easy to handle in the macho world of football.

[4]Again, as it turned out, England lost. At least they got as far as a penalty shoot-out.

newspaper and television editors worldwide, and even in England the team's performance was soon pushed back to the specialist sports pages. Gazza's tears were a clear example of the difference between MediaSport and pure sport; they became a common cultural reference point rather than a specialised activity.

MOTIVATIONS FOR VIEWING AND ENJOYING SPORT

Why has sport become such a phenomenal media success? The answer may take in various economic and structural explanations, such as the potential exposure for advertisers and its ability to fill "dead" airtime for relatively little financial outlay, but there is no escaping the fact that sport is *popular.*

Research in the uses and gratifications tradition has examined media sport in terms of motives for viewing. Gantz (1981) identified three main motivations. Chief among these is "fanship" (or fandom), interpreted as the desire "to thrill in victory"; also important is the desire to "let loose," suggesting a kind of cathartic function for sport and, to a lesser extent, the desire to learn skills and tactics by watching top performers. We need to elaborate further on these, particularly because the viewing context is surely important; as Sapolsky and Zillmann (1978) found, viewing enjoyment of mediated sport differs between people watching at home and those watching in bars, and there are certainly differences between solitary and group viewing at home.

Fandom clearly plays a central role in media sports, as it does in sport more generally. Cialdini et al. (1976) noted that the supporters of college (American) football teams demonstrated higher affiliation with their sides after victories than after defeats. Cialdini et al. referred to this as a "basking" effect, whereby the team would be referred to as "we"—a practice that would be described within social identity theory as identification with a successful group in order to promote a positive self-image (Tajfel & Turner, 1979). In MediaSport, fan affiliation is different from actual sport; sports fans who attend matches often refer derisively to media sports fans as "armchair supporters." Here, "basking" is perhaps even more important, because there are relatively few teams to support who appear regularly on television, and they tend to be the most successful ones. Furthermore, many of the reasons for affiliating with actual sports teams rest with regional pride (i.e., supporting your local team), whereas MediaSport is conducted in the virtual world where proximity to a television or radio set is the only geographical factor.

Dechesne, Greenberg, Arndt, and Schimel (2000) argued that sports fandom can be explained in terms of terror management theory. Identification with winning teams, they suggested, produces a degree of self-worth that acts as a shield against the fear of dying. This was demonstrated in an experiment in which Dutch students were asked to predict the result of a forthcoming international football match against Germany. Half the students were also asked questions about their own death (what would it be like to die, what happens afterwards, etc.). It was this group that predicted significantly more goals for the Dutch team than did the control group (1.61 compared to 1.08), although the number of German goals was similar (1.20/1.25). A similar study was conducted with basketball fans in Arizona, where it was found that affiliation was stronger for the local basketball team after the local football team had lost, suggesting that glory seeking can cut across personal interests and preferences. This is certainly true of media sports coverage, in which popular sports may be interrupted to bring reports of national team victories in minority sports.

Although studies of terror management and basking may explain loose allegiances to sports teams, their findings may not necessarily explain the behaviour of committed sports fans. For example, it is highly unusual for sports fans (except, perhaps, young children) to change allegiances simply because their team loses. Indeed, the tenacity of sports fans resembles nothing so much as the ties of kinship (or "unreasonable care," as parenting researchers describe parent–child relations). Fandom is a core characteristic of identity and, in relation to mediated sport, spreads the basking effect more generally—it does not matter whether our team wins or loses so long as it makes the headlines. Writer Nick Hornby captured the effect perfectly in the book *Fever Pitch* (1992), his autobiographical account of life as a fan of English football team Arsenal:

> You know that on nights like the '89 championship night, or on afternoons like the afternoon of the 1992 Wrexham disaster, you are in the thoughts of scores, maybe even hundreds, of people . . . old girlfriends and other people you have lost touch with and will probably never see again are sitting in front of their TV sets and thinking, momentarily but *all at the same time*, Nick, just that, and are happy or sad for me. (pp. 194–195)

Hornby's affiliation with Arsenal is an essential part of his social identity. Such attachments may explain all manner of fandoms, within sport and outside it, and is not reliant on the object of identification necessarily being successful. However, it is unlikely that an "armchair supporter" will choose initially to associate with a losing side.

It has been argued that affiliation with winning teams has less to do with social identity and more to do with individual well-being. Various studies have examined the effect of sports results on self-reported mood. Schwarz, Strack, Kommer, and Wagner (1987) noted that a victory for the (West) German football team resulted in significantly higher levels of global well-being, job satisfaction, and political optimism than did a disappointing draw. In a study in the early 1990s (Schweitzer, Zillmann, Weaver, & Luttrell, 1992), American college students were asked questions about the possibility of conflict in the Gulf after watching their local football teams either winning or losing. Compared with controls, the losing supporters were more likely to predict the possibility of war, and predicted far higher war casualties than did winning supporters (69,300 U.S. soldiers to be killed in action, compared with 22,800). These findings suggest that depressed mood caused by watching your team lose has a more profound effect than does elated mood caused by victory.

Cooper-Chen (1994) suggested a number of additional features that make MediaSport so attractive. One is that (live) sport has *immediacy*; it takes place in real time, unlike scripted drama. This means, as much as anything, that it has a heightened level of realism—as we see in chapter 15, one of the defining characteristics of soaps is the sense of a parallel universe in which action is unfolding simultaneously with our own lives. In sport, however, there is nothing "parallel" about the universe it describes; its universe is shared by the viewers. This lends MediaSport the quality of *independence*; unlike drama, sport seems to exist regardless of media involvement, and the media create the impression of simply being bystanders to record the action. As a result, sport has the air of *purity*; it is not scripted by a producer, but instead is contained by its own set of rules and any result is the outcome of luck or skill. Finally, sport results in *closure*—at the end of viewing, there is a result, and each fixture leads on clearly to the next.[5]

In addition to the features just discussed, a key element in sport is its status as a "mythic ritual" (Real, 1977). Events such as the football World Cup final and Wimbledon singles finals offer live cultural experiences that are shared simultaneously by television viewers around the world. At the national level, events like the Superbowl (in the United States) and the FA Cup final (in the United Kingdom) likewise constitute an "imaginary community" that carries patriotic overtones, particularly when the events are idiosyncractic, such as the Oxford versus Cambridge boat race (viewed by millions who have no particular interest in rowing the rest of the year round). Such is the cultural importance of these events that in the 1990s the British government labelled them the "crown jewels" in the state-owned BBC's annual schedule, and the corporation has since fought tooth and nail against commercial television to maintain exclusive rights.[6]

[5]This does not apply to all sports; cricket test matches, for example, are spread across 5 days, and may be drawn—a result, of course, but one that fails to provide satisfactory closure for the unconverted.

[6]Not always successfully; gradually the financial clout of commercial television is winning out. Home cricket test matches, long held to be central to BBC programming, were finally sold to Channel 4 and BskyB in 1999.

PROBLEMATIC ASPECTS OF SPORT IN THE MEDIA

Although sport is a source of enjoyment and often elation for millions of media users across the world, inevitably psychological and communications research have focused on its less positive aspects. The literature can be roughly divided into three areas of negative aspects of media sport: the "effects" of sporting aggression on spectator and viewer behaviour, its role in promoting inequalities in gender, and its contribution to xenophobia and even racism.

Violence

Sport-related violence comes in many forms, from rule-bound aggressive contact in sports such as boxing and rugby, to on-field breaches of the rules in football and ice hockey, and off-field conflict between rival groups of fans. The boundary between the first two types is blurred, with opinion sharply divided within and without the sporting community as to the status of boxing as a sport. Almost every casualty in a major boxing bout is followed by calls from medical authorities and various media commentators for a ban on boxing, but prize money continues to call the tune. Furthermore, the world of boxing is so loosely structured that it is hard to see how a ban could be enforced without breaching other liberties.

Violence in ice hockey has long been a problem in the sport, and yet it is clear that for many spectators is it not only acceptable but it also forms an integral part of the excitement generated by the game. The use of the "sin bin"—where offending players are sent to cool off for a period of time—seems only to contribute to the expectation that violence will occur (in most sports, violent acts are punished by dismissing the miscreants from the game altogether). In rugby and American football, so much aggressive contact is allowed by the rules that it has proved easy for players to sneak in punches and stamps undetected. Squeezing opponents' testicles during the scrum has long been part of rugby's traditions, although camera close-ups are making even these transgressions increasingly risky.

Concern for the welfare of sports performers has not been the main focus of the limited research on the psychological effects of sports violence; like research into media violence more generally, the fear is that the sight of men bashing one another around the head will inspire viewers, especially young ones, to do likewise in the street or home. Bryant, Zillmann, and Raney (1998) found a clear linear relationship between the amount of aggression in sport and the level of spectator enjoyment, particularly for men (but note that the overall trend is similar for women). If the catharsis theory is correct, sport should have a pacifying effect, although some research has linked on-field violence to off-field trouble (Celozzi, Kazelskis, &

Gutsch, 1981). The excitation transfer hypothesis (see chap. 4) suggests that play need not be violent but simply exciting, to stir up aggression, and this may account for some early reports of violence at football games in the United Kingdom. However, football hooliganism has since become a far more complex issue, and today has little connection with on-field activity except in terms of overall result (hooliganism tends to be worst when the team supported by the hooligans has lost[7]).

One of the more interesting aspects of sport-related violence is the part played by the media. As hinted in the vignette at the start of this chapter, media coverage of sport is usually only imported into the mainstream from the specialist media when something controversial occurs. Partly this is because such incidents cross the divide between sport and everyday life. However, there is a tendency even in the sports media to dwell on transgressions of the rules and on disciplinary issues. Several studies suggest that match commentary is a major factor in promoting sport as an aggressive spectacle. An experiment by Comisky, Bryant, and Zillmann (1977) discerned a direct correspondence between the commentator's emphasis on rough play and participants' own perceptions of roughness. When the commentary dwelled on aggressive incidents, they were seen by viewers as aggressive; if the commentary ignored them, they were not noted by viewers as aggressive incidents. A related study (Bryant, Brown, Comisky, & Zillmann, 1982) found that even in a noncontact sport (tennis), when the commentary described two opponents as bitter enemies, viewers rated the match as more hostile and tense. Any criticism that the viewers' level of interest and knowledge about these sports may have influenced results was dealt with in a study by Sullivan (1991), who, using a similar experimental paradigm, noted that even experienced fans were strongly influenced by commentary on a basketball game.

In terms of crowd violence, it has long been thought by television producers that trouble was exacerbated by media coverage. This was clearly the case in some early incidents of football hooliganism in England in the 1970s, in which the popular tabloid newspaper the *Daily Mirror* unwittingly put together a "league of violence" based on numbers of fans arrested at

---

[7]Nick Hornby (1992) made the interesting point that football hooliganism at club level in England seems to correspond with the clubs' declining fortunes. Manchester United were the first club to become strongly related to hooliganism after being relegated from the old First Division in 1973. Other clubs with notorious fan reputations earned these during periods outside the top flight—notably West Ham, Millwall, Birmingham City, and Chelsea. Although Man Utd and Chelsea seem to have shed their hooligan following, Millwall and Birmingham held on to theirs for longer, possibly due to their relatively low status. At international level, England's hooligan problems seem to be related to their relative lack of success on the world stage, although clearly poor results cannot explain the continuation of violence, which is related to xenophobia and may be habitual as much as anything (media expectations of trouble do not always help matters).

each club. The *Mirror's* intention was to shame fans into good behaviour; unsurprisingly, it seemed to provoke them into further misdeeds by rewarding the leading clubs' hooligan element with a hierarchical status. As Dunning, Murphy, and Williams (1988) pointed out, this amounted to nothing less than a *celebration* of hooligan reputations by the media. Despite media interest in the more salacious aspects of sport violence, television producers have maintained a prudishness about audience misbehaviour whereby, even today, fans who invade the field of play are pointedly ignored by the cameras and commentators, often to the point of absurdity (as when there is no explanation given for crowd excitement with the cameras focused on, say, a long-distance shot out of the stadium).

Gender

For some academic scholars, that sport should be riven with excess aggression and violence is hardly surprising. Watching sport is largely a male activity; indeed, as Condry (1989) commented, it is the only television genre for which male viewers outnumber females. Furthermore, there is a serious underrepresentation of women in sport media, even when actual participation in sport is more equal; this has been termed the "symbolic annihilation" of women in sport (Gerbner, 1978). Of the cover stars of *Sports Illustrated* magazine between 1954 and 1978, only 5% were female. For Hargreaves (1986), this situation benefits men; women are excluded from sport in order to maintain it as a prime site for displays of male power. Although men are in control, Hargreaves asserted, sport is governed by the virtues of muscularity and strength, in which women are clearly inferior, with statistics to prove it.

Would greater female representation in media sport force an appreciation of elegance and other "feminine" virtues? Hargreaves' theory is not shared by all feminist authors, some of whom maintain that women are held back from serious competition from an early age and thus never acquire the musculature necessary for top-level participation. Creedon (1994) argued that the problem for women sports performers is that they are always judged against male norms: if women play as well as men, they are judged as aberrant. Interestingly, a series of experiments found that although both men and women participants judged women's sport as inferior in terms of skill and excitement, both genders were more appreciative if the objective was to *learn* from viewing sport. In other words, they could admire the technique of the female sports performers, even if the overall spectacle was rated as less attractive.

Much of the research into the representation of gender in media sports has focused on underrepresentation. Not only are women featured less often than men, but when they are featured there is a tendency to dwell on nonathletic aspects of the stars, such as their off-field relationships. Alternatively, coverage of female athletes is limited to "feminine" sports such as ice skating and gymnastics (Kane & Greendorfer, 1994). Although there has been more coverage of women's participation in sports such as football in the 1990s and early 21st century, a recent Swedish study still found that less than 2% of airtime was devoted to women playing traditionally "masculine" sports (Koivula, 1999). Much coverage of sporting success by Swedish females was relegated to end-piece status within sports reports ("and to end with, some good news—the Swedish women's team have won a medal in X"), and even when live events were covered, the production was often considerably poorer than for men's sport, with limited camera angles and other technological resources.

When female athletes finally attract the attention of the media, it often dwells on intrinsically "feminine" aspects of their personalities. Kane and Greendorfer (1994) compared the media coverage of the American sprinter Florence Griffith-Joyner ("FloJo") during the 1988 and 1992 Olympics with that of heptathlete Jackie Joyner-Kersee (FloJo's sister-in-law). Despite the fact that the latter won gold medals at both tournaments, there was substantially more coverage for FloJo, much of it focusing on her fashion sense, notably her elongated fingernails. More recently, the coverage of glamorous Russian tennis star Anna Kournikova has vastly outweighed that of far more successful players. For example, Kournikova withdrew at the start of the 2001 Wimbledon championships due to a foot injury, yet she still commanded more front-page coverage than did the players who remained in the tournament.

Like other cases of under- and misrepresentation (see chap. 10), it seems that women's status in sports media will only change when women comprise a more substantial force at the level of production. The last 10 years have seen more and more women obtaining roles as sports presenters (although fewer as commentators and pundits), but even some of the successes can be attributed more to telegenic factors than to expertise. However, it does seem that things are at last moving in the right direction.

Xenophobia and Racism

The power of sport to unite a nation has underpinned much of its success in the media. Alas, patriotism often begets xenophobia, and although sport manages to bring different cultures and nations together, the media coverage of international sport frequently descends into crude stereotyping and even outright racism.

Blain et al. (1993) conducted a broad investigation of national representations in sport-related media and found that sport presents media in general with a tremendous opportunity to reproduce xenophobic or stereotypical discourses about national identity to a remarkably consistent degree across Europe. For example, different European media outlets tended to deploy the same representations of African sports performers, and even tended to deploy the same representations of each other. Although stereotyping seemed to be universal, the English media (notably its tabloid newspapers) were found to be uniquely unpleasant, particularly toward close neighbours France and Germany.

In the English media, much stereotyping could be seen as attempts to excuse poor performance without crediting opposing teams. For example, English teams were often characterised as lacking the "killer instinct" necessary for sporting success. However, teams that possess killer instinct seem to lose out in other departments—hence, the Germans are framed as overserious, humourless, and ruthlessly efficient, whereas other teams' will to win is characterised as irrational, resulting from a surfeit of passion (attributed in the case of the Pakistani cricket team to religious fanaticism). Blain et al. discerned that specific devices were employed in international sports media that had the effect of implying inferiority. One such device is the use of the term *temperament*, which is rarely used approvingly. Typically, *temperament* is invoked to account for negative behaviour; for example, a "Latin temperament" implies passion and a lack of self-control, resulting in bursts of temper, extravagant gesticulations, and unpredictable mood swings. Players from Central and South America such as the West Indies cricketers and Brazilian footballers are admired for their "natural athleticism" but are also prone to "temperamental outbursts."

One of the most problematic issues surrounding representations of different ethnic groups in sports is the debate about the apparent natural superiority of athletes of African descent. A cursory glance at athletics competition leaves the casual onlooker in little doubt about this. The vast majority of successful international sprinters are Black, whether they represent the United States, West Indies, or European nations. Ergo, Black people must be superior in terms of the musculature required for running fast. Indeed, many serious articles have appeared in various sport media offering theories about muscle fibres and other biological factors that contribute to Black athletic success. Roger Bannister, the (White) British runner who famously broke the 4-minute mile barrier, delivered a speech to the British Association for the Advancement of Science in 1995 in which he forwarded a (speculative) theory that people of African descent had a longer heel bone that gave them an advantage in athletics (Hoberman, 1997).

However, the various theories fail to account for a number of anomalies regarding ethnicity and sport. They do not explain why the apparent Black superiority in sprinting fails to transfer to any other athletics events, or indeed other sports generally. Furthermore, as biological theories, they should predict clear differences between athletes of direct African descent and those with mixed ethnic background, although such a "hierarchy of Blackness" does not appear to operate in sport, even in sprinting. The "superior natural athleticism" argument is part of a wider racist discourse that has evolved over the last few centuries as a tactic for White supremacy and Eurocentrism more generally. It is interesting how many variations on the theme can be employed to counter disconfirming evidence. The history of Afro-Caribbean players in British football has been accompanied by many different variations of the same tune in the media.

CONCLUSION

Given sport's violent and bloody history, back to the days of mediaeval jousting and Roman gladiators, one might argue that it could be treated under the banner of "media violence." Yet, with the exception of boxing, the two have rarely been studied together by media researchers. There are many grounds for arguing that, psychologically, media sport and media violence have common appeal, and this may explain why we become so absorbed in cases in which sports performers break the rules and dabble in controversial behaviour. Our fascination with these matters is captured perfectly by that hilarious caricature of professional sport, the World Wrestling Federation. The action in the ring, which is effectively masterful choreography, takes place to the accompaniment of a commentary concerning almost anything other than the action; it usually focuses on the "rivalry" between the wrestlers, which invariably erupts in full-scale violence, with referees being assaulted and opponents chased out of the ring and into the audience. This is accompanied by much verbal bravado in which contestants seize the broadcasting equipment to harangue one another (and the commentators), parodying the rhetorical jousting that precedes professional boxing bouts.

Much as sporting purists might disagree, the living soap that surrounds the on-field action is an intrinsic element in the attraction of MediaSport. It produces a drama that is acted out in the media generally (in news bulletins and other current affairs programming), often to the irritation of the performers themselves. In this way, the appeal of sport is not dissimilar to that of fictional drama.

Chapter 14

Audience Participation and Reality TV

During the late 1990s, Maureen Rees, a woman from Cardiff in Wales, became a national superstar in the United Kingdom after appearing on a BBC series, *Driving School.* This series followed the experiences of driving instructors by recording some of their lessons and tracking selected learners through to their tests. Maureen was a student who presented her instructor with a major challenge: She appeared incapable of mastering the basic skills of driving, but was desperate to pass her test. Gritty determination paid off and, on her eighth attempt, she finally passed the test in a car with an automatic gearbox. What gripped the series' producers, and eventually the watching millions, were Maureen's practice sessions, filmed in her own car with her husband Dave in the passenger seat, where she was seen weaving dangerously in and out of busy traffic lanes—horns blaring from all sides—and mounting the pavement in an attempt to reverse around a corner. By the end of 1997, Maureen had been featured in most national newspapers and on other television shows, and had become a celebrity as well known, for a limited period, as leading politicians and artistic and sporting achievers.

We are growing increasingly familiar with seeing "ordinary" people on television. Audience participation shows now constitute a substantial portion of programming, from long-standing game shows to audience "talk" shows, "docusoaps,"[1] fly-on-the-wall documentaries, and "makeover" shows. In recent years the expression "reality TV" has been coined as an umbrella

[1]Not to be confused with "docudramas," which are reconstructions of actual events, such as Jimmy McGovern's TV drama *Hillsborough* (1996) that recreated the 1989 Hillsborough football stadium tragedy in Sheffield. These are not audience-participation shows and really

term for audience-participation shows, although it has been applied largely to shows such as *Big Brother*, originally a Dutch game show in which ordinary members of the public (and occasionally celebrities) share living space for several weeks, the winner decided by the television audience. The format has since been exported to many other countries, and has been modified to produce variations such as *Survivor* and *Castaway* (set on remote islands). The contestants of these shows have become national celebrities in their respective countries.

The popularity of this type of programming raises a number of psychological issues, for both participants and the watching audience. Which aspects of reality TV shows appeal most to audiences, and why? What motivates individual viewers to participate in these shows, and what are the psychological consequences of participation? Finally, what does this genre tell us about the relationship between public and private life, and the nature of reality itself in the context of media? Unfortunately, psychology has been as slow to pick up on this aspect of media as on any other, perhaps understandably cautious of a television genre that may prove to be short lived. Even if this is the case, audience-participation media in general provide some fascinating snapshots of human behaviour, making excellent material for psychological research.

AUDIENCE-PARTICIPATION MEDIA: A HISTORY

As mass media, television and radio were introduced with the idea that they would convey information from authority to a viewing public; King George V was one of the first figures to speak on BBC television. In the 1930s, BBC radio in Manchester presented shows in which presenter Frank Nicholls, under the guise of "Harry Hopeful," interviewed members of the public about their daily activities. The series was broadcast live in front of a studio audience, although much of the material was recorded in interviewees' houses (Scannell, 1996). During World War II, in an attempt to boost national morale, the BBC took their outside broadcast unit around the country, finding and reporting on important contributions to the "war effort." In shows such as *Go To It!* and *We Speak for Ourselves*, working-class people were interviewed in factories by well-known Yorkshire presenter Wilfred Pickles. After the war, *Have a Go!* (also fronted by Pickles) turned this basic format into a quiz show, creating the formula for audience-participation media to come.

---

belong to the genre of news and current affairs, although their dramatised nature—and their impact on the viewing public—raise some interesting questions about truth and reality. See Paget (1998) for a lively discussion of the issues and some detailed examples.

Even the basic dialogue in *Have a Go!* paralleled that of many of today's audience-participation shows, in that guests were introduced to the listeners in a formal style that displayed "the minimal components of any person's identity-kit in our kind of society" (Scannell, 1996, p. 55). Details such as name, address, and occupation are obtained, followed by more exploratory questions about favourite foods, embarrassing moments, and romantic status. An extract from a typical show was reported by Scannell (p. 53):

Pickles	And that brings our first er personality to the microphone and she's a very charming lady with nice grey hair and a very nice grey frock. It's very nice to have you here will you tell me your name?
Florrie	Mrs Florence Holt.
Pickles	Mes (.) Florence?
Florrie	Yes.
Pickles	'Ave a go Flo! [*Shrieks of laughter*]
Pickles	Mrs Florence Holt and where where d'you live?

It was clear right from the start of audience-participation media that although they were genuine "members of the public," the contestants were handpicked inasmuch as they were felt to be representative of the population (i.e., the residents of the locale) and that listeners would be able to identify with them. They also had to sound good on the radio; thus, they would be screened to some extent for their performative abilities. During this period, quiz shows began to appear regularly on radio stations in the United States, where members of the studio audience would compete for small cash prizes (even the BBC awarded cash in its earliest shows). The show *Dr. IQ*, presented by Lew Valentine, asked simple questions of selected audience members and, if the contestants answered correctly, paid them in silver dollars on the spot (Goedkoop, 1985). Some shows specialised in a particular field, such as musical knowledge; others, such as *Quiz Kids*, featured child contestants. The first television quiz show was broadcast by the BBC in 1938; entitled *Spelling Bee*, it involved members of the public attempting to spell difficult words. Not surprisingly, it had a very short run.

Television Game Shows

Despite attempts, few of the popular American radio shows transferred successfully to television, but during the 1950s the quiz show format became extremely successful, and by 1957 half of the 10 highest-rated network shows were quiz shows (Goedkoop, 1985). Probably the most well known of these is *The $64,000 Question*, adapted from a radio show with a top prize of a mere $64. It attracted sponsorship from the cosmetics company Revlon, made stars out of "ordinary" contestants, and scooped 85% of the viewing audience. However, in 1958 it was cancelled, along with several other popular quiz shows, following a "rigging" scandal that led to the producer of *Twenty-One* being charged with perjury. It later emerged that many contestants on *Twenty-One* had been offered bribes and advance information in order to keep them appearing on the show and thus become recognisable figures for the viewing audience.

Partly as a result of the rigging scandal, the makers of 1960s game shows began to dream up nonmonetary prizes. One big success during this period was *The Dating Game*, in which a contestant asked questions of three hidden competitors and eventually selected one to join him or her on an exotic romantic outing. The formula was recycled in the 1980s by the U.K. company Granada in the guise of *Blind Date*, which became one of the United Kingdom's longest-running and most popular television shows. Indeed, numerous game shows around the world are variants on U.S. shows from the 1950s and 1960s. One difference between game shows from early periods and later shows is that the originals were usually screened live, and thus offered audiences many of the gratifications provided by live sporting events, such as unpredictability and the air of authenticity. This may explain why the United States was so shocked by the rigging scandal, leading President Eisenhower to declare it "a terrible thing to do to the American people" (Wheen, 1985). The "live" feel has been retained in later variations, even though most game shows are now prerecorded, suggesting that it forms a key element of the appeal of such programming.[2]

The basic game show format had been stretched beyond all recognition by the early 21st century, although remaining extremely popular with audiences.[3] Many contemporary game shows based on the traditional format tend to involve celebrity panelists, although some of the most popular include traditional quiz shows such as *Who Wants to Be a Millionaire?* (at its peak attracting 30 million viewers per show in the United States) and *The Weakest Link.* However the most controversial game show format in recent years is the reality TV genre, in which members of the public compete against each other for monetary prizes based on audience popularity. *Big Brother*, the first such show, was aired in Holland, and was quickly adopted by many other American and European countries. In the United Kingdom, the press attention for the first two series (and a celebrity version for charity) has been phenomenal, turning nearly all the contestants into major

[2]This can be seen most clearly in *Who Wants to Be a Millionaire?*, where ad breaks are organised around key moments when contestants are on the verge of answering big-money questions (an ingenious way of retaining the suspense intrinsic to the quiz show format).

[3]Popular with television bosses too, because they represent one of the cheapest forms of the medium.

personalities, and attracting a barrage of critical opinion on everything from the show's ethics to the worthlessness of modern celebrity. Among the show's innovations, some versions have allowed computer users round-the-clock access to WebCams set up in the house (supplemented by live coverage on cable TV).

The reality genre has taken root in modern television as other producers have dreamed up real-life scenarios in which an element of competition can be introduced. A Swedish TV show, *Expedition Robinson,* sent a group of young contestants to live on a remote island for 40 days, and the final episode of the first series of its U.S. version, *Survivor,* attracted 50 million viewers. The BBC version, *Castaway,* was more ambitious, placing several families on a Scottish island for a whole year. In 2000, ITV screened *PopStars,* a competition among young people to put together a singing group; this was immensely popular with the viewing audience as the initial contestants were whittled down to the final lineup, who have since gone on, perhaps predictably, to enjoy considerable chart success.

Talk Shows

A separate, although ultimately related, development over the years has been the emergence of the "talk show" as a major genre of television programming. The category talk show covers a wide range of shows that, like game shows, are oriented around a single personality or host who presides over the contribution of a participating audience, but without any element of competition. The earliest precursor of talk shows was probably *Broadway Open House* (first screened in 1950), on which comedian Jerry Lester hosted a late-night variety show that involved celebrity guests and some audience participation (Rose, 1985). Steve Allen presented a similar show in the mid-1950s, albeit with some outrageous stunts, including occasional forays into the studio audience for comments. Around this time, however, came the rise of the "chat show," in which a host would conduct conversation with invited celebrity guests; this type of programme became very popular in Europe as well, making stars out of hosts such as Johnny Carson, Michael Parkinson, and Russell Harty.

The talk show of today has its origins with *The Phil Donahue Show* in the 1960s. Donahue was a newscaster who began to run audience discussion shows in which he would roam around the studio audience, carrying a microphone and inviting questions directed at the celebrity or expert guests seated on stage (and taking a certain number of calls from viewers). Soon the audience contribution began to dictate the schedule in its own right. Because the audience was 99% female, many of the discussion topics centred on women's interests, and the show attained a certain notoriety for covering sexual topics in some detail. Unlike game shows—which, with a few exceptions, tend to be presented by a male host—talk shows became a popular site for female presenters, such as Oprah Winfrey, Vanessa Feltz, and Ricki Lake (Shattuc, 1997).

In the United Kingdom during the late 1980s, former MP Robert Kilroy-Silk began a long-running morning discussion show (*Kilroy*) on which serious political and social issues—such as working mothers, state benefits, racism, and homophobia—were debated alongside "lighter" issues such as psychic phenomena and sexual preferences. During the 1990s, however, there was a gradual weighting toward the latter category, as talk show topics move from the political to the personal. Hosts have become increasingly young and more "ordinary," moving away from the authoritative tone of Kilroy, Oprah, and other figures with backgrounds in serious programming, toward figures with whom the audience could identify directly. As an example, here are the themes from some late-1990s episodes of *The Ricki Lake Show* (from Shattuc, 1998):

Listen family, I'm gay . . . it's not a phase . . . get over it!
Girl, you're easy because you're fat . . . respect yourself ASAP
Someone slap me! Today I meet my all-time favorite star

The colloquial English in these titles indicates the informal nature of the contemporary discussion show, and the titles' directness is a signal for potential conflict. Security guards have reportedly confiscated guns from audience members, and their presence in the audience seems to invite hostility among guests. On *The Jerry Springer Show,* conflict is more than merely suggested; indeed, that particular show has been criticised as "voyeuristic" entertainment. Many critics are concerned about the way that such shows seem to goad some of the poorest and most volatile members of society—"trailer-park trash and ghetto kids" as one producer referred to the audience (Gamson, 1998)—into bad behaviour: "It is not that *Ricki Lake* is beset by aggressive viewers; the show actively constructs them" (Shattuc, 1998, p. 218).

The rigging scandal has also reared its head again in the controversy over "fake" guests on talk shows. In recent years, U.K. shows *Vanessa* and *Trisha* have both been accused of presenting guests who lied about their relationship (e.g., one episode of *Vanessa* featured two women who falsely claimed to be sisters, although the researcher who booked them denied all knowledge of their fake status).[4] There is something almost Barnumesque about the appeal of viewers debating whether certain audience members have been planted by the show's producers, or whether they are acting up for the cameras. As Shattuc (1998) pointed out, however, there is a very thin line between the authenticity of fake guests and those who are simply

[4]Indeed, the researcher has since accepted libel damages following a national news story that she had been implicated in planting these fakes.

revelling in performance. She described a punk/Gothic couple on *Jerry Springer* in complete "regalia," one of whom entered the stage "sashaying to the rhythmic beat of the audience clapping while tossing confetti" (p. 220).

"Candid Video"

A third form of audience participation media has emerged largely through the availability of technological equipment that enables members of the public (i.e., untrained television producers) to acquire footage of their own activities. O'Sullivan (1998) called this genre "candid video," which refers to the technology of the video camera but also to the guiding inspiration behind much of this sort of television: the *Candid Camera* show, first aired as a segment in a variety show by producer Allen Funt back in 1948. *Candid Camera* set up discreet recording equipment to film unsuspecting members of the public blundering into booby traps set up by the show's producers (e.g., a motor showroom salesperson selling a car to a client and removing the engine before the client attempted to drive it away). Later on the same format, supplemented with superior technological equipment (although a somewhat less naïve public) was used by British presenter Jeremy Beadle in the show *Beadle's About.*

Up to this point, the audience participation in such programming had been mostly passive, as compliant (with regard to allowing film to go out) victims of producers' pranks. However, the prevalence of handheld camcorders led Beadle to put together a new show, *You've Been Framed,* which invited viewers to send in footage of their own blunders and mistakes. Audiences responded enthusiastically, and a whole new genre sprung up involving homemade television. Serious programmes were also made, such as the BBC series *Video Diaries* and *Video Nation,* to which members of the public sent in short, soapbox-style clips of themselves discussing their everyday lives or their opinions on a topical social issue. In some ways this style of programming completes a nice circle from the Harry Hopeful radio series, just dispensing with the interviewer en route.

"Makeover Television"

A final audience participation genre has emerged in recent years in which members of the public appear alongside experts from fields such as cookery, DIY, gardening, estate management, and fashion. The object of most of these shows is for the expert to display his or her skills while at the same time providing a service for a member of the public. For example, in the BBC series *Ground Force,* a team of gardening and/or construction experts descend on the home of an unsuspecting viewer while he or she is away from home (typically, a member of a couple whose partner has contacted the show and is often present during early stages of filming). The experts then gradually transform the viewer's existing garden into a state-of-the-art showcase, with the producer capturing their comments on the decision-making process and the camera recording them in the act of planting shrubs, laying decking, painting fences blue, and so on. The show's climax arrives when the unsuspecting viewer returns home, usually having been stalled by his or her partner, and whose response is filmed at the moment of revelation.

An early example of this genre is *Style Challenge,* perhaps the first true "makeover" show, which began life as a slot in a daytime magazine programme, drawing on traditions from U.S. talk shows that often feature a "makeover" slot in which an audience member is restyled with the latest hairstyle and a designer outfit (Moseley, 2000). A popular subgenre in the United Kingdom (cashing in on the 1990s property boom) consists of shows on which property experts find homes for househunters, or transform their interiors to add value to their existing properties. There is even a cable channel devoted to makeover and similar programmes (UK Style).

In traditional documentary programming and game shows it has long been customary to film members of the public trying their hand at new skills and tasks. *The Generation Game,* for example, would contain at least one round in which contestants would be required to emulate the skilled performance of an expert (e.g., paper folding or cookery); the winner would be the contestant whose effort was judged to be closest to the model, affording much hilarity at the expense of less dextrous performers. A recent variant on this, *Can't Cook, Won't Cook,* involves participants attempting to prepare a gourmet meal. These shows have always provided popular entertainment, although they are never empowering for participants; instead they are merely platforms for the celebrity presenters.

A more recent trend is for audience/expert collaborations to provide some benefit for the participant. In some cases, this involves learning a new skill, but in most it is a matter of a novice participant benefiting from the experts' contributions. An additional element in makeover programming is that they are closely tied to sponsorship and marketing opportunities—there is much product placement. Shows like *Ground Force* and *Changing Rooms* (its DIY interior equivalent) advertise home improvement more generally, and have been credited with the DIY boom in the United Kingdom in the 1990s. Househunting and selling shows perform a similar function in relation to the property market. At their most extreme, makeover shows intend to benefit participants in the longer term, because they acquire training for new skills, often social skills. A very popular Channel 4 series *Faking*

It (2000) documented, among other transformations, the successful attempts of two female house DJs (and a performance coach) to transform a young classical cellist into a credible nightclub DJ within a month.

THE APPEAL OF AUDIENCE-PARTICIPATION MEDIA

As far as television companies are concerned, audience-participation programming has many benefits: It tends to be cheap, especially when the users are also the producers (e.g., *Video Diaries,* although there is no real sign of any increase in this type of programme), and it is certainly popular. Many television personalities have been created through the shows—usually the presenters, but also certain experts and, occasionally, members of the public (particularly in reality TV shows). For the audience, the main attraction is clearly the participation of members of the public, which has the effect of breaking down the private/public barrier. This raises numerous issues for media psychology.

Parasocial Interaction and Identification

Undoubtedly the basis of the appeal of audience-participation television is that viewers recognize versions of themselves on screen. As discussed in chapter 11, there are several processes operating here, which can be broadly defined as "parasocial" interaction. However, it is likely that identification is a key process, at least in the sense that viewers relate to and can empathise with the members of the public who appear in these shows.[5] It is therefore essential that viewers identify guests as belonging to a shared category of "the audience"; this is one of the reasons why fakery and inauthenticity are so problematic for this type of programme.

Livingstone and Lunt (1994), in their analysis of talk shows (or "audience-discussion programmes"),[6] viewed such programmes as a revival of the "public sphere." This concept, from Habermas (1989), describes the public sphere as a social realm uniting individuals into a larger body through which public opinion is formed. Habermas argued that the media has effectively killed off such a sphere, reducing us all to passive, isolated

[5]An interesting paper by Horton and Strauss (1957) discussed the phenomenon of parasocial interaction with audience-participation media, concentrating mainly on game show hosts.

[6]Mostly *Kilroy,* which, although still running, is somewhat different from the majority of 1990s talk shows in that it often deals with serious political and social issues; typically, politicians and professionals are engaged in heated debate with members of the public. The evolution of talk shows since the mid-1990s, particularly in the United States, suggests that their vision of the reawakening of the public sphere may prove to be somewhat optimistic.

spectators, unwilling to act politically. Livingstone and Lunt maintained that the talk show actually gives the public a voice that empowers minority groups (among others) and acts as a vital forum for public debate and a mouthpiece for opinion. At the same time, talk shows are necessarily heavily scripted, and may be capable of stifling anything too radical.

Ultimately, the public/private distinction arises from the way in which audience participation shows are constructed. Livingstone and Lunt described how Kilroy-Silk introduces "experts" into the discussion, plays them off against the audience and each other, and how the show as a whole constructs the studio audience as the "ordinary" public. This is a clear example of the way in which identity is often the result of locally negotiated discourse (Antaki, Condor, & Levine, 1996). A medical doctor appearing on *Kilroy* may be constructed as an expert in a discussion on doctor–patient interaction, but the same individual could just as easily be cast as an ordinary member of the public in a discussion about nuclear waste.

Although group identification may be essential for the enjoyment of audience participation shows, it is not necessary for viewers to identify with each individual. Indeed, the talk show in particular is a genre whose appeal is best described by a more general sense of parasocial interaction. The talk show acts as a "surrogate salon" (Greenfield, 1977), that creates a sense of "presence"—the feeling that we are *there* (Lombard & Ditton, 1997). As one viewer put it, "It's as though I'm having an argument with some people" (Livingstone & Lunt, 1994, p. 84). Uses-and-gratifications theorists have argued that parasocial interaction may be used to compensate for lack of social contact, and indeed studies of talk radio have found that enthusiasts prefer to listen alone, even if only during the context of the broadcast (Bierig & Dimmick, 1979).

In other forms of audience-participation television, certain members of the public clearly stand out and become memorable, perhaps because they share some of the characteristics of the viewing audience who can thus empathise with their experiences (e.g., Maureen Rees in *Driving School*, Helen from the 2001 U.K. *Big Brother*), or because they have an exceptional ability or personality. One of the first celebrities to emerge as a direct result from appearing in an audience-participation show was Gino Prato, a shoe repairman from the Bronx, who appeared on *The $64,000 Question* and became renowned as an expert on opera; likewise, in the United Kingdom, London taxi driver Fred Housego became *MasterMind* champion.

One of the problems for members of the public who become famous in this way is that they often struggle, after an initial honeymoon phase, to maintain their celebrity status, particularly when the cause of their fame has long passed. Several of the contestants on the U.K. version of *Big Brother* found it hard to cope with their declining fame, especially having become used to the "limo culture" of celebrity in the months following their appearance on the show. In extreme cases, the fickle trajectory of fame may cause extreme distress: American paramedic Robert O'Donnell committed suicide several years after becoming a national hero for rescuing an 18-month-old girl who had fallen down a mineshaft, largely as a result of his fading star (Braudy, 1997).

Revelation and Authenticity

Moseley (2000) argued that the defining moment of makeover television is the revelation at the end of each show, when the members of the public respond to the transformation in front of them. In *Style Challenge*, this moment occurs when the participant is allowed to see him- or herself, for the first time since the makeover began, in a mirror. In *Ground Force*, it occurs as the "victim" returns home and sees the transformed garden, unaware that anything will have changed. The reaction is often highly emotional: An appreciative participant may be overcome with gratitude, whereas a disappointed one may well respond angrily.

These reactions are typically accompanied by demonstrations of emotion that are unusual in the British and are uncomfortable for some viewers (see Fig. 14.1). Lusted (1998) described the distancing effect that such displays may have on White, middle-class intellectuals, leading them to define the moments in terms of "taste" and seeing such displays as sentimental. This reaction may spring from an inability to identify with the participants (as "ordinary," usually working-class, members of the public). It does however mean that academics and other middle-class critics frequently regard audience-participation shows as essentially vulgar, forcing them into "a retreat into a position of class- and taste-based superiority" (Moseley, 2000, p. 314). This occurs particularly when the participants are largely drawn from the lowest social classes or from minority groups; the sternest criticism of talk shows, for example, concerns their potentially "corrupting influence" on viewers (Rössler & Brosius, 2001). The same arguments could be applied to gender, too: Displays of emotion are usually considered to be unmasculine, and the female appeal of audience-participation television sets male critics (generally the most scathing) at an even greater distance.

The moment of revelation is not peculiar to makeover shows; it is a staple of many audience-participation shows. Similar revelations can be found in "candid video" shows, when the key moment is the unmasking of the presenter (Jeremy Beadle, or whomever) and the exposure of the contrivance. Again, these moments are invariably accompanied by high emotional display on behalf of the duped participants. Such scenes are routinely described as "voyeuristic" by critics but, again, this may be the result of discomfort in the viewing context; ethical (legal) requirements, although not

FIG. 14.1. A contestant "loses it" in Channel 5's *Hot Property* (2001), a U.K. audience participation show in which young couples try to guess the market value of featured homes in order to win the property. Such public displays of emotion were once thought to be inappropriate for television. Here, not only does the camera keep running, but the footage is preserved in a tightly edited, 30-minute programme. Producers have realised that emotional display is a useful indicator of public participants' authenticity.

a strong point of audience participation programming, usually prevent the use of footage unless participants give their willing consent.

Shows like *Blind Date* also pivot on a moment of revelation, when both partners who were previously "blind" to each other's identity meet, creating a double revelation that provides viewers with the opportunity for much amateur psychology (does he fancy her? is she pleased with her choice? etc.) As in the theatre of "MediaSport," much of our pleasure in audience-participation media derives from the reading of "character"—of estimating attitudes, motives, and intentions, and identifying verbal and nonverbal clues from the behaviour of people onscreen. We scrutinize every facial expression that Chris Tarrant makes before disclosing the correct answer in *Who Wants to Be a Millionaire?* We analyse the interaction of the contestants in *Mr and Mrs* and other "couple" shows in order to construct our diagnoses of their relationships.

One of the most important function of makeover shows, argued Moseley (2000), is that audiences believe in the *credibility* of the members of the public who appear on them, because they have "an intense desire for . . . authenticity" (p. 314). Without this credibility, the appeal of such shows may vanish, as happened to U.S. quiz shows (for a time) following the 1950s rigging scandal. If participants are simply "plants," and their emotional displays part of the script, then the element of identification is lost and we are unmoved by their reactions.

Why have such scandals not affected the popularity of the contemporary talk show, however? Perhaps the most spectacular revelations of all arise in *Jerry Springer* and other, similar, talk shows, where, say, a jilted partner is joined on stage first by his or her wayward lover, then, later, by his or her deadliest rival (described by Shattuc, 1997, as "ambush disclosure"). These revelations only achieve their full effect if the audience is under the impression that the first guest is ignorant of the others' looming presence. However, the format of such shows is so familiar that it is unlikely that participants are ever naïve, and it often seems to viewers as if all involved are willing contributors to on-air conflict and uproar.

Joshua Gamson (1998), in a provocative discussion of 1990s talk shows, maintained that credibility is not necessarily the defining feature of such shows. In earlier work, he advanced a theory that audiences may actually revel in the artifice behind media productions; they are not repelled by the fact that they can see the strings and observe all the manipulations—indeed, these things are part of the pleasure of celebrity spectatorship (Gamson, 1994). With regard to talk shows at least, the familiarity of the typical sequence of events may override notions of authenticity; the Jerry Springer audience is there to see a fight, and is rarely disappointed. The appeal of such shows, therefore, may be closer to that of boxing than to the more genteel pleasures of *Ground Force.*

This leads on to the oft-asked question: Are talk shows *bad* for us? Postmodern writers such as Munson (1994) celebrated the talk show as a rare example of "carnival" in media culture, whereas Livingstone and Lunt (1994) saw their evocation of the public sphere as a democratic symbol. Gamson (1998, p. 4) was not so sure: "They seem as much about democracy as *The Price Is Right* is about mathematics." However, much of the criticism of talk shows has concerned their portrayal of gay and ethnic minority participants, leading to accusations of "freakery" by commentators on all sides of the political spectrum. Gamson argued that, in some respects, the freakery is welcome, because it pushes noncomformity closer to normality. As he noted, "Over time, the talk shows have managed to do for their audiences what no-one else has: to make homosexuality, and even transsexualism and bisexuality, basically dull" (1998, p. 217).

CONCLUSION

The advent of digital television has resulted in an explosion of cheap programming throughout the world, and lifestyle programming in particular. In most of these productions, members of the public appear alongside media employees: They are cheaper to use than celebrities, the viewing audience can identify with them, and occasionally they provide the industry with new celebrities and talking points. But we can only identify with public participants if we believe that they are the genuine article, and audience participation media fail when participants are revealed as "plants" or fakes, except where their appeal is based in ironic appreciation (e.g., *The Jerry Springer Show*). This has led producers to explore new ways of demonstrating participants' authenticity—hence the interest in emotional display and intimate disclosure that characterizes both lifestyle programming and reality TV. Inevitably, the lingering eye of the camera in these instances has led to charges of voyeurism and exploitation; these accusations are hard to defend, but they are equally impossible to prove. Perhaps a clear code of ethics, like those drawn up by professional psychology bodies, is the next step, but in the fragmented world of media, how easily could such a code be enforced?

Chapter 15

Soaps

In audience participation media, it seems, there is a great need for members of the public to appear credible on screen, and rooting out the "fakes" is an important activity for viewers and producers alike. But what happens when all the people on screen are fakes? The popularity of fictional media rivals that of any other genre, so clearly credibility, in the sense of authenticity, is not a barrier to the enjoyment of film and television in general. In this chapter, I focus on a particularly successful form of fictional media—the soap opera[1]—where "faking it" is a full-time occupation for actors and actresses, who spend much of their careers playing a single character in a parallel universe.

Soap is a genre that attracted much attention from European media scholars in the 1980s, particularly from a feminist perspective, but as a genre it is constantly in flux. Arguably, soaps today have much more mainstream appeal than did those discussed by feminist writers during the 1980s, and there is an enormous diversity of long-running fictional series throughout the world. In some countries, such as Brazil, time stands still for soap viewing; in others, such as rural India, soap has acted as a catalyst for social change. Ultimately, however, the appeal of soaps is fundamentally

[1]The term *soap opera* has uncertain origins—one suggestion is that it emerged during the 1930s as a deliberately ironic juxtaposition of high- and low-cultural imagery (soap = advertising, low culture; opera = high culture), so that "the highest of dramatic art forms is made to describe the lowest" (Allen, 1995, p. 4). Today it is more usual to refer to "soaps," as I have done in this book, although, as I go on to explain, the diversity of serial dramas both within and between international media cultures makes it problematic to characterise soap as a catchall category.

psychological, resting in our ability to bring fictional creations to life in our cognitive activity and in our talk.

SOAPS: A HISTORY

The long-running dramatic fictional serial has been a feature of almost all media cultures, from the instalment fiction of Victorian magazines in the United Kingdom to modern television and radio networks across the globe. Charles Dickens and Thomas Hardy, among other novelists from the 19th century, published their novels in regular magazine episodes, which accounts for the size of their works and some of their more incredulous fictional aspects, with editors demanding cliffhanging endings for each instalment. Elsewhere, serial dramas have included modern interpretations of ancient religious epics, known in India as "sacred soaps"; such is the popularity of these programmes, and the intensity with which they are followed, that viewing has become a religious ritual in itself, with the television set placed on a sanctified altar (Lutgendorf, 1995).

The archetypal soap opera, however, began life as radio drama during the 1930s in the United States. Several series started during that decade, most of them based around a single central character, such as *Just Plain Bill* ("the man who might be your next door neighbour"), *The Romance of Helen Trent* ("romance can begin at 35"), and *Ma Perkins* (Cassata, 1985). The hallmark of such serials was that the characters were intended to be "everyday folk" with whom listeners could identify. Such listeners were typified as housewives, once the soap's evening popularity led to them being broadcast during the working day.

The involvement of sponsors of household goods, such as Lever Brothers and Procter & Gamble (and several food companies), further consolidated the female stereotype of the listener, and heralded the introduction of the label "soap opera." Before long, a clear formula was defined for soaps, with four "cornerstones" established for a successful serial: first, characters needed to be simple enough to become predictable; second, they should find themselves in "understandable predicaments"; third, female characters should be central; and finally, they needed to have "philosophical relevance," meaning they should be in tune with contemporary issues of morality (Cassata, 1985). Broadly similar criteria applied when television began to broadcast soaps in 1951, with *Search for Tomorrow.*

Something of a soap decline set in during the 1960s. The last four surviving radio series ended on the same day, whereas many of the new television soaps failed to last into the next decade. Meanwhile, the soap opera began to appear in other countries, notably the United Kingdom, where BBC radio began broadcasting *The Archers* in 1951, and *Coronation Street* was launched by ITV in 1960; both series remain hugely popular today. This was followed by another ITV series, *Crossroads,* which was later relaunched after a 13-year gap (from 1988 to 2001). Television soaps in the United States did not really come of age until the 1970s, when *Dallas* drew huge audiences and broadened soap's appeal, introducing younger audiences to the genre. *Dallas* was successfully exported, and enjoyed enormous popularity across the world.

South of the United States, in Mexico and other Latin American countries, a slightly different dramatic tradition was taking place. As in North America, soap companies were involved in sponsoring serial drama during the 1950s in Mexico, but the format was slightly different, and by the 1970s several Latin American countries were broadcasting *telenovelas,* which became immensely popular throughout the region. The key difference between telenovelas and soaps is that the former are "closed" serials, rarely lasting longer than 6 months at a time (Trinta, 1998). They have also, over the years, attained a different artistic status than soaps. They are to Latin America what Hollywood movies are to the United States—the pinnacle of achievement for actors and producers, with the status of the *writers* equivalent to that of leading Hollywood directors. The cultural impact of these shows has been tremendous, particularly in Cuba, where Brazilian telenovelas were introduced during the 1980s following decades of low-budget local programming (Lopez, 1995).

In these and other parts of the world, serial drama has been used as a vehicle for disseminating educational material about health, environmental, and egalitarian issues. Terms like *prosocial soap opera* and *entertainment-education* are widely used to describe these forms (Sherry, 1998; Singhal & Rogers, 1999). Typically, at least one educational issue will be introduced per storyline, such as birth control, adult literacy, or HIV prevention. In the late 1990s, women in some northern Indian villages openly rejected the dowry system following gender equality storylines in the radio drama *Tinka Tinka Sukh* ("Happiness Lies in Small Pleasures"). Another series promoting environmental issues resulted in collective action regarding fuel conservation, sanitation, and tree growing (Papa et al., 2000).

Social issues have also played a large part in the British soap tradition. The pioneering Channel 4 show *Brookside* was the first to incorporate explicitly topical storylines during the 1980s, when issues such as trade unionism, sexual harassment, and unemployment featured heavily in the storylines. The hugely successful BBC series *EastEnders,* launched in 1985, continued this tradition, with storylines concerning breast cancer, schizophrenia, and AIDS. In recent years, the proliferation of channels has resulted in an ever-increasing number of soaps, some short-lived, and a greater diversity of forms. Although the archetypal soap is one that is primarily situated in a residential community (e.g., Albert Square in *East-*

Enders), many new series have taken elements of soap and reproduced these in occupational settings. A good example is the ITV series *The Bill*, a twice-weekly drama set in a police station, with a soap-style cast of characters, that has been running continuously since 1988. Such shows are rarely thought of as soaps because of their setting,[2] but they bear all the other hallmarks of the genre.

FORMAL FEATURES OF SOAPS

The plethora of forms that soap can take has made it very difficult to pinpoint its essential characteristics. Nevertheless, many media scholars have identified a number of common soap features in an attempt to explain their popularity, although these have dated rapidly with the expansion of the genre. Ang (1996) identified three formal characteristics of soap: first, personal life as the "core problematic" (e.g., J.R.'s oil business in *Dallas* takes second place to family issues); second, soaps are marked by melodramatic excess, necessary for their emotional impact; and third, soaps lack narrative resolution, thereby maintaining their continuous existence. Although it is possible to think of soaps that lack one or two of these features, it is unlikely that a show could lack all three and still be classed as a soap.

Allen (1995) listed a number of more specific features that differentiate between "open" soaps and closed serials such as telenovelas. One particular feature involves situations that are contrived to bring together a regular cast of characters, particularly important for big-city soaps such as *EastEnders* where such regular encounters involving a small number of people would be extremely unlikely. Soaps manage this by focusing on specific locations such as (community-based) pubs, hospitals, or offices, which have a relatively restricted number of people in attendance. Characters' occupations are also restricted to allow maximum opportunities for talk, with a predominance of health and legal professionals (but very few computer programmers), and to facilitate the introduction of new characters (e.g., new neighbours in *Brookside*, a new doctor in *Casualty*). One ingenious example of the latter is the widespread fostering practice in the Australian soap *Home and Away*, enabling a continuous turnover of teenage characters to keep the young audience involved.

---

[2]One exception to the rule, certainly in the United Kingdom, concerns imported series from Australia and New Zealand, which frequently have occupational settings (e.g., *Prisoner (Cell Block H)*, *Shortland Street*, and *The Young Doctors*), yet are widely classed as soaps. Possibly this reflects cultural snobbery toward these countries' media products, their position in the schedule (typically, midafternoon), and soaps in general; usually, the label "soap" is only applied as a last resort, when a show cannot be described by any other generic term.

Soap characters need to be dramatic, but they also need to be reasonably attractive to viewers, even as villains. It has been hard, for example, to tackle issues such as racism, child abuse, or political extremism in soaps, because this would require making a regular character thoroughly objectionable, thus running the risk of alienating viewers. When racism is introduced into a series such as *EastEnders*, it tends to be imported from outside the community, which weakens the impact of the storyline and presents it as an "alien" issue rather than one contained in the social fabric. Common villainy is acceptable, especially because it allows the creation of dramatic storylines (murder mysteries, etc.). Allen argued that the big climax, the overly dramatic incident, is more typical of closed serials like telenovelas (where cities practically come to a standstill when a final episode is broadcast). However, sensational storylines are not uncommon in British soaps, where they are often used as ploys to revive slack viewing ratings, or to compete with popular material on alternative channels.

When it comes to soap characters, the overall structure varies among series, although there are common features. Livingstone (1988, 1989) examined this by asking viewers of a number of soaps to sort the characters into groups on the basis of similar characteristics. She found that characters in *Dallas* were classified along two dimensions—morality (good/bad) and occupation (business/leisure). When three new characters replaced old ones, the basic structure remained the same. However, *Coronation Street* characters were represented on different dimensions, with gender emerging as a more important characteristic, and outlook (traditional/modern). The same features were also salient for *EastEnders*, suggesting a fundamental U.S./U.K. distinction.

SOAP FANS, STIGMA, AND FEMINISM

Traditionally, soap has been regarded as an overwhelmingly female concern, with its focus on the family and the local community over occupational settings and stories, and its predominance of female characters. Soap fans have long been regarded by (largely male) academics and by the general public as shallow, sentimental, and even pathological; such was the disapproval attached to their enthusiasms that Cassata (1985) described the typical soap fan from the pre-*Dallas* period as a "closet" listener or viewer. In the 1940s, an American psychiatrist published a speculative article in which he assessed soap fans as "emotionally distorted" and voyeuristic. These ruminations were picked up by the media and publicised as "scientific findings," leading to a general impression that soaps satisfied some basic need or lack in the female audience, but this was never taken seriously enough to warrant any empirical research (Allen, 1995).

It was against such a backdrop that feminist critics began to study soap seriously in the 1980s, with British scholars Charlotte Brunsdon and Dorothy Hobson analysing the appeal of *Crossroads*, and Tania Modleski in the United States writing about *Dallas* and *Dynasty*. For Brunsdon (1981) and Hobson (1982), the general abuse hurled at *Crossroads* in the British press represented the epitome of antisoap snobbery; they saw the attacks on the show as fundamentally misogynistic, and attempts to deny female viewing pleasures. For these writers, television and media in general were dominated by a masculine worldview, which held up news and current affairs as serious and important, and rejected drama and audience participation shows as trivial and inconsequential, even feeble-minded. They argued for a reappraisal of soap as psychological drama, a point which I return to later in the chapter.

Not all feminist critics were quite so positive about soap. Modleski (1979) characterised the typical soap viewer as the "ideal mother," able to indulge herself in the business of her "children" but without any of the real-life repercussions of maternal responsibility for their moral weakness and bad behaviour. Ultimately, Modleski saw soap viewing as a consolatory activity for women, who in an ideal world would have something more important to get on with. Similar sentiments were expressed by feminist scholars writing about women's fiction more generally, such as Radway's (1987) work on the romance novel and Winship's (1987) study of women's magazines. In each case, the act of reading was seen as more important than the material itself; Winship characterised magazines as women's "refuge" from the masculine world, containing important "survival" information.

This group of feminist scholars has since been criticised by various writers on soap, who viewed them as tacitly accepting masculine cultural hierarchies. Ang (1991) and Geraghty (1991) were more concerned with the recognition of women's pleasure in viewing soap as culturally important. Geraghty was particularly scathing toward the producers of *Crossroads*, whom she accused of betraying women by writing out the strong central female characters and replacing them with laddish males and sexually alluring minor female characters in order to appeal to a wider audience, thus leading to the show's (temporary) demise at the end of the 1980s. Geraghty even wondered, as a result, whether soap could survive as a genre in the 1990s (apparently it did!).

The diversity of series in the 1990s and early 2000s has perhaps challenged the concept of soap as a predominantly female pursuit. Less than 10 years on, Gauntlett and Hill (1999), in their broad study of British television viewers, found little support for this position in relation to soap, describing the earlier "gender essentialism" of authors like Geraghty as "laughable." In a later work, Brunsdon (2000) also acknowledged the narrowness of the 1980s vision of soap viewers as middle-class suburban housewives, arguing for a more pluralistic and global perspective on the genre.

THE VIEWER AS PSYCHOLOGIST: IDENTIFICATION AND PARASOCIAL INTERACTION

Much feminist analysis of soap was based around the idea of identification—the argument that women viewers enjoy soap because it is one of the few fictional genres to feature central female characters, particularly those living alone or without a male partner (Geraghty, 1991). But is identification truly necessary for the enjoyment of soap? Might other cognitive processes be equally important?

In an ethnographic study of Punjabi youngsters in the United Kingdom, Gillespie (1995) noted that one of their most popular programmes was the Australian soap *Neighbours*, which features a lot of teenage characters in a residential setting. Identification theory might find few reasons why young Punjabis should relate to, or derive gratifications from, a show featuring predominately White characters from a distant culture. Gillespie argued, however, that the (perhaps contrived) community of Ramsay Street was not dissimilar to the neighbourhood of Southall in which her participants lived, with strong kinship networks and family-based activities. Furthermore, many characters in *Neighbours* seemed to be analogues of people whom the youngsters encountered in everyday life—such as the local busybody or gossip, staunchly traditional adults and rebellious teenagers. She suggested that, in this instance, *associationism* was a more appropriate term than *identification.*

Nevertheless, television producers have often felt that identification was the primary explanation for soap appeal. When the BBC launched *EastEnders* in the mid-1980s, it was allocated a 7 p.m. weekday slot, the rationale being that it would attract a largely working-class audience because it was set in a working class area of London, with strong Cockney accents and close community ties.[3] Competition from a rival ITV soap forced the BBC to switch to a 7.30 p.m. slot, resulting in a spectacular rise in ratings; whereas 13 million watched the first episode, the figures peaked at 23 million within a year. Buckingham (1987) maintained that the time switch was more attractive to a (middle-class) commuter audience, and early demographic viewing information suggested that its audience was more diverse than anticipated. Clearly the appeal of *EastEnders* reached far beyond the working-class audience.

A survey of *EastEnders* viewers conducted by Middleham and Wober (1997) examined the reasons given for enjoying the series. Very few respondents cited identification as a factor, disagreeing with the suggestion

[3]Unrealistically close for 1985; many commentators have suggested that when identification takes place for the *EastEnders* audience it is in a largely nostalgic context, with older viewers reminiscing about the community spirit of pre- and post-World War II London.

that the series reflected real life in any way. Most viewers' appreciation was based around the quality of the acting, reflecting a significant shift in the public perception of soap from the era of *Crossroads*, when wobbling scenery and fluffed lines were felt to be the defining characteristics of the genre. But *EastEnders* is no costume drama; its concerns are essentially those of soaps through the ages, of "everyday folk," albeit with a bit more crime and violence than in previous decades. What impressed Middleham and Wober's respondents was the *realism* of the acting, the convincing portrayal of emotion and the depth of character. Contrary to the idea that soap appeal rests in identification, some of the most admired *EastEnders* characters are those whom the audience likes, and identifies with, the least—the charismatic villains.

Although identification may explain the appeal of *some* soap characters, it would appear that the broader concept of parasocial interaction is needed to explain the appeal of soap in general. In a study of student soap fans, Perse and Rubin (1989) found that parasocial interaction with their favourite characters was strongest when they were most able to predict the feelings and attitudes of those characters. They explained this in terms of uncertainty reduction theory (Berger & Calabrese, 1975), a cognitive process found to be important for forming ordinary social relationships. Reduced uncertainty about a person makes it easier to anticipate his or her responses to social situations, and this results in "attributional confidence"—the feeling that we know what makes a person tick. Uncertainty reduction was measured in Perse and Rubin's study by the length of time a participant had spent viewing a character, which may explain why many soap fans become strongly attached to long-standing soap characters.

In her early writing on *Crossroads*, Brunsdon (1981) made a similar point about soap fans. She argued that the key question for a soap viewer—as opposed to a general drama viewer—is not "what happens next" but "what kind of person is this?" Essentially the appeal of soap is not unlike that of detective fiction, in which the viewer turns psychologist, analysing characters' motives for behaviour and predicting their emotional responses. This task is accomplished by drawing on two important sources of information. First, viewers have biographical knowledge about the characters concerning their relationship histories, including previous activities that may be unknown to other characters (e.g., a clandestine sexual liaison with another character that has resulted in uncertain parentage). Second, viewers may have access to some of the characters' most private moments. To an extent this is true of all fictional drama (think, e.g., of Hamlet's soliloquies), but in soap we are able to see the private tears of a cuckold, or intepret a longing glance or pensive expression.

Soap's appeal may lie in the fact that this information is very rarely accessible in real life. Anyone who has ever stolen a glance through a friend's private diary will know that the disclosure of private sentiments is very often unpalatable to us. Modleski's (1979) "ideal mother" theory, if we de-gender the concept, contains an important idea—that soap's enjoyment results in part from the lack of responsibility that viewers have for the characters. It allows us to indulge our social curiosity without ever experiencing the repercussions. It also allows us to discuss the characters and their activities with fellow soap viewers, which is an essential aspect of soap appeal. In a study of Trinidadian soap viewers, Miller (1995) argued that soap facilitates *safe gossip*—no harm can be done in casting aspersions about the intentions or morals of a soap character. Gillespie (1995) found a similar function of soap in her Punjabi sample, where soap was used as a way of solving family problems in a culture in which *izzat,* a code of honour, prohibits discussion of such issues outside the family.

Ultimately, the success of soap lies in its ability to permeate everyday conversation between viewers. This is the context in which parasocial relationships are formed and in which fictional creations come to life; in Livingstone's (1998a, p. 61) words, "After a while, the characters do become real people and we are concerned for their well-being just as we are for our friends and colleagues."

FANTASY AND REALISM

The perceived superiority of the obviously and tangibly "real" may explain the disdain with which soaps have been viewed over the years. It may well be a feature of masculinity; traditionally, male media users have preferred more realistic media such as news, current affairs, and sport. It may also reflect an empiricist bias in Western culture more generally, whereby factual entertainment is held to be more trustworthy, serious, and meaningful than is fictional entertainment, except where fiction is venerated as art. At the same time, soaps have traditionally been derided for their concern with the everyday and mundane.

The root of soap appeal lies within this combination of the mundane and the fantastic. Geraghty (1991) argued that the main achievement of soap is the production of a parallel universe through a series of ingenious contrivances. The pacing of a soap—the regularity of the episodes (many soaps are now broadcast 4 nights a week, in addition to "omnibus" editions at weekends)—creates a "sense of endless but organised time . . . which shapes the way in which we respond to their narratives" (1991, p. 11). It is the space *between* episodes that is important, creating the sense that although we watch other programmes, or continue with our own lives, life continues in Albert Square or Ramsay Street or wherever, and that the next half-hour segment is effectively an "edited highlights" of that day or the previous day's events. This format has been used by the producers of reality TV shows, and it will be interesting to see if this example of life imitating art has the effect of reinforcing the realism of soaps for a modern audience.

The tendency to pathologise soap fans as addicts, inadequate, or shallow has, over the years, received considerable support from numerous instances in which viewers behaved as though the fantasy/reality division has become blurred. Geraghty (1991) listed a number of such well-publicised instances; during the 1970s, several viewers applied for jobs at the *Crossroads* motel, and when a *Coronation Street* storyline focused on the character Hilda Ogden losing her raincoat, several viewers posted replacements to Granada studios. Many other such incidents have been recounted over the years. It is not uncommon for viewers to send flowers to sick or bereaved characters, or for soap actors and actresses to be berated in public for their character's behaviour in the show. Are such incidents evidence of individuals' delusional belief systems or pathologically low intelligence? Geraghty asserted that this cannot be the case, because viewers are fully aware of the formal features of soap. It is extremely unlikely that a modern media-savvy audience truly believes that a given soap is anything but a cleverly scripted, often brilliantly acted work of fictional drama.

CONCLUSION

The challenge of soap is perhaps the most intriguing one facing the media psychologist. Do soap fans really "believe" in the characters, in the way that their behaviour often suggests, and what mechanisms do the producers of soap use to construct such convincing creations? These apparent breaches of the fantasy–reality boundary may be best explained with reference to active audience theory, and the idea that viewers make their own meanings from the media text rather than decoding an unambiguous, predefined message. Clearly the "preferred reading" of any soap is that the characters are played by actors, the plots and dialogue are tightly scripted, and the locations are simply outdoor studios. But it may be important for soap to succeed if viewers make other readings, whereby the issue of "unreality" is very much a secondary concern. Participating in the fictional reality of soap may even be seen as a form of *play*. In any case, the behaviour of the soap audience, and of fan culture more generally, raises questions that media psychologists struggle to answer without a full ethnographic engagement with the audience. Research in this tradition may eventually provide an explanation of how children learn about media culture, and how that culture is gradually integrated into everyday behaviour.

Part VI

THE FUTURE OF MEDIA PSYCHOLOGY

Chapter 16

The Internet

As pointless as it may be to speculate about the future, it is necessary to round off here by considering some of the more recent developments in media that have implications for a psychology of media, possibly forcing it to redefine its boundaries. In this chapter I consider the extent to which Internet technology complicates some of the issues discussed so far in the book, whereas in the final chapter I discuss psychology's role in the media, and what psychological research may be able to contribute in an applied context.

THE INTERNET: ONE MEDIUM OR SEVERAL?

The Internet is a global computing network that connects local computing networks to one another. It is therefore not a medium in the usual sense of the word. In its entirety the Net is more like the kind of literal medium that McLuhan had in mind when he described the car and the electric light as media—anything that communicates meaning or purpose, or rather anything to which we can attach meaning. Just as the electric light enabled us to continue working into the night and supply pizza 24 hours a day, so the Internet has enabled us to send a text message whistling through cyberspace within seconds to a friend on the other side of the world.

However, the definition of media outlined in the first chapter of this book causes problems when we start to consider the Internet. There, I suggested that a mass medium was one that brought together technology, culture, and mass communication. The Internet does all three, certainly, but it does a lot more besides. This means that it needs unpacking. As Morris and Ogan (1996) put it, it is a "multifaceted medium" comprising a number of discrete functions: e-mail, which is primarily a communication medium analogous to the telephone and fax machine, so in itself should not trouble us here; usenet/chat environments, which are again communication media allowing synchronous or asynchronous communication; and the World Wide Web, an information medium that is more like the traditional media discussed so far in this book.

Nevertheless, the Internet has long been discussed as though it is a single medium, and most of the academic literature on the topic has ignored these boundaries when discussing psychological factors. Thus, in this chapter I consider aspects of Internet use that may fall beyond the usual boundaries of media psychology, such as online interpersonal communication. I also briefly consider some aspects of modern technology that are not directly concerned with the Internet, such as virtual reality. This is the inevitable consequence of historical change; the academic literature on the Internet has rapidly mushroomed across disciplines in such a way as to make it very hard to extract what is truly psychological, and what is truly concerned with "media." However, these are important challenges for media psychology as we progress through the new century.

A BRIEF HISTORY OF THE NET

Before examining psychological aspects of the Internet in any detail, it may be useful to consider how the Internet and its various functions came about. It is now generally accepted that its origins lay in 1960s military technology; specifically, out of the desire to have a communications system that could survive nuclear war and would be under no overall control (Gackenbach & Ellerman, 1998). This led to the development of a network of computers that were linked to each other (known as ARPANET), and at first this was limited largely to academia (four U.S. universities in 1969, but this had spread to 37 "nodes" by 1972). As the 1970s progressed it began to expand rapidly, particularly within academia, so much so that the military split off to develop its own network.

As the academic Internet expanded, it began to incorporate a variety of communicative environments. One of the earliest of these was Usenet, a bulletin board on which people could post information. By the late 1980s this had grown out of all recognition and was being used for discussion groups by people outside academia as well. This led in 1989 to the creation of the World Wide Web (WWW) that set universal standards (such as html authoring) and allowed users to link documents through *hypertext* (highlighted text that gives users access to other websites). Soon browsers were developed, such as *Netscape*, allowing easy access to multiple sites, followed by search engines that were themselves linked to thousands of sites. The installation of fibre-optic cable in the 1990s also allowed television networks to utilise Internet technology, providing online shopping and video games.

In addition to bulletin board functions, the Internet also carried synchronous communication environments, which have provided much of the psychological interest in the Net. These include *chat rooms*, where users can communicate with up to hundreds of others simultaneously, and MUDs, which are text-based virtual reality environments, used largely for game playing; the acronym MUD stands for "multi-user dungeon," reflecting the technology's initial association with the game Dungeons and Dragons (Wallace, 1999). Finally, the development of the webcam, cameras that can transmit pictures in (almost) real time to other connected computers, has opened up new possibilities for Internet communication in the future.

THE INTERNET IN RESEARCH

Research on the various aspects of the Internet has been a growth area within academia in the last 10 or 20 years, although it has not been as prolific in some areas as we might expect. Morris and Ogan (1996) suggested that the lack of media and communications research on the Internet stems from the scepticism of early communications researchers about the computer's potential as a mass medium, although a number of other factors are likely to be more important. As I suggested in chapter 1, media in general are treated with suspicion within academia because of their sheer speed of technological change in relation to the funereal pace of academic research and publishing. Quite reasonably, researchers and their benefactors will wait for a medium to have a profound impact on society before investing time and effort into studying what may turn out to be a fleeting phenomenon, or where the pace of change may outstrip the usefulness of the findings.

At the same time, two other traditions can be identified within which Internet research has blossomed. First, the computer science literature has obviously kept abreast of developments within technology, and in order to remain contemporary there has been a gradual shift from hard-copy publishing to online literature. In IT-related social science areas journals such as the *Journal of Computer-Mediated Communication* began to appear during the 1990s in response to the need for rapid dissemination of research in this area. The interest in these areas has focused largely on the social potential of new forms of technology, such as virtual reality and immersive television (Freeman et al., 2001), rather than the Internet as such, but the potential issues for media psychology are similar.

The second tradition of research relating to the Internet comes from the direction of the arts and humanities, and has brought together philosophers, psychoanalysts, and social theorists into a broad consideration of the more exotic implications of modern technology. This tradition ranges from fairly conventional applications of social theory to the impact of new media on human culture to postmodernist speculation bordering on science fiction ("cyberpunk"). In psychology, a very small field has emerged that describes itself as "cyberpsychology" (Gordo-Lopez & Parker, 2000), consisting largely of theoretical considerations of the implications of virtual technology for the body, identity, and human nature in general.

It is also possible to identify a third tradition of Internet literature within media studies, although this is (at the time of writing) somewhat embryonic. Nevertheless, the provocative collection *web.studies* (Gauntlett, 2000) highlights a number of important issues, notably a rejection of traditional media studies in favour of the rather sexier proposition of "new media studies." As I argued in chapter 1, Gauntlett's dismissal of pre-2000 media studies rather hands the baton on to psychology, because his chief concerns were that the discipline has bitten off more than it can chew by introducing the "ethnographic" study of real audiences in addition to media texts. But Gauntlett also derided traditional media scholarship for its hard-copy-fixated sluggishness, arguing that real progress lies in cyberspace and the Internet. Although this type of revisionism is clearly designed to appeal to a new logged-on generation of students, it also smacks of the technophilia of the 1998–99 period that had already begun to sound dated by the dawn of the 21st century. Nevertheless, it is a bold move, and one that many feel was long overdue in media and communications research.

Within psychology itself, most of the interest in the Internet has, rather disappointingly, been restricted to its use as a tool for conducting research. For example, Buchanan and Smith (1999) and Senior and Smith (1999) examined the advantages and disadvantages of online surveys and experiments. Here, the interest was not in media use as such, but in the potential of the Net as a means of facilitating data collection in conventional psychological projects. Although such matters do not by themselves fall within media psychology's remit, a number of interesting phenomena crop up indirectly. For example, Joinson (1998) found a tendency for Internet users to disclose more personal information and generally communicate in a less inhibited fashion than in face-to-face interaction; this may create confounding factors for researchers who are just hoping that the Internet can be treated as an unproblematic vehicle for speeding up research.

ATTITUDES AND THEORIES TOWARD THE NET

The literature on the Internet is so diverse that it is almost futile to attempt to integrate it into any coherent set of theories about the Internet that might be of use to media psychology. However, through all the exotica and hyperbole there are some quite distinct positions that different writers hold in relation to cyberculture and Internet technology. Some of these positions echo those relating to traditional media, and there are quite close analogies between recent discussions about the Internet and responses to the introduction of media such as radio and television.

As with traditional media, most writers about the Internet can be broadly classified as either positive or negative. Generally the former outweigh the latter in academia, largely because people who are not excited by the prospect of cyberculture or "the digital age" are much less inclined to research and write about it. Negative attitudes toward the Net can be found in books such as Steinberg and Kincheloe's (1997) *Kinderculture,* in which digital media are demonised along with more traditional forms of media as part of a capitalist conspiracy. Elsewhere, concern about the Internet largely focuses on popular fears about the easy distribution of unsavoury information, from right-wing propaganda and terrorist information (e.g., bomb-making sites) to unacceptable forms of pornography. Many of these concerns are simply updated versions of early (and late) fears about radio and television content.

There is far more positive thinking in relation to the Internet than to other existing media forms, although this may be part of a more general optimism regarding the possibilities of new technological forms. Specifically, Internet enthusiasts see it as opening up opportunities in the educational field in particular, creating an "information-rich" society in which we can all be educated at the click of a mouse. Rushkoff (1996) and Tapscott (1998) both heralded the Net as the inspiration for a new "digital generation" of children who end up actually teaching their parents how to get the most out of technology (and, by implication, of life). Although their optimism is infectious, other scholars have warned of the dangers of "technological determinism," whereby too much causative power is handed over to the media. Significantly, Boiarsky (1997) urged new media scholars to consider psychological aspects of new technology, querying claims made by many proponents of Internet technology that computer use actually sharpens cognitive skills. At the same time, however, it is equally important to avoid a biological determinism that maintains that human performance is unaffected by the cultural environment.

Gackenbach and Ellerman (1998) equated the ambivalence toward the Internet with attitudes toward radio at its inception at the beginning of the

20th century. Indeed, the similarities between the two media are quite striking: Both were developed initially for military communication purposes, only to be claimed by the general public as a "people's medium" until commercial interest took hold, at which point fears grew about their use as disseminators of unsavoury propaganda. The authors did, however, make the point that although radio was a "one-way" technology once it fell into the hands of state or private ownership, the Internet continues to be a two-way, interactive technology. This is true up to a point, in that anyone can easily add material to the Web, or open an e-mail account; however, much of the information available on the Web is provided by the same institutions that provide information in other media. The real difference between the two is that radio was never anything more than a mode of broadcasting, whereas the Internet is multifunctional.

One of the attractions of the Internet for its champions is its apparently democratic status, which have led to such descriptions as "liberating" and "emancipatory." Much of the writing envisages the Net as a global meeting place for marginalized groups and alienated individuals who can enter into a virtual community that knows no geographical or spatial bounds. Some critics argue that the enthusiasm of its users has blinded them to the economic realities of Internet culture. For example, the software and hardware are manufactured by profit-making organisations who deliberately update materials at regular intervals to keep computer owners' hands in their pockets. Franklin (1990) asserted that the introduction of new technology is carefully staggered to boost profit margins and phase out old technology at a gradual rather than sudden rate. The automated banking machine ("cashpoint") is an example of a technology that was introduced as a cutting-edge optional facility but became effectively obligatory once human cashiers began to be laid off (in the United Kingdom, this process is taking rather longer). It is not the technology that is driving change, but the market. Other sceptics have queried whether the Internet, far from being a liberating technology, may eventually end up as the ultimate surveillance tool, raising the spectre of Orwell's *1984.*

INDIVIDUAL ASPECTS OF INTERNET USE

In these next two sections I have tried to condense the broad findings of Internet-related research into two areas of relevance for psychology: individual and social aspects of Internet technology. Individual aspects are those that deal with the behaviour and cognitions of the private computer user, although it could be argued that many of the issues I have listed under "social" concern the self-identity of the private user. In a traditional social sense, Internet use is invariably a private matter, because each keyboard is controlled by an individual user, and each log-on identity is an analogue of an individual human user (however many virtual environments we inhabit at any given point in time).

In the 1990s, media researchers were interested in the factors that persuaded individuals to "go online." What sort of people adopted the Internet? A telephone survey conducted in the Midwest of the United States during 1996 found that most Internet subscribers fitted the typical description of "innovative" media users—young, affluent, educated, and mostly male (Atkin, Jeffres, & Neuendorf, 1998). As time goes by, and the Internet finds its way into people's homes via more traditional media (digital television, etc.), the characteristics of the audience will presumably change. However, a major flaw with this survey (and many others) was that it failed to differentiate between "Internet adoption" at home and at work. Atkins et al.'s "Internet adopters" may have had little choice if their employers chose to thrust adoption on them.

The Internet comes under the control of the user in a way that differs sharply from traditional media such as newspapers, radio, and television. This is likely to have a major impact on the "effects" of its content and, as Morris and Ogan (1996) pointed out, it makes the uses and gratifications approach a natural perspective for Internet research. Ferguson and Perse (2000) applied this approach to Internet use by examining the Web as a "functional alternative" to television. They carried out a diary study and questionnaire with a number of adolescent Internet users and noted that although the Web could be seen to compete with television for entertainment purposes, it was unable to meet other functions of television, notably its relaxation value and its use as a vehicle for passing the time. The authors also found, perhaps surprisingly, that teenagers did not use the Internet for informational purposes. These findings may be somewhat disappointing for those who champion the Net as an educational medium, although results may be somewhat different for adult users.

But what about the Web's use as a news and current affairs medium? This is one area in which there is much optimism about the future of interactive media as a way of creating an information-rich society that avoids the potential propaganda effect of traditional broadcast media. Interactive news bulletins allow a user to dictate the content of the news stories, tailoring information to personal interests and also, perhaps, to ideological perspectives. Sundar and Nass (2001) conducted an experimental study to investigate the appeal of self-selection of news stories in which the user could attribute the choice of story to one of three possible sources: self, other users (audience), or gatekeeper (editor). In each case the stories were identical, although this was not apparent to the participants. Surprisingly, when they came to rate their level of interest and enjoyment in the stories, participants who believed they had selected the stories themselves delivered the lowest ratings (those believed to be selected by the audience were the most preferred).

This finding suggests that Internet users perceive no real advantage in having so much control over media content, certainly when it comes to news. It may not be the same for other kinds of material; after all, as we saw in chapter 12, users need to trust news sources, and part of that trust comes from the expert status that we attribute to news gatherers and editors. If agenda setting is left to the user, many of the functions of news (e.g., the surveillance function) are potentially lost, and doubt creeps in. Sundar and Nass suggested that poor ratings for self-selected news stories may simply be due to users' expectations about how interesting self-selected material will be. If so, this is presumably an artifact of the experimental design, because questions about users' enjoyment of news hardly seem appropriate to real-world newsreading!

One of the more negative behaviours that have been associated with Internet use concerns the overinvolvement of users with the medium; when taken to a pathological degree, this activity may be described as "addiction." Griffiths (1999) listed a number of "core components" of addictions that may be exhibited by heavy Internet users, including salience (the Internet is the most important thing in their life), mood modification (the user receives a "buzz" from Internet use), and tolerance (where the user becomes habituated to this buzz and requires greater use to reexperience it). For some individuals, Internet use is a full-time occupation; in one study nearly 400 users were identified as "Internet dependent" with an average weekly online time exceeding 38 hours (Young, 1998).

What do Internet users spend all this time doing? One of the unique features of hypertext is the ability to hop from web page to web page in rapid succession (depending on the quality of your browser) in a manner that is referred to as "surfing," and the sheer quantity of information on the Web makes it hard to close off the search for material as new page after page opens up. This is often reinforced by the activation of new windows, often connected to the link for advertising purposes; try searching under "clip-art" for some infuriating examples of this!

However, it seems more likely that excessive Internet use is social rather than informational; most of the case studies reported by Griffiths and Young concerned users of online chat facilities, dating agencies, and MUDs rather than idle browsing. In such cases, online relationships are formed and reinforced through constant visits to specific sites. For some individuals, cyber-communication has distinct advantages (albeit in the immediate short term) over face-to-face communication, for reasons that are discussed in the next section. However, there are some studies of Internet use producing conflict in users' social relationships, often reflecting the social nature of the online relationships (e.g., jealousy on behalf of users' partners).

SOCIAL ASPECTS OF INTERNET USE

Online Relationships

Much of the research into the psychology of the Internet has focused on the nature of online communication. For some authors, the experience of socialising via computer is barely distinguishable from face-to-face interaction. Reeves and Nass (1996) described this as "the media equation," whereby we anthropomorphise machines and media, treating them as though human—for example, saying "thank you" to an automated banking machine as it spews out cash. One way of accounting for this behaviour is to think of such instances as the operation of long-established social scripts, which offers an alternative explanation for the development of parasocial relationships. However, there is a qualitative difference between the type of parasocial relationship that exists, say, between a fan and his or her idol, and a fully reciprocal dyadic interaction between two computer users. Therefore, human–computer interaction in the sense of online communication cannot really be classed as "parasocial" (Nass & Steuer, 1993).

Nevertheless, online communication is profoundly different from face-to-face interaction. Anyone who has sent a joke e-mail around a user group that has unintentionally ruffled a few feathers will be fully aware of the limitations of Internet communication for subtle interaction (e.g., irony and sarcasm). In cyberspace, we must do without the gestural and other nonverbal cues that convey paralinguistic information to supplement the verbal content of our communication. A shrug of the shoulders, a head nod, a wink, or an apologetic grin are all unavailable online, although "emoticons" [e.g., :-)] have evolved as a partial substitution for such gestures. Prosodic cues—emphasis on certain words, mimicked accents, pauses, and other paralinguistic verbal utterances (um, ah, etc.)—that also add meaning to the words we speak are likewise absent in online interaction. All we have left are the bare bones of the verbal text itself, although we persist in bringing oral social conventions into this written communication.

For some users, as I suggested in the previous section, freedom from these visual and oral modes of communication may actually bring benefits. Our appearance may profoundly affect the nature of our face-to-face interaction: Our bodies convey information about age, gender, ethnicity, attractiveness, and fashion sense, and interactants enter into conversation fully armed with a panoply of preconceptions. Even if we are invisible, our manner of speaking can fill some of the gaps, betraying our ethnic, social class, and cultural background through our accents; our social competence and confidence through our articulation; and our personality characteristics through our immediate real-time answers to questions. Without these potentially disabling and stigmatising cues, Internet users have the potential to present a version of self that is confident and eloquent, without being hampered by shyness, inarticulacy, or face-to-face prejudices. Furthermore, online communication is extremely important for individuals who are unable to meet other people in conventional settings for reasons of physical mobility or geographical isolation.

A number of studies have examined this "empowering" quality of Internet communication. McKenna and Bargh (1998) found that it was particularly helpful for users who felt marginalized in face-to-face interaction, either for concealed reasons, such as sexuality, or conspicuous reasons, such as ethnicity or obesity. Drawing on Tajfel's social identity theory, the authors maintained that belonging to newsgroups increased self-esteem through group membership. They described cases of gay users who had "come out" in a face-to-face context after gaining confidence from interacting with other gay users online. A different sort of empowerment occurs where societies have become dispersed across the globe (e.g., people from the Indian subcontinent), and the Internet has allowed the creation of "diasporic cybercommunities" in which Indian users in Australia can interact with users of similar ethnic origin in the United Kingdom, United States, India, or Pakistan (Mitra, 1997).

The text-based nature of online communication may bestow advantages over face-to-face communication for some Internet users. But how far can cyber-relationships really replace the real thing? For some champions of the Internet, this question is meaningless: Cyber-relationships are just different, and their unique nature has the potential to change the way humans interact in general. Parks (1996) argued that cyber-relationships necessitate a rethinking of traditional relationship theory—for example, direct exchange and reciprocal feedback need no longer be thought of as essential for successful interaction. However, in many cases online relationships actually develop into face-to-face relationships; in Parks' newsgroup sample, a third of the participants had made actual contact, and another third had communicated via other media, such as the telephone or letter. Similar findings were obtained in a study by Drees (1998), in which surprisingly large numbers of users had gone on to form romantic social relationships after meeting on the Internet.

Generally, then, it seems that the Internet is a good place for people to strike up conversation without being hampered by bodily or prosodic cues; however, it will take some time to establish to what extent people are satisfied with relationships that remain solely online, and whether tapping at a computer keyboard can ever really compensate for the lack of physically proximate human interaction.

The Internet as "Identity Laboratory"

Probably the psychological topic that has generated most discussion among Internet enthusiasts is the potential of cyberspace for reconstructing identity. A key issue in postmodernism is that the "essential" version of the self—the one that psychologists have studied through tests, scales, and interviews—is fast becoming extinct. Cyberspace offers the potential for a completely new concept of self, in which we are no longer constrained by geography, embodiment, personal history, and so on. In this parallel universe we can reinvent ourselves and nobody can tell. Gergen (1991) asserted that in an everyday sense our selves are distributed across a variety of media—for instance, we leave part of our self behind when we record an ansaphone message. Rom Harré (1983) presented a similar concept, "file selves"—versions of the self that we set loose to interact without our physical presence (e.g., a job application form). Both ideas are relevant to cyberpsychology in that we can create all kinds of selves to interact in virtual environments, such as chat rooms and MUDs.

Chat rooms and MUDs are, however, not typical activities for most Internet users, whose representation of self is confined to nothing more exotic than a personal home page. Even here, it has been suggested that the home page presents "emancipatory" opportunities for differing presentations of self (Cheung, 2000), although most of us are forced to commit to a fairly mundane version of self through professional obligations. Indeed, a counterargument is that, contrary to postmodernist theory, personal home pages actually create the reverse effect; instead of fragmenting the individual self, they glorify or exaggerate it (Wallace, 1999).

The issue of multiple Internet identities has led to some interesting possibilities. In some ways the opportunities for identity reconstruction may be seen as liberating (Turkle, 1995). Other authors have referred to the Net as an "identity laboratory" (Wallace, 1999) where we can play around with versions of ourselves. This "liberating" activity can occasionally get us into trouble. There is a well-documented example of a New York male psychiatrist who created a self as a disabled lesbian and managed to get some very intimate disclosures from other Net users before he was uncloaked. This case raised the ethical issue of deception, which places severe curbs on such identity experiments. The psychiatrist's fellow users felt he had severely violated their trust, but other cases have seen women pose as men without much disgruntlement.

The "fragmented self" is a contentious issue in social psychology. Although the liberating potential of cyberspace may offer hope to those of us who feel hampered by our personal histories, it raises again the question of how far this potential is simply compensatory—how many of us are really content with invisible, exploratory cyber-communication except as a precursor to actual contact? The findings of Parks (1996) and Drees (1998) suggest that most Internet users feel a need to meet their cyber-friends in person at some point. Although these studies may simply reflect the use of a medium in its early stages, before it has had a chance to actually shape the way we think about relationships, they may also highlight potential pitfalls of cyber-relationships for those who invest the most optimism in the medium. Physically unattractive users might portray themselves as online sex gods or goddesses, but how long is it before the well of hope runs dry?

CONCLUSION

The more extravagant fanfares promoting the Internet have started to die down to some extent. As Parks (1996) wrote, cyberspace is rather less glamorous and mysterious than the purple proselytes have made out. Furthermore, the Internet is no longer something that will change the future but instead is a phenomenon that is very much a part of the present. The speed of technological change makes research redundant very quickly, and even some of the studies conducted during the late 1990s are beginning to look dated. For example, studies of "Internet adoption" may have little currency by the time this text is published; at the time of writing, the British government is hoping to phase out broadcast media in favour of digital media by the year 2005. With television and Internet services gradually converging, "adoption" may not remain obligatory for long.

It seems likely that the future of the Internet will depend on which bit of it we are discussing. E-mail has established itself as a communication medium par excellence alongside the telephone, although we are still working out how to use it effectively without upsetting one another. User groups, chat rooms, and MUDs still exist, but among today's Internet users they are exotica rather than typical activities. In either case, it seems that it is the Web and its various interactive offshoots that hold the most interest for media psychologists.

Chapter 17

Psychology in the Media

Think back a few years, a few decades perhaps, to when you were a high school or sixth-form student wondering what it must be like to be a psychologist. Did we all wear white lab coats and have grey beards? Did we lurk in dark recesses scribbling notes on eccentric human activity? Did we attempt to analyse strangers at parties immediately after meeting them? Whatever image you had then of psychologists and psychology is highly likely to have been influenced by what you have seen and read about them in the media. How much has that image changed through studying psychology and, in many cases, becoming a psychologist yourself?

The presentation of psychology in the media is a vastly underrated issue in the psychological literature, although both the APA and BPS (and, no doubt, most other professional bodies) have addressed it both directly, through their codes of conduct, and indirectly, through training psychologists in dealing with the media. In this chapter I discuss the attempt in some areas of psychology to turn media psychology into a practice rather than (or as well as) a branch of the academic discipline. In some respects this is unavoidable, because psychology has application to the media just as it does to areas such as health and business. However, in order for such a practice to be at all successful, it needs to attend to research and theoretical issues about the nature of the media and the media's impact on psychology in return.

The main topics of interest in this chapter are how the media (where psychologists themselves are either absent or present) represents psychology in particular and academic research in general, and the ways in which psychologists can best present themselves and their discipline in the media.

The key question is to what extent the one influences the other: How much control do psychologists have over their media representation? In what ways, if any, can we influence the public face of the discipline?

PSYCHOLOGISTS IN THE MEDIA

In the United States, there has been a long tradition of psychologists appearing in the media in a variety of guises—pundits offering insight on news stories, talk show guests giving advice to the studio audience, or even as presenters of radio and television shows whom members of the public call for on-air therapy. The extent to which psychologists can actively "practise" counselling skills in a public domain is questionable. During the 1980s a group of radio psychologists formed the Association for Media Psychology, which then became an official division (number 46) of the APA (Broder, 1999). For these psychologists, "media psychology" meant the practise of psychology through media outlets, rather than the systematic study of behavioural aspects of the media, rather in the way that "clinical psychology" refers to the medium in which therapies are practised rather than a study of "the clinic" as such.

Many of the psychologists who practise on the air in the United States have turned it into a full-time profession. Joyce Brothers began her own talk radio show at the start of the 1960s, and was followed by others such as Sonya Friedman, Toni Grant, and Lawrence Balter (Friedland & Koenig, 1997). Some have left academic posts or private practice to become, in effect, full-time broadcasters and journalists; others continue to lecture and practise part time. Most of the time, professional ethics restrict them from doing little more than offering "advice" to viewers or listeners, much in the same way as medical experts cannot diagnose a caller's illness but can make sensible suggestions based on more than common sense.

In the United Kingdom and Europe, psychologists have proved to be less attractive to media producers, or maybe they have been less forthright in promoting themselves. The exception here is in print journalism, in which a small number of psychologists, such as Maryon Tysoe, have been able to forge a career. Nevertheless, psychologists are much in evidence as "experts," appearing as guests on talk shows, or being quoted in newspapers and magazines, either in relation to their research or to provide commentary on topics of public interest. My own research, particularly on psychological aspects of fame and celebrity, has generated a fair amount of coverage in print media, radio, and television, but nobody has ever offered me a show of my own. Perhaps the nearest British psychologists have come to regular media work are the regular appearances of Geoff Beattie as behavioural commentator for reality-TV game show *Big Brother*, or consultant psychiatrist Raj Persaud's slot on morning television. In general, it seems, neither producers nor psychologists in the United Kingdom are falling over one another to get psychology on air in the way it has taken off in North America.

THE ACADEMIA/MEDIA RELATIONSHIP

One of the main concerns for academic psychologists considering media work is the response of their peers. As suggested in chapter 1, academia has not had a particularly happy relationship with the media over the years. The media are held responsible, partly if not wholly, for the alleged "dumbing down" of society over the last century, reducing complex and serious issues to the level of soundbites and generally poking fun at academics, portraying them at best as amiable buffoons, at worst as idle wasters of public money. In return, media producers tend to see academics as self-important, oversensitive, and out of touch with public interests and current affairs. However, research by Fenton, Bryman, and Deacon (1998) suggests that the academia/media relationship may not be quite as prickly as imagined, certainly not as far as social science is concerned.

First of all, there are enormous differences between the working practices of academic researchers and journalists. The most profound difference probably concerns the speed with which work is published in the two domains. Journalists work to deadlines, which means they rarely have longer than a week in which to produce copy; news editors in broadcast media have literally hours in which to conduct research, record interviews, and draw conclusions. The same processes can take 2 or 3 years in academic research, longer if money is needed for funding the project in the first place. The immediacy of daily news means that stories are discarded if not used immediately, which means that much research is wasted; meanwhile, accepted articles pile up in academic publishing, creating a logjam that may take years to clear.

The speed of media research means that sacrifices need to be made that break many of the rules of academic research. Competition for column space and airtime means that hurriedly compiled, sensational stories are prized above well-researched, although less spicy items. Although newspaper websites now make it easy to recover archival material, traditionally media material has a very short shelf life, being forgotten barely a day later; the only way of assessing the long-term impact of newspaper stories is by the trail of commentary and discussion left behind in columns and features, whereas academic journal articles can be and often still are cited extensively by researchers for decades.

The differences between academia and media are often exaggerated when the two are brought together. This happens frequently in television talk shows when academics appear as experts to field questions from members of the public, particularly those with relatively serious discussion topics, such as the BBC show *Kilroy*. Livingstone and Lunt (1994) conducted a close analysis of this show, with particular regard to the way in which experts were managed by the host, Robert Kilroy-Silk. They found that, on average, four experts would be present in a discussion, and psychology was frequently represented. However, in the talk show environment, experts were "deprived . . . of their expert discourse, technical paraphernalia and peer group context" (p. 97), and often found themselves played off against one another. Kilroy himself usually took the side of the (nonexpert) audience, prioritising anecdotal evidence and personal experience over statistics and scientific findings; at one point an expert's statement "That's a fact" was countered with "Well, that's one view, are there any others?" (p. 104).

Not surprisingly, academics who have been involved in such programmes are frequently disappointed by the experience. They find themselves in positions that are alien to their authoritative standing within the campus environment, having to compete for the floor with lay audience members. Even when invited to speak, they have a matter of seconds in which to get complex or sensitive points across, and are often forced to simplify their comments to a degree that makes those comments easy to counter or painfully bland. Worse still, when back in the bosom of academia, the academics are scorned by their colleagues who mistrust their motives for appearing, suspecting them of personal glorification rather than taking an opportunity to disseminate research or contribute expertise for the public good. Nevertheless, television researchers rarely need to struggle to find academics willing to offer their services, suggesting that the glamour of appearing in the media tends to outweigh the negative aspects.

SCIENCE IN THE MEDIA

Relatively little research has been conducted on the representation of social science, including psychology, in the media. However, there is a small literature concerned with science in general and the media. Public dissemination of scientific and health research is considered very important within the media; many big news stories rely on scientific research, and so most newspapers in the United States and Europe employ a specialist "science editor" (by contrast, "social science" editors are practically unheard of). In recent years in the United Kingdom, scientists have been summoned to comment on topics such as germ warfare, BSE, genetic engineering, foot-and-mouth disease, global warming, and genetically modified food.

In the majority of cases such stories begin life as political news. Most of the topics listed in the previous paragraph only attracted widespread media attention after politicians had become embroiled in controversy. For example, BSE (perhaps better known as "mad cow disease") only became a major news story when it was feared that the disease might be transmitted to humans through their unknowing consumption of infected meat. For several years, opinions have yo-yoed back and forth from one expert to another, with media stories usually appearing on the back of published research reports in scientific journals. Typically, a scientist releases some data that indicate, say, a link between BSE and CJD (the supposed human equivalent), which is then turned into a news story along the lines of "NEW LINK IDENTIFIED."

Nelkin (1987) argued that science stories in the media tend to have a consistent formulaic structure. They are usually built around a "discovery" or "breakthrough" motif, with the scientist cast as hero or explorer. Very little information is provided about the actual procedures of research—methodology or analysis—or the people involved in the process. It is rare to find any researchers named apart from the lead author or most senior member of the research team. The whole emphasis is on unearthing the "truth" about the topic, which is why conflicting evidence so exasperates reporters and readers.

Once a concept becomes ingrained in the public consciousness, scientific opinion may be sought on matters that are entirely independent of published research. A good example here is the global warming phenomenon. Dramatic weather conditions in the United Kingdom invariably bring to life a variety of stories about global warming, whether "DROUGHTS SET TO TURN SOUTHERN ENGLAND INTO DUST BOWL" or "FLOODS SET TO SUBMERGE HALF OF SOUTHERN ENGLAND" (other parts of the British Isles are usually spared such fates, or simply ignored). Here, a climatologist or meteorologist may be quoted, however tenuous the link between yesterday's weather and the long-term climate. In the United Kingdom and Norway, most science stories are of this nature; scientists themselves generate only about 25% of them (Fenton et al., 1998).

The purpose of scientists' contribution here seems to be largely rhetorical. A comment from a lofty academic source can serve to rubber-stamp what would otherwise be dismissed as reporter bias—a classic example of "stake inoculation" (Edwards, 1997). For a full "white coat" effect, certain conditions need to be met—titles such as Doctor or Professor are essential, as are the names of reputable research institutions, the more prestigious the better. Ultimately, however, the academics play little part in the construction of the story.

SOCIAL SCIENCE IN THE MEDIA

Social science coverage, in the U.K. media at least, seems to mirror that of science coverage, according to Fenton et al. (1998). Again, where social scientists are most in evidence is in an advisory category, providing supporting quotes for journalists' stories rather than generating coverage through research findings. However, the percentage of social science publication-generated stories is somewhat higher than for science (43%). Most of these were the results of surveys or press releases concerning research; a surprisingly small number (3%) of stories were generated by conferences, although these were mostly psychological in nature.

Like the scientists mentioned in general science stories, the social scientists themselves tended to be somewhat invisible. Co-authors of research were ignored in 59% of cases, whereas funding bodies and methods were rarely discussed (in 17% and 29% of stories, respectively). Most stories concerned politics, economics, and health, although crime, sex, lifestyles, and relationships were also featured occasionally. Psychologists were referred to more often than academics from any other social science discipline (32%, compared to 14% for sociologists), although Fenton et al. argued that sociologists were inferred in over half of the stories.[1] The range of institutions represented was very restricted. Oxford University was mentioned in 21% of stories; the London School of Economics in 18%. Surprisingly, Cambridge was somewhat lower (6%), perhaps reflecting institutional structure.

Generally, Fenton et al. maintained, social science gets a fair treatment at the hands of the media, perhaps fairer than most social scientists might believe. Certainly, there are many psychologists who can relate horror stories involving media coverage of their research, in which they were quoted out of context, or their findings were distorted to the point of absurdity. Others may recall broad attacks on their discipline by individual journalists; the British Psychological Society's annual conference always seems to attract at least one column along the lines of "THESE PEOPLE ARE WASTING TAX-PAYERS' MONEY."

However, less than 10% of social science stories present a negative picture of the research or the scientists involved. Negative coverage tends to fall into two categories. First, findings that seem "commonsensical" are lampooned along "waste of money" lines, the argument being that public money should be spent on something more worthwhile than simply confirming what people "already know." The second type of negative story concerns findings that are counterintuitive, where, like Kilroy when confronted by an unpopular expert, the "hard facts" are dismissed as subjectivity, and personal experience is privileged over academic theory. These stories usually follow a "whatever will they think of next?" line of argument that presents scientists as out-of-touch eccentrics.

---

[1]Fenton et al. put this down to the positivistic bias of journalists, who prefer the "hard facts" of science to the qualified musings of "soft" social science, thus privileging psychology over sociology. It is difficult to infer discipline from topic area, although the same biases can be observed working against psychology on other topics. For example, I have yet to hear a single psychologist invited to discuss genetic issues in the media, even when contentious topics such as mental illness and sexuality are on the agenda. When genetics is concerned, it seems, geneticists suddenly become experts on all manner of human behaviour.

Although 10% may represent a low proportion of negative stories, social scientists' impressions of the media tend mostly to be unfavourable. They insist that journalists neglect important details of research and lack sensitivity to the research context. Media coverage of social science is also perceived to be inaccurate, although an interesting study by Weiss and Singer (1988) found a large discrepancy between social scientists' general impression of media inaccuracy and the impressions of stories in which they were featured themselves. Only 19% of social science stories overall were perceived to be accurate, compared with 88% of stories featuring their own research. This suggests that academic distrust of journalists may well be unfounded.

Along with a distrust of journalists goes a similar distrust of fellow academics who appear in the media. Terms like *media tart* and *prostitute* are not unknown in academic circles, fostered by the dual impression that any academic who has deigned to appear on television or radio is doing it solely for vanity, and in the process somehow devalues the credibility of the profession. Many of Fenton et al.'s sample simply failed to see publicity as part of their job, although academic institutions in some countries require their members to disseminate their research as widely as possible. Derision often comes tinged with envy, as academics wonder why the media seem to have passed them over in favour of their colleagues. Envy can spill over into outright contempt when the chosen party is felt to lack credentials; Fenton et al. (1998, p. 90) quoted a psychologist who, after scanning a selection of publicised stories featuring fellow psychologists, complained that the sources were all unknown in the profession and that they would probably "give an opinion on anything."

Source credibility is not quite the same for journalists, who often prefer to rely on trusted contacts rather than take the trouble to seek out genuine experts. This is particularly true when they want academics to perform in an "advisory" role, for which a quote attributed to an authoritative source is sufficient; "Dr. X, a psychologist" will often suffice in such instances. There is a hierarchy in operation whereby contacts at more prestigious institutions are prized over less well-connected sources, and titled academics prized over untitled ones. This hierarchy can, however, be overridden when the researcher him- or herself initiates the story, particularly if he or she is sensitive to the requirements of the media.

GUIDELINES AND TRAINING FOR MEDIA PERFORMANCE

Suspicion of "quackery" in the practice of media psychology has inspired professional bodies to issue strict advice about the behaviour of their members when appearing in the media. The BPS, for instance, published a set of guidelines for dealing with media enquiries in the March 1996 edition of its journal *The Psychologist* (pages 101–102). These included various tips on dealing with interviewers from different media sources. A similar set of guidelines were published in the United States by Keith-Spiegel and Koocher (1985).

Preparation is extremely important, particularly for on-air interviews. The BPS recommends that psychologists enter into a media interview only once they have established the purpose of the interview, the questions they can expect to answer, and the appropriateness of their expertise for the subject matter. It is also useful to know beforehand whether the interview will be live or recorded, whether you will be a lone guest or in the company of other (possibly hostile!) experts, and how you will be introduced (as a psychologist, lecturer, author, or whatever).

Both the BPS and the APA advocate that research psychologists stick to topics on which they have personal expertise. The APA's ethics code (section 3.04)[2] recommends that statements made by psychologists in the media be "based on appropriate psychological literature and practice." They also attempt to restrict the extent to which psychologists can discuss living individuals, a caveat arising largely from instances of disclosure relating to high-profile clients. In the BPS guidelines, it was stated that psychologists should not attempt to comment on the state of an individual's "mind" or even on their "body language," which, for some interviewers, might defeat the whole object of inviting a psychologist onto their show!

Not surprisingly, it is very difficult to enforce some of these requirements. The issue of expertise is one that is impossible to police, simply because it is so hard to determine how one qualifies to be an expert on a specific topic in the first place. Psychologists are routinely contacted by journalists for comments on a plethora of topics, most of which have never generated academic research, never mind research by the psychologist concerned. And what constitutes sufficient research on a topic? A close familiarity with the literature on a topic may be a better qualification for expertise than a one-off empirical study with limited application. Journalists rarely request precise details; most of the time, what is sought is the kind of generalised statement that academics are reluctant to make.

The BPS and other bodies are, however, keen to improve relations between psychologists and the media, and offer various training for fledgling researchers with little media experience. Mostly this consists of making psychologists more aware of the demands of the media, and cultivating their ability to present research to a lay audience—skills that are rarely taught in the university.

---

[2]The APA's ethics code can be accessed at http://www.apa.org/ethics/code.html

How much training should be given for media work? Tanenbaum (1997) listed a number of verbal, nonverbal, and visual aspects of television performance that are clearly aimed at psychologists who harbour ambitions of becoming major television personalities, some of which seem ludicrously dated. For instance, psychologists with "strong regional accents" are advised to "visit a speech therapist or voice coach" (p. 167)! Farberman (1999) provided a much more realistic list of suggestions. She began by advising readers to anticipate key questions and to prepare and fine-tune some "quotable phrases" (i.e., "soundbites"). Request questions in advance, if possible. During the interview, if it is live, set your own pace and do not allow the interviewer to rush you. Don't be afraid to say "I don't know," and use verbal bridges to move away from unwanted topics.

In some respects, the most important thing for psychologists appearing in the media is to be familiar with the nature of the show or publication concerned. Supplying information for a magazine article is different from an interview for a news story in a daily paper. The former medium allows you to develop your subject matter in much more depth. Similarly, there is a big difference between live broadcasting and recorded material. Skilful editing can make recorded interviews sound much more fluent than they seem at the time; on the other hand, there is more opportunity for phrases to be taken out of context. Live broadcasting is more nerve-wracking but in a sense you have more control over your presentation. Television is another matter again, where eccentric mannerisms and inappropriate gestures may result in your contribution being edited out of the final show, before it is broadcast.

Another issue for psychologists to consider is payment for their appearances. Journalists and researchers will not mention payment unless you bring the subject up, and it is probably best to negotiate this as early as possible in the conversation. Of course, if you are just starting out and are happy to provide your services free of charge, this is not a problem! However, it is important that academics are not exploited by the media, and there is a tendency for us to undersell what we do. I have spent many hours talking to television researchers about my research interests in the anticipation that I will be asked to appear in the show they are putting together, but have never heard from them again. Such phone calls have amounted to 30 minutes or more of free consultancy, for which experts in other fields would have charged vast sums of money.

Finally, there is always a temptation to do the thing yourself. Rather than be misquoted, taken out of context, or have your research inaccurately reported, why not practise writing for a lay audience and produce your own article? If your research is newsworthy, somebody somewhere will be more than happy to pay you a "kill fee" for rights to the piece, and—who knows—you may end up with a lucrative sideline as a freelance journalist! For some excellent advice on how to enter into the media yourself as a writer, and general tips on dealing with journalists, see White, Evans, Mihill, and Tysoe (1993).

CONCLUSION

Scientists frequently complain about the way they are (mis)represented by the media but, as I have argued throughout this book, the distinction between reality and representation is much less clear than we often imagine. When psychologists appear in the media, we usually imagine that this constitutes an uncluttered channel of communication through which we can give audiences a clear glimpse of our research findings or theories. In practice this rarely happens: No matter how well the recorded interview has gone, a producer might later slap an inappropriate job title under our talking head, or snip our contribution at a vital point, or juxtapose our contribution with misleading visual footage. Or we might find ourselves on a talk show where the host chooses to turn us against the lay audience members, for no better scientific reason than to provide the viewing audience at home with a livelier show. We can exert some influence over these decisions by making life easier for journalists and producers—writing entertaining press releases and delivering useful soundbites—but, as with all social groups, we only achieve full representation by taking charge of the forces of production themselves, and becoming the editors, writers, and producers.

References

Abrams, K. K., Allen, L. R., & Gray, J. J. (1993). Disordered eating attitudes and behaviors, psychological adjustment, and ethnic identity: A comparison of Black and White female college students. *International Journal of Eating Disorders, 14,* 49–57.

Adams, W. J. (2000). How people watch television as investigated using focus group techniques. *Journal of Broadcasting and Electronic Media, 44,* 78–93.

Adorno, T. (1991). *The culture industry: Selected essays on mass culture.* London: Routledge.

Age Concern. (1999). *Too old for TV? The portrayal of older people on television.* London: Age Concern and the Communications Research Group.

Ajzen, I., & Fishbein, M. (1972). Attitudes and normative beliefs as factors influencing behavioural intentions. *Journal of Personality and Social Psychology, 21,* 1–9.

Alasuutari, P. (1995). *Researching culture: Qualitative method and cultural studies.* London: Sage.

Allen, M., Emmers, T., Gebhardt, L., & Giery, M. A. (1995). Exposure to pornography and acceptance of rape myths. *Journal of Communication, 45,* 5–26.

Allen, R. C. (1995). Introduction. In R. C. Allen (Ed.), *To be continued . . . soap operas around the world* (pp. 1–26). London: Routledge.

Alperstein, N. (1991). Imaginary social relationships with celebrities appearing in television commercials. *Journal of Broadcasting and Electronic Media, 35,* 43–58.

Altman, I. (1975). *The environment and social behaviour: Privacy, personal space, territoriality and overcrowding.* Monterrey, CA: Brooks/Cole.

Aluja-Fabregat, A., & Torrubia-Beltri, R. (1998). Viewing of mass media violence, perception of violence, personality, and academic achievement. *Personality and Individual Differences, 25,* 973–989.

Amis, M. (2001, March 17). A rough trade. *Guardian Weekend,* p. 5.

Andersen, A. E., & DiDomenico, L. (1992). Diet vs. shape content in popular male and female magazines: A dose-response relationship to the incidence of eating disorders? *International Journal of Eating Disorders, 11,* 283–287.

Anderson, C. A., & Dill, K. E. (2000). Video games and aggressive thoughts, feelings and behavior in the laboratory and in life. *Journal of Personality and Social Psychology, 78,* 772–790.

Anderson, D. R., Collins, P., Schmitt, K. L., & Jacobvitz, R. S. (1996). Stressful life events and television viewing. *Communication Research, 23,* 243–260.

Anderson, R. C., & Pichert, J. W. (1978). Recall of previously unrecallable information following a shift in perspective. *Journal of Verbal Learning and Verbal Behavior, 17,* 1–12.

Ang, I. (1991). *Desperately seeking the audience.* London: Routledge.

Ang, I. (1994). In the realm of uncertainty: The Global Village and capitalist postmodernity. In D. Mitchell & D. Crowley (Eds.), *Communication theory today* (pp. 193–213). Cambridge: Polity.

Ang, I. (1996). *Living room wars: Rethinking media audiences for a postmodern world.* London: Routledge.

Antaki, C., Condor, S., & Levine, M. (1996). Social identities in talk: Speakers' own orientations. *British Journal of Social Psychology, 35,* 173–192.

Ariès, P. (1962). *Centuries of childhood: A social history of family life* (R. Baldick, Trans.). New York: Random House.

Aron, A., Aron, E. N., Tudor, M., & Nelson, G. (1991). Close relationships as including other in the self. *Journal of Personality and Social Psychology, 60,* 241–253.

Asbach, C. (1994). Media images and personality development: The inner image and the outer world. In J. Bryant & A. C. Huston (Eds.), *Media, children and the family: Social scientific, psychodynamic and clinical perspectives* (pp. 117–130). Hillsdale, NJ: Lawrence Erlbaum Associates.

Astington, J. W., & Jenkins, J. M. (1995). Theory of mind development and social understanding. *Cognition and Emotion, 9,* 151–165.

Atkin, D. J., Jeffres, L. W., & Neuendorf, K. A. (1998). Understanding Internet adoption as telecommunications. *Journal of Broadcasting and Electronic Media, 42,* 475–490.

Austin, E. W. (1993). Exploring the effects of active parental mediation of television content. *Journal of Broadcasting and Electronic Media, 37,* 147–158.

Austin, E. W., Bolls, P., Fujioka, Y., & Engelbertson, J. (1999). How and why parents take on the tube. *Journal of Broadcasting and Electronic Media, 43,* 175–192.

Austin, E. W., Roberts, D. F., & Nass, C. I. (1990). Influences of family communication on children's television-interpretation processes. *Communication Research, 17,* 545–564.

Auter, P. J. (1992). TV that talks back: An experimental validation of a parasocial interaction scale. *Journal of Broadcasting and Electronic Media, 36,* 173–181.

Auter, P. J., & Palmgreen, P. (2000). Development and validation of a parasocial interaction measure: The audience–persona interaction scale. *Communication Research Reports, 17,* 79–89.

Babrow, A. S., O'Keefe, B. J., Swanson, D. L., Meyers, R. A., & Murphy, M. A. (1988). Person perception and children's impressions of television and real peers. *Communication Research, 15,* 680–698.

Ball, S., & Bogatz, G. A. (1970). *The first year of* Sesame Street*: An evaluation.* Princeton, NJ: Educational Testing Service.

Ball-Rokeach, S., & DeFleur, M. L. (1976). A dependency model of mass media effects. *Communication Research, 3,* 3–21.

Balter, R. (1999). From stigmatization to patronization: The media's distorted portrayal of physical disability. In L. L. Schwartz (Ed.), *Psychology and the media: A second look* (pp. 147–172). Washington, DC: American Psychological Association.

Bandura, A. (1973). *Aggression: A social learning analysis.* Englewood Cliffs, NJ: Prentice-Hall.

Bandura, A. (2001). Social cognitive theory of mass communication. *Media Psychology, 3,* 265–299.

Bandura, A., Ross, D., & Ross, S. A. (1963). Imitation of film-mediated aggressive models. *Journal of Abnormal and Social Psychology, 66,* 3–11.

Baran, S. J., Chase, L. J., & Courtright, J. A. (1979). Television drama as a facilitator of prosocial behaviour: *The Waltons. Journal of Broadcasting, 23,* 265–276.

Barker, M. (1997). The Newson report: A case study in "common sense." In M. Barker & J. Petley (Eds.), *Ill effects: The media/violence debate* (pp. 12–31). London: Routledge.

Barker, M., & Petley, J. (1997). *Ill effects: The media/violence debate.* London: Routledge.

Baron, R. M., & Kenny, D. A. (1986). The moderator–mediator distinction in social psychological research: Conceptual, strategic, and statistical considerations. *Journal of Personality and Social Psychology, 51*, 1173–1182.

Barr, R., & Hayne, H. (1999). Developmental changes in imitation from television during infancy. *Child Development, 70*, 1067–1081.

Basil, M. D. (1995). Secondary reaction-time measures. In A. Lang (Ed.), *Measuring psychological responses to media* (pp. 85–98). Hillsdale, NJ: Lawrence Erlbaum Associates.

Baudrillard, J. (1985). The ecstasy of communication. In H. Foster (Ed.), *Postmodern culture* (pp. 126–134). London: Pluto.

Baudrillard, J. (1988). *Selected writings.* Cambridge: Polity.

Bearison, D. J., Bain, J. M., & Daniele, R. (1982). Developmental changes in how children understand television. *Social Behavior and Personality, 10*, 133–144.

Beck, U. (1992). *Risk society: Towards a new modernity.* London: Sage.

Berelson, B. (1952). *Content analysis in communication research.* New York: Free Press.

Berg, B. L. (1995). *Qualitative research methods for the social sciences.* New York: Allyn & Bacon.

Berger, A. A. (1995). *Essentials of mass communication theory.* Thousand Oaks, CA: Sage.

Berger, A. A. (2000). *Media and communication research methods: An introduction to qualitative and quantitative approaches.* Thousand Oaks, CA: Sage.

Berger, C. R., & Calabrese, R. J. (1975). Some explorations in initial interaction and beyond: Towards a development theory of interpersonal communication. *Human Communication Research, 1*, 99–112.

Berkowitz, L. (1984). Some effects of thoughts on the anti- and prosocial influences of media events: A cognitive neoassociationistic analysis. *Psychological Bulletin, 95*, 410–427.

Berkowitz, L., & Rawlings, E. (1963). Effects of film violence on inhibitions against subsequent aggression. *Journal of Abnormal and Social Psychology, 66*, 405–412.

Berry, C., Scheffler, A., & Goldstein, C. (1993). Effects of text structure on the impact of heard news. *Applied Cognitive Psychology, 7*, 381–395.

Bettelheim, B. (1976). *The uses of enchantment: The meaning and importance of fairy tales.* New York: Random House.

Bianculli, D. (1992). *Tele-literacy: Taking television seriously.* New York: Continuum.

Bierig, J., & Dimmick, J. (1979). The late night radio talk show as interpersonal communication. *Journalism Quarterly, 56*, 92–96.

Billig, M. (1999). Commodity fetishism and repression: Reflections on Marx, Freud, and the psychology of consumer capitalism. *Theory and Psychology, 9*, 313–329.

Biocca, F., & Levy, M. R. (1995). Virtual reality as a communication system. In F. Biocca & M. R. Levy (Eds.), *Communication in the age of virtual reality* (pp. 15–31). Hillsdale, NJ: Lawrence Erlbaum Associates.

Blackman, L., & Walkerdine, V. (2001). *Mass hysteria: Media studies and critical psychology.* Basingstoke: Palgrave.

Blain, N., Boyle, R., & O'Donnell, H. (1993). *Sport and national identity in the European media.* Leicester: Leicester University Press.

Bloom, P., & German, T. P. (2000). Two reasons to abandon the false belief task as a test of theory of mind. *Cognition, 77*, 25–32.

Bogart, L., & Tolley, B. S. (1988, April/May). The search for information in newspaper advertising. *Journal of Advertising Research*, pp. 9–19.

Boiarsky, G. (1997). The psychology of new media technologies: Lessons from the past. *Convergence, 3*, 109–126.

Borzekowski, D. L. G., Robinson, T. N., & Killen, J. D. (2000). Does the camera add 10 pounds? Media use, perceived importance of appearance, and weight concerns among teenage girls. *Journal of Adolescent Health, 26*, 36–41.

Botta, R. A. (2000). The mirror of television: A comparison of black and white adolescents' body image. *Journal of Communication, 46*, 144–159.

Boynton, P. M. (1999). "Is that supposed to be sexy?" Women discuss women in "top shelf" magazines. *Journal of Community and Applied Social Psychology, 9,* 449–461.

Bransford, J. D., & Johnson, M. K. (1972). Contextual prerequisites for understanding: Some investigations of comprehension and recall. *Journal of Verbal Learning and Verbal Behavior, 11,* 717–726.

Braudy, L. (1997). *The frenzy of renown: Fame and its history* (2nd ed.). New York: Vintage.

Bretherton, I., & Beeghly, M. (1982). Talking about internal states: The acquisition of an explicit theory of mind. *Developmental Psychology, 18,* 906–921.

Broder, M. S. (1999). So you want to work in the media? 21 things I wish I had known when I first asked myself that question. In L. L. Schwartz (Ed.), *Psychology and the media: A second look* (pp. 25–36). Washington, DC: American Psychological Association.

Brown, J. D., Dykers, C. R., Steele, J. R., & White, A. B. (1994). Teenage room culture: Where media and identities intersect. *Communication Research, 21,* 813–827.

Brown, J. D., & Schulze, L. (1990). The effects of race, gender and fandom on audience interpretations of Madonna's music videos. *Journal of Communication, 36,* 94–106.

Brown, W. J., & Cody, M. J. (1991). Effects of a prosocial television soap opera in promoting women's status. *Human Communication Research, 18,* 114–142.

Bruner, J. S. (1990). *Acts of meaning.* Cambridge, MA: Harvard University Press.

Brunsdon, C. (1981). Crossroads: Notes on soap opera. *Screen, 22,* 32–37.

Brunsdon, C. (2000). *The feminist, the housewife, and the soap opera.* Oxford: Oxford University Press.

Bryant, J., Brown, D., Comisky, P. W., & Zillmann, D. (1982). Sports and spectators: Commentary and appreciation. *Journal of Communication, 32,* 109–119.

Bryant, J., & Zillmann, D. (Eds.). (1994). *Media effects: Advances in theory and research.* Hillsdale, NJ: Lawrence Erlbaum Associates.

Bryant, J., Zillmann, D., & Raney, A. A. (1998). Violence and the enjoyment of media sports. In L. A. Wenner (Ed.), *MediaSport* (pp. 252–265). London: Routledge.

Bryce, J. W., & Leichter, H. J. (1983). The family and television: Forms of mediation. *Journal of Family Issues, 4,* 309–328.

Buchanan, T., & Smith, J. (1999). Using the internet for psychological research: Personality testing on the World Wide Web. *British Journal of Psychology, 90,* 125–144.

Buckingham, D. (1987). *Public secrets:* EastEnders *and its audience.* London: British Film Institute.

Buckingham, D. (2000). *After the death of childhood: Growing up in the age of electronic media.* Cambridge: Polity.

Buller, D. B., Borland, R., & Burgoon, M. (1998). Impact of behavioral intention on effectiveness of message features: Evidence from the Family Sun Safety Project. *Health Communication, 24,* 433–453.

Burt, M. R. (1980). Cultural myths and support for rape. *Journal of Personality and Social Psychology, 38,* 217–230.

Bushman, B. J. (1995). Moderating role of trait aggressiveness in the effects of violent media on aggression. *Journal of Personality and Social Psychology, 69,* 950–960.

Bushman, B. J. (1998). Effects of television violence on memory for commercial messages. *Journal of Experimental Psychology: Applied, 4,* 291–307.

Bushman, B. J., & Stack, A. D. (1996). Forbidden fruit versus tainted fruit: Effects of warning labels on attraction to television violence. *Journal of Experimental Psychology: Applied, 2,* 207–226.

Butter, E. J., Popovich, P. M., Stackhouse, R. H., & Garner, R. K. (1981). Discrimination of television programs and commercials by preschool children. *Journal of Advertising Research, 21,* 53–56.

Cacioppo, J. T., & Petty, R. E. (1982). The need for cognition. *Journal of Personality and Social Psychology, 42,* 116–131.

Cacioppo, J. T., Petty, R. E., Kao, C. F., & Rodriguez, R. (1986). Central and peripheral routes to persuasion: An individual difference perspective. *Journal of Personality and Social Psychology, 51,* 1032–1043.

Cairns, E., Hunter, D., & Herring, L. (1980). Young children's awareness of violence in Northern Ireland: The influence of Northern Irish television in Scotland and Northern Ireland. *British Journal of Social and Clinical Psychology, 19,* 3–6.

Cameron, D., & Frazer, E. (2000). On the question of pornography and sexual violence: Moving beyond cause and effect. In D. Cornell (Ed.), *Feminism and pornography* (pp. 240–253). Oxford: Oxford University Press.

Cameron, G. T., & Frieske, D. A. (1995). The time needed to answer: Measurement of memory response latency. In A. Lang (Ed.), *Measuring psychological responses to media* (pp. 149–164). Hillsdale, NJ: Lawrence Erlbaum Associates.

Cantril, H., & Allport, G. (1935). *The psychology of radio.* New York: Harper & Brothers.

Cantril, H., Gaudet, H., & Herzog, H. (1940). *The invasion from Mars: A study in the psychology of panic.* Princeton, NJ: Princeton University Press.

Cassata, M. B. (1985). The soap opera. In B. G. Rose (Ed.), *TV genres: A handbook and reference guide* (pp. 131–150). Westport, CT: Greenwood Press.

Cassidy, T., & Waugh, K. (1997). *Can your idol make you ill? Teenage idols, adjustment and health.* Paper presented at the Annual Conference of the British Psychological Society, Herriot-Watt University, 3–6 April.

Caughey, J. L. (1984). *Imaginary social worlds: A cultural approach.* Lincoln: University of Nebraska Press.

Celozzi, M. J., Kazelskis, R., & Gutsch, K. U. (1981). The relationship between viewing televised violence in ice hockey and subsequent levels of personal aggression. *Journal of Sport Behavior, 4,* 157–162.

Centerwall, B. S. (1993). Television and violent crime. *The Public Interest, 111,* 56–71.

Charlton, T., Gunter, B., & Lovemore, T. (1998). Television on St. Helena: Does the output give cause for concern? *Medien Psychologie, 10,* 183–203.

Check, J., & Guloine, T. (1989). Reported proclivity for coercive sex following repeated exposure to sexually violent pornography, non-violent dehumanising pornography, and erotica. In D. Zillmann & J. Bryant (Eds.), *Pornography: Recent research, interpretations, and policy considerations* (pp. 159–184). Hillsdale, NJ: Lawrence Erlbaum Associates.

Cheung, C. (2000). A home on the web: Presentations of self on personal homepages. In D. Gauntlett (Ed.), *web.studies: Rewiring media studies for a digital age* (pp. 43–51). London: Arnold.

Chippindale, P., & Horrie, C. (1992). *Stick it up your punter! The rise and fall of* The Sun. London: Mandarin.

Christensen, P. G., & Roberts, D. F. (1983). The role of television in the formation of children's social attitudes. In M. J. A. Howe (Ed.), *Learning from television: Psychological and educational research* (pp. 79–99). London: Academic.

Christenson, P. G. (1992). The effects of parental advisory labels on adolescent music preferences. *Journal of Communication, 42,* 106–113.

Cialdini, R., Borden, R., Thorne, A., Walker, M., Freeman, S., & Sloan, L. (1976). Basking in reflected glory: Three (football) field studies. *Journal of Personality and Social Psychology, 34,* 366–375.

Clark, C. (1969). Television and social controls: Some observation of the portrayal of ethnic minorities. *Television Quarterly, 8,* 18–22.

Cole, M., & White, S. H. (1996). *Cultural psychology.* Cambridge, MA: Harvard University Press.

Cole, T., & Leets, L. (1999). Attachment styles and intimate television viewing: Insecurely forming relationships in a parasocial way. *Journal of Social and Personal Relationships, 16,* 495–511.

Coleman, J. C., & Hendry, L. B. (1990). *The nature of adolescence* (2nd ed.). London: Routledge.

Coltrane, S., & Messineo, M. (2000). The perpetuation of subtle prejudice: Race and gender imagery in 1990s television advertising. *Sex Roles, 42,* 363–389.

Comisky, P., Bryant, J., & Zillmann, D. (1977). Commentary as a substitute for action. *Journal of Broadcasting, 27,* 150–153.

Comstock, G., & Scharrer, E. (1999). *Television: What's on, who's watching, and what it means.* San Diego, CA: Academic.

Condry, J. (1989). *The psychology of television.* Hillsdale, NJ: Lawrence Erlbaum Associates.

Connell, R. W. (1995). *Masculinities.* Cambridge: Polity.

Cook, G. (1992). *The discourse of advertising.* London: Routledge.

Cook, T. D., Appleton, H., Conner, R. F., Schaffer, A., Tabkin, G., & Weber, J. S. (1975). Sesame Street *revisited.* New York: Sage.

Cooper-Chen, A. (1994). Global games, entertainment and leisure: Women as TV spectators. In P. J. Creedon (Ed.), *Women, media and sport: Challenging gender values* (pp. 257–272). Thousand Oaks, CA: Sage.

Corder-Bolz, C. R. (1980). Mediation: the role of significant others. *Journal of Communication, 30,* 106–118.

Corner, J. (2000). Mediated persona and political culture: Dimensions of structure and process. *European Journal of Cultural Studies, 3,* 386–402.

Craig, S. (1992). Introduction: Considering men and the media. In S. Craig (Ed.), *Men, masculinity, and the media* (pp. 1–5). Thousand Oaks, CA: Sage.

Creedon, P. J. (1994). Women, media and sport: Creating and reflecting gender values. In P. J. Creedon (Ed.), *Women, media and sport: Challenging gender values* (pp. 3–27). Thousand Oaks, CA: Sage.

Crigler, A. N., Just, M., & Neuman, W. R. (1994). Interpreting visual versus audio messages in television news. *Journal of Communication, 44,* 132–149.

Cumberbatch, G., & Negrine, R. (1992). *Images of disability on television.* London: Routledge.

Cusumano, D. L., & Thompson, J. K. (1997). Body image and body shape ideals in magazines: Exposure, awareness and internalisation. *Sex Roles, 37,* 701–721.

Danziger, K. (1990). *Constructing the subject: Historical origins of psychological research.* New York: Cambridge University Press.

Danziger, K. (1997). *Naming the mind: How psychology found its language.* Thousand Oaks, CA: Sage.

Davis, M. H. (1980). A multidimensional approach to individual differences in empathy. *JSAS Catalog of Selected Documents in Psychology, 10,* 85.

Davis, M. H. (1983). Measuring individual differences in empathy: Evidence for a multidimensional approach. *Journal of Personality and Social Psychology, 44,* 113–126.

de Bourdeaudhuij, I., & van Oost, P. (2000). Personal and family determinants of dietary behaviour in adolescents and their parents. *Psychology and Health, 15,* 751–770.

Dechesne, M., Greenberg, J., Arndt, J., & Schimel, J. (2000). Terror management and the vicissitudes of sports fan affiliation: The effects of mortality salience on optimism and fan identification. *European Journal of Social Psychology, 30,* 813–835.

DeFleur, M. L., & Ball-Rokeach, S. (1989). *Theories of mass communication* (5th ed.). White Plains, NY: Longman.

Demare, D., Lips, H. M., & Briere, J. (1993). Sexually violent pornography, anti-women attitudes and sexual aggression: A structural equation model. *Journal of Research in Personality, 27,* 285–300.

Denski, S., & Scholle, D. (1992). Metal men and glamour boys: Gender performance in heavy metal. In S. Craig (Ed.), *Men, masculinity, and the media* (pp. 41–60). Thousand Oaks, CA: Sage.

Dickerson, P. (1996). Let me tell us who I am: The discursive construction of viewer identity. *European Journal of Communication, 11,* 57–82.

Diener, E., & DuFour, D. (1978). Does television violence enhance program popularity? *Journal of Personality and Social Psychology, 36,* 333–341.

Dietz, P. E., Matthews, D. B., Van Duyne, C., Martell, D. A., Parry, C. D. H., Stewart, T., Warren, J., & Crowder, J. D. (1991). Threatening and otherwise inappropriate letters to Hollywood celebrities. *Journal of Forensic Sciences, 36,* 185–209.

Dietz, W. H. (1990). You are what you eat—what you eat is what you are. *Journal of Adolescent Health Care, 11,* 76–81.

Dittmar, H., Lloyd, B., Dugan, S., Halliwell, E., Jacobs, N., & Cramer, H. (2000). The "body beautiful": English adolescents' images of ideal bodies. *Sex Roles, 42,* 887–913.

Donnerstein, E., & Berkowitz, L. (1981). Victim reactions in aggressive erotic films as a factor in violence against women. *Journal of Personality and Social Psychology, 41,* 710–724.

Donnerstein, E., & Smith, S. L. (1997). Impact of media violence on children, adolescents, and adults. In S. Kirschner & D. A. Kirschner (Eds.), *Perspectives on psychology and the media* (pp. 29–68). Washington, DC: American Psychological Association.

Dorr, A., Graves, S. B., & Phelps, E. (1980). Television literacy for young children. *Journal of Communication, 30,* 71–83.

Draine, S. C., & Greenwald, A. G. (1998). Replicable unconscious semantic priming. *Journal of Experimental Psychology: General, 127,* 286–303.

Drees, D. (1998, March 28). *The mystery of relationships by e-mail.* Paper presented at the Annual Conference of the BPS Student Members Group, Brighton Conference Centre.

Drèze, X., & Zufryden, F. (1999, May/June). Is internet advertising ready for prime time? *Journal of Advertising Research,* pp. 7–18.

Duck, J. M., Hogg, M. A., & Terry, D. J. (1999). Social identity and perceptions of media persuasion: Are we always less influenced than others? *Journal of Applied Social Psychology, 29,* 1879–1899.

Dunn, J., Brown, J., Slomkowski, C., Tesla, C., & Youngblade, L. (1991). Young children's understanding of other people's feelings and beliefs: Individual differences and their antecedents. *Child Development, 62,* 1352–1366.

Dunning, E., Murphy, P., & Williams, J. (1988). *The roots of football hooliganism: An historical and sociological study.* London: Routledge & Kegan Paul.

Dworkin, A. (2000). Pornography and grief. In D. Cornell (Ed.), *Feminism and pornography* (pp. 39–44). Oxford: Oxford University Press.

Dyer, G. (1982). *Advertising as communication.* London: Methuen.

Dyer, R. (1993). *The matter of images: Essays on representations.* London: Routledge.

Eagle, M., Wolitzky, D. L., & Klein, G. S. (1966). Imagery: Effect of a concealed figure in a stimulus. *Science, 151,* 837–839.

Edwards, D. (1997). *Discourse and cognition.* London: Sage.

Edwards, D., & Potter, J. (1992). *Discursive psychology.* London: Sage.

Einsiedel, E. F. (1988). The British, Canadian, and U.S. pornography commissions and their use of social science research. *Journal of Communication, 38,* 108–121.

Elliott, P. (1974). Uses and gratifications research: A critique and sociological alternative. In J. G. Blumler & E. Katz (Eds.), *The uses of mass communications: Current perspectives on gratifications research* (pp. 249–268). Beverly Hills, CA: Sage.

Emmison, L., & Goldman, L. (1996). What's that you said Sooty? Puppets, parlance and pretence. *Language and Communication, 16,* 17–35.

Emmison, L., & Goldman, L. (1997). *The Sooty Show* laid bear: Children, puppets, and make-believe. *Childhood: A global journal of child research, 4,* 325–342.

Entman, R. M. (1991). Framing U.S. coverage of international news: Contrasts in narratives of the KAL and Iran Air incidents. *Journal of Communication, 41,* 6–27.

Enzensberger, H. M. (1974). *The consciousness industry: On literature, politics and the media.* New York: Seabury.

Erikson, E. H. (1968). *Identity: Youth and crisis.* New York: Norton.

Eron, L. D. (1993). *The problem of media violence and children's behaviour.* New York: Henry Frank Guggenheim Foundation.

Esser, F., & Brosius, H. B. (1996). Television as arsonist? The spread of right-wing violence in Germany. *European Journal of Communication, 11,* 235–260.

Fairclough, N. (1995). *Media discourse.* London: Edward Arnold.

Fairclough, N. (2000). *New Labour, new language?* London: Routledge.

Fairclough, N. (2001). The discourse of New Labour: Critical discourse analysis. In M. Wetherell, S. Taylor, & S. J. Yates (Eds.), *Discourse as data: A guide for analysis* (pp. 229–266). London: Sage.

Farberman, R. K. (1999). What the media need from news sources. In L. L. Schwartz (Ed.), *Psychology and the media: A second look* (pp. 9–24). Washington, DC: American Psychological Association.

Feldman, C. F. (1992). The new theory of theory of mind. *Human Development, 35,* 107–117.

Fenton, N., Bryman, A., & Deacon, D. (1998). *Mediating social science.* London: Sage.

Ferguson, D. A., & Perse, E. M. (2000). The world wide web as a functional alternative to television. *Journal of Broadcasting and Electronic Media, 44,* 155–174.

Fernbach, M. (2002). The impact of a media campaign on cervical screening knowledge and self-efficacy. *Journal of Health Psychology, 7,* 85–97.

Feshbach, N. D. (1975). Empathy in children: Some theoretical and empirical considerations. *The Counseling Psychologist, 4,* 221–226.

Feshbach, N. D., & Feshbach, S. (1997). Children's empathy and the media: Realising the potential of television. In S. Kirschner & D. A. Kirschner (Eds.), *Perspectives on psychology and the media* (pp. 3–28). Washington, DC: American Psychological Association.

Festinger, L. (1954). A theory of social comparison processes. *Human Relations, 7,* 117–140.

Fisch, S., Truglio, R. T., & Cole, C. F. (1999). The impact of *Sesame Street* on preschool children: A review and synthesis of 30 years' research. *Media Psychology, 1,* 165–190.

Fisher, W. A., & Grenier, G. (1994). Violent pornography, antiwomen thoughts, and antiwomen acts: In search of reliable effects. *Journal of Sex Research, 31,* 23–38.

Fiske, J. (1987). *Television culture.* London: Methuen.

Fiske, J. (1989). Moments of television: Neither the text nor the audience. In E. Seiter, H. Borchers, G. Kreutzner, & E. Warth (Eds.), *Remote control: Television, audiences and cultural power* (pp. 56–78). London: Routledge.

Flavell, J. H., Flavell, E. R., & Green, F. L. (1983). Development of the appearance–reality distinction. *Cognitive Psychology, 15,* 95–120.

Flavell, J. H., Flavell, E. R., Green, F. L., & Korfmacher, J. E. (1990). Do young children think of television images as pictures or real objects? *Journal of Broadcasting and Electronic Media, 34,* 399–419.

Fowler, R. (1991). *Language in the news: Discourse and ideology in the press.* London: Routledge.

Fowles, J. (1996). *Advertising and popular culture.* Thousand Oaks, CA: Sage.

Fowles, J. (1999). *The case for television violence.* Thousand Oaks, CA: Sage.

Franklin, U. (1990). *Real world of technology.* Toronto: CBC Enterprises.

Franzini, L. R., & Grossberg, J. M. (1995). *Eccentric and bizarre behaviors.* New York: John Wiley.

Freedman, J. L. (1984). Effect of television violence on aggression. *Psychological Bulletin, 96,* 227–246.

Freedman, J. L. (1986). Television and aggression: A rejoinder. *Psychological Bulletin, 100,* 372–378.

Freeman, J., Lessiter, J., & IJsselsteijn, W. (2001). Immersive television. *The Psychologist, 14,* 190–194.

Freud, S. (1930). *Civilisation and its discontents.* London: Hogarth.

Friedland, L., & Koenig, F. (1997). The pioneers of media psychology. In S. Kirschner & D. A. Kirschner (Eds.), *Perspectives on psychology and the media* (pp. 121–140). Washington, DC: American Psychological Association.

Friedrich-Cofer, L., & Huston, A. C. (1986). Television and aggression: The debate continues. *Psychological Bulletin, 100,* 364–371.

Frow, J. (1998). Is Elvis a god? Cult, culture, questions of method. *International Journal of Cultural Studies, 1,* 197–210.

Furnham, A., Gunter, B., & Walsh, D. (1998). Effects of programme content on memory of humorous television. *Applied Cognitive Psychology, 12,* 555–567.

Gackenbach, J., & Ellerman, E. (1998). Introduction to psychological aspects of internet use. In J. Gackenbach (Ed.), *Psychology and the internet* (pp. 1–28). San Diego, CA: Academic.

Gamson, J. (1994). *Claims to fame: Celebrity in contemporary America.* Berkeley: University of California Press.

Gamson, J. (1998). *Freaks talk back: Tabloid talk shows and sexual nonconformity.* Chicago: University of Chicago Press.

Gantz, W. (1981). An exploration of viewing motives and behaviors associated with television sports. *Journal of Broadcasting, 25,* 263–275.

Garner, D. M., Garfinkel, P. E., Schwartz, D., & Thompson, M. (1980). Cultural expectations of thinness in women. *Psychological Reports, 47,* 483–491.

Gauntlett, D. (1995). *Moving experiences: Understanding television's influences and effects.* London: John Libbey.

Gauntlett, D. (Ed.). (2000). *web.studies: Rewiring media studies for the digital age.* London: Arnold.

Gauntlett, D., & Hill, A. (1999). *TV living: Television, culture and everyday life.* London: Routledge.

Geiger, S., & Reeves, B. (1993). The effects of scene changes and semantic relatedness on attention to television. *Communication Research, 20,* 155–175.

Geraghty, C. (1991). *Women and soap opera.* Cambridge: Polity.

Gerbner, G. (1978). The dynamics of cultural resistance. In G. Tuchman, A. K. Daniels, & J. Benet (Eds.), *Hearth and home: Images of women in the mass media* (pp. 46–50). New York: Oxford University Press.

Gerbner, G. (1997). Gender and age in prime-time television. In S. Kirschner & D. A. Kirschner (Eds.), *Perspectives on psychology and the media* (pp. 69–94). Washington, DC: American Psychological Association.

Gerbner, G., & Gross, L. (1976). Living with television: The violence profile. *Journal of Communication, 26,* 173–199.

Gerbner, G., Gross, L., Eleey, M., Jackson-Beeck, M., Jeffries-Fox, S., & Signorielli, N. (1978). Cultural indicators: Violence profile #9. *Journal of Communication, 28,* 176–207.

Gerbner, G., Gross, L., Morgan, M., & Signorielli, N. (1980). The mainstreaming of America: Violence profile #11. *Journal of Communication, 30,* 10–29.

Gerbner, G., Gross, L., Morgan, M., & Signorielli, N. (1994). Growing up with television: The cultivation perspective. In J. Bryant & D. Zillmann (Eds.), *Media effects: Advances in theory and research* (pp. 17–43). Hillsdale, NJ: Lawrence Erlbaum Associates.

Gergen, K. (1991). *The saturated self.* New York: Basic.

Gibson, B., & Maurer, J. (2000). Cigarette smoking in the movies: The influence of product placement on attitudes toward smoking and smokers. *Journal of Applied Social Psychology, 30,* 1457–1473.

Giddens, A. (1991). *Modernity and self-identity: Self and society in the late modern age.* Cambridge: Polity.

Giles, D. C. (2000). *Illusions of immortality: A psychology of fame and celebrity.* Basingstoke: Macmillan.

Giles, D. C. (2002a). *Advanced research methods in psychology.* London: Routledge.

Giles, D. C. (2002b). Parasocial interaction: A review of the literature and a model for future research. *Media Psychology, 4,* 279–305.

Giles, D. C., & Naylor, G. C. Z. (2000a, Sept. 13–16). *Self-construal and the private bedroom: The effect of domestic environment on idiocentrism-allocentrism in British adolescents.* Poster presentation, BPS Developmental Section Annual Conference, University of Bristol.

Giles, D. C., & Naylor, G. C. Z. (2000b, Dec. 19–20). *The construction of intimacy with media figures in a parasocial context.* Oral presentation, BPS London Conference, Institute of Education.

Giles, D. C., Naylor, G. C. Z., & Sutton, J. (2000, Sept. 6–8). *Psychological correlates of parasocial interaction: Attachment style, empathy and theory of mind.* Oral presentation, BPS Social Section Annual Conference, Nottingham Trent University.

Gill, R., McLean, C., & Henwood, K. (2000, Dec. 19–20). *Advertising as a technology of gender: Men's responses to idealised male body imagery.* Paper presented at the BPS London conference, Institute of Education.

Gillespie, M. (1995). *Television, ethnicity and cultural change.* London: Routledge.

Glascock, S. (2001). Gender roles on prime-time network television: Demographics and behavior. *Journal of Broadcasting and Electronic Media, 45,* 656–669.

Goedkoop, R. (1985). The game show. In B. G. Rose (Ed.), *TV genres: A handbook and reference guide* (pp. 287–306). Westport, CT: Greenwood.

Goffman, E. (1979). *Gender advertisements.* Cambridge, MA: Harvard University Press.

Goldman, R. (1992). *Reading ads socially.* London: Routledge.

Goldstein, J. H. (1998a). Immortal Kombat: War toys and violent video games. In J. H. Goldstein (Ed.), *Why we watch: The attractions of violent entertainment* (pp. 53–68). New York: Oxford University Press.

Goldstein, J. H. (Ed.). (1998b). *Why we watch: The attractions of violent entertainment.* New York: Oxford University Press.

Goldstein, J. H. (1999). Children and advertising—the research. *Advertising & Marketing to Children, 1,* 113–118.

Gordo-Lopez, A., & Parker, I. (Eds.). (2000). *Cyberpsychology.* Basingstoke: Macmillan.

Gramsci, A. (1985). *Selections from cultural writings.* London: Lawrence & Wishart.

Grant, A., Guthrie, K., & Ball-Rokeach, S. J. (1991). Television shopping: A media dependency perspective. *Communication Research, 18,* 773–798.

Greenberg, B. S. (1980). *Life on television: Content analysis of U.S. TV drama.* Norwood, NJ: Ablex.

Greenberg, B. S. (1988). Some uncommon television images and the Drench Hypothesis. In S. Oskamp (Ed.), *Television as a social issue* (pp. 88–102). Newbury Park, CA: Sage.

Greene, A. L., & Adams-Price, C. (1990). Adolescents' secondary attachment to celebrity figures. *Sex Roles, 22,* 335–347.

Greenfield, J. (1977). *Television: The first 25 years.* New York: Harry Abrams.

Greenfield, P. M. (1984). *Mind and media.* London: Fontana.

Greenfield, P. M., Bruzzone, L., Koyamatsu, K., Satuloff, W., Nixon, K., Brodie, M., & Kinsgsdale, D. (1987). What is rock music doing to the minds of our youth? A first experimental look at the effects of rock music lyrics and music videos. *Journal of Early Adolescence, 7,* 315–329.

Greenwald, A. G., Spangenberg, E. R., Pratkanis, A. R., & Eskenazi, J. (1991). Double-blind tests of subliminal self-help audiotapes. *Psychological Science, 2,* 119–122.

Griffiths, M. (1997). Video games and aggression. *The Psychologist, 10*, 397–401.

Griffiths, M. D. (1999). Internet addiction: Fact or fiction? *The Psychologist, 12*, 246–251.

Griffiths, M. (2001, March). Letter to *The Psychologist*, p. 123.

Groth, A. N. (1979). *Men who rape: The psychology of the offender.* New York: Plenum.

Gunter, B. (1985a). *Dimensions of television violence.* Aldershot: Gower.

Gunter, B. (1985b). News sources and news awareness: A British survey. *Journal of Broadcasting, 29*, 397–406.

Gunter, B. (1987). *Poor reception: Misunderstanding and forgetting broadcast news.* Hillsdale, NJ: Lawrence Erlbaum Associates.

Gunter, B. (1994). The question of media violence. In J. Bryant & D. Zillmann (Eds.), *Media effects: Advances in theory and research* (pp. 163–212). Hillsdale, NJ: Lawrence Erlbaum Associates.

Gunter, B. (1995). *Television and gender representation.* London: John Libbey.

Gunter, B. (1997). *Measuring bias on television.* Luton: University of Luton Press.

Gunter, B. (2000a). *Media research methods: Measuring audiences, reactions and impact.* London: Sage.

Gunter, B. (2000b) Avoiding unsavoury television. *The Psychologist, 13*, 194–199.

Gunter, B. (2002). *Media sex: What are the issues?* Mahwah, NJ: Lawrence Erlbaum Associates.

Gunter, B., Berry, C., & Clifford, B. (1981). Release from proactive interference with television news items: Evidence for encoding dimensions within televised news. *Journal of Experimental Psychology: Human Learning and Memory, 6*, 216–223.

Gunter, B., & Furnham, A. (1984). Perceptions of television violence: Effects of programme genre and physical form of violence. *British Journal of Social Psychology, 23*, 155–184.

Gunter, B., & Furnham, A. (1998). *Children as consumers: A psychological analysis of the young people's market.* London: Routledge.

Gunter, B., & McAleer, J. (1997). *Children and television* (2nd ed.). London: Routledge.

Habermas, J. (1989). *The structural transformation of the public sphere: An inquiry into a category of bourgeois society* (T. Burger with F. Lawrence, Trans.). Cambridge, MA: MIT Press.

Hall, S. (1980). Encoding/decoding. In S. Hall, D. Hobson, A. Lowe, & P. Willis (Eds.), *Culture, media, language* (pp. 128–138). London: Hutchinson.

Hall, S. (1981). The whites of their eyes: Racist ideologies and the media. In G. Bridges & R. Brunt (Eds.), *Silver linings* (pp. 28–52). London: Lawrence & Wishart.

Hall, S. (Ed.). (1997). *Representation: Cultural representations and signifying practices.* London: Sage.

Hamilton, K., & Waller, G. (1993). Media influences on body size estimation in anorexia and bulimia: An experimental study. *British Journal of Psychiatry, 162*, 837–840.

Hammersley, M., & Atkinson, P. (1996). *Ethnography: Principles in practice* (2nd ed.). London: Routledge.

Hansen, A., Cottle, S., Negrine, R., & Newbold, C. (1999). *Mass communication research methods.* Basingstoke: Macmillan.

Hargreaves, J. A. (1986). Where's the virtue? Where's the grace? A discussion of the social production of gender through sport. *Theory, Culture, and Society, 3*, 109–121.

Harré, R. (1983). *Personal being.* Cambridge, MA: Harvard University Press.

Harris, P. L. (1994). Understanding pretence. In C. Lewis & P. Mitchell (Eds.), *Children's early understanding of mind: Origins and developments* (pp. 235–259). Hove: Lawrence Erlbaum Associates.

Harris, R. J. (1999). *A cognitive psychology of mass communication* (3rd ed.). Mahwah, NJ: Lawrence Erlbaum Associates.

Harrison, K. (1997). Does interpersonal attraction to thin media personalities promote eating disorders? *Journal of Broadcasting and Electronic Media, 41*, 478–500.

Harrison, K., & Cantor, J. (1997). The relationship between media consumption and eating disorders. *Journal of Communication, 47*, 40–67.

Harrower, J. (1995). The dubious nature of Mrs. Doubtfire—yet another case of mal de mère? *Feminism and Psychology, 5,* 419–425.

Hebditch, D., & Anning, N. (1988). *Porn gold: Inside the pornography business.* London: Faber & Faber.

Heilman, E. E. (1998). The struggle for self: Power and identity in adolescent girls. *Youth and Society, 30,* 182–208.

Heinberg, L. J., & Thompson, J. K. (1992). Social comparison: Gender, target importance ratings and relation to body image disturbance. *Journal of Social Behavior and Personality, 7,* 335–344.

Henderson-King, E., & Henderson-King, D. (1997). Media effects on women's body esteem: Social and individual difference factors. *Journal of Applied Social Psychology, 27,* 399–417.

Hennigan, K. M., Del Rosario, M. L., Heath, L., Cook, T. D., Wharton, J. D., & Calder, B. J. (1982). Impact of the introduction of television on crime in the U.S.: Empirical findings and theoretical implications. *Journal of Personality and Social Psychology, 42,* 461–477.

Hewstone, M., & Stroebe, W. (Eds.). (2001). *Introduction to social psychology: A European perspective* (3rd ed.). Oxford: Blackwell.

Hill, A. (1997). *Shocking entertainment: Viewer response to violent movies.* Luton: Luton University Press.

Himmelweit, H. T., Oppenheim, A. N., & Vince, P. (1958). *Television and the child: An empirical study of the effect of television on the young.* London: Oxford University Press.

Hinerman, S. (1992). "I'll be here with you": Fans, fantasy and the figure of Elvis. In L. A. Lewis (Ed.), *The adoring audience: Fan culture and popular media* (pp. 107–134). London: Routledge.

Hoberman, J. (1997). *Darwin's athletes: How sport has damaged black America and preserved the myth of race.* New York: Houghton Mifflin.

Hoberman, J. (1998). "A test for the individual viewer": *Bonnie and Clyde's* violent reception. In J. Goldstein (Ed.), *Why we watch: The attractions of violent entertainment* (pp. 116–143). New York: Oxford University Press.

Hobson, D. (1980). Housewives and the mass media. In S. Hall, D. Hobson, A. Lowe, & P. Willis (Eds.), *Culture, media, language: Working papers in cultural studies 1972–79* (pp. 105–116). London: Hutchinson.

Hobson, D. (1982). *Crossroads: The drama of a soap opera.* London: Methuen.

Hodge, B., & Tripp, D. (1986). *Children and television: A semiotic approach.* Cambridge: Blackwell.

Hoffner, C., & Cantor, J. (1985). Developmental differences in responses to a television character's appearance and behaviour. *Developmental Psychology, 21,* 1065–1074.

Hoffner, C., Plotkin, R. S., Buchanan, M., Anderson, J. D., Kamigaki, S. K., Hubbs, L. A., Kowalczyk, L., Silberg, K., & Pastorek, A. (2001). The third person effect in perceptions of the influence of television violence. *Journal of Communication, 51,* 283–299.

Hogg, M. A., & Vaughan, G. M. (1998). *Social psychology* (2nd ed.). Hemel Hempstead: Prentice-Hall.

Höijer, B. (1992). Socio-cognitive structures and television reception. *Media, Culture and Society, 14,* 583–603.

Honeycutt, J. M., & Wiemann, J. M. (1999). Analysis of functions of talk and reports of imagined interactions (IIs) during engagement and marriage. *Human Communication Research, 25,* 399–419.

Hopkins, R., & Fletcher, J. E. (1995). Electrodermal measurement: Particularly effective for forecasting message influence on sales appeal. In A. Lang (Ed.), *Measuring psychological responses to media* (pp. 113–132). Hillsdale, NJ: Lawrence Erlbaum Associates.

Hornby, N. (1992). *Fever pitch.* London: Victor Gollancz.

Horton, D., & Strauss, A. (1957). Interaction in audience-participation shows. *American Journal of Sociology, 62,* 579–587.

Horton, D., & Wohl, R. R. (1956). Mass communication and para-social interaction. *Psychiatry, 19,* 215–229.

Hovland, C. I., Lumsdaine, A. A., & Sheffield, F. D. (1949). *Experiments in mass communication.* Princeton, NJ: Princeton University Press.

Howitt, D. (1995). *Paedophiles and sexual offences against children.* Chichester: Wiley.

Howitt, D. (1998). *Crime, the media and the law.* Chichester: Wiley.

Howitt, D., & Cumberbatch, G. (1975). *Mass media violence and society.* London: Elek.

Huesmann, L. R. (1986). Psychological processes promoting the relation between exposure to media violence and aggressive behaviour by the viewer. *Journal of Social Issues, 42,* 125–139.

Huesmann, L. R., Lagerspetz, K., & Eron, L. D. (1984). Intervening variables in the TV violence–aggression relation: Evidence from two countries. *Developmental Psychology, 20,* 746–775.

Hughes, M., & Grieve, R. (1980). On asking children bizarre questions. *First Language, 1,* 149–160.

Hume, S. (1992, May 25). "Best ads don't rely on celebrities." *Advertising Age,* p. 20.

Hunt, L. (2000). Obscenity and the origins of modernity, 1500–1800. In D. Cornell (Ed.), *Feminism and pornography* (pp. 355–380). Oxford: Oxford University Press.

Huston, A. C., & Wright, J. C. (1998). Television and the informational and educational needs of children. *The Annals of the American Academy of Political and Social Science, 557,* 9–23.

Huston, A. C., Wright, J. C., Alvarez, M., Truglio, R., Fitch, M., & Piemyat, S. (1995). Perceived television reality and children's emotional and cognitive responses to its social content. *Journal of Applied Developmental Psychology, 16,* 231–251.

Hutchby, I., & Wooffitt, R. (1998). *Conversation analysis.* Cambridge: Polity.

Isler, L., Popper, E. T., & Ward, S. (1987). Children's purchase requests and parental responses: Results from a diary study. *Journal of Advertising Research, 27,* 28–39.

Itzin, C. (Ed.). (1992). *Pornography: Women, violence and civil liberties—a radical new view.* New York: Oxford University Press.

Jaglom, L. M., & Gardner, H. (1981). The preschool television viewer as anthropologist. In H. Kelly & H. Gardner (Eds.), *New directions in child development: Viewing children through television* (pp. 9–30). San Francisco: Jossey-Bass.

Jagose, A. (1996). *Queer theory: An introduction.* New York: New York University Press.

Jaynes, J. (1976/1990). *The origin of consciousness in the breakdown of the bicameral mind.* London: Penguin.

Jenkins, H. (1992a). *Textual poachers: Television fans and participatory culture.* New York: Routledge, Chapman & Hall.

Jenkins, H. (1992b). "Strangers no more, we sing": Filking and the social construction of the science fiction fan community. In L. A. Lewis (Ed.), *The adoring audience: Fan culture and popular media* (pp. 208–236). London: Routledge.

Jhally, S. (1990). *The codes of advertising.* London: Routledge.

Jindra, M. (1994). *Star Trek* fandom as a religious phenomenon. *Sociology of Religion, 55,* 27–51.

Jo, E., & Berkowitz, L. (1994). A priming effect analysis of media influence: An update. In J. Bryant & D. Zillmann (Eds.), *Media effects: Advances in theory and research* (pp. 43–60). Hillsdale, NJ: Lawrence Erlbaum Associates.

Johnson, B. T., & Eagly, A. H. (1989). Effects of involvement on persuasion: A meta-analysis. *Psychological Bulletin, 106,* 290–314.

Johnson, D., Flora, J. A., & Rimal, R. N. (1997). HIV/AIDS public service announcements around the world: A descriptive analysis. *Journal of Health Communication, 2,* 223–234.

Johnson, J. D., Trawalter, S., & Davidio, J. F. (2000). Converging interracial consequences of exposure to violent rap music on stereotypical attributions of blacks. *Journal of Experimental Social Psychology, 36,* 233–251.

Johnston, D. D. (1995). Adolescents' motivation for viewing graphic horror. *Human Communication Research, 21,* 522–552.

Johnston, W. M., & Davey, G. C. L. (1997). The psychological impact of negative TV news bulletins: The catastrophizing of personal worries. *British Journal of Psychology, 88,* 85–91.

Joinson, A. (1998). Causes and implications of disinhibited behaviour on the internet. In J. Gackenbach (Ed.), *Psychology and the internet* (pp. 43–60). San Diego, CA: Academic Press.

Josephson, W. L. (1987). Television violence and children's aggression: Testing the priming, social script, and disinhibition predictions. *Journal of Personality and Social Psychology, 53,* 882–890.

Kane, M., & Greendorfer, S. L. (1994). The media's role in accommodating and resisting stereotyped images of women in sport. In P. J. Creedon (Ed.), *Women, media and sport: Challenging gender values* (pp. 28–44). Thousand Oaks, CA: Sage.

Katz, E., Blumler, J. G., & Gurevitch, M. (1974). Utilisation of mass communication by the individual. In J. G. Blumler & E. Katz (Eds.), *The uses of mass communication: Current perspectives on gratifications research* (pp. 19–32). Beverly Hills: Sage.

Kaufman, G. (1999). The portrayal of men's family roles in television commercials. *Sex Roles, 41,* 439–458.

Keith-Spiegel, P., & Koocher, G., (1985). *Ethics in psychology: Professional standards and cases.* New York: Random House.

Kenrick, D. T., Gutierres, S. E., & Goldberg, L. L. (1989). Influence of popular erotica on judgments of strangers and mates. *Journal of Experimental Social Psychology, 25,* 159–167.

Kepplinger, H. M., & Daschmann, G. (1997). Today's news—tomorrow's context: A dynamic model of news processing. *Journal of Broadcasting and Electronic Media, 41,* 548–565.

Key, W. B. (1989). *The age of manipulation: The con in confidence, the sin in sincere.* Lanham, MD: Madison.

Kirschner, S., & Kirschner, D. A. (Eds.). (1997). *Perspectives on psychology and the media.* Washington, DC: American Psychological Association.

Klapper, J. T. (1960). *The effects of mass communication.* New York: Free Press.

Koivula, N. (1999). Gender stereotyping in televised media sport coverage. *Sex Roles, 41,* 589–604.

Korhonen, T., Uutela, A., Korhonen, H. J., & Puska, P. (1998). Impact of mass media and interpersonal health communication on smoking cessation attempts: A study in North Karelia, 1989–1996. *Journal of Health Communication, 3,* 105–118.

Krcmar, M., & Greene, K. (1999). Predicting exposure to and uses of television violence. *Journal of Communication, 49,* 24–45.

Kristeva, J. (1980). *Desire in language: A semiotic approach to literature and art.* New York: Columbia University Press.

Krugman, H. E. (1965). The impact of television advertising: Learning without involvement. *Public Opinion Quarterly, 29,* 349–356.

Kunkel, D. (1988). From a raised eyebrow to a turned back: The F.C.C. and children's product-related programming. *Journal of Communication, 38,* 90–108.

Kutchinsky, B. (1973). The effect of easy availability of pornography on the incidence of sex crimes: The Danish experience. *Journal of Social Issues, 29,* 162–181.

Kutchinsky, B. (1991). Pornography and rape: Theory and practice? Evidence from crime data in four countries where pornography is easily available. *International Journal of Law and Psychiatry, 14,* 147–164.

Kvale, S. (Ed.). (1992). *Postmodernism and psychology.* London: Sage.

Lagerspetz, K. M. J., Waldroos, C., & Wendelin, C. (1978). Facial expressions of pre-school children while watching television violence. *Scandinavian Journal of Psychology, 19,* 213–222.

Lang, A. (1994). What can the heart tell us about thinking? In A. Lang (Ed.), *Measuring psychological responses to media* (pp. 99–112). Hillsdale, NJ: Lawrence Erlbaum Associates.

Larson, R. W., & Verma, S. (1999). How children and adolescents spend time across the world: Work, play and developmental opportunities. *Psychological Bulletin, 125,* 701–736.

Laspsley, R., & Westlake, M. (1988). *Film theory: An introduction.* Manchester: Manchester University Press.

Lasswell, H. D. (1935). *World politics and personal insecurity: A contribution to political psychiatry.* New York: McGraw-Hill.

Latané, B., & Darley, J. (1970). *The unresponsive bystander: Why doesn't he help?* New York: Appleton-Century-Crofts.

Lavine, H., Sweeney, D., & Wagner, S. H. (1999). Depicting women as sex objects in television advertising: Effects on body dissatisfaction. *Personality and Social Psychology Bulletin, 25,* 1049–1058.

Lazarsfeld, P. F., & Merton, R. K. (1948). Mass communication, popular taste and organised social action. In L. Bryson (Ed.), *The communication of ideas* (pp. 95–118). New York: Harper & Bros.

Leavis, F. R., & Thompson, D. (1933). *Culture and environment: The training of critical awareness.* London: Chatto & Windus.

Lemish, D., & Tidhar, C. E. (2001). How global does it get? The *Teletubbies* in Israel. *Journal of Broadcasting and Electronic Media, 45,* 558–574.

Leong, E. K. F., Huang, X., & Stanners, P.-J. (1998, Sept./Oct.). Comparing the effectiveness of the web site with traditional media. *Journal of Advertising Research,* pp. 44–51.

Leslie, A. M. (1987). Pretense and representation: The origins of "theory of mind." *Psychological Review, 94,* 412–426.

Levin, S. R., Petros, T. V., & Petrella, F. W. (1982). Preschoolers' awareness of television advertising. *Child Development, 53,* 933–937.

Levy, M. R. (1979). Watching TV news as para-social interaction. *Journal of Broadcasting, 23,* 69–80.

Lewis, J. (1991). *The ideological octopus: An exploration of television and its audiences.* New York: Routledge.

Lewis, M. (1994). Good news, bad news. *The Psychologist, 7,* 157–159.

Leyens, J., Camino, L., Parke, R. D., & Berkowitz, L. (1975). Effects of movie violence on aggression in a field setting as a function of group dominance and cohesion. *Journal of Personality and Social Psychology, 32,* 346–360.

Liebes, T., & Katz, E. (1990). *The export of meaning: Cross-cultural readings of Dallas.* New York: Oxford University Press.

Lillard, A. S. (1993). Young children's conceptualisation of pretense: Action or mental representational state? *Child Development, 64,* 348–371.

Lindlof, T. R. (Ed.). (1987). *Natural audiences: Qualitative research of media uses and effects.* Norwood, NJ: Ablex.

Linz, D., & Donnerstein, E. (1988). The methods and merits of pornography research. *Journal of Communication, 38,* 180–184.

Linz, D., Donnerstein, E., & Penrod, S. (1984). The effects of multiple exposures to filmed violence against women. *Journal of Communication, 34,* 130–147.

Linz, D., & Malamuth, N. (1993). *Pornography.* Newbury Park, CA: Sage.

Linz, D., Malamuth, N., & Beckett, K. (1992). Civil liberties and research on the effects of pornography. In P. Tetlock & P. Suedfeld (Eds.), *Psychology and social advocacy* (pp. 149–164). New York: Hemisphere.

Livingstone, S. (1988). Why people watch soap opera. *European Journal of Communication, 3,* 55–80.

Livingstone, S. (1989). Interpretive viewers and structured programs: The implicit representation of soap opera characters. *Communication Research, 16,* 25–57.

Livingstone, S. (1998a). *Making sense of television: The psychology of audience interpretation* (2nd ed.). London: Routledge.

Livingstone, S. (1998b). Mediated childhoods: A comparative approach to young people's changing media environment in Europe. *European Journal of Communication, 13,* 435–456.

Livingstone, S. (1999). Audience research at the crossroads: The "implied audience" in media and cultural theory. *European Journal of Cultural Studies, 1,* 193–217.

Livingstone, S., & Bovill, M. (1999). *Young people, new media.* Report of the research project: Children, Young People and the Changing Media Environment. London: London School of Economics.

Livingstone, S., & Green, G. (1986). Television advertisements and the portrayal of gender. *British Journal of Social Psychology, 25,* 149–154.

Livingstone, S., & Lunt, P. (1994). *Talk on television: Audience participation and public debate.* London: Routledge.

Lockwood, P., & Kunda, Z. (1999). Increasing the salience of one's best selves can undermine inspiration by outstanding role models. *Journal of Personality and Social Psychology, 76,* 214–228.

Lombard, M., & Ditton, T. (1997). At the heart of it all: The concept of presence. *Journal of Computer-Mediated Communication, 3.* Retrieved 15 July 2002 from http://www.ascusc.org/jcmc/vol3/issue2

Lonner, W. J., Thorndike, R. M., Forbes, N. E., & Ashworth, C. (1985). The influence of television on measured cognitive abilities: A study with native Alaskan children. *Journal of Cross-Cultural Psychology, 16,* 355–380.

Lopez, A. M. (1995). Our welcomed guests: Telenovelas in Latin America. In R. C. Allen (Ed.), *To be continued . . . Soap operas around the world* (pp. 256–275). London: Routledge.

Lorch, E. P., Bellack, D. R., & Augsbach, L. H. (1987). Young children's memory for televised stories: Effects of importance. *Child Development, 58,* 453–463.

Low, J., & Durkin, K. (2000). Event knowledge and children's recall of television based narratives. *British Journal of Developmental Psychology, 18,* 247–267.

Lull, J. (1987). *Popular music and communication.* Newbury Park, CA: Sage.

Lull, J. (1990). *Inside family viewing.* London: Routledge.

Lunt, P., & Livingstone, S. (1996). Rethinking the focus group in media and communications research. *Journal of Communication, 46,* 79–98.

Lusted, D. (1998). The popular culture debate and light entertainment on television. In C. Geraghty & D. Lusted (Eds.), *The television studies book* (pp. 175–197). London: Arnold.

Lutgendorf, P. (1995). All in the (Raghu) family: A video epic in cultural context. In R. C. Allen (Ed.), *To be continued . . . Soap operas around the world* (pp. 321–353). London: Routledge.

Mackinnon, C. A. (2000). Only words. In D. Cornell (Ed.), *Feminism and pornography* (pp. 94–120). Oxford: Oxford University Press.

Makkar, J. K., & Strube, M. J. (1995). Black women's self-perceptions of attractiveness following exposure to White versus Black beauty standards: The moderating role of racial identity and self esteem. *Journal of Applied Social Psychology, 25,* 1547–1566.

Malamuth, N. M. (1996). Sexually explicit material, gender differences and evolutionary theory. *Journal of Communication, 46,* 8–31.

Malamuth, N. M., & Billings, V. (1984). Why pornography? Models of functions and effects. *Journal of Communication, 34,* 117–129.

Malamuth, N. M., & Check, J. V. P. (1980). Penile tumescence and perceptual responses to rape as a function of victim's perceived reactions. *Journal of Applied Social Psychology, 10,* 528–547.

Malamuth, N. M., Check, J. V. P., & Briere, J. (1986). Sexual arousal in response to aggression: Ideological, aggressive, and sexual correlates. *Journal of Personality and Social Psychology, 50,* 330–340.

Malamuth, N. M., & Donnerstein, E. (1982). The effects of aggressive-pornographic mass media stimuli. In L. Berkowitz (Ed.), *Advances in experimental social psychology* (Vol. 15, pp. 103–136). New York: Academic.

Malamuth, N. M., Heim, M., & Feshbach, S. (1980). Sexual responsiveness of college students to rape depictions. *Journal of Personality and Social Psychology, 38,* 399–408.

Maloney, J. (1994). The first 90 years of advertising research. In E. M. Clark, T. C. Brock, & D. W. Stewart (Eds.), *Attention, attitude and affect in advertising* (pp. 13–54). Hillsdale, NJ: Lawrence Erlbaum Associates.

Mann, C., & Stewart, F. (2000). *Internet communication and qualitative research: A handbook for researching online.* London: Sage.

Markus, H. R., & Nurius, P. (1986). Possible selves. *American Psychologist, 41,* 954–969.

Marsh, P., Rosser, E., & Harré, R. (1978). *The rules of disorder.* London: Routledge & Kegan Paul.

Martin, M. C. (1997). Children's understanding of the intent of advertising: A meta-analysis. *Journal of Public Policy and Marketing, 16,* 205–216.

Martin, M. C., & Kennedy, P. F. (1993). Advertising and social comparison: Consequences for female preadolescents and adolescents. *Psychology and Marketing, 10,* 513–530.

McCaul, K. D., Jacobson, K., & Martinson, B. (1998). The effects of a state-wide media campaign on mammography screening. *Journal of Applied Social Psychology, 28,* 504–515.

McCombs, M. (1994). News influence on our pictures of the world. In J. Bryant & D. Zillmann (Eds.), *Media effects: Advances in theory and research* (pp. 1–16). Hillsdale, NJ: Lawrence Erlbaum Associates.

McDonald, D. G., & Kim, H. (2001). When I die, I feel small: Electronic game characters and the social self. *Journal of Broadcasting and Electronic Media, 45,* 241–258.

McGuire, W. J. (1974). Psychological motives and communication gratification. In J. G. Blumler & E. Katz (Eds.), *The uses of mass communications: Current perspectives on gratifications research* (pp. 167–196). Beverly Hills, CA: Sage.

McGuire, W. J. (1985). The nature of attitudes and attitude change. In G. Lindzey & E. Aronson (Eds.), *Handbook of social psychology* (Vol. 4, pp. 233–346). Reading, MA: Addison-Wesley.

McGuire, W. J. (1986). The myth of massive media impact: Savagings and salvagings. In G. Comstock (Ed.), *Public communication and behavior* (Vol. 1, pp. 173–257). New York: Academic.

McKee, R. (2002). *Developmental differences in the recognition of print advertisements.* Unpublished BA dissertation, Department of Psychology, University of Sheffield.

McKenna, K. Y. A., & Bargh, J. A. (1998). Coming out in the age of the internet: Identity "demarginalization" through virtual group participation. *Journal of Personality and Social Psychology, 75,* 681–694.

McLuhan, M. (1964). *Understanding media: The extensions of man.* London: Routledge & Kegan Paul.

McQuail, D. (1997). *Audience analysis.* Thousand Oaks, CA: Sage.

McQuail, D., Blumler, J. G., & Brown, J. R. (1972). The television audience: A revised perspective. In D. McQuail (Ed.), *Sociology of mass communications: Selected readings* (pp. 135–165). Harmondsworth: Penguin.

McQuail, D., & Windahl, S. (1993). *Models of mass communication* (2nd ed.). New York: Longman.

McRobbie, A. (1994). *Postmodernism and popular culture.* London: Routledge.

Meehan, M. (2000, Dec. 19–20). *Measuring presence objectively.* Paper presented at the British Psychological Society London conference, Institute of Education.

Merton, R. K., Fiske, M., & Curtis, M. (1957). *The focussed interview. A manual of problems and procedures.* Glencoe, IL: The Free Press.

Messaris, P. (1997). *Visual persuasion: The role of images in advertising.* Thousand Oaks, CA: Sage.

Messenger Davies, M. (1997). *Fake, fact and fantasy: Children's interpretations of television reality.* Mahwah, NJ: Lawrence Erlbaum Associates.

Messenger Davies, M., & Machin, D. (2000). "It helps people make their decisions": Dating games, public service broadcasting and the negotiation of identity in middle childhood. *Childhood, 7,* 173–191.

Meyers, M. (Ed.). (1999). *Mediated women: Representations in popular culture.* Cresskill, NJ: Hampton.

Middleham, G., & Wober, J. M. (1997). An anatomy of appreciation and of viewing amongst a group of fans of the serial *EastEnders. Journal of Broadcasting and Electronic Media, 41,* 330–347.

Middlestadt, S. E., Fishbein, M., & Chan, D. K. (1994). The effect of music on brand attitudes: Affect- or belief-based change? In E. M. Clark, T. C. Brock, & D. W. Stewart (Eds.), *Attention, attitude and affect in advertising* (pp. 149–168). Hillsdale, NJ: Lawrence Erlbaum Associates.

Miller, D. (1995). The consumption of soap opera: *The Young and the Restless* and mass consumption in Trinidad. In R. C. Allen (Ed.), *To be continued . . . Soap operas around the world* (pp. 213–232). London: Routledge.

Mitra, A. (1997). Diasporic web sites: Ingroup and outgroup discourse. *Critical Studies in Mass Communication, 14,* 158–181.

Modleski, T. (1979). The search for tomorrow in today's soap opera. *Film Quarterly, 33,* 12–21.

Morgan, D. L. (1988). *Focus groups as qualitative research.* Newbury Park, CA: Sage.

Morley, D. (1980). *The "Nationwide" audience.* London: British Film Institute.

Morley, D. (1986). *Family television: Cultural power and domestic leisure.* London: Comedia.

Morris, M., & Ogan, C. (1996). The internet as mass medium. *Journal of Communication, 46,* 39–50.

Morrison, D. E. (1999). *Defining violence: The search for understanding.* Luton: University of Luton Press.

Moseley, R. (2000). Makeover takeover on British television. *Screen, 41,* 299–314.

Mullen, B., Futrell, D., Stairs, D., Tice, D. M., Baumeister, R. F., Dawson, K. E., Riordan, C. A., Radloff, C. E., Goethals, G. R., Kennedy, J. G., & Rosenfeld, P. (1986). Newscasters' facial expressions and voting behaviour of viewers: Can a smile elect a president? *Journal of Personality and Social Psychology, 51,* 291–95.

Mulvey, L. (1975). Visual pleasure and narrative cinema. *Screen, 16,* 6–18.

Mundorf, N., & Zillmann, D. (1991). Effects of story sequencing on affective reactions to broadcast news. *Journal of Broadcasting and Electronic Media, 35,* 197–211.

Munson, W. (1994). *All talk: The talkshow in media culture.* Philadelphia: Temple University Press.

Myers, P. N., & Biocca, F. A. (1992). The elastic body image: The effect of television advertising and programming on body image distortion in young women. *Journal of Communication, 42,* 108–133.

Nass, C., & Steuer, J. (1993). Voices, boxes, and sources of messages: Computers and social actors. *Human Communication Research, 19,* 504–527.

Nathanson, A. I., & Cantor, J. (2000). Reducing the anger-promotion effect of violent cartoons by increasing children's fictional involvement with the victim: A study of active mediation. *Journal of Broadcasting and Electronic Media, 44,* 125–142.

Neisser, U. (1976). *Cognition and reality.* San Fransisco: Freeman.

Nelkin, D. (1987). *Selling science: How the press covers science and technology.* New York: W. H. Freeman.

Newhagen, J. E. (1998). TV news images that induce anger, fear, and disgust: Effects on approach-avoidance and memory. *Journal of Broadcasting and Electronic Media, 42,* 265–276.

Newhagen, J. E., & Reeves, B. (1992). The evening's bad news: Effects of compelling negative television news images on memory. *Journal of Communication, 42,* 25–41.

Newson, E. (1994a). Video violence and the protection of children. *The Psychologist, 7,* 272–274.

Newson, E. (1994b). Ordeal by media: A personal account. *The Psychologist, 7,* 275–276.

Oates, C., Blades, M., & Gunter, B. (2002). Children and television advertising: When do they understand persuasive intent? *Journal of Consumer Behaviour, 1,* 238–245.

Olshavsky, R. W. (1994). Attention as an epiphenomenon: Some implications for advertising. In E. M. Clark, T. C. Brock, & D. W. Stewart (Eds.), *Attention, attitude and affect in advertising* (pp. 97–106). Hillsdale, NJ: Lawrence Erlbaum Associates.

O'Sullivan, T. (1998). Nostalgia, revelation and intimacy: Tendencies in the flow of modern popular television. In C. Geraghty & D. Lusted (Eds.), *The television studies book* (pp. 198–211). London: Arnold.

O'Sullivan, T., Dutton, B., & Rayner, P. (1998). *Studying the media* (2nd ed.). London: Arnold.

Paget, D. (1998). *No other way to tell it: Dramadoc/docudrama on television.* Manchester: Manchester University Press.

Paik, H., & Comstock, G. (1994). The effects of television violence on antisocial behaviour: A meta-analysis. *Communication Research, 21,* 516–546.

Palmer, P. (1986). *The lively audience: A study of children around the television set.* North Sydney: Allen & Unwin.

Palmgreen, P., Wenner, L. A., & Rayburn, J. D. (1980). Relations between gratifications sought and obtained: A study of television news. *Communication Research, 7,* 161–192.

Papa, M. J., Singhal, A., Law, S., Pant, S., Sood, S., Rogers, E. M., & Shefner-Rogers, C. L. (2000). Entertainment-education and social change: An analysis of parasocial interaction, social learning, collective efficacy, and paradoxical communication. *Journal of Communication, 50,* 31–55.

Papachrissi, Z., & Rubin, A. M. (2000). Predictors of internet use. *Journal of Broadcasting and Electronic Media, 44,* 175–196.

Parker, I., Georgaca, E., Harper, D., McLaughlin, T., & Stowell-Smith, M. (1995). *Deconstructing psychopathology.* London: Sage.

Parks, M. R. (1996). Making friends in cyberspace. *Journal of Communication, 46,* 80–97.

Pasquier, D., Buzzi, C., d'Haenens, L., & Sjöberg, U. (1998). Family lifestyles and media use patterns: An analysis of domestic media among Flemish, French, Italian and Swedish children and teenagers. *European Journal of Communication, 13,* 503–519.

Patterson, J. E., Field, J., & Pryor, J. (1994). Adolescents' perceptions of their attachment relationships with their mothers, fathers and friends. *Journal of Youth and Adolescence, 23,* 579–600.

Perner, J., Ruffman, T., & Leekam, S. R. (1994). Theory of mind is contagious: You catch it from your sibs. *Child Development, 65,* 1228–1238.

Perse, E. M., & Rubin, R. B. (1989). Attribution in social and parasocial relationships. *Communication Research, 16,* 59–77.

Peters, P. D., & Ceci, S. J. (1982). Peer-review practices of psychological journals: The fate of published articles, submitted again. *Behavioral and Brain Sciences, 5,* 187–255.

Petty, R. E., & Cacioppo, J. T. (1981). *Attitudes and persuasion: Classic and contemporary approaches.* Dubuque, IA: Brown.

Petty, R. E., & Cacioppo, J. T. (1990). Involvement and persuasion: Tradition versus integration. *Psychological Bulletin, 107,* 367–374.

Phillips, D. P. (1983). The impact of mass media violence on U.S. homicides. *American Sociological Review, 48,* 560–568.

Philo, G., & The Glasgow Media Group (1996). *Media and mental distress.* Harlow: Addison-Wesley-Longman.

Piaget, J., & Inhelder, B. (1969). *The psychology of the child.* New York: Basic.

Picirillo, M. S. (1986). On the authenticity of televisual experience: A critical exploration of para-social closure. *Critical Studies in Mass Communication, 3,* 337–355.

Pine, K., & Nash, A. (2001, March 28–31). *The effects of television advertising on young children.* Paper presented at the British Psychological Society Centenary Conference, SECC, Glasgow.

Pingree, S., & Hawkins, R. (1981). U.S. programs on Australian television: The cultivation effect. *Journal of Communication, 31,* 97–105.

Podlas, K. (2000). Mistresses of their own domain: How female entrepreneurs in cyberporn are initiating a gender power shift. *Cyberpsychology and Behavior, 3,* 847–854.

Potter, J. (1996). *Representing reality.* London: Sage.

Potter, W. J. (1991). Examining cultivation from a psychological perspective: Component subprocesses. *Communication Research, 18,* 77–102.

Potter, W. J. (1999). *On media violence.* Thousand Oaks, CA: Sage.

Premack, D., & Woodruff, G. (1978). Does the chimpanzee have a theory of mind? *Behavioral and Brain Sciences, 1,* 515–526.

Prinsky, L. E., & Rosenbaum, J. L. (1987). "Leer-ics" or lyrics? Teenage impressions of rock 'n' roll. *Youth and Society, 18,* 384–397.

Quinsey, V. L., Steinman, C. M., Bergersen, S. G., & Holmes, T. F. (1975). Penile circumference, skin conductance, and ranking responses of child molesters and "normals" to sexual and nonsexual visual stimuli. *Behavior Therapy, 6,* 213–219.

Radway, J. (1987). *Reading the romance: Women, patriarchy and popular literature.* Chapel Hill: University of North Carolina Press.

Real, M. R. (1977). *Mass-mediated culture.* New Jersey: Prentice-Hall.

Rebello, S. (1990). *Alfred Hitchcock and the making of Psycho.* London: Marion Boyars.

Rees, L. (1992). *The myth of the leader.* London: BBC Books.

Reeves, B., & Anderson, D. R. (1991). Media studies and psychology. *Communication Research, 18,* 597–600.

Reeves, B., & Greenberg, B. (1977). Children's perceptions of television characters. *Human Communication Research, 3,* 113–117.

Reeves, B., Lombard, M., & Melwani, G. (1992, May). *Faces on the screen: Pictures or natural experience?* Paper presented to the biannual conference of the International Communication Association, Miami.

Reeves, B., & Lometti, G. (1979). The dimensional structure of children's perceptions of television characters: A replication. *Human Communication Research, 5,* 247–256.

Reeves, B., & Nass, C. (1996). *The media equation: How people treat computers, television and new media like real people and places.* New York: Cambridge University Press.

Reeves, B., Newhagen, J., Maibach, E., Basil, M., & Kurz, K. (1991). Negative and positive television messages: Effects of message type and context on attention and memory. *American Behavioral Scientist, 34,* 679–694.

Reith, M. (1999). Viewing of crime drama and authoritarian aggression: An investigation of the relationship between crime viewing, fear and aggression. *Journal of Broadcasting and Electronic Media, 43,* 211–221.

Rice, M. L., Huston, A. C., Truglio, R., & Wright, J. (1990). Words from *Sesame Street*: Learning vocabulary while viewing. *Developmental Psychology, 26,* 421–428.

Robinson, J. P., & Davis, D. K. (1990). Television news and the informed public: An information processing approach. *Journal of Communication, 40,* 106–119.

Robson, C. (1993). *Real world research: A resource for social scientists and practitioner-researchers.* Oxford: Blackwell.

Roe, K. (1995). Adolescents' use of socially disvalued media: Towards a theory of media delinquency. *Journal of Youth and Adolescence, 24,* 617–631.

Rose, B. G. (1985). The talk show. In B. G. Rose (Ed.), *TV genres: A handbook and reference guide*, (pp. 329–352). Westport, CT: Greenwood.

Rose, D. (1998). Television, madness, and community care. *Journal of Community and Applied Social Psychology, 8,* 213–228.

Rosen, C. S., Schwebel, D. C., & Singer, J. L. (1997). Preschoolers' attribution of mental states in pretense. *Child Development, 68,* 1133–1142.

Rosengren, K. E., & Windahl, S. (1972). Mass media consumption as a functional alternative. In D. McQuail (Ed.), *Sociology of mass communications: Selected readings* (pp. 119–134). Harmondsworth: Penguin.

Rosenkoetter, L. I. (1999). The television situation comedy and children's prosocial behaviour. *Journal of Applied Social Psychology, 29,* 979–993.

Ross, B. L. (2000). "It's merely designed for sexual arousal": Interrogating the indefensibility of lesbian smut. In D. Cornell (Ed.), *Feminism and pornography* (pp. 264–317). Oxford: Oxford University Press.

Rössler, P., & Brosius, H. (2001). Do talk shows cultivate adolescents' views of the world? A prolonged-exposure experiment. *Journal of Communication, 51,* 143–163.

Rubin, A. M., & Perse, E. M. (1987). Audience activity and soap opera involvement: A uses and effects investigation. *Human Communication Research, 14,* 246–268.

Rubin, A. M., Perse, E. M., & Powell, R. A. (1985). Loneliness, parasocial interaction, and local television news viewing. *Human Communication Research, 12,* 155–180.

Rubin, A. M., West, D. V., & Mitchell, W. S. (2001). Differences in aggression, attitudes towards women, and distrust as reflected in popular music preferences. *Media Psychology, 3,* 25–42.

Rubin, R., & McHugh, M. (1987). Development of parasocial interaction relationships. *Journal of Broadcasting and Electronic Media, 31,* 279–292.

Ruddock, A. (2001). *Understanding audiences: Theory and method.* London: Sage.

Rushkoff, D. (1996). *Playing the future: How kids' culture can teach us to thrive in an age of chaos.* New York: HarperCollins.

Russell, D. E. H. (2000). Pornography and rape: A causal model. In D. Cornell (Ed.), *Feminism and pornography* (pp. 48–93). Oxford: Oxford University Press.

Sanders, M. R., Montgomery, D. J., & Brechman-Toussaint, M. L. (2000). The mass media and the prevention of child behaviour problems: The evaluation of a television series to promote positive outcomes for parents and their children. *Journal of Child Psychology and Psychiatry, 41,* 939–948.

Sapolsky, B. S., & Zillmann, D. (1978). Enjoyment of televised sport contests under different conditions of viewing. *Perceptual and Motor Skills, 46,* 29–30.

Scannell, P. (1989). Public service broadcasting: The history of a concept. In A. Goodwin & G. Whannel (Eds.), *Understanding television* (pp. 11–29). London: Routledge.

Scannell, P. (1996). *Radio, television, and modern life.* Oxford: Blackwell.

Scannell, P., & Cardiff, D. (1991). *A social history of British broadcasting: Volume 1, 1922–1939, Serving the nation.* Oxford: Blackwell.

Schachter, S., & Singer, J. (1962). Cognitive, social and physiological determinants of emotional state. *Psychological Review, 69,* 379–399.

Schlesinger, P. (1978). *Putting reality together: BBC news.* London: Methuen.

Schlesinger, P., Dobash, E., Dobash, R. P., & Weaver, K. C. (1992). *Women viewing violence.* London: British Film Institute.

Schlesinger, P., Haynes, R., Boyle, R., McNair, B., Dobash, E., & Dobash, R. P. (1998). *Men viewing violence.* London: Broadcasting Standards Council.

Schutte, N. S., Malouff, J. M., Post-Gorden, J. C., & Rodasta, A. L. (1988). Effects of playing video games on children's aggression and other behaviours. *Journal of Applied Social Psychology, 18,* 454–460.

Schwartz, L. L. (Ed.). (1999). *Psychology and the media: A second look.* Washington, DC: American Psychological Association.

Schwarz, N., Strack, F., Kommer, D., & Wagner, D. (1987). Soccer, rooms, and the quality of your life: Mood effects on judgements of satisfaction with life in general and with specific domains. *European Journal of Social Psychology, 17,* 69–79.

Schweitzer, K., Zillmann, D., Weaver, J. B., & Luttrell, E. S. (1992). Perception of threatening events in the emotional aftermath of a televised college football game. *Journal of Broadcasting and Electronic Media, 36,* 75–82.

Scott, W. D. (1908). *The psychology of advertising.* Boston: Small Maynard.

Segal, L. (1990). *Slow motion: Changing masculinities, changing men.* London: Virago.

Senior, C., & Smith, M. (1999). The internet . . . a possible research tool? *The Psychologist, 12,* 442–445.

Shapiro, L. R., & Hudson, J. A. (1991). Tell me a make-believe story: Coherence and cohesion in young children's picture-elicited narratives. *Developmental Psychology, 27,* 960–974.

Shattuc, J. (1997). *The talking cure: TV talk shows and women.* New York: Routledge.

Shattuc, J. (1998). "Go Rikki": Politics, perversion and pleasure in the 1990s. In C. Geraghty & D. Lusted (Eds.), *The television studies book* (pp. 212–227). London: Arnold.

Shaw, R. L. (2001). *Vicarious violence and its context: An inquiry into the psychology of violence.* Unpublished doctoral dissertation, De Montfort University, Leicester.

Sheras, P. L., & Sheras, P. R. (1999). Using the media to promote positive images of couples: A multi-level approach. In L. L. Schwartz (Ed.), *Psychology and the media: A second look* (pp. 53–75). Washington, DC: American Psychological Association.

Sherry, J. L. (1998). Prosocial soap operas for development: A review of research and theory. *Journal of International Communication, 48,* 75–101.

Shoemaker, P. J. (1996). Hardwired for news: Using biological and cultural evolution to explain the surveillance function. *Journal of Communication, 46,* 32–47.

Signorielli, N. (1989a). Television and conceptions about sex roles: Maintaining conventionality and the status quo. *Sex Roles, 21,* 341–360.

Signorielli, N. (1989b). The stigma of mental illness on television. *Journal of Broadcasting and Electronic Media, 33,* 325–331.

Signorielli, N., & Bache, A. (1999). Recognition and respect: A content analysis of prime-time television characters across three decades. *Sex Roles, 40,* 527–544.

Signorielli, N., Gerbner, G., & Morgan, M. (1995). Violence on television: The cultural indicators project. *Journal of Broadcasting and Electronic Media, 39,* 278–283.

Signorielli, N., & Morgan, M. (Eds.). (1990). *Cultivation analysis: New directions in media effects research.* New York: Sage.

Silverstein, B., Perdue, L., Peterson, B., & Kelly, E. (1986). The role of the mass media in promoting a thin standard of attractiveness for women. *Sex Roles, 14,* 519–532.

Silverstone, R. (1993). Television, ontological security and the transitional object. *Media, Culture, and Society, 15,* 573–598.

Sims, V. K., & Mayer, R. E. (2002). Domain specificity of spatial expertise: The case of video game players. *Applied Cognitive Psychology, 16,* 97–115.

Singer, J. L., Singer, D. G., & Rapaczynski, W. S. (1984). Family patterns and television viewing as predictors of children's beliefs and aggression. *Journal of Communication, 34,* 73–89.

Singhal, A., & Rogers, E. M. (1999). *Entertainment-education: A communication strategy for social change.* Mahwah, NJ: Lawrence Erlbaum Associates.

Slade, J. W. (1984). Violence in the hard-core pornographic film: A historical survey. *Journal of Communication, 34,* 148–163.

Smith, D. D. (1976). The social content of pornography. *Journal of Communication, 26,* 16–24.

Sneegas, J. E., & Plank, T. A. (1998). Gender differences in pre-adolescent reactance to age-categorized television advisory labels. *Journal of Broadcasting and Electronic Media, 42,* 423–434.

Snyder, M., & de Bono, K. G. (1985). Appeals to image and claims about quality: Understanding the psychology of advertising. *Journal of Personality and Social Psychology, 49,* 586–597.

Spangler, L. C. (1992). Buddies and pals: A history of male friendships on prime-time television. In S. Craig (Ed.), *Men, masculinity, and the media* (pp. 93–110). Thousand Oaks, CA: Sage.

Sperling, G. (1960). The information available in brief visual presentations. *Psychological Monographs, 74*(11, Whole No. 498).

Sprafkin, J. N., & Rubenstein, E. A. (1979). Children's television viewing habits and prosocial behaviour: A field correlational study. *Journal of Broadcasting, 23,* 265–276.

St. Peters, M., Fitch, M., Huston, A. C., Wright, J. C., & Eakins, D. J. (1991). Television and families: What do young children watch with their parents? *Child Development, 62,* 1409–1423.

Steele, J. R., & Brown, J. D. (1995). Adolescent room culture: Studying media in the context of everyday life. *Journal of Youth and Adolescence, 24,* 551–576.

Steinberg, L., & Silverberg, S. (1986). The vicissitudes of autonomy in adolescence. *Child Development, 57,* 841–851.

Steinberg, S. R., & Kincheloe, J. L. (Eds.). (1997). *Kinderculture: The corporate construction of childhood.* Boulder, CO: Westview.

Stevenson, N., Jackson, P., & Brooks, K. (2000). The politics of "new" men's lifestyle magazines. *European Journal of Cultural Studies, 3,* 366–385.

Strasburger, V. C. (1995). *Adolescents and the media: Medical and psychological impact.* Thousand Oaks, CA: Sage.

Strate, L. (1992). Beer commercials: A manual on masculinity. In S. Craig (Ed.), *Men, masculinity, and the media* (pp. 78–92). Thousand Oaks, CA: Sage.

Strauss, A., & Corbin, J. (1998). *Basics of qualitative research: Grounded theory procedures and techniques* (2nd ed.). Thousand Oaks, CA: Sage.

Suess, D., Suoninen, A., Garitaonandia, C., Juaristi, P., Koikkalainen, R., & Oleaga, J. A. (1998). Media use and the relationships of children and teenagers with their peer groups: A study of Finnish, Swedish and Swiss cases. *European Journal of Communication, 13,* 521–538.

Sullivan, O. B. (1991). Commentary and viewer perception of player hostility: Adding punch to televised sport. *Journal of Broadcasting and Electronic Media, 35,* 487–504.

Sundar, S. S., & Nass, C. (2001). Conceptualizing sources in online news. *Journal of Communication, 51,* 52–72.

Tajfel, H., & Turner, J. C. (1979). An integrative theory of intergroup conflict. In W. G. Austin & S. Worchel (Eds.), *The social psychology of intergroup relations* (pp. 33–47). Monterey, CA: Brooks/Cole.

Tanenbaum, R. (1997). The media psychologist on TV. In S. Kirschner & D. A. Kirschner (Eds.), *Perspectives on psychology and the media* (pp. 157–172). Washington, DC: American Psychological Association.

Tapscott, D. (1998). *Growing up digital: The rise of the net generation.* New York: McGraw-Hill.

Tatar, M. (1998). "Violent delights" in children's literature. In J. H. Goldstein (Ed.), *Why we watch: The attractions of violent entertainment* (pp. 69–87). New York: Oxford University Press.

Taylor, M., & Carlson, S. M. (1997). The relation between individual differences in fantasy and theory of mind. *Child Development, 68,* 436–455.

Taylor, M., & Thompson, S. C. (1982). Stalking the elusive "vividness" effect. *Psychological Review, 89,* 155–181.

Tedesco, N. (1974). Patterns in prime-time. *Journal of Communication, 74,* 119–124.

Thomas, S. (1994). Artifactual study in the analysis of culture: A defense of content analysis in a postmodern age. *Communication Research, 21,* 683–697.

Thompson, J. K., Heinberg, L. J., Altabe, M., & Tantleff-Dunn, S. (1999). *Exacting beauty: Theory, assessment and treatment of body image disturbance.* Washington, DC: American Psychological Association.

Thorson, E. (1995). Using eyes on screen as a measure of attention to television. In A. Lang (Ed.), *Measuring psychological responses to media* (pp. 65–84). Hillsdale, NJ: Lawrence Erlbaum Associates.

Tiggemann, M., & Pickering, A. S. (1996). Role of television in adolescent women's body dissatisfaction and drive for thinness. *International Journal of Eating Disorders, 20,* 199–203.

Trinta, A. R. (1998). News from home: A study of realism and melodrama in Brazilian *Telenovelas*. In C. Geraghty & D. Lusted (Eds.), *The television studies book* (pp. 275–286). London: Arnold.

Trostle, L. C. (1993). Pornography as a source of sex information for university students: Some consistent findings. *Psychological Reports, 72,* 407–412.

Tuan, Y. (1982). *Segmented worlds and self.* Minneapolis: University of Minnesota Press.

Tuchman, G. (1978). The symbolic annihilation of women by the mass media. In G. Tuchman, A. Daniels, & J. Benet (Eds.), *Hearth and home: Images of women in the mass media* (pp. 3–38). New York: Oxford University Press.

Tudor, A. (1974). *Image and influence.* London: Allen & Unwin.

Tulloch, J. (1990). Television and black Britons. In A. Goodwin & G. Whannel (Eds.), *Understanding television* (pp. 141–152). London: Routledge.

Tulloch, J. (2000). *Watching television audiences: Cultural theories and methods.* London: Arnold.

Turkle, S. (1995). *Life on the screen: Identity in the age of the internet.* New York: Simon & Schuster.

Turner, J. R. (1993). Interpersonal and psychological predictors of parasocial interaction with different television performers. *Communication Quarterly, 41,* 443–453.

Turow, J. (2001). Family boundaries, commercialism and the internet: A framework for research. *Journal of Applied Developmental Psychology, 22,* 73–86.

Unnikrishnan, N., & Bajpai, S. (1996). *The impact of television advertising on children.* New Delhi: Sage.

Valkenburg, P. M., & Cantor, J. (2001). The development of a child into a consumer. *Journal of Applied Developmental Psychology, 22,* 61–72.

Valkenburg, P. M., Krcmar, M., Peeters, A. L., & Marseille, N. M. (1999). Developing a scale to assess three styles of television mediation: "Instructive mediation," "Restrictive mediation," and "Social coviewing." *Journal of Broadcasting and Electronic Media, 43,* 52–66.

Valkenburg, P. M., & van der Voort, T. H. A. (1995). The influence of television on children's daydreaming styles: A one-year panel study. *Communication Research, 22,* 267–287.

van den Broeck, P., Lorch, E. P., & Thurlow, R. (1996). Children's and adult's memory for television stories: The role of causal factors, story grammar categories and hierarchical level. *Child Development, 67,* 3010–3028.

Van den Bulck, J. (2000). Is television bad for your health? Behaviour and body image of the adolescent "couch potato." *Journal of Youth and Adolescence, 29,* 273–288.

van der Voort, T. H. A., Beentjes, J. W. J., Bovill, M., Gaskell, G., Koolstra, C. M., Livingstone, S., & Marseille, N. (1998). Young people's media ownership and uses of new and old forms of media in Britain and the Netherlands. *European Journal of Communication, 13,* 457–477.

van der Voort, T. H. A., & Valkenburg, P. M. (1994). Television's impact on fantasy play: A review of research. *Developmental Review, 14,* 27–51.

van Dijk, T. (1988). *News as discourse.* Hillsdale, NJ: Lawrence Erlbaum Associates.

van Dijk, T. (1998). *Ideology: A multidisciplinary approach.* Thousand Oaks, CA: Sage.

Vermorel, F., & Vermorel, J. (1985). *Starlust: The secret fantasies of fans.* London: W. H. Allen.

Vine, I. (1997). The dangerous psycho-logic of media effects. In M. Barker & J. Petley (Eds.), *Ill effects: The media/violence debate* (pp. 125–146). London: Routledge.

Vygotsky, L. S. (1978). *Mind in society: The development of higher psychological processes.* Cambridge, MA: Harvard University Press.

Walker, M., Langmeyer, L., & Langmeyer, D. (1992). Celebrity endorsers: Do you get what you pay for? *Journal of Consumer Marketing, 9,* 69–76.

Wallace, P. (1999). *The psychology of the internet.* Cambridge: Cambridge University Press.

Walsh, A. (1999). Life history theory and female readers of pornography. *Personality and Individual Differences, 27,* 779–787.

Ward, L. M., & Greenfield, P. M. (1998). Designing experiments on television and social behavior: Developmental perspectives. In J. K. Asamen & G. L. Berry (Eds.), *Research paradigms, television and social behavior* (pp. 67–108). Thousand Oaks, CA: Sage.

Warm, A. (2000, Sept. 6–8). *Video game violence and aggression: A study of adolescents.* Paper presented at the BPS Social section annual conference, Nottingham Trent University.

Watt, J. H. (1995). Detection and modelling of time-sequenced processes. In A. Lang (Ed.), *Measuring psychological responses to media* (pp. 181–208). Hillsdale, NJ: Lawrence Erlbaum Associates.

Weaver, J. (1991). Responding to erotica: Perceptual processes and dispositional implications. In J. Bryant & D. Zillmann (Eds.), *Responding to the screen: Reception and reaction processes* (pp. 329–354). Hillsdale, NJ: Lawrence Erlbaum Associates.

Weaver, J. B., Masland, J. M., & Zillmann, D. (1984). Effects of erotica on young men's aesthetic perception of their female sexual partners. *Perceptual and Motor Skills, 58,* 929–930.

Weiss, C. H., & Singer, E. (1988). *Reporting of social science in the national media.* New York: Russell Sage Foundation.

Wenner, L. A. (Ed.). (1998). *MediaSport.* London: Routledge.

Wernick, A. (1987). From voyeur to narcissist: Imaging men in contemporary advertising. In M. Kaufman (Ed.), *Beyond patriarchy: Essays by men on pleasure, power, and change.* Toronto: Oxford University Press.

Westen, D. (1999). *Psychology: Mind, brain, and culture* (2nd ed.). New York: Wiley.

Wetherell, M., Taylor, S., & Yates, S. J. (Eds.). (2001a). *Discourse theory and practice: A reader.* London: Sage.

Wetherell, M., Taylor, S., & Yates, S. J. (Eds.). (2001b). *Discourse as data: A guide for analysis.* London: Sage.

Wheen, F. (1985). *Television: A history.* London: Guild.

White, S., Evans, P., Mihill, C., & Tysoe, M. (1993). *Hitting the headlines: A practical guide to the media.* Leicester: BPS Books.

Wiegman, O., Kuttschreuter, M., & Baarda, B. (1992). A longitudinal study of the effects of television viewing on aggressive and prosocial behaviours. *British Journal of Social Psychology, 31,* 147–164.

Wiggins, S., Potter, J., & Wildsmith, A. (2001). Eating your words: Discursive psychology and the reconstruction of eating practices. *Journal of Health Psychology, 6,* 5–15.

Wilcox, K., & Laird, J. D. (2000). The impact of media images of super-slender women on women's self-esteem: Identification, social comparison, and self-perception. *Journal of Research in Personality, 34,* 278–286.

Williams, C. (2001). Does it really matter? Young people and popular music. *Popular Music, 20,* 223–242.

Williams, R. (1962). *Communications.* Harmondsworth: Penguin.

Williams, R. (1974). *Television: Technology and cultural form.* London: Fontana.

Willis, P. (1990). *Common culture: Symbolic work at play in the everyday cultures of the young.* Milton Keynes: Open University Press.

Wilson, B. J., Kunkel, D., Linz, D., Potter, J., Donnerstein, E., Smith, S. L., Blumenthal, E., & Berry, M. (1998). Violence in television programming overall: University of California, Santa Barbara study. *National television violence study* (Vol. 2, pp. 3–204). Thousand Oaks, CA: Sage.

Wilson, B. J., Kunkel, D., Linz, D., Potter, J., Donnerstein, E., Smith, S. L., Blumenthal, E., & Gray, T. (1997). Television violence and its context: University of California, Santa Barbara study. *National television violence study* (Vol. 1, pp. 3–268). Thousand Oaks, CA: Sage.

Wilson, C., Nairn, R., Coverdale, J., & Panapa, A. (2000). How mental illness is portrayed in children's television. *British Journal of Psychiatry, 176,* 440–443.

Wimmer, H., & Perner, J. (1983). Beliefs about beliefs: Representation and constraining function of wrong beliefs in young children's understanding of deception. *Cognition, 13,* 103–128.

Winship, J. (1987). *Inside women's magazines.* London: Pandora.

Winterhoff-Spurk, P. (Ed.). (1995). *Psychology of media in Europe: The state of the art, perspectives for the future.* Opladen: Westdeutscher Verlag.

Winterhoff-Spurk, P., & van der Voort, T. H. A. (Eds.). (1997). *New horizons in media psychology: Research cooperation and projects in Europe.* Opladen: Westdeutscher Verlag.

Wiseman, C. V., Gray, J. J., Mosimann, J. E., & Ahrens, A. H. (1990). Cultural expectations of thinness in women: An update. *International Journal of Eating Disorders, 11,* 85–89.

Wober, J. M. (1992). Violence and appreciation: The broken chain. *Medienpsychologie, 4,* 15–24.

Wober, J. M. (1997). Violence or other routes to appreciation: TV program makers' options. *Journal of Broadcasting and Electronic Media, 41,* 190–202.

Wober, J. M., Brosius, H. B., & Weinmann, G. (1996). The European election of 1989: British television viewers' knowledge, attitudes and voting behaviour. *British Journal of Social Psychology, 35,* 233–244.

Wood, J. V. (1989). Theory and research concerning social comparisons of personal attributes. *Psychological Bulletin, 106,* 231–248.

Wood, W., Wong, F. Y., & Chachere, J. G. (1991). Effects of media violence on viewers' aggression in unconstrained social interaction. *Psychological Bulletin, 109,* 371–383.

Worchel, S. (1972). The effect of films on the importance of behavioural freedom. *Journal of Personality, 40,* 417–435.

Wright, J. C., Huston, A. C., Reitz, A. L., & Piemyat, S. (1994). Young children's perceptions of television reality: Determinants and developmental differences. *Developmental Psychology, 30,* 229–239.

Young, B. (1990). *Children and television advertising.* Oxford: Clarendon.

Young, K. (1998). *Caught in the net.* Chichester: Wiley.

Yue, X. D., & Cheung, C. (2000). Selection of favourite idols and models among Chinese young people: A comparative study in Hong Kong and Nanjing. *International Journal of Behavioural Development, 24,* 91–98.

Yuill, N. (1992). Children's conception of personality traits. *Human Development, 35,* 265–279.

Zillmann, D. (1971). Excitation transfer in communication-mediated aggressive behaviour. *Journal of Experimental Social Psychology, 7,* 419–434.

Zillmann, D. (1991). Empathy: Affect from bearing witness to the emotions of others. In J. Bryant & D. Zillmann (Eds.), *Responding to the screen: Reception and reaction processes* (pp. 135–168). Hillsdale, NJ: Lawrence Erlbaum Associates.

Zillmann, D., & Bryant, J. (1975). Viewers' moral sanction of retribution in the appreciation of dramatic presentations. *Journal of Experimental Social Psychology, 11,* 572–582.

Zillmann, D., & Bryant, J. (1984). Effects of massive exposure to pornography. In N. Malamuth & E. Donnerstein (Eds.), *Pornography and sexual aggression* (pp. 115–138). New York: Academic.

Zillmann, D., & Bryant, J. (1986). Shifting preferences in pornography consumption. *Communication Research, 13,* 560–578.

Zillmann, D., & Bryant, J. (1988). Pornography's impact on sexual satisfaction. *Journal of Applied Social Psychology, 18,* 438–453.

Zillmann, D., Katcher, A. H., & Milavsky, B. (1972). Excitation transfer from physical exercise to subsequent aggressive behaviour. *Journal of Experimental Social Psychology, 8,* 247–259.

Zillmann, D., & Wakshlag, J. (1985). Fear of victimization and the appeal of crime drama. In D. Zillmann & J. Bryant (Eds.), *Selective exposure to communication* (pp. 141–155). Hillsdale, NJ: Lawrence Erlbaum Associates.

Zillmann, D., & Weaver, J. B. (1997). Psychoticism in the effect of prolonged exposure to gratuitous media violence on the acceptance of violence as a preferred means of conflict resolution. *Personality and Individual Differences, 22,* 613–627.

Zillmann, D., & Weaver, J. B. (1999). Media violence on provoked and unprovoked hostile behaviour. *Journal of Applied Social Psychology, 29,* 145–165.

Author Index

C

D

E

F

G

H

I

J

M

N

O

P

Q–R

S

T

U

V

W

Y

Z

Subject Index

D–E

F–G

H–I

L–M

N

P

Q–R

S